THE BRITISH WAY IN WARFARE: POWER AND THE INTERNATIONAL SYSTEM, 1856–1956

The British Way in Warfare: Power and the International System, 1856–1956

Essays in Honour of David French

EDITED BY
KEITH NEILSON AND GREG KENNEDY
Royal Military College of Canada and King's College London

ASHGATE

Published by
Ashgate Publishing Limited
Wey Court East
Union Road
Farnham
Surrey, GU9 7PT
England

Ashgate Publishing Company
Suite 420
101 Cherry Street
Burlington
VT 05401-4405
USA

www.ashgate.com

British Library Cataloguing in Publication Data
The British way in warfare : power and the international system, 1856–1956 :
essays in honour of David French.
 1. Great Britain–Military policy. 2. Great Britain–Foreign relations–1837–1901.
 3. Great Britain–Foreign relations–1910-1936. 4. Great Britain–Foreign relations
 –1936–1945. 5. Great Britain–History, Military–19th century. 6. Great Britain–
 History, Military–20th century.
 I. French, David, 1954– II. Neilson, Keith. III. Kennedy, Greg.
 355'.0335'41–dc22

Library of Congress Cataloging-in-Publication Data
The British way in warfare : power and the international system, 1856-1956 :
essays in honour of David French / Keith Neilson and Greg Kennedy [editors].
 p. cm.
 ISBN 978-0-7546-6593-9 (hardcover : alk. paper) 1. Great Britain—Military policy.
 2. Great Britain—History, Military—19th century. 3. Great Britain—History,
 Military—20th century. 4. Great Britain—Armed Forces—History—19th century.
 5. Great Britain—Armed Forces—History—20th century. 6. Great Britain—
 Foreign relations—19th century. 7. Great Britain—Foreign relations—20th century.
 I. Neilson, Keith. II. Kennedy, Greg. III. French, David, 1954–
 UA647.B856 2009
 355'.033541—dc22

                                                                    2009034597
ISBN 9780754665939 (hbk)
ISBN 9780754699590 (ebk)

Printed and bound in Great Britain by
MPG Books Group, UK

Contents

Introduction

Keith Neilson and Greg Kennedy

When David French began his post-graduate studies in the 1970s, he did so at a propitious time. In the 1960s and early 1970s, the study of British military history generally had taken a new direction. Long derided as 'drum and trumpet history', it was emerging as a serious academic discipline. This was due to a number of things. At a general level, the work of such luminaries as Michael Howard in the Department of War Studies at King's College London, was as careful, thoughtful and sophisticated as studies produced in other historical disciplines. The new work insisted that the study of military history needed to go far beyond examinations of great men and battles and deal with such matters as war planning, munitions, economics and finance. This was particularly notable with respect to the First World War, interest in which had been stimulated by the acrimonious debate over war guilt caused by the publication of Fritz Fischer's *Griff nach der Weltmacht* in 1961. At the level of the battlefield, the stereotypical view of the Great War as a futile and unmitigated disaster, in which troops were led into battle by such 'donkeys' as Sir Douglas Haig, was being challenged in books like John Terraine's *Douglas Haig: the Educated Soldier*. Revisions of the existing orthodoxy were increasingly possible due to opening of the archives under the Public Records Act (1968) and the work of the Historical Manuscripts Commission, which allowed the new generation of historians to bring a wealth of primary material to bear on the conflict on the Western front.[1]

Thus, it was not surprising that French, stimulated by his undergraduate interest in German and military history, chose as a thesis topic – fittingly undertaken at King's College London under Brian Bond (Howard's successor as the leading military historian on the Strand) – an examination of British planning for war in the decade before 1914. This work, which was published in 1982 as *British Economic and Strategic Planning 1905–1915*, marked David out as one of the bright young historians whose work over the next decade was going to transform our understanding of the First World War.[2] It also gave an indication of the sort

---

[1] The 'battle' for the public view of the First World War in the 1960s is nicely set out in Alex Danchev, '"Bunking" and Debunking: The Controversies of the 1960s', in Brian Bond, ed., *The First World War and British Military History* (Oxford, 1991), 263–88. The entire volume illustrates the rapid expansion of academic work on the Great War. The growth has continued unabated to the present.

[2] David French, *British Economic and Strategic Planning 1905–1915* (London, 1982).

of approach that is the hallmark of French's subsequent work. David stepped outside the usual narrow range of sources – primarily the documents of the War Office and Admiralty and a narrow range of military private papers – that many historians had consulted when discussing military matters and examined Treasury, Home Office and Board of Trade sources (as well as the private papers of major political figures) to show what sort of pre-war planning had been done, and how and why the national policy of 'business of usual' had to be adjusted to once war was declared.

As David pursued the usual academic trek of the freshly minted PhD in search of employment – temporary posts at North London Polytechnic, the University of Newcastle upon Tyne and Herriot-Watt University, before finding a permanent post at University College London in 1981 – he wrote several articles that showed his wide concept of what constituted matters military. An important article linked the problems of British munitions production with the state of military affairs.[3] A particular interest was intelligence history, itself an emerging field that was gaining academic respectability under the encouragement of Christopher Andrew. French demonstrated how pre-war British concerns about mostly fictitious German spies created a public anti-German atmosphere that increased the depth of anti-German feeling when war came.[4] Intelligence was a continuing interest. As time passed, David wrote on such matters as the embryonic secret service created on the Western front and how British intelligence interpreted events during the Great War itself.[5] He also wrote about the origins of the First World War, demonstrating that Fritz Fischer's contention that domestic politics had led to the outbreak of hostilities did not apply to Britain.[6]

However, while this was going on, David's primary research goal was to answer the questions that his first book had raised as to just what was British strategy in the First World War. While he was preparing the first of two volumes on this subject, he continued to write insightful articles dealing with particular matters that required explication but could not be dealt with at length in a book. These articles, on such matters as the controversies surrounding the Dardanelles campaign and the reputation of Sir Douglas Haig, gave an indication of the

---

[3]   David French, 'The Military Background to the "Shell Crisis" of May 1915', *Journal of Strategic Studies*, 2, 2 (1979), 192–205.

[4]   David French, 'Spy Fever in Britain, 1900–1915', *Historical Journal*, 21, 2 (1978), 355–70.

[5]   David French, 'Watching the Allies: British Intelligence and the French Mutinies of 1917', *Intelligence and National Security*, 6, 3 (1991), 573–92; 'Failures of Intelligence: The Retreat to the Hindenburg Line and the March 1918 Offensive', in Michael Dockrill and David French, eds, *Strategy and Intelligence: British Policy during the First World War* (London and Rio Grande, 1996), 67–95.

[6]   David French, 'The Edwardian Crisis and the Origins of the First World War', *International History Review*, 4, 2 (1982), 207–21.

wide sweep of David's conception of what a study of British strategy involved.[7] However, it was the publication of his second book that firmly cemented French's reputation as the foremost student of British strategy in the First World War. Here, French debunked a number of orthodoxies and showed a willingness to revise some of his own opinions – the latter a demonstration of David's intellectual honesty and uncompromising adherence to the results of further research.[8] Discarding as inadequate the existing interpretative frameworks that had explained the making of British strategy in terms either of varying military views ('easterners' versus 'westerners') or of civil-military relations ('brass hats' versus 'frocks'), French instead developed an approach showing that British policies were constructed within the constraints of its alliance with France and Russia. This 'alliance' approach took into account foreign, economic and financial policy, providing a nuanced explanation for British policy, one that raised military history to a more sophisticated level and has become the standard for understanding Britain's contribution to the total war of 1914–1918. It also helped to rehabilitate the reputation of Lord Kitchener and made him one of the architects of the 'alliance' approach – something that had not emerged in David's first book.

French applied this same method to a second volume that took his story from the fall of the Asquith government to the end of the war.[9] His examination of the functioning of the Lloyd George coalition, Britain's relations to its allies, war aims and peace terms illustrated the broader principle that countries fight wars with the hope of emerging from them at least as well off as they began. While preparing this volume, David cleared away some misconceptions regarding British strategy and military affairs. In a seminal article, he teased out the various meanings of that much used (and maligned) but little understood term, attrition.[10] He also demonstrated how issues of Empire and prestige played into the war, with regard to such diverse matters as naval supremacy and the British campaigns in the Middle East.[11]

---

[7]   David French, 'The Origins of the Dardanelles Campaign Reconsidered, *History*, 68, 223 (1983), 210–24; *idem*, 'Sir Douglas Haig's Reputation: A note', *Historical Journal*, 28, 4 (1985), 953–60.

[8]   David French, *British Strategy and War Aims 1914–1916* (London and Boston, 1986).

[9]   David French, *The Strategy of the Lloyd George Coalition, 1916–1918* (Oxford, 1995).

[10]   David French, 'The Meaning of Attrition, 1914–1916', *English Historical Review*, 103, 407 (1988), 385–405.

[11]   David French, 'The Royal Navy and the Defense of the British Empire, 1914–1918', in Keith Neilson and Elizabeth Jane Errington, eds, *Navies and Global Defense: Theories and Strategy* (Westport, CT, and London, 1995), 117–38; *idem*, 'The Dardanelles, Mecca and Kut: Prestige as a Factor in British Eastern Strategy, 1914–1916', *War and Society*, 5, 1 (1987), 45–62.

However, the path between his two volumes on the First World War was not an unbroken one. In 1988–89, David was a Woodrow Wilson Fellow in Washington DC. During this time, he gained a reputation among the other Fellows as a Stakhanovite for his strict regimen of reading and writing, something that was interrupted only by his unrelenting assault on the second-hand bookstores of Georgetown. At the end of the Fellowship, David had finished his third book, *The British Way in Warfare*, an examination of three centuries of British strategy.[12] The title of this book – alluding to Sir Basil Liddell Hart's famous volume of the same name – reflected the fact that French wished to consider whether the paradigms usually invoked to explain how British policy worked were valid. His conclusion, based on his extensive reading and his own archival research, was that British decision-makers pursued the country's best interests, alternating between a navalist approach and a commitment to the Continent as appropriate, but always attempting to do so at the least cost (in a broad sense) to Britain.

Having dealt comprehensively with the First World War and taken a longer view of British strategy, David pursued his interest in the British army into the post-1918 period. The result was *Raising Churchill's Army* (the title itself a bow to the familiar phrase used to describe the formation of Kitchener's armies in 1914–18), a comprehensive look at the inter-war army and its effectiveness in the Second World War.[13] Here, David was treading in the footsteps of his mentor, Brian Bond, whose survey of the topic written twenty years earlier had opened up the topic.[14] This vast subject required a number of things to be cleared away. In a series of important articles, David dealt with the morale and ideological commitment of the British soldiers of the Second World War, deepening our understanding of how combat affects the individual.[15] Several myths – that the British had not learned any military lessons in 1914–18, that it was slow to mechanise during the inter-war period, that the British army in the Second World War was staffed by Colonel Blimps – needed to be examined (and often discarded).[16] *Raising Churchill's Army*

---

[12]   David French, *The British Way in Warfare, 1688–2000* (London and Boston, 1990).

[13]   David French, *Raising Churchill's Army: The British Army and the War Against Germany 1919–1945* (Oxford, 2000).

[14]   Brian Bond, *British Military Policy between the Two World Wars* (Oxford, 1980).

[15]   David French, '"Tommy is No Soldier": The Morale of the Second British Army in Normandy, June–August 1944', *Journal of Strategic Studies*, 19, 4 (1996), 154–78; *idem*, 'Discipline and the Death Penalty in the British Army in the War against Germany during the Second World War', *Journal of Contemporary History*, 33, 4 (1998), 531–45; *idem*, '"You Cannot Hate the Bastard Who is Trying to Kill You …" Combat and Ideology in the British Army in the War Against Germany, 1939–45', *Twentieth Century British History*, 11, 1 (2000), 1–22.

[16]   David French, 'Doctrine and Organization in the British Army, 1919–1939', *Historical Journal*, 44, 2 (2001), 497–515; *idem*, 'The Mechanization of the British Cavalry between the World Wars', *War in History*, 10, 3 (2003), 298–320; *idem*, 'Colonel

was widely hailed, and received the 2000 Templer Medal as the outstanding book dealing with the history of the British Army. Just two years later, David (along with Brian Holden Reid) won a second Templer Medal for editing (and contributing to) a festschrift in honour of Brian Bond, a book that dealt with the history of the British General Staff.[17]

At this point Professor French, as David had become, looked for new worlds to conquer. He soon hit upon a topic that combined a number of his long-standing interests in an innovative fashion. Always wanting to determine just what made the British way in warfare different from that of other countries and building upon the extensive work that he had done regarding the morale and education of the British Army, David turned his attention to a history of the British regimental system.[18] This was David's most ambitious book, a complex and sophisticated analysis of the various aspects of the British regiment, a formation long regarded as the unique feature of the British Army. Not only does *Military Identities* provide a history of the changes in the use, function and composition of British regiments, but also it delves into the private lives of its members. This approach, utilising regimental histories and records as well as the Sound Records of the Imperial War Museum puts a human face on the generalities of regimental life. It is an admirable blend of military, organisational and social history. Naturally, it was the recipient of yet another Templer Medal, prompting calls from the jealous that French's work should be banned from any consideration for the prize in future!

In 2008, at an absurdly young age (and to the envy of many of his colleagues) David chose to take advantage of University College's offer of early retirement in order to concentrate his efforts on writing. At present, as he 'commutes three yards from the kitchen to [his] study', David is writing a book tentatively entitled *Army, Empire and Cold War, 1945–71*, a volume that will open up the post-war study of the British army.[19] While he does this, we hope that he will enjoy the chapters in this book, contributions written by his friends, admirers and colleagues, dealing with aspects of David's own interest in the British way in warfare.

Blimp and the British Army: British Divisional Commanders in the War against Germany, 1939–1945', *English Historical Review*, 111, 444 (1996), 1182–201; *idem*, '"An Extensive Use of Weedkiller": Patterns of Promotion in the Senior Ranks of the British Army, 1919–1939', in David French and Brian Holden Reid, eds, *The British General Staff. Reform and Innovation, 1890–1939* (London and Portland, OR, 2002), 159–74; *idem*, 'Officer Education and Training in the British Regular Army, 1919–1939', in Gregory C. Kennedy and Keith Neilson, eds, *Military Education Past, Present, and Future* (Westport, CT and London, 2002), 105–28.

[17]   French and Holden Reid, *British General Staff*.

[18]   David French, *Military Identities. The Regimental System, the British Army, and the British People c. 1870–2000* (Oxford, 2005).

[19]   D. French to K. Neilson, 8 December 2008; French's book is to be published by Oxford University Press.

Chapter 1

The British Way in Warfare and Russia

Keith Neilson

David French has argued that neither the 'navalist' argument made by Basil Liddell Hart (the original 'British way in warfare') nor the 'mixed paradigm' put forward by others adequately explains how Britain has fought her opponents. 'The only generalization which is valid for the whole period', he has asserted in his *The British Way in Warfare 1688–2000*, 'is that British strategic policy was essentially adaptive.' British 'policy-makers', he concluded, 'pursued policies which seemed to be best calculated to achieve their dominant policy aims at minimum cost'.[1]

Anglo-Russian relations in the century from the Crimean War to at least 1957 provide us with an opportunity to examine the validity of these competing paradigms. Perhaps no other of Britain's bilateral relationships better illustrates the variety of ways in which Britain has pursued her interests in both war and peace. In the century and a half since the Crimean conflict, Russia has been at the centre of British strategic foreign policy – albeit playing sharply different roles throughout. In the First and Second World Wars, Russia was a British ally against Germany and the latter's supporters. However, with the exception of the seven years (1914–17 and 1941–45) that the two countries fought alongside each other, Russia has been viewed as a threat to British security. Indeed, it would be fair to argue that the Anglo-Russian relationship in the past one hundred and fifty years has been one of near-unbroken enmity, a state of affairs interrupted only briefly by collaboration against the threat that Germany has posed to them both.[2]

The Crimean War would seem to support the ideas advanced by the 'mixed paradigm' school, in that Britain not only utilised her naval forces to harass Russia on a global scale, but also sent a substantial army to the Continent to operate alongside an ally.[3] However, a careful look at the agreements signed at the end of

---

[1] David French, *The British Way in Warfare 1688–2000* (London, 1990), xv–xvii, quotations from 232. An excellent overview of the arguments about the topic is Hew Strachan, 'The British Way in Warfare Revisited', *Historical Journal*, 26, 2 (1983), 447–61.

[2] For an insightful analysis of the nature of the Anglo-Russian relationship, see Edward Ingram, 'Great Britain and Russia', in William R. Thompson, ed., *Great Power Rivalries* (Columbia, SC, 1999), 269–305.

[3] For a robust argument that the naval side of the British effort predominated during the Crimean conflict, see Andrew D. Lambert, *The Crimean War: British Grand Strategy against Russia, 1853–56* (Manchester and New York, 1990). For aspects of the global

the war sheds a different light on British motives. The first arrangement reached was the Declaration of Paris, dealing with maritime law, signed in April 1856.[4] While the Declaration gave up Britain's traditional maritime rights with respect to privateering, the war had demonstrated that blockade and in-shore bombardment provided sufficient naval means for Britain to deal with Russia. The second agreement was the Treaty of Paris, which formally ended the war. From a British perspective, its key terms were decidedly naval. The neutralisation of the Black Sea meant that Russia was unable to use that body of water as an enclosed harbour from which its fleet could issue into the Mediterranean to harass British ships secure in the knowledge that, when superior British forces were encountered, the Russian fleet could retreat to fortified anchorages. A similar case emerged about the Baltic. There, the related provisions of 1856 demilitarised the Åland islands, something that prevented Russia from making the eastern Baltic into a secure base for operations.[5]

After the Crimean War, Russian foreign policy in Europe took a pacific turn. With the country's weaknesses exposed by the conflict, Russia turned its attention to domestic reform and the repair of its armed forces.[6] Russia's withdrawal from international affairs was not complete. When her own interests were involved – such as in the Polish insurrection of 1863 – St Petersburg moved quickly. However, Russia was no longer willing to play the role of 'gendarme of Europe', as she had under Nicholas I. This meant that the shadowy Anglo-Russian condominium that had underpinned the settlements reached at Vienna in 1815 was no more.[7] In turn,

---

nature of Britain's naval response, see C.I. Hamilton, 'Sir James Graham, the Baltic Campaign and War Planning at the Admiralty in 1854', *Historical Journal*, 19 (1967), 89–112; J.J. Stephan, 'The Crimean War in the Far East', *Modern Asian Studies*, 3 (1969), 257–77; E. Anderson, 'The Role of the Crimean War in the Baltic', *Scandinavian Studies*, 41 (1969), 263–75. Lambert has argued broadly that the threat of naval intervention was the underpinning of British diplomacy in the nineteenth century, see his 'The Royal Navy, 1856–1914: Deterrence and the Strategy of World Power', in Keith Neilson and Elizabeth Jane Errington, eds, *Navies and Global Defense: Theories and Strategy* (Westport, CT and London, 1995), 69–92, and 'Winning without Fighting: British Grand Strategy and its Application to the United States, 1815–65', in Bradford A. Lee and Karl F. Walling, eds, *Strategic Logic and Political Rationality* (London and Portland, OR, 2003), 164–95.

[4]   Lambert, *Crimean War*, 333–34; C.I. Hamilton, 'Anglo-French Seapower and the Declaration of Paris', *International History Review*, 4, 2 (1982), 166–90.

[5]   J. Barros, *The Åland Islands Question: Its Settlement by the League of Nations* (New Haven, 1960), 1–19.

[6]   For Russian foreign policy, see Dietrich Geyer, *Russian Imperialism. The Interaction of Domestic and Foreign Policy, 1860–1914* (Leamington Spa, Hamburg and New York, 1987).

[7]   The argument made in Paul Schroeder, 'Did the Vienna System Rest Upon a Balance of Power?', *American Historical Review*, 97 (1992), 683–706; and see *idem*, 'The Nineteenth Century System: Balance of Power or Political Equilibrium?', *Review of International Studies*, 15 (1989), 135–53.

this also meant that British influence on the Continent would have to depend on what maritime pressure London could bring to bear against the European states or what alliances she could find, since Russian arms were no longer available to ensure the stability of the post-Napoleonic settlement.

As a result of the need for reform, Russia played a passive role in both the Italian and German wars of unification. However, Russia did not remain quiescent without exacting a price. In the latter conflict, the Russians received a Prussian agreement to the abrogation of the Black Sea clauses of the Treaty of Paris as recompense for their agreeing to remain neutral.[8] The abrogation was counter to British interests. As the Permanent Undersecretary at the Foreign Office, Edmund Hammond, noted, 'it is a matter of no small moment for the maritime Powers that Russia should not be allowed to maintain a fleet of unlimited strength in a secure basin, inaccessible to the navies of other Powers who are excluded from the Black Sea by the Treaty'. Further, this would allow Russia to threaten the Suez Canal, all the while maintaining the security of her own route to India.[9] But the fact that London was isolated diplomatically limited its course of action to mere protest. Lacking a Continental ally, the British could bring only sea power to bear on the Russians, and this was not felt either worth the cost or likely to be effective, particularly given public opinion.[10]

However, the British inability to affect Russia's naval efforts in the Mediterranean was only temporary. The aftermath of the Russo-Turkish War of 1877–78 provided an opportunity to compensate for the abrogation of the Black Sea clauses and to curb Russian aspirations in the Balkans. The treaty of San Stefano, which ended the conflict between the Russians and Turks, was widely viewed as unsatisfactory. For the British, the prospect of Russia's having access to the Mediterranean via a 'Big Bulgarian' port on the Aegean and the Russian acquisition of Batum (Batumi) in the Black Sea, was particularly unwelcome, raising as it did the spectre of Russia's becoming an Eastern Mediterranean naval power and one able to threaten the newly-opened Suez Canal. However, British plans to counter Russia by moving Indian troops to Malta and threatening to blockade both the Black Sea and the Baltic were fraught with difficulties. It was not clear that a British fleet could force the Straits, while the military strength available – 7,000 men – was inadequate to effect a landing on the Black Sea Coast.[11] While the Mediterranean fleet did eventually go into the Sea of Marmora,

---

[8]   W.E. Mosse, 'The End of the Crimean System: England, Russia and the Neutrality of the Black Sea, 1870–1', *Historical Journal*, 4 (1961), 164–90;

[9]   As quoted in Barbara Jelavich, 'British Means of Offense against Russia in the Nineteenth Century', *Russian History*, 1, 2 (1974), 122. For more on Hammond's views, see Keith Neilson and T.G. Otte, *The Permanent Under-Secretary for Foreign Affairs, 1854–1946* (New York and London, 2009), 28–29.

[10]   W.E. Mosse, 'Public Opinion and Foreign Policy: The British Public and the War-scare of November 1870–1', *Historical Journal*, 6, 1 (1963), 38–58.

[11]   Jelavich, 'British Means of Offence', 125–27.

this was viewed as a risky business.[12] As a result, the British Foreign Secretary, Lord Salisbury, moved to check Russia by other means. He did so by signing a secret agreement with Russia on 31 May 1878, giving the latter Batum in exchange for St Petersburg's surrendering the idea of 'Big Bulgaria'. Four days later, he checked the strategic advantage that Russians had gained at Batum by obtaining the right from the Turks to maintain British forces in Cyprus in exchange for a British guarantee of Asiatic Turkey against Russia.[13]

Further manoeuvrings occurred at the Congress of Berlin, which opened on 13 June 1878. This meeting, called by German Chancellor, Otto von Bismarck, was designed to find a settlement to replace San Stefano. At it, the Russians attempted to evade the ramifications of the secret agreement with the British, but to no avail. Salisbury took advantage of the general anti-Russian feeling at the Congress and declared that Britain would respect the right of the Sultan to prohibit warships entering the Black Sea only when London was convinced that this decision had been made independently. This meant, in effect, that the Royal Navy would be able to move into the Black Sea to check Russia at any time that it was judged in London that St Petersburg posed a threat to British interests.[14] Diplomacy had secured the necessary conditions for British sea power to continue to be a major weapon against Russia.

However, the major British concern about Russia after 1856 was not in regard to the Balkans, but, rather, the defence of India.[15] While Russia had pursued a quiescent policy in Europe, she had followed an aggressive policy in Central Asia. Beginning in the 1860s, Russia had moved steadily into the Eurasian heartland. Her advances had raised concerns in both London and Simla about the security of British India, something already stimulated by the Great Mutiny of 1857 and by the unstable frontier with Afghanistan.[16] Beginning in 1865, these fears took on greater significance as the Russian advance into Central Asia began.[17] The latter

---

[12]   Matthew Allen, 'The British Mediterranean Squadron during the Great Eastern Crisis of 1876–9', *Mariner's Mirror*, 85, 1 (1999), 53–67.

[13]   Barbara Jelavich, 'Great Britain and the Russian Acquisition of Batum, 1878–1886', *Slavonic and East European Review*, 48, 110 (1970), 44–56.

[14]   For how this was to be done, see Adrian Preston, 'Frustrated Great Gamesmanship: Sir Garnet Wolseley's Plans for War against Russia, 1873–1880', *International History Review*, 2, 1 (1980), 237–65.

[15]   For how the Franco-Prussian war shifted the emphasis in Anglo-Russian relations to the North-West frontier, see Adrian Preston, 'The Eastern Question in British Strategic Policy during the Franco-Prussian War', (Canadian) *Historical Papers* (1972), 55–88.

[16]   Edward Ingram, *The Beginning of the Great Game in Asia, 1828–34* (Oxford, 1979); *idem*, *In Defence of British India: Great Britain in the Middle East, 1775–1842* (London, 1984); G.J. Alder, 'The Key to India?: Britain and the Herat Problem 1830–1863', Parts I and II, *Middle Eastern Studies*, 10, 2 (1974), 186–209, and ibid., 10, 3 (1974), 287–311.

[17]   A.P. Thornton, 'The Reopening of the Central Asian Question, 1864–9', *History*, 41 (1956), 120–22; G.J. Alder, 'India and the Crimean War', *Journal of Imperial and*

raised serious difficulties for British defence planners. Whereas Russian aggression either against the Great Powers or against the Ottoman Empire was sure to generate support among the European Powers for British efforts to curtail it, the same could not be said for Russian threats to India. Equally, maintaining an Indian army sufficient to defend the North-West Frontier against Russia was expensive. Nor could naval power be used to deter Russia, except possibly by entering the Black Sea and threatening Russia's lines of communication. As Salisbury had noted in 1877, Russia was 'unassailable by us'; there was 'absolutely no point at which we could attack her with any chance of doing serious injury'.[18] The concessions that Salisbury had gained in 1878 only eased, but did not obviate, the difficulties in dealing with Russia by maritime means.

This problem grew worse over time. The steady Russian advance into Central Asia, despite St Petersburg's denials of such intentions both before and during the Congress of Berlin, created increasing Anglo-Russian enmity.[19] British concern grew as the Russian incursions approached Afghanistan. In the second half of 1878, the Russians sent an envoy to Kabul, something that seemed to foreshadow the creation of a Russian sphere of influence in Afghanistan. The response of the Viceroy, Lord Lytton, was to initiate the Second Afghan War (1878–80), despite the fact that Salisbury (then Secretary of State for India) had contended three years earlier that, 'We cannot conquer it [Afghanistan]; we cannot leave it alone. We can only spare to it our utmost vigilance.'[20] The result of the war was to extend a shadowy British protectorate over Afghanistan. In this relationship, the British promised to defend Afghanistan's territorial integrity against Russian encroachments; in return, Afghanistan's external relations were to be supervised by the British. This did not, however, end the question of how to defend India against a Russian threat and raised the additional question of just how Afghanistan's territory was to be maintained.

For this, there were two schools of thought.[21] One – the so-called 'defence-in-depth school' – believed that India was best defended by using Afghanistan

---

Commonwealth History, 2 (1973), 15–37; Firuz Kazemzadeh, *Russia and Britain in Persia, 1864–1914* (New Haven and London, 1968).

[18] Salisbury to Lytton (Viceroy, India), 22 June 1877, as cited in B.J. Williams, 'The Approach to the Second Afghan War: Central Asia during the Great Eastern Crisis, 1875–8', *International History Review*, 2 (1980), 216.

[19] A.P. Thornton, 'Afghanistan in Anglo-Russian Diplomacy, 1869–1873', *Cambridge Historical Journal*, 11, 2 (1954), 204–18; John Lowe Duthie, 'Pragmatic Diplomacy or Imperial Encroachment?: British Policy towards Afghanistan, 1874–1879', *International History Review*, 5, 4 (1983), 475–95.

[20] Salisbury to Northbrooke, 5 March 1875, as cited in E.D. Steele, 'Salisbury at the India Office', in Lord Blake and Hugh Cecil, *Salisbury: the Man and his Policies* (Basingstoke and London, 1987), 128.

[21] For an introduction, see M.A. Yapp, 'British Perceptions of the Russian Threat to India', *Modern Asian Studies*, 21, 4 (1987), 646–65, and, more broadly, *idem, Strategies of*

as a buffer state, strengthening the Indian Army and meeting any attack at the Indian border itself. The other, the 'forward school', preferred to push actively into Afghanistan itself to establish the so-called 'Scientific Frontier' and prevent any Russian advances from reaching India at all.[22] Each of these approaches had problems. Opponents of the defence-in-depth school argued that an unopposed Russian presence in Afghanistan would act as a catalyst for native unrest in British India. On the other hand, proponents of the forward school – best exemplified by the British Quarter-Master General in India (1880–85), Sir Charles MacGregor, and the British Commander-in-Chief in India (1885–1893), Lord Roberts – had to justify the enormous cost of establishing and maintaining a presence in Afghanistan.[23] Costs of plans for the defence of India tended to be somewhat vague; however, MacGregor's plans called for 65,000 British and 220,000 Native reinforcements to maintain an Indian Army of 120,000 on a war footing, figures so vast that the Secretary of State for India, Lord Kimberley, noted 'I have never read anything wilder'.[24]

The next flashpoints in Anglo-Russian relations occurred in 1885, with the Bulgarian crisis and the Penjdeh incident. [25] These two events underlined the difficulties of dealing with Russia. The year before, these problems had been outlined by the War Office. The Assistant Quarter-Master General, Major J.S. Rothwell, had concluded a long study of 'England's Means of Offence against Russia' by noting that 'simple blockade would be useless' although 'under exceptional circumstances' amphibious military operations were possible in the Baltic. Only at Batum might the British hope to attack with any real chance of affecting Russia.[26] Thus, in 1885, with regard to Bulgaria, the British had no means of becoming involved, except by joining with the other Powers, something that many in the Cabinet were reluctant to do. As to Penjdeh, while it provided Roberts with another opportunity to press for the 'scientific frontier' of the Hindu

---

British India: Britain, Iran and Afghanistan, 1898–1850 (Oxford, 1980).

[22]   For a good summary of this debate, see R.A. Johnson, '"Russians at the Gates of India"? Planning the Defence of India, 1885–1900', *Journal of Military History*, 67 (2003), 697–744, which forms the basis for the following.

[23]   Ibid. and Adrian Preston, 'Sir Charles MacGregor and the Defence of Indian, 1857–1887', *Historical Journal*, 12, (1969), 58–77. There were also those in the India Office who advocated a 'forward' policy; see John Lowe Duthie, 'Pressure from Within: The "Forward" Group in the India Office During Gladstone's First Ministry', *Journal of Asian History*, 15, 1 (1981), 36–74.

[24]   Kimberley to Ripon, 2 October 1884, as cited in Preston, 'Sir Charles MacGregor', 76.

[25]   For the two, see C.J. Lowe, *The Reluctant Imperialists. British Foreign Policy 1878–1902* (London, 1967), 99–108, and R.A. Johnson, 'The Penjdeh Incident 1885', *Archives*, 29, 100 (2004), 28–48.

[26]   'England's Means of Offence Against Russia', 7 July 1884, secret, J.S. Rothwell, printed in Barbara Jelavich, *The Ottoman Empire, the Great Powers, and the Straits Question 1870–1887* (Bloomington and London, 1973), 189–98.

Kush, the means to implement his plans were lacking. While Salisbury (as prime minister) was sympathetic to Roberts' arguments, in 1885 diplomacy had to make do where material force was lacking.[27]

And, this inability tended to become greater. The growth of railways diminished the logistical advantage that British sea power had enjoyed against Russia. Even the perennial idea of entering the Black Sea and attacking Batum became less attractive after the Franco-Russian rapprochement of 1892, something that finally resulted in the signing of the Franco-Russian Alliance two years later. This latter regrouping of the Powers meant that any British naval action in the Black Sea would likely involve the French as well as the Russian fleet, and to force the Straits also would require some 10,000 men.[28] Indeed, by 1896, the Director of Military Intelligence, Sir John Ardagh, argued that, as Russia could take the Straits whenever she was so inclined, the British policy should now be to open the Straits to all. While this would allow the Russian fleet to aid the French fleet in the Mediterranean (to Britain's possible detriment), it would also allow the Royal Navy unfettered access to the Black Sea where it could both threaten the Russian lines of communication to Central Asia and prevent the Russians from being able to coerce the Sultan unopposed.[29]

The switch of Russia's diplomatic interests from the Balkans to the Far East in the early 1890s – something reflecting the initiation of the building of the Trans-Siberian railway in 1891 – changed the venue for British concerns about Russia. In that region, the British found that their ability to challenge any Russian advances was limited.[30] Naval power could find no place to operate effectively. British pressure against Russia in Central Asia was never contemplated, despite Russian concerns that this might occur. This left diplomacy. Britain's initial efforts were to find some sort of agreement with Russia with regard to China. However, outside of a limited agreement with regard to railway concessions, this came to naught. London next turned to Berlin. However, the negotiations with the Germans in 1900 and 1901 foundered on the *Kaiserreich*'s excessive demands: a British willingness to remain neutral in any European war as the price of an alliance. Stymied at Berlin, the British looked next at Tokyo. The result was the Anglo-Japanese alliance of 1902. This agreement, often mistakenly seen as resulting from Britain's need to

---

[27]   Johnson, '"Russians at the Gates"', 717–19.

[28]   Memorandum by E.F. Chapman (Director of Military Intelligence) and Cyprian A.G. Bridge (Director of Naval Intelligence), 18 March 1892, and a covering memorandum by Salisbury, 4 June 1892, both printed in Lowe, *Reluctant Imperialists*, 355–61, and the discussion in Keith Neilson, '"Greatly Exaggerated": The Myth of the Decline of Great Britain before 1914', *International History Review*, 13, 4 (1991), 711–13.

[29]   'The Eastern Question in 1896', secret, Ardagh, October 1896, Ardagh Papers, PRO 30/40/14.

[30]   For complementary overviews, see Keith Neilson, *Britain and the Last Tsar: British Policy and Russia, 1894–1917* (Oxford, 1995), 147–238, and T.G. Otte, *The China Question: Great Power Rivalry and British Isolation, 1894–1905* (Oxford, 2007).

concentrate her efforts (particularly, naval forces) against a rising Germany, was, in fact, the result of London's inability to check Russia in any other fashion.[31]

The Anglo-Japanese alliance did not bring an end to British concerns about Russia. Until the outbreak of the Russo-Japanese war in 1905, Russia continued to reject British overtures for a settlement of their outstanding colonial differences. In addition, the growth of the Russian navy continued. This was worrying, since the British two-power standard was based on the strength of the combined French and Russian fleets. In 1898, the First Lord of the Admiralty, George Goschen, had confessed himself 'compelled' by the Russian building programme to insist on increased naval estimates.[32] Indeed, by 1901, the new First Lord of the Admiralty, Lord Selborne, contended that the expansion of the Russian fleet meant that Britain would have to build beyond the two-power standard.[33] All of this involved expense, something that the cost of the Boer War made even less palatable than usual.

How to defend India against Russian incursion again came to the fore as the Trans-Siberian railway, with a spur line from Orenberg to Tashkent, neared completion. This line eliminated the logistical advantage that British India had enjoyed thanks to the ability of the British to move reinforcements to India quicker by sea than Russia could transport troops to the North-West Frontier by land.[34] The British response was to build their own lines towards Afghanistan, but this did not reduce the number of troops that were required to meet any Russian advance.[35] In 1903, it was deemed that the standing garrison in India would require 30,000 reinforcements four months after the outbreak of war. The figure was increased to 135,614 a year later and to 211,824 by 1905. This number of men could not be raised without conscription, something that was anathema to Liberals before 1914, and, even if the men could be found, the cost of doing so was equally unappealing.

How to deal with Russia clearly required something more than military and naval means – although concerns about the Russian naval threat were temporarily ended by the catastrophic defeat of the Russian fleet at Tsushima. A patch was put

[31]   Keith Neilson, 'The Anglo-Japanese Alliance and British Strategic Foreign Policy, 1902–1914', in Phillips Payson O'Brien, ed., *The Anglo-Japanese Alliance, 1902–1922* (London, 2004), 48–63.

[32]   'Russian Naval construction', Goschen, 6 June 1898, Cab 37/47/39 and 'Navy Estimates and Ship-Building Programme, 1898–9', Goschen, 17 February 1898, Cab 27/46/20.

[33]   See the discussion of this in Neilson, *Britain and the Last Tsar*, 118–21.

[34]   See Keith Neilson, 'The Baghdad to Haifa Railway: The Culmination of Railway Planning for Imperial Defence East of Suez', in T.G. Otte and Keith Neilson, eds, *Railways and International Politics. Paths of Empire, 1848–1945* (London and New York, 2006), 156–61.

[35]   What follows is based on Neilson, *Britain and the Last Tsar*, 126–32 and *idem*, '"Greatly Exaggerated"', 713–17.

on the defence of India by means of the provisions of the renewed Anglo-Japanese alliance of 1905.[36] Under the terms of the new treaty, Japanese troops would help defend India against Russia, but the British had second thoughts about the wisdom of using non-European troops in India and the Japanese made it clear that their troops would be better used to attack Russia in Korea. This left diplomacy. Russia's weakness after the Russo-Japanese War made her more willing to listen to British overtures. The result was the Anglo-Russian Convention of 1907 that brought an end to the quarrels about the North-West frontier. With the Convention in sight, the last British discussion of the defence of India simply concluded that 100,000 reinforcements would be required if war were to break out and the matter was left there.[37]

The fact that the Anglo-Russian Convention was by no means an alliance meant that when Britain and Russia became allies in 1914, the functioning of the coalition had to be worked out on the fly and was characterised by a series of ad hoc measures shaped by the exigencies of the conflict.[38] However, this does not mean that Russia was a negligible factor in the British way in warfare during the First World War. Indeed, British strategy in the war can be understood only in the context of its functioning within an alliance structure, something that David French has emphasised.[39] Initially, the British intended to fight the war by limited means: sending an expeditionary force to the Continent and utilising naval power to blockade the Central Powers. In this war, the Russian 'steamroller' was to provide the troops necessary for victory. However, as the war became a long one, a total war that tested the economic, financial and manpower resources of the belligerents, the British role in the conflict changed. This was nowhere more noticeable than in the functioning of the Anglo-Russian portion of the coalition.

With respect to strategy, the Russian influence was evident in two aspects. The first was in regard to the British Gallipoli campaign. While not the only reason why the British attacked the Dardanelles, the fact that a successful assault there would eliminate the Russian Caucasian front and open up a means for Russia to renew her external trade was an important factor in the British decision to attempt to force the

---

[36] Ian Nish, *The Anglo-Japanese Alliance: The Diplomacy of Two Island Empire 1894–1907* (London, 1966), 317–35.

[37] 'The Military Requirements of the Empire as Affected by the Defence of India', Morley (Secretary of State for India), 1 May 1907, Cab 16/2.

[38] The standard study of the wartime relationship is Keith Neilson, *Strategy and Supply: The Anglo-Russian Alliance 1914–17* (London, 1984); see also, *idem*, 'Managing the War: Britain, Russia and Ad Hoc Government', in Michael Dockrill and David French, eds, *Strategy and Intelligence: British Policy during the First World War* (London and Rio Grande, OH, 1996), 96–118. My account of the functioning of the alliance is based on these two sources unless otherwise noted.

[39] See his magisterial two volumes: *British Strategy and War Aims 1914–1916* (London, 1986) and *The Strategy of the Lloyd George Coalition, 1916–1918* (Oxford, 1995).

Straits. The second impact of Russia was more general. The lack of coordination among the Allies during the first two campaigning seasons led the Russians, in the autumn of 1915, to insist that any attack by the Central Powers against one of the coalition members should be met, as soon as possible, by a countervailing blow against Germany by the other partners. A concern to coordinate her military effort with Russia thus helped to shape British military decisions in 1916 and 1917 – the former out of a desire to coordinate with the Brusilov offensive and the latter out of concern that a failure to launch an offensive while Russia was (it was hoped, temporarily) *hors de combat* due to the March revolution would allow Germany a much-needed respite to recoup her strength.

Such things were the norm of coalition warfare and not particular to the way in which Britain pursued her wars. Another aspect of the Anglo-Russian alliance, however, was more unique to the British way in warfare. As the war progressed, Russia found herself both short of munitions and short of the means to obtain them from overseas. Britain, with her vast financial resources and extensive merchant marine, became Russia's financier and armourer. This began early in the war. In the autumn of 1914, the British extended a loan of £20 million to Russia, and began negotiations for a further £40 million. In February 1915, the British lent a further £25 million. The Russian need for munitions of war was the driving force behind these loans, and a complex series of committees grew up between Russia and Britain to coordinate purchasing abroad, particularly in the United States. In addition to financing Russian purchasing, the British provided the shipping necessary to transport the war materiel to Russia, primarily through the port of Archangel, although a significant amount of was trans-shipped via Sweden and other goods went via Vladivostok.[40]

The alliance did not always run smoothly. The Russians were suspicious that the British were willing to fight to the last drop of Russian blood, given the disparity in size between their two armies. Equally, the Russians resented the control that the British exercised over purchasing, finances and shipping. For Petrograd, British claims that such resources were finite, and that limitations had to be imposed for the sake of the long-term viability of the Entente's finances and transportation, were no more than excuses and reflected a lack of appreciation of the Russian *effort du sang*. Despite Russian mutterings, however, the British contribution to Russia was substantial. Russia was loaned some £571.6 million by Britain during the First World War, just more than 30 per cent of the total of British lendings in the conflict and more than 50 per cent greater than France received from London.[41]

But, even while the Anglo-Russian alliance was in full operation, the longer-term Anglo-Russian enmity was not forgotten. British war aims and diplomacy during the First World War were underpinned by concerns about Imperial defence

---

[40]   For the context, see Keith Neilson, 'Reinforcements and Supplies from Overseas: British Strategic Sealift in the First World War', in Greg Kennedy, ed., *The Merchant Marine in International Affairs, 1850–1950* (London and Portland, OR, 2000), 31–58.

[41]   Neilson, *Strategy and Supply*, 316.

and British security generally, in which Russia figured prominently.[42] In 1915, the Russians insisted that the promise made in November 1914 that Constantinople would be Russian after the war was made formal.[43] While the British had decided before the war that denying Constantinople to Russia was no longer necessary for British security in the Mediterranean, many believed that, if the Tsarist state held the Ottoman capital, then the British must hold Alexandretta in order to threaten the Russian flank should a descent on India occur. Equally, it was important that any Russian gain be balanced by the British acquisition of Mesopotamia. At the meetings of the de Bunsen Committee, a body created to establish the British desiderata in the negotiations, the Director of Military Operations, Sir Charles Callwell, reminded the members that they needed to 'bear in mind in the future … the possibility of war with Russia'.[44]

This was not the end to concerns about Russia and the post-war situation. In 1916, similar fears about future Russian aggression against India were raised in a discussion of whether to extend British railways from British India towards Persia. While this was felt necessary in order to deal with the German-Turkish forces in Persia, such a rail line potentially would be able to link up with the Russian Trans-Persian line. In turn, this would provide the Tsarist state with a means of aggression against India after the war. The Chief of the Imperial General Staff (CIGS), Sir William Robertson, made the point that, as the war-time alliance with Russia was only ephemeral, British policy should be based on long-term considerations.[45] Such an approach also was to the fore when Europe's future was discussed. When British war aims were discussed in 1916, one of the essential factors was deemed to be the maintenance of the balance of power in Europe. As part of this, the British opposed giving all of Poland to Russia, since extending the Tsarist state 'within 125 miles of Berlin' would prevent post-war Germany from being able to check Russian aggression.[46] While close Anglo-Russian relations

---

[42]   The following discussion, except where otherwise noted, is based on Keith Neilson, '"For Diplomatic, Economic, Strategic and Telegraphic Reasons": British Imperial Defence, the Middle East and India, 1914–1918', in Greg Kennedy and Keith Neilson, eds, *Far-Flung Lines: Essays on Imperial Defence in Honour of Donald Mackenzie Schurman* (London and Portland, OR, 1997), 103–24.

[43]   G. Paget, 'The November 1914 Straits Agreement and the Dardanelles-Gallipoli Campaign', *Australian Journal of History and Politics*, 33 (1987), 253–60, and A.L. Macfie, 'The Straits Question in the First World War, 1914–18', *Middle Eastern Studies*, 19 (1983), 43–74.

[44]   Callwell's remarks, 13 April 1915, minutes of the 2nd meeting, Cab 27/1.

[45]   'Extension of the Quetta-Nushki Railway to Seistan', Robertson, 16 August 1916, Cab 6/4/108-D; John Fisher, 'Lord Curzon and British Strategic Railways in Central Asia before, during and after the First World War', in Otte and Neilson, *Railways and International Politics*, 146–48.

[46]   'Suggested Basis for a Territorial Settlement in Europe', Tyrrell and Paget, 7 August 1916, Cab 29/1. For the context, see V.H. Rothwell, *British War Aims and Peace Diplomacy, 1914–1918* (Oxford, 1971), 42–49, and Lorna S. Jaffe, *The Decision to Disarm*

were to be maintained if possible (and were the preferred means of maintaining a stable Europe), considerations of a possible end to the good relations that had existed since 1907 were paramount.[47]

Such thinking continued after the First World War. The Bolshevik revolution and subsequent Civil War made any discussion of Russia at the Paris Peace Conference essentially theoretical.[48] How to treat with Russia, however, never strayed far from concerns about British strategic policy. The defence of India continued to intrude, as there were those, like the Secretary of State for Foreign Affairs, Lord Curzon, who wished to establish the British in the formerly Russian areas of the Caucasus (or, at least, to support the independence of the nascent states there) in order to prevent a recrudescence of the Russian menace to India. Others worried that to support separatist movements would result, should Russia recover her strength, in creating permanent enmity between Britain and whatever polity emerged out of the former Tsarist state. This latter possibility also carried with it the likelihood that there would be a re-emergence of a German-Russian axis reminiscent of the Great Power alignment that had been a feature of the Bismarckian era, something that would rob the Allies of the fruits of the victory that that they had achieved in 1918.

In the end, all depended on events. By 1922, the Bolsheviks had established themselves in Russia. While the new communist state was too weak – as the Russo-Polish War demonstrated – to expand militarily into Central Europe, it was a formidable threat to Britain and the Empire.[49] In the domestic turmoil following the First World War, there was a widely perceived 'red menace' in Britain. More importantly, Soviet Russia was an ideological threat in the British Empire, an empire already under stress due to the heightened expectations of greater political independence that its participation in the First World War had created.[50] Throughout the 1920s, Anglo-Soviet relations oscillated between attempts to establish – mainly via trade agreements – a reasonably amicable relationship, and

---

Germany: British Policy towards Post-war German Disarmament (London and Boston, 1985), 24–25, 27–28 and 31–32.

[47]   'Views of the Foreign Office Representatives on the Question of the Retention of the German Colonies', TC-17, Tyrrell, Mallet, Clerk, 21 January 1917, Cab 16/36.

[48]   For a discussion, see Keith Neilson, '"That elusive entity British policy in Russia": the Impact of Russia on British Policy at the Paris Peace Conference', in Michael Dockrill and John Fisher, eds, *The Paris Peace Conference, 1919: Peace without Victory?* (Basingstoke and New York, 2001), 67–102.

[49]   Keith Neilson, *Britain, Soviet Russia and the Collapse of the Versailles Order, 1919–1939* (Cambridge, 2006), 43–47.

[50]   John Gallagher, 'Nationalisms and the Crisis of Empire, 1919–1922', *Modern Asian Studies*, 15, 3 (1931), 355–68; John Darwin, 'Imperialism in Decline? Tendencies in British Imperial Policy between the Wars', *Historical Journal*, 23, 3(1980), 657–79; Ronald Hyam, *Britain's Declining Empire. The Road to Decolonisation 1918–1968* (Cambridge, 2006), 30–83.

periods when diplomatic relations were broken off due to the ideological antipathy between the two and the continued Soviet attempts to undermine both Britain and the Empire.

While the ideological threat was mainly the province of the British secret service – an early 'cold war' of code breaking and counter-espionage – there remained the physical threat of Soviet Russia.[51] As in the past, the defence of India was the central issue. The key to this defence was Afghanistan.[52] In 1926, the Chiefs of Staff stated that, should Soviet Russia attack and seize northern Afghanistan, it would be difficult to dislodge her. And, in contradistinction to pre-1914 views, the Chiefs were positive that naval raids and blockades of Russia 'would entail great efforts, and would yield comparatively small results'. The new possibilities of striking Russia via air attacks would 'certainly not be expected to produce decisive results' and any military effort 'conducted by the British Empire alone against European Russia would have no military effect whatsoever on the situation in Asia'.[53] This bleak assessment was repeated the following year. At that time, the Indian General Staff and the British CIGS, General Milne, argued about where to situate the boundary at which Afghanistan would be defended – a variation of the Victorian argument about 'forward defence' – but both were pessimistic about their ability to repel the Russians. While Milne's view that all of Afghanistan would have to be defended became policy, the difficulties of doing so were immense.

And Afghanistan was not the only region that would have to be defended against Soviet depredations. In 1928, a subcommittee of the Committee of Imperial Defence (CID) was created to examine the question of the defence of Persia.[54] This was necessary, the COS argued, because Persia was not strong enough 'to act as an effective buffer against Russian aggression'.[55] The means of doing so were varied, but involved attacks against the Soviet periphery. These included incursions in the Black Sea and attacks from Iraq and Persia itself. Naval blockade, that staple of Indian defence, was no longer advocated, since it was no longer likely to be able to affect Russia.[56] In 1931, the COS undertook further examination of the means

[51]   Christopher Andrew, *Secret Service: The Making of the British Intelligence Community* (London, 1985), 203–45; 259–338.

[52]   What follows is based, except where otherwise noted, on Keith Neilson, '"Pursued by a Bear": British Estimates of Soviet Military Strength and Anglo-Soviet Relations, 1922–1939', *Canadian Journal of History*, 28 (1993), 194–203.

[53]   'Afghanistan. Second (Interim) Report', COS 48, Beatty (1st Sea Lord), Milne (CIGS) and Trenchard (CAS), 29 July 1926, Cab 53/12.

[54]   The minutes of the Persian Gulf Sub-Committee are in Cab 16/93; the memoranda are in Cab 16/94.

[55]   'Report by the Chiefs of Staff Sub-Committee', COS 179, Trenchard (CAS), Madden (First Sea Lord) and Milne, 11 October, Cab 53/16.

[56]   'Russia – Possible Subsidiary Operations Against', JP 31, R.H. Peck, 12 December 1927, Cab 55/5; 'Subsidiary Operations in the Black Sea', JP 34, Admiralty (Plans

of striking a blow against Russia in the region. The War Office and Air Ministry based their plans on seizing an advanced base in Persia and operating from it. The Admiralty, however, preferred to defend the Persian oil fields from the Gulf, where naval power could play a more significant role.[57] A deadlock ensued, and the entire matter was not discussed again until 1933.[58]

By that time, the increased threats from Japan and Germany shunted considerations of defence against Soviet Russia to the background. The Defence Requirements Sub-Committee, which reported in 1934 on Britain's military needs, put the defence of India into third place, well behind the need to prepare to meet the challenges of Japan and Germany.[59] This meant that Soviet Russia was now considered in the context of how it could aid Britain in dealing with these threats. In the Far East, the British utilised the on-going quarrel between Tokyo and Moscow in Manchuria to their own advantage. While unable and unwilling to reach any formal agreement with the Russians, the British were quick to encourage Tokyo in the belief that the European powers (and the United States) presented a united front against Japanese aggression.[60] In Europe, repeated Soviet demands for a 'united front against fascism' were met with scepticism by the British.[61] This resulted from a number of things. The first was a suspicion that Soviet Russia merely wanted to foment trouble between Nazi Germany and Britain and would take no action against Berlin unless Soviet interests were directly involved. And, after the Purges that decimated the Soviet armed forces in 1937, there was little confidence that the Red Army could do anything to check Hitler. These beliefs underpinned the British attitude towards Russia during the Munich crisis.

In 1939, however, things changed. Faced with imminent peril, the British opened alliance talks with Russia in the spring.[62] Mutual suspicion prevented any agreement from being reached. British evaluations of Russian strength changed

---

Division), 8 February 1928, Cab 55/5; 'Russia – Plan for Subsidiary Operations against Russia in Perso-Iraq Area', JP 45, C.L.N. Newall (Director of Operations and Intelligence, Air Staff), 29 January 1930.

[57]   'Plan for Subsidiary Operations Against Russia in the Perso-Iraq Area', DMO & I (WO) and DOI (Air Ministry), 11 December 1930, Cab 53/22; minutes 48th meeting JPC, 10 December 1931, Cab 55/1.

[58]   The Russian threat to India was not reconsidered until 1938; see Pradeep Barua, 'Strategies and Doctrines of Imperial Defence: Britain and India, 1919–45', *Journal of Imperial and Commonwealth History*, 25, 2 (1997), 240–66; Milan Hauner, 'The Soviet Threat to Afghanistan and India, 1938–1940', *Modern Asian Studies*, 15, 2 (1982), 287–309.

[59]   For the workings of the DRC, see Keith Neilson, 'The Defence Requirements Sub-Committee, British Strategic Foreign Policy, Neville Chamberlain and the Path to Appeasement', *English Historical Review*, 118, 477 (2003), 651–84.

[60]   Greg Kennedy, '1935: A Snapshot of British Imperial Defence in the Far East', in Kennedy and Neilson, eds, *Far-Flung Lines*, 190–216.

[61]   Neilson, *Britain, Soviet Russia*, 120–253 forms the basis of my discussion.

[62]   Ibid., 254–317.

in the spring of 1939. The Soviet regime was now thought capable of providing sufficient aid to Poland to allow the latter to resist German aggression long enough for Britain and France to be able to implement their long-term policies of establishing a Western front and strangling the Nazi regime economically.

The signing of the Nazi-Soviet Pact and the subsequent outbreak of war changed the status of Soviet Russia in British eyes from potential ally to malignant neutral.[63] Indeed, Soviet actions in the autumn of 1939 – the Russo-Finnish War and the Soviet supply of vital war material to Germany – led many to consider that Moscow was an enemy in all but name. If this was so, the performance of the Red Army in Poland did not cause a great deal of concern for British military observers. They believed that the Red Army could not undertake an offensive and could offer little help to the Germans in any joint operations. Indeed, the Soviet forces were felt 'capable of taking hard blows but is not capable of delivering them'.[64] In fact, by the end of October, the COS were discussing the effect of Britain's declaring war on Russia. Here, the main concern was that the Soviets might strike 'against Iran, Iraq and India', but, given Britain's existing commitments, the Chiefs opposed London's initiating hostilities.[65] By the beginning of 1940, however, plans were afoot for taking action against Russia. These involved air attacks against the Russian oil wells at Baku and instituting a blockade of Vladivostok, two actions that would plug the hole in the British blockade and stop the flow of fuel to Germany.[66] The end to the Russo-Finnish War and the subsequent German invasion of Norway meant that these operations never left the planning stage, but the fact that they were seriously considered underlines the animosity that the British felt towards Russia.

After the fall of France, the British interest in Soviet Russia focused on the inadvertent assistance that Moscow could extend to the British war effort. In the Far East, continuing Soviet aid to China was useful in that it helped to keep

---

[63]   The best coverage is in Michael J. Carley, '"A Situation of Delicacy and Danger": Anglo-Soviet Relations, August 1939–March 1940', *Central European History*, 2 (1999), 175–208, which is expanded in his *1939: The Alliance that Never Was and the Coming of World War II* (Chicago, 1999), 213–59. Carley's treatment of the Soviet position is more sympathetic than my own.

[64]   The opinions of British military attachés in Moscow, in Seeds to FO, dispatch 303, 20 October 1939, FO 371/23678/N5778/57/38 and, for the quotation, 'The Red Army', secret, MI 2(b), 22 November 1939, WO 193/642.

[65]   'Soviet Aggression Against Finland or other Scandinavian Countries', WP (39) 107, 31 October 1939, Cab 66/3.

[66]   For these plans, see Brock Millman, 'Toward War with Russia: British Naval and Air Planning for Conflict in the Near East, 1939–40', *Journal of Contemporary History*, 29 (1994), 261–83; Patrick R. Osborn, *Operation Pike: Britain Versus the Soviet Union, 1939–1941* (Westport, CT, 2000), 139–56; C.O. Richardson, 'French Plans for Allied Attacks on the Caucasus Oil Fields, January–April 1940', *French Historical Studies*, 8 (1973), 130–56; Talbot Imlay, 'A Reassessment of the Anglo-French Strategy during the Phony War, 1939–1940', *English Historical Review*, 119, 481 (2004), 362–70.

Tokyo stuck in the Chinese bog.[67] In Europe, it was hoped that Russia might act as a barrier to German expansion in the Balkans, although the War Office was convinced that the Red Army was in no condition to prevent such an advance.[68] In these circumstances, the British began to divert troops away from Egypt to Greece in an attempt to buoy the latter against Italy and any expected German involvement. This proved inadequate, and the German invasion of Yugoslavia on 6 April led to a rapid collapse of any Balkan barrier.

When Germany invaded Soviet Russia in June 1941, Britain and Russia were once again allies.[69] But, to borrow a felicitous phrase, they were only 'allies of a kind'. As in the First World War, the two countries lacked a common front and the Soviets shared the Tsarist belief that the British would fight to the last drop of Soviet blood. This belief was compounded by the fact that there was no Western front in the fashion of 1914–1918. The Soviet demand that the Western Allies open a 'second front' was, in fact, a major point of contention. In the initial phases of the war, in 1941, Stalin suggested that British forces open a second front either in France or the Balkans; alternatively 25–30 British divisions could be sent to Russia, via either Iran or Archangel, to aid in the defence of Moscow. These suggestions were given an anodyne reply, since British troops had their hands full in the Middle East, and the size of the commitment that the Soviets requested was out of the realm of possibility.[70] The British were, in fact, at this time determined to defend the 'Northern Front' of the Middle East against a German assault if Soviet Russia collapsed.[71] In 1942 and 1943, there were rumours that Moscow contemplated making a separate peace with Germany, something that helped to push the British towards a reluctant acceptance of a cross-Channel invasion.[72] Behind the British

[67]   See the scattered remarks in Antony Best, *Britain, Japan and Pearl Harbour. Avoiding war in East Asia, 1936–1941* (London and New York, 1995), and *idem*, *British Intelligence and the Japanese Challenge in Asia, 1914–1941* (Basingstoke and New York, 2002).

[68]   Gabriel Gorodetsky, *Grand Delusion: Stalin and the German Invasion of Russia* (New Haven and London, 1999) 89–154; 'Will Stalin Fight', Lt-Col. D.A. Mackenzie (MI 2), 8 January 1941, WO 208/1758.

[69]   The best studies of the wartime relationship are Victor Rothwell, *Britain and the Cold War 1941–1947* (London, 1982) and Martin Kitchen, *British Policy Towards the Soviet Union during the Second* World *War* (London, 1986).

[70]   John Erickson, 'Stalin, Soviet Strategy and the Grand Alliance', in Ann Lee and Howard Temperley, eds, *The Rise and Fall of the Grand Alliance, 1941–45* (London, 1995), 140–41.

[71]   Nicholas Tamkin, 'Britain, the Middle East, and the "Northern Front", 1941–1942', *War in History*, 15, 3 (2008), 314–36.

[72]   Vojtech Mastny, 'Stalin and the Prospects of a Separate Peace in World War II', *American Historical Review*, 77, 5 (1972), 1365–88; H.W. Koch, 'The Spectre of a Separate Peace in the East: Russo-German "Peace Feelers", 1942–44', *Journal of Contemporary History*, 10, 3 (1975), 531–49; Keith Sainsbury, '"Second front in 1942" – A Strategic Controversy Revisited', *British Journal of International Studies*, 4 (1978), 47–58 and

unwillingness to consider the second front, lay two things. First, there was the manifest difficulty of so doing, something that Churchill never tired of telling to both Stalin and Roosevelt. The other was the fact that the British plans for winning the war were based on the long-term weapons of blockade and strategic air attack. This was a strategy that fit British pre-war planning, economically and financially.[73] British strategy was not going to be deflected by Soviet Russia; only the United States had the requisite influence to push Churchill towards the Continent.

What the British were willing to do was to provide Soviet Russia with as many supplies as possible.[74] The problems involved in doing so were reminiscent of the First World War. The Soviets complained that Britain did not send as much as promised as quickly as was wanted. The British complained of Soviet obstructionism and secrecy. And there was the difficulty of getting the supplies to Russia, something solved by the convoys to Murmansk and Archangel, as well as by the overland route through Iran. Despite these difficulties, the British contribution to Soviet Russia was enormous. From October 1941 to the end of March 1946, the British sent £308 millions' worth of military equipment and £112 million of other materiel.[75] While the exact impact of British (and American) aid to Russia has been a matter of debate, it is clear that Soviet advances against Germany would have been substantially delayed had foreign supplies not been forthcoming.

The needs of coalition warfare did not mean that British attitudes towards Russia had changed. Once Russia had entered the war, efforts were made to pursue a policy of cooperation and to ignore the difficulties that Russian attitudes introduced in the functioning of the alliance. However, at Yalta and Potsdam, it was clear that such a policy had borne no fruit. Soviet insistence on control of Eastern Europe in any peace settlement (and American acceptance of this) led to a hardening of attitudes in London.[76] At the Foreign Office, this trend continued after

---

Tuvia Ben-Moshe, 'Winston Churchill and the "Second Front": A Reappraisal', *Journal of Modern History*, 62 (1990), 503–17. Ironically, Stalin feared that the British might make a separate peace and leave Russia to fight alone; see Jonathan Haslam, 'Stalin's Fears of a Separate Peace, 1942', *Intelligence and National Security*, 8, 4 (1993), 97–99.

[73] G.C. Peden, *Arms, Economics and British Strategy* (Cambridge, 2007), 199–217.

[74] What follows is based on John Daniel Langer, 'The Harriman-Beaverbrook Mission and the Debate over Unconditional Aid for the Soviet Union, 1941', *Journal of Contemporary History*, 14 (1979), 463–82; Joan Beaumont, *Comrades in Arms: British Aid to Russia, 1941–1945* (London, 1980); Mark Harrison, 'The Soviet Economy and Relations with the United States and Britain, 1941–45', in Lane and Temperley, *Grand Alliance*, 69–89. The latter is also found in slightly modified form in Mark Harrison, *Accounting for War: Soviet Production, Employment, and the Defence Burden, 1940–1945* (Cambridge, 1996), 128–54.

[75] Beaumont, *Comrades*, 202–03.

[76] Michael Dockrill, 'Defending the Empire or Defeating the Enemy: British War Aims 1938–47', in Peter Catterall with C.J. Morris, *Britain and the Threat to Stability in Europe, 1918–45* (London and New York, 1993), 117–21; Norman A. Graebner, 'Yalta,

the war. Opinion there was fuelled by reports from the heads of British military occupation forces in Europe, who believed that any chance of cooperation with the Soviets was illusory. While the British Foreign Secretary, Ernest Bevin, attempted to pursue an even-handed course, by the end of 1947, he had come to share the view that Britain must oppose Soviet efforts globally in order to check communist expansion.[77]

How was this to be done?[78] In 1947, the COS produced the Overall Strategic Plan, outlining Britain's defence position in the post-war.[79] They argued that Soviet attacks anywhere on the globe would have to be met by massive air strikes. While the perimeter of Empire had been reduced when India and Pakistan became independent in 1947, this did not mean that the new Commonwealth members were not threatened by Russia.[80] The locations from which air strikes could be launched – Britain itself, the Middle East and West Pakistan – underlined where the British felt it likely that it would have to face Soviet aggression.[81] In addition, Britain would require allies, particularly the United States, since it was deemed impossible to check any Russian advance by British efforts alone. In 1950, after the formation of the North Atlantic Treaty Organization (NATO), a second study re-emphasised many of these conclusions.[82] With allies available to help defend

---

Potsdam, and Beyond: The British and American Perspectives', in Lane and Temperley, *Grand Alliance*, 226–54; Graham Ross, 'Foreign Office Attitudes to the Soviet Union 1941–45', *Journal of Contemporary History*, 16 (1981), 521–40; P.G.H. Holdich, 'A Policy of Percentages? British Policy and the Balkans after the Moscow Conference of October 1944', *International History Review*, 9, 1 (1987), 28–47. For what the Soviets intended, Jonathan Haslam, 'Soviet War-Aims', in Lane and Temperley, *Grand Alliance*, 22–42.

[77]   Ray Merrick, 'The Russia Committee of the British Foreign Office and the Cold War, 1946–47', *Journal of Contemporary History*, 20 (1985), 453–68; Sean Greenwood, 'Frank Roberts and the "Other" Long Telegram: The View from the British Embassy in Moscow, March 1946', *Journal of Contemporary History*, 25 (1990), 103–22.

[78]   For useful introductions to the various problems of imperial defence after 1945, see the contributions by John Kent, David French, Greg Kennedy, James Corum and Ashley Jackson, all in Greg Kennedy, ed, *Imperial Defence: The Old World Order 1856–1956* (London and New York, 2008), which introduce the literature.

[79]   'The Overall Strategic Plan', DO(47), May 1947, published in Julian Lewis, *Changing Direction: British Military Planning for Post-war Strategic Defence 1942–1947* (London, 1988), 370–87.

[80]   On the shrinking of Empire, see A.G. Hopkins, 'Rethinking Decolonization', *Past and Present*, 200 (2008), 211–47, which also introduces the vast literature.

[81]   For an examination of part of this, see Richard Aldrich and Michael Coleman, 'Britain and the Strategic Air Offensive Against the Soviet Union: the Question of South Asian Air Bases, 1945–9', *History*, 74 (1989), 400–426; Simon J. Ball, 'Bomber Bases and British Strategy in the Middle East, 1945–1949', *Journal of Strategic Studies*, 14, 4 (1991), 515–33.

[82]   'Defence Policy and Global Strategy', DO (50), 45, 7 June 1950, printed in *Documents on British Policy Overseas* (London, 1991), series 2, vol. 4, 411–31.

Europe, Britain should focus on the ability to strike a strategic blow against Russia from the United Kingdom itself, all the while holding its base in Egypt.[83] Two years later, the Global Strategy Paper made the British position clear.[84] The Soviet Union was clearly identified as Britain's most dangerous enemy. While an imminent Soviet attack was unlikely, the COS were determined that Moscow needed to be deterred by the threat of nuclear weapons. Much of this, due to the economic constraints that hobbled British defence in the era, would be furnished by the United States. However, the British would maintain their own independent deterrent – a justification for a British nuclear force that would be used in concert with the greater American capacity.[85]

This British approach reached its apotheosis in 1957. The White Paper of that year, introduced by the Secretary of Defence, Duncan Sandys, argued that British defence must be based – *pace* Neville Chamberlain in the 1930s – on the country's economic strength and financial resources.[86] Any Russian advances would be met by a nuclear response, and, as a consequence, conventional forces could be reduced. This approach was necessitated by economic considerations, but also reflected a belief that thermonuclear weapons had brought about an end to a direct Soviet threat in Europe. What needed to be dealt with were 'proxy wars' sponsored by the Soviet Union, something that would require rapid-reaction forces similar to those that were such a feature of British Imperial defence in the nineteenth century. However, while much was made of the independence that this makeover of British defence policy gave to London, Sandys – particularly in the aftermath of Suez – was determined that Britain would go to war only in conjunction with allies, particularly the United States. If the Soviet Union were to be contained globally, this would be done in the context of an alliance.

What does this examination of British strategic foreign policy with respect to Russia tell us about the 'British way in warfare'? Essentially, it suggests that the competing paradigms, those of the 'navalist', 'Continentalist' and even the 'mixed' variety, are inadequate explanations. One problem is that two of them are time bound; affected by the 'presentist' concerns of the day. Liddell Hart, writing in the aftermath of the Great War, was determined that Britain should not commit itself to the Continent again with the attendant casualties of 1914–18. Correlli Barnett, writing in the midst of the Cold War, in a period of British economic decline, and

---

[83]   On the need for Egypt, John Kent, 'The Egyptian Base and the Defence of the Middle East, 1945–54', *Journal of Imperial and Commonwealth History*, 21 (1993), 45–65.

[84]   John Baylis and Alan Macmillan, 'The British Global Strategy Paper of 1952', *Journal of Strategic Studies*, 16, 2 (1993), 200–226.

[85]   For the economic constraints, Peden, *Arms, Economics*, 229–71.

[86]   What follows is based on Wyn Rees, 'The 1957 Sandys White Paper: New Priorities in British Defence Policy', *Journal of Strategic Studies*, 12, 1 (1989), 215–29; also germane here is Martin S. Navias, 'Strengthening the Deterrent? British Medium Bomber Forces Debate, 1955–56', *Journal of Strategic Studies,* 11, 2 (1988), 203–19.

where the assistance of the United States was integral to any attempt to check the world's other superpower, failed to consider that these circumstances were not timeless when he argued that Britain had to commit itself to the Europe for its own safety. The 'mixed' paradigm – that naval power was important for colonial matters, but inadequate to safeguard Britain against a Continental opponent is more attractive, but also fails to explain the Russian case.

When evaluating such explanations that are meant to have universal application for an understanding of the British way in warfare the study of Russia raises several points. The first is that to create models that deal only with countries with whom Britain actually fought, is to consider things too narrowly, and to assume that British strategic foreign policy was influenced by only those states. While they never fought (except in the Crimea, a particular case), Russia was Britain's primary opponent in the global context – and Britain was a global power – for more than one hundred years, and considerations of that state shaped British defence policy at least as much as did any other Power.

A second shortcoming is to ignore geography. As a result of geography, Anglo-Russian relations were different from those between Britain and the other major European powers, and the fact that the generalisations about British defence policy have as their historical basis wars with such western European states as Spain, France and Germany has distorted our understanding of that policy. While Britain and Russia both had European interests, they were unlikely to come to blows directly on that continent, the sole exception being after 1945, when the Fulda Gap replaced the North-West frontier as the most likely site of direct Anglo-Russian confrontation. Thus for Britain, when dealing with Russia, a Continental commitment was a matter of choice, since she could be certain that she would not have to face that country alone in the unlikely circumstances that Russia could threaten to reach the Channel. Before 1914, the balance of power meant that any Russian aggression in the European context would generate opposition from the other Great Powers. In the inter-war period, Soviet Russia was incapable of threatening Western Europe. After 1945, NATO provided the necessary assistance, although Britain's Army of the Rhine gave substance to Stanley Baldwin's pronouncement that Britain's frontier now lay on that river and to the later Continentalist argument.

A third issue involves both geography and Empire. Because Britain could not strike a direct blow at Russia on the Continent, this meant that London was forced to adopt a 'peripheral' strategy when dealing with that country in either its Tsarist or Soviet guise. This took a naval form in the nineteenth century, with the British determined to strike maritime blows globally against Russia. Between the wars, this policy was augmented by possible air strikes launched from Imperial outposts against the Russian borderlands. After 1945, such air assaults became the preferred option, with the increased range of British aircraft making it possible to hit the Soviet Union from Britain itself. But, if the Empire provided useful bases for prodding the bear, it also was a hostage to ursine attacks. The defence of India was an unsolvable problem. The cost of doing so was high and the likelihood of assistance was nil. This Imperial aspect alone makes the impact of Russia on British defence planning completely different from that of any other Power, and suggests that none of the paradigms discussed above is an adequate tool for analysing British policy.[87]

Instead, the only explanation that is able to deal with the Russian case is French's assertion that British policy was both 'adaptive' and designed to achieve her security ends at a minimum cost, the latter widely defined. This is far more than a policy of muddling through. What it reflects, and what an examination of Anglo-Russian relations reveals, is that British circumstances were unique. As a global power for the entire period under consideration, Britain had to adjust how she dealt with Russia according to power-political circumstances that were constantly changing yet in an unvarying geographical context. A hard and fast definition of the British way in warfare remains elusive.

---

[87] Nor does the interesting concept of an 'Anglo-Saxon' way in warfare put forward by Walter Russell Mead, *God and Gold: Britain, America and the Making of the Modern World* (London, 2007), 85–191, though it provides a fascinating point of departure.

Chapter 2

Some Principles of Anglo-American Strategic Relations, 1900–1945

Greg Kennedy

I

The work of David French has often involved the way in which Britain has constructed wartime alliances, a key component of the British Way of Warfare.[1] Britain's need for allies to maintain its position within the ranking structure of the Great Powers was absolute. And nowhere was this need more apparent than in the twentieth century. Faced with fighting two world wars, with prosecuting an extended Cold War, and with maintaining its position as a global player within the post-Cold War international system, Britain could not, and did not, overcome these challenges alone. This chapter will investigate Great Britain's most important alliance in that century: the Anglo-American strategic relationship.[2]

---

[1]   David French, *British Strategy and War Aims*, (London, 1986); *idem, The British Way in Warfare, 1688–2000* (London, 1990); *idem, Military Identities: the Regimental System, the British Army, and the British People, c. 1870–2000* (Oxford, 2005); *idem, Raising Churchill's Army: The British Army and the War Against Germany, 1919–1945* (Oxford, 2000); *idem, The Strategy of the Lloyd George Coalition, 1916–1918* (Oxford, 1995).

[2]   Joel H. Wiener and Mark Hampton eds, *Anglo-American Media Interactions, 1850–2000* (Basingstoke, 2007); Jonathan Hollowell ed., *Twentieth Century Anglo-American Relations* (Basingstoke, 2001); David Reynolds, Warren Kimball and A.O. Chubarian, eds, *Allies at War: the Soviet, American and British Experience, 1939–1945* (New York, 1994); Alex Danchev, *On Specialness: Essays in Anglo-American Relations* (New York, 1998); Alan Dobson, *US Wartime Aid to Britain, 1940–1946* (New York, 1986); William H McNeill, *America, Britain and Russia: Their Co-operation and Conflict, 1941–1946* (Oxford, 1953); Warren F. Kimball ed., *Churchill and Roosevelt: The Complete Correspondence, Vol. I, Alliance Emerging, October 1933–November 1942* (Princeton, 1984); Mark A. Stoler, *The Politics of the Second Front: American Military Planning and Diplomacy in Coalition Warfare, 1941–1943* (Westport, CT, 1977); *idem, Allies in War: Britain and America Against the Axis Powers, 1940–1945* (London, 2005); Randall B. Woods, *A Changing of the Guard: Anglo-American Relations, 1941–1946* (Chapel Hill, NC, 1990); Terry H. Anderson, *The United States, Great Britain and the Cold War, 1944–1947* (Columbia, 1981); David B. Woolner ed., *The Second Quebec Conference Revisited: Waging War, Formulating Peace: Canada, Great Britain and the United States, 1944–1945*

It is unquestionably the case that the relationship between Great Britain and the United States of America was the most important strategic partnership of the last century, and, some would argue, even beyond that.[3] The 1900s were the Anglo-American century. Militarily, economically, industrially and geographically dominant, the two nations were the main determiners that dictated the pattern of conflict for the century. And, at present, that truism is no less apparent, particularly given the nature of the conflicts which have occurred over the past fifteen years.[4] No other pair of nations have collaborated, competed, and conspired to the same extent, on such a wide array of issues, over such an extended period of time. There is, indeed, something special about that relationship. However, special does not mean inevitable, nor does it mean right or natural. Today the debate still rages as to whether Britain is better off with Europe than with America, or, indeed, whether America even appreciates its relationship with the middle power, Britain. The closeness of this strategic relationship creates jealousy, animosity, anger and suspicion, as well as loyalty, tolerance, admiration and understanding, all within the same social, economic and ethnic classes.[5]

(New York, 1988); Donald Cameron Watt, 'Britain and the Historiography of the Yalta Conference and the Cold War', *Diplomatic History*, Vol. 13 (Winter, 1989), pp. 67–98; Greg Kennedy, *Anglo-American Strategic Relations, 1933–1939: Imperial Crossroads* (London, 2002); Iestyn Adams, *Brothers Across the Ocean: British Foreign Policy and the Origins of the Anglo-American 'Special Relationship' 1900–1905* (New York, 2005); William H. Becker and Samuel F. Wells Jr, *Economics and World Power: An Assessment of American Diplomacy Since 1789* (New York, 1984); Robert Self, *Britain, America and the War Debt Controversy: The Economic Diplomacy of an Unspecial Relationship, 1917–1941* (London, 2006); G.C. Peden, *Arms, Economics and British Strategy: From Dreadnoughts to Hydrogen Bombs* (Cambridge, 2007).

[3] Walter Russell Mead, *God and Gold: Britain, America, and the Making of the Modern World* (New York, 2007).

[4] Lawrence Freedman, *The Transformation of Strategic Affairs* Adelphi Paper 379 (London, 2006); Bernard Porter, *Empire and Superempire: Britain, America and the World* (New Haven, 2006); Niall Ferguson, *Empire: How Britain Made the Modern World* (London, 2003); *idem, Colossus: The Rise and Fall of the American Empire* (New York, 2004); Charles S. Maier, *Among Empires: American Ascendancy and Its Predecessors* (Cambridge, MA, 2006).

[5] Gary Hart, *The Fourth Power: A Grand Strategy for the United States in the Twenty-First Century* (Oxford, 2004); Stephen M. Walt, 'Why Alliances Endure or Collapse', *Survival*, Vol.39, No.1 (Spring 1997), pp. 156–79; James B. Steinberg, 'An Elective Partnership: Salvaging Transatlantic Relations', *Survival*, Vol.45, No.2 (Summer, 2003), pp. 113–46; Ivo H. Daalder, 'The End of Atlanticism', *Survival*, Vol.45, No.2 (Summer, 2003), pp. 147–66; Lawrence Freedman, 'The Transatlantic Agenda: Vision and Counter-Vision', *Survival*, Vol.47, No.4 (Winter, 2005–06), pp. 19–38; James Dobbins, 'New Directions for Transatlantic Security Cooperation', i, Vol.47, No.4 (Winter, 2005–06), pp. 39–54; Jeffrey D. McCausland and Douglas T. Stuart, eds., *US–UK Relations at the Start of the 21st Century* (Carlisle, 2006).

The most important part of that relationship's development is to be found in the formative period, in the first half of the twentieth century, before the static forces of the Cold War locked many strategic elements into place in a new, and artificial international system. The demands of that bipolar relationship not only froze the antagonists into place, arresting the progress of regional relations, but also constrained alliance relationships. In the period between 1900 and 1945, and in particular the period from 1914 to 1943, the bedrock of the strategic culture that utilised the principles of the Anglo-American strategic relationship was formed.[6] It was that relationship which would be subject to glacial changes over the period from 1945 to 1990. And those influences, those principles, can still be found wandering the corridors of Whitehall and the British policymaking process even today, as ideas such as wars of humanity, force for good, and concepts of crusades and imperialism, still abound in modern journals and books that form the basis of the intellectual environment of Anglo-American strategic policymaking. In Washington, as well, the hand of history touches contemporary American policymakers, as debates about imperialism, special relations, and coalitions swirl around the corridors of power.[7]

In this chapter what is meant by 'principles' and 'strategic' is important for the reader. Firstly, principles are not laws. They are assessments of a combination of elements that are as the basis for prediction and assumption, but they are not either permanent or absolute. With regard to Anglo-American strategic relations in the period under review here, several principles were key aspects of that relationship. They represented sensitive areas of interaction, which, if treated crudely or tactfully, properly or improperly, affected the very nature of that relationship. Most importantly, the primary use of these principles was to create closer, more open and more reliable strategic relations. The management of these key areas and the operational working of these principles was the purview of official and unofficial networks, working primarily in the areas of foreign, economic and defence policy. They were areas governed and run by elites, who, while part of a democratic society, had to acknowledge the boundaries of public opinion on their policymaking, but did not have to abide by the fickle nature of the populace to oversee the daily running of those policies.

---

[6]   Colin S. Gray, *Strategy and History: Essays on Theory and Practice* (London, 2006); Richard Lock-Pullan, *US Intervention Policy and Army Innovation: from Vietnam to Iraq* (London, 2005); Lawrence Sondhaus, *Strategic Culture and Way of War* (London, 2006); Asle Toje, *America, the EU and Strategic Culture: Renegotiating the Transatlantic Bargain* (London, 2008); Alan Macmillan, 'Strategic Culture and National Ways in Warfare: The British Case', *Royal United Services Institute Journal* (October, 1995), pp. 32–42.

[7]   Christopher Meyer, *DC Confidential: The Controversial Memoirs of Britain's Ambassador to the United States of 9/11 and the Run-up to the Iraq War* (London, 2005); Gideon Rachman, 'Is the Anglo-American Relationship Still Special?', *Washington Quarterly* (Spring, 2001), pp. 7–20; Robin Niblett, 'Choosing Between American and Europe', *International Affairs*, Vol.83, No.4 (2007), pp. 627–35.

Those principles were several. First, money was the most important source of both cooperation and tension. Second, the most constructive strategic relations, particularly in peace time, took place at the periphery of each nation's core strategic interests: in the imperial, not the European, areas of intersection. Third, maritime power was the basis of each nation's military power internationally and thus was the key source of military power interactions. Army and air force relations were not as important. Fourth, the sharing of military technology to promote confidence building between administrations/elites that were suspicious of one another was a cheap way to smooth relations and give public opinion positive issues on which to focus. As well, such sharing created confusion in other nations as to the exact nature of Anglo-American relations. That uncertainty was a useful diplomatic tool for influencing, coercing and deterrence. Fifth, both nations were aware of the need to never embarrass or lead the other government about international topics that the public were not likely to support, thus avoiding exposing the relationship to public debate. This meant ensuring that the public was not introduced to areas of contention until the parameters of each nation's position were determined by the elites so it could be handled by government officials with the media in each country. Sixth, the need to understand one another was not equally important for both sides, nor was it pursued equally. Britain attempted to influence America more so than the reverse, because of an American lack of appreciation of any need to employ this soft power option at the time. Finally, the British cared more about what America thought of it than vice versa; this was true with respect to both the public and the elites.[8]

So what then is meant by strategic? The concept of strategic relations used here is an all-encompassing one. There is only one strategic level, which by its very nature covers the coordination of all strategic elements. There is no Grand Strategic or Military Strategic level of war. To separate these areas artificially is to violate the very thing that is supposed to, and must, occur: that is, the consideration of all aspects of concern to the conflict at hand. This approach is historically accurate. The British and American strategic policymaking processes discussed here did not make that sort of artificial divide. While the British system of decision-making was markedly superior to the American throughout this entire period, employing a more comprehensive means of information gathering and processing for strategic planning purposes, that fact is not relevant here.[9] In both countries, the process of strategic policymaking had the same aim: the creation of a global strategy incorporating all aspects of power within the national framework.

---

[8]   Stephen Badsey, 'Propaganda and the Defence of Empire, 1856–1956', in Greg Kennedy ed., *Imperial Defence: the Old World Order, 1956–1956* (London, 2008), pp. 218–33.

[9]   W.R. Rock, *British Appeasement in the 1930s* (London, 1977); Gaines Post Jr, *Dilemmas of Appeasement: British Deterence and Defense, 1934–1937* (Ithaca, NY, 1993).

II

This study will concentrate on three main areas of interaction, or centres of gravity, between the two nations and the Ambassadors who managed those issues: economics, maritime power and the mental maps and morals of the two nations' foreign policy. The first two are relatively self-explanatory. In this period the maritime component was the key military aspect of the strategic policymaking. The economic power of each was also a constant source of power, a form of power that was as equally able to coerce, deter, embrace, bribe, and attack, as the maritime component. Indeed, the links between each nation's economic and maritime power were absolute, thus forming an important conjunction of commonality between the two systems. This conjunction allowed close cooperation (perhaps uniquely special cooperation) but also evoked equally protectionist and hostile response to any attempts by the other to interfere with the other's management of the maritime or economic environment globally. However, it is with respect to the third aspect, the creation of strategic foreign policy, that there is some need for further clarification. Within that process, the concepts of motives, public opinion and geography are key points for analysis, as are the institutional cultures of the professional bodies charged with implementing policy. As the key institutional links between the two nations, the British Ambassadors had to deal with all these strategic factors constantly.

When historians view the nature of the strategic relationship which existed between these two English-speaking nations, trying to trace its evolution, they must overcome a number of contemporary influences. The first is the belief that there was somehow a 'natural' or pre-ordained rise of the United States to the status of 'leader of the free world' or hegemon.[10] This determinism has been contributed to in large part by American historians seeking to persuade others that the exceptionalism and Darwinian selectionism that is the American experience will be inevitably triumphant. The American path throughout the twentieth century is portrayed as an inexorable journey to the position of being the world's most powerful nation. Most importantly, this journey is seen as being an individual role: saviour of Europe twice; overseer of Latin American freedom and stability; and policeman of the Far East. Seldom do studies of the American involvement in any but total war conflicts portray America's role as either subservient or subsidiary.[11]

---

[10]   Niall Ferguson, *Empire: How Britain Made the Modern World* (London, 2004); Michael Howard, *The Continental Commitment: The Dilemma of British Defence Policy in the Era of Two World Wars* (London, 1972); W. Wark, *The Ultimate Enemy: British Intelligence and Nazi Germany, 1933–39* (Ithaca, NY, 1985); B.J.C. McKercher, *Transition of Power: Britain's Loss of Global Pre-eminence to the United States, 1930–1945* (Cambridge, 1999).

[11]   John Baylis, *Anglo-American Defence Relations, 1939–1980* (London, 1981); Wayne S. Cole, *Determinism and American Foreign Relations During the Franklin D. Roosevelt Era*, (Lanham, MD, and London, 1995); J.D. Doenecke and J.E. Witz, *From*

On the other side of the equation, the British role in its relationship with America is often portrayed as one of inevitable decline. From being the world's greatest power to becoming a junior partner dwarfed by the massive armies and industries of America and the Soviet Union in 1945, Great Britain's empire was doomed to implode upon itself in a chaotic rubble of imperial overstretch, organisational malaise, class division, technological ineptitude and competing visions of empire.[12] As for the United States, the jury is divided. Some historians bemoan the fact that the young, Anglo-Saxon nation did not rush immediately to the aid of its Atlantic cousin in both World Wars. American aid was instead only given grudgingly and sporadically to noble Britain. What is more galling to these Atlantic Bloc advocates is the fact that such aid had conditions attached, conditions that were to the benefit of the American strategic position. In the light of such betrayal, many argue, Great Britain would have been better off to abandon France and the rest of Europe to German design and strike a separate peace. In so doing, goes this illogical thinking, the British Empire would have been protected and valuable British blood and treasury would not have been wasted while America lapped up the unguarded remnants of the Empire. Such attempts to argue for the continued 'Greatness' of Great Britain and its empire through isolation fail to understand how the British Empire influenced and controlled the international system of this period for its national interests. Those interests were protected through the control of key maritime and economic aspects of the system and, thus, through those global linkages, the empire had to maintain the very fabric of this inter-connected system. And, in the British efforts of the first half of the twentieth century to maintain that status quo, the United States, as a maritime power, as a democratic, capitalist, industrial state, and as a non-European, English-speaking nation, geographically isolated and with similar but not identical values towards the international system, was the key part of British global security needs.

A key point in all of this is to determine what sort of imperial powers the United States and Britain were in this period. The British were a conscious and unashamed imperial power, comfortable at all levels of government and society with that system of economic and security provision. The United States, however, was an unconscious and embarrassed imperial power that found its need for such imperial policies, as the Monroe Doctrine, post-Spanish American war possessions and the Open Door in China, uncomfortable truths it would have to

---

Isolationism to War, 1931–1941 (Arlington Heights, IL, 1991); Walter LaFeber, *The Clash: US–Japanese Relations Throughout History* (New York, 1997).

[12]   John Charmley, *Splendid Isolation? Britain and the Balance of Power 1874–1914* (London, 1999); Lawrence James, *The Rise and Fall of the British Empire* (London, 1994); Anil Seal ed., *The Decline, Revival and Fall of the British Empire: The Ford Lectures and Other Essays* (Cambridge, 1982); Paul Kennedy, *The Rise and Fall of the Great Powers: Economic Change and Military Conflict from 1500–2000* (London, 1988).

manage if it was to be more than a continental power.[13] Given the need for the rejection of Imperial Britain, and old Europe in general, if the American national identity myth was to flourish, it was not easy to allow ideas of being an empire just like Britain to be formal or public policy.[14] President Theodore Roosevelt ran great risks in taking his expansionist message to a conservative Midwest, and a cautious Eastern-Seaboard. But the vigour of Western expansion and the concept of Darwinian Manifest Destiny combined, along with the reaction to the Spanish-American experience, to galvanise enough of the American public into believing that, if the United States did not take on this greater interest in the far-flung regions of the world, particularly in China and the Far East, then unrestricted European expansionism would be allowed to work against America's long-term economic and strategic interests. Thus, ideas such as 'Dollar Diplomacy' or 'Missionary Diplomacy' were created, the equivalents of the White Man's Burden or Imperial Preference, thus creating a palatable face of imperialism for the American domestic markets.

Competition between American interests and other Europeans, such as Spain and then Germany in the period before the First World War, created a greater tolerance in America towards Britain. North American hemispheric issues necessary for closer Anglo-American relations included the Panama Canal and continued access to it, and safe-guarding the sovereignty of the Canadian position, as well as encouraging America to help exclude other Europeans from the Latin American area in general.[15] The Venezuelan dispute of 1903 and its eventual resolution was a good example of that coordination of interests, even though animosity towards the upstart American position had some backers in Britain who were worried about the effect of potential American industrial and maritime power on British security. However, on the points concerning maritime and economic power in the period preceding the 1914–18 war, some contemporary commentators and their views are worth noting, as an illustration that the idea of an Anglo-American alliance was a living concept within various British policymakers and influencers.

---

[13]   P.J. Cain and A.G. Hopkins, *British Imperialism, 1688–2000* 2nd edn (London, 2000); Andrew Thompson, *The Empire Strikes Back?: The Impact of Imperialism on Britain from the Mid-Nineteenth Century* (London, 2005); Bernard Porter, *The Absent-Minded Imperialists: What the British Really Thought about Empire* (Oxford, 2004); Carl Bridge and Kent Fedorowich, eds, *Special Issue of the Journal of Imperial and Commonwealth History, 'The British World: Diaspora, Culture and Identity'*, Vol.31, No.2 (May 2003).

[14]   Richard F. Hamilton, *President McKinley, War and Empire, vol. 2: President McKinely and America's 'New Empire'* (Edison, NJ, 2007); Hal M. Friedman, *Creating an American Lake: United States Imperialism and Strategic Security in the Pacific Basin, 1945–1947* (Westport, CT, 2001); David Harvey, *The New Imperialism* (Oxford, 2003); Chalmers Johnson, *The Sorrows of Empire: Militarism, Secrecy and the End of the Republic* (London, 2004); Frank A. Ninkovich, *The United States and Imperialism* (Malden, MA, 2001); Anne Rice Pierce, *Woodrow Wilson and Harry Truman: Mission and Power in American Foreign Policy* (New Brunswick, NJ, 2007).

[15]   Iestyn Adams, *Brothers Across the Ocean* (New York, 2005).

In May 1902, the publisher Sir Henry Newbolt asked the naval historian Julian Corbett to write an article on the Atlantic Trust, a project which Corbett told Newbolt he was thinking of doing himself in any case. The request prompted Corbett to comment to Newbolt that the two of them had 'only one brain between us'. He went on to tell the publisher:

> It has stuck me that there was an important aspect of the case which on one had called attention to. It is this: our great danger in case of war is the stoppage of our food and raw material and especially that which comes across the Atlantic. Now if this trade is to be in the hands of an Anglo-American syndicate how is a European army to stop it? By a stroke of the pen such ships as may remain under the English flag could be transferred to the American with perfect plausibility and if the European enemy refused to recognize the transfer it would mean almost certain war with America as well as ourselves. The Atlantic trade is certainly something they would fight for. They nearly did in 1794 while their debt to France was still warm. France had to give way or they would have fought her by our side, over this very question. The rule would apply vice versa for America's benefit and then I see in it not only our capital coming back to us after many days but also the first step to our real angle. Saxon krieg-bund – not depending on a mere treaty but on commercial unity, which once formed in this way can never be broken. If one is hit both must be hit and hard enough for both hitting back. That is the general idea. It wants thinking out. If you feel there is nothing in it – please say so. Anyway it is free trade carried in extremes. I see Amcrica not conquering us but binding herself to the wheels of our chariot and bind away say I.[16]

This sort of maritime imperialism, with strong elements of both racial and economic determinism, was echoed in the writings of Mahan in the United States and taken up by such important political figures as President Theodore Roosevelt. His use of the US Navy, in particular the sailing of the Great White Fleet, had economic as well and military connotations for the future use of both sets of power by the United States.[17] This event would be not only a marking of America's interest and commitment to the protection of its Far Eastern interests, but also a clear declaration of the co-joined approach of the American and British empires to

---

[16]   Sir Julian Stafford Corbett Papers, Queen's University, Kingston, Ontario, Folder 3, Corr. with Newbolt, Letter from Corbett to Newbolt, 3 May 1902.

[17]   James R. Reckner, *Teddy Roosevelt's Great White Fleet* (Annapolis, MD, 1988); Kenneth Wimmel, *Theodore Roosevelt and the Great White Fleet: American Sea Power Comes of Age* (Washington, DC, 1998); Nathan Miller, *Theodore Roosevelt: A Life* (New York, 1992); Daniela Rossini, *From Theodore Roosevelt to FDR: Internationalism and Isolationism in American Foreign Policy* (Keele, UK, 1999); William N. Tilchin and Charles E. Neu, eds, *Artists of Power: Theodore Roosevelt, Woodrow Wilson, and Their Enduring Impact on US Foreign Policy* (Westport, CT, 2006).

the region: the maintenance of the Open Door and the rights of non-Asian powers to dictate the development of the region.[18] The Great White Fleet could not have undertaken its world cruise without the aid and permission of Great Britain for it to visit and use Royal Navy facilities. This close cooperation between the two navies did not go unnoticed in the capitals of Japan, Russia and Germany. Further, President Roosevelt ensured that American newspapers made certain that the close ties between the two nations and their navies were not overlooked.[19]

In Great Britain, Prime Minister Arthur Balfour was favourably disposed to close and sustained Anglo-American strategic cooperation. His comments in June 1905 were symbolic of many of the British desires for closer relations, but also an awareness of the dangers that could be created by expressing that desire openly and in public:

> I have spoken, not infrequently, in public upon Anglo-American relations, and have never concealed the strength of the convictions which have all my life animated me, even in the now far-distant days before I entered parliament and was a student, not an actor, in the sphere of politics. But I have always been careful to make my words, strong though they have been, less strong than my convictions; for (as it seems to me) the feeling that the two great co-heirs of Anglo-Saxon freedom and civilisation have a common mission, has more quickly developed on this side of the Atlantic than on the other, – at least among the general mass of the population, and that there is therefore some danger lest phrases which are suitable enough in Great Britain may seem excessive in America, and may excite, not sympathy, but suspicion or ridicule. There is, in truth, an element of sentiment in the views which I, and many others, hold on this subject which supplies an easy mark for criticism. But I console myself by remembering that easy criticism is usual bad criticism.[20]

He continued to hold this view throughout the pe-war period, writing to Philip Kerr (later Lord Lothian), in March 1911, after Kerr had written to criticise him for what Kerr thought were unnecessary slights of the United States in public addresses, that:

> I cannot conceive what speeches the Union leaders have made which can justly 'embitter' the United States. I am certainly quite unconscious of having made any myself. I am, and always have been, a Pan-Anglican; – that is I have always held that the English-speaking peoples have traditions, interests, and ideals

[18] Walter LaFeber, *The Clash: US–Japanese Relations Throughout History* (New York, 1997).

[19] For views of Roosevelt's appreciation of Britain in American foreign affairs, see David H. Burton, *Cecil Spring Rice: A Diplomat's Life* (London, 1990), pp. 121–50.

[20] Balfour Papers, British Library, London, Add MSS 49742, Balfour to Choate, 1 June 1905.

which should Unite them in common sentiments, and, in not inconceivable eventualities, in common action. I am the very last man living who would desire to offend the susceptibilities of the USA. But surely if there has been recklessness of speech it has not been on this side of the Atlantic.[21]

Race, then, was a key element in the moral landscape that tempered both American and British views of each other's role in the international system, not only with respect to one another, but in relation to the rest of the world. Because of the ability to identify with each other linguistically and culturally on so many levels, it is not a surprise that many Anglo-American commentators saw a combination of the two nations as a natural 'racial' event. However, race was not the supreme element in that relationship. What was supreme was the way each nation perceived the other's actions in the international system: the mental map of whether those acts were cooperative or competitive.

Comments by Foreign Office officials in this period, from 1902, involving the Anglo-Japanese Alliance and the 1905 Treaty of Portsmouth, as well as the events surrounding the Latin American tension in 1903, have led some observers of the Foreign Office's attitude to claim that it was particularly anti-American in its attitude. This was certainly not the case with regard to James Bryce, one of the most influential pre-First World War British observers of the American condition.

Bryce, British Ambassador to the United States from 1907 to 1913, had already formulated his views of the American condition in his classic study, *The American Commonwealth*. In those two large volumes he dissected the American democratic experiment, weighing carefully the utility of the American experience to the needs of the British Empire's future. In particular he concentrated on the role of the public and public opinion in American policymaking, a trait and focus which was handed down not just to his immediate successor, Cecil Spring-Rice, but also to subsequent British Ambassadors to the United States, Esme Howard and Ronald Lindsay. Bryce's understanding of the link between maritime power and Britain's fiscal power were of great benefit to his interactions with the Americans. Such pro-American leanings as Bryce's were also evident in other strands of the British policymaking elite prior to the First World War.

Sir George Paish was an economist and one of three editors of the *Statist* in 1899. In the first decade of the twentieth century he spent a good deal of time in America studying the system of railway financing practised there.[22] He became an unofficial adviser to the future Prime Minister, Lloyd George, regarding City matters in 1909, often arguing against the Treasury's official view of the strength of Britain's economy and trade, and winning. Paish believed there was a 'fanatical

---

[21]   Balfour Papers, British Library, London, Add MSS 49797, Balfour to Kerr, 18 March 1911.

[22]   Sir George Paish Papers, British Library of Economic and Political Science, Coll Misc 621, 621/1 – Memoir.

jealousy' towards Britain among German bankers and businessmen. As a result of that antagonism, he went to the USA in 1909 to:

> suggest to President Taft that he should form a World Police Force so strong that no one would dare attack it. I hoped that this force would at least make Germany pause before plunging the world into the horrors of war. I arrived in Washington early in December, 1909, with this purpose in view and was taken to the President by my friend, Mr. George E. Roberts, Director of the Mint. Mr. Taft was receptive, and after our talk asked me to see the Assistant Secretary of State [Huntington Wilson].[23]

Paish's efforts coincided with the overall British effort for closer Anglo-American strategic relations.

By 1914, then, Anglo-American strategic relations had progressed to a condition of mutual understanding and respect, but not full agreement, on each other's global needs in the areas of maritime, economic, and foreign policies. The Far East was an area where cooperation and contention were both apparent, depending on which level of the relationship one looked. At the operational level – that of banks, businesses and financial institutions – there was fierce competition in the region, with both American and British businessmen lobbying their respective governments for greater protection or support in the face of the other's perceived advantages. The realities of a stronger British economic presence, in partnership with a larger and more effective merchant shipping fleet, meant that the British position was the dominant one, and it was the American reaction to that situation that was usually the source of any tensions at the governmental or strategic level. In most cases, as in disputes over railway loans or unfair banking practices, aimed at such companies as Jardine Mathieson, the preferred solution by both the Foreign Office and the State Department was to let matters run their own course. The State Department had a great deal of admiration for, and envy of, the power and resources of the Foreign Office, and often felt itself to be, in both administrative and organisational ways, much the inferior of the two. And this perception was correct. In terms of telegraph (that is, reach), research, linguistic capability, cryptographic ability and secretarial support, the Foreign Office and its global network was far in advance of the smaller and cash-starved State Department. This, however, worked in an odd way. British representatives abroad could create better Anglo-American relations by volunteering or giving an informal offer of sharing or providing of information and intelligence with American colleagues. Such an informal approach avoided any hint of official cooperation, although the latter did take place in times of crisis. This formal education of the American contingents throughout the Far East, and other parts of the world, was in complete compliance with Bryce's calls for the continued education of not only the American people but also their policymaking elites to Britain's needs. Bryce accurately assessed the reality of Anglo-American

---

[23] Ibid.

strategic relations as being very much a one-way street where, unless brought into stark relief by actions or words, American interest in the British world was not in any way similar to the attention paid by British official and unofficial observers to the American condition.

III

The First World War changed that dynamic quickly and drastically. The key strategic British weapon of that war, the blockade, threatened both the economic and maritime power sources of the United States, and violated core freedoms of movement and action on the high seas in a way that the American public could not help but notice, even without German agents whipping up outrage towards the Allied blockade. The management of that blockade was the first serious test of how, in total war, Britain could manage its strategic relationship with America. For the British Empire, fighting a major European war meant being able to obtain vast amounts of war material from the far-flung reaches of that Empire.[24] Manpower, raw materials, finished goods, and stable fiscal strength were vital to British plans for prosecuting and winning such a conflict. There was also the need to deny such vital resources to any Continental enemy. Blockade was a traditional weapon of choice for the British Empire when at war with a major European power. The lessons of the French Revolution, as well as the American Civil War, were embedded in a strategy that saw blockade as a major component of a war-winning strategy. This played into Anglo-American relations. During his consideration of Anglo-American strategic relations and the effects of the British blockade policy, Foreign Secretary Sir Edward Grey consistently portrayed British blockade policy and its legal and strategic position in terms of the US history of blockade. He made his case, both to his own decision-making elite and to American representatives, clearly and carefully using the American Civil War experience and their use of belligerent rights in that conflict to help make the British case.[25]

The United States was seen as being a potential source of war material by Great Britain, but, it was also a possible supplier to the German war effort. In the period from 1914 to 1916, British strategic policy-makers faced the problem of how to deal with the United States during any blockade of Germany. That issue had two sides: how to keep the USA from cutting off support to Great Britain if America's rights and freedom of the seas were impinged upon; and, how to implement a

---

[24]   I would like to thank the Canadian High Commission in London for awarding me a Faculty Research Program Award for doing research on this topic in Canada and the British Academy for a Small Grant during my sabbatical which enabled me to do much of the British research on this topic.

[25]   Foreign Office (FO) 382/2/282/17792 (National Archive, Kew, London), 15 Feb. 1915, confidential memo to American Ambassador to England, Walter H. Page from Sir E. Grey

blockade policy that would be effective against Germany and not drive the United States into the German camp through its implementation.[26] For President Woodrow Wilson and his Administration, the issue was one of maintaining American freedom of the seas in spite of British attempts to prevent the United States from exercising those rights.[27] This conflicting set of strategic mandates requires some thought to be given to how each nation viewed the other in order to make a better evaluation of the obstacles to full Anglo-American cooperation. In particular, the views from the American and British embassies in London and Washington, are important in this regard. As part of the British system of observation and influence, as well as being a separate element of that Anglo-American strategic relationship, certain aspects of the Canadian participation in this area are also important.[28]

Great Britain's Ambassador to the United States, Sir Cecil Spring Rice, was the most important observer of the effect of the blockade on Anglo-American relations in the first two years of the war.[29] In January 1915, it was his belief that the United States and Great Britain had successfully negotiated agreements dealing with many disputes. Congress had stepped aside and allowed private companies and various interests to conduct private and separate negotiations on

---

[26]   See, C.M. Mason, 'Anglo-American Relations: Mediation and "Permanent Peace"', in F.H. Hinsley ed., *British Foreign Policy Under Sir Edward Grey* (Cambridge, 1977), pp. 466–87; Arthur Marsden, 'The Blockade' in Hinsley, pp. 488–515; Marion C. Siney, 'The Allied Blockade Committee and the Inter-allied Trade Committees: the Machinery of Economic Warfare, 1917–1918', in K. Bourne and D.C. Watt, eds, *Studies in International History: Essays Presented to W. Norton Medlicott* (London, 1967), pp. 330–44; John W. Coogan, *The End of Neutrality: The United States, Britain, and Maritime Rights 1899–1915* (Ithaca, NY, 1981); Paul Hayes, 'Britain, Germany, and the Admiralty's Plans for Attacking German Territory, 1906–1915', in Lawrence Freedman, Paul Hayes and Robert O'Neill, eds, War, *Strategy, and International Politics: Essays in Honour of Sir Michael Howard* (Oxford, 1992), pp. 95–116; Lord Hankey, *The Supreme Command, 1914–1918*, 2 vols (London, 1961); David French, *British Economic and Strategic Planning, 1905–1915* (London, 1982), pp. 112–18; Keith Neilson, '"The British Empire Floats on the British Navy": British Naval Policy, Belligerent Rights, and Disarmament, 1902–1909', in B.J.C. McKercher, ed., *Arms Limitation and Disarmament: Restraints on War, 1899–1939* (Westport, CT, 1992), pp. 21–43.

[27]   See Arthur S. Link, *Wilson: The Struggle for Neutrality 1914–1915* (Princeton, NJ, 1960); Ethel C. Phillips, 'American Participation in Belligerent Commercial Controls 1914–1917', *The American Journal of International Law*, Vol.27 (1933), pp. 675–93; David F. Trask, *Captains and Cabinets: Anglo-American Naval Relations, 1917–1918* (Columbia, MO, 1972), pp. 54–89.

[28]   See my articles on Blockade: 'Strategy and Power: The Royal Navy, the Foreign Office and the Blockade, 1914–1917', *Journal of Defence Studies*, Vol.8 , No.2 (June 2008), pp. 190–206, and 'Anglo-American Strategic Relations and the Blockade, 1914–1916', *Journal of Transatlantic Studies*, Vol.6, No. 1 (April 2008), pp. 22–33.

[29]   David H. Burton, *Cecil Spring Rice: A Diplomat's Life* (London, 1990), pp. 152–81.

some matters related to contraband. The Wilson Administration was extremely anxious to maintain its attitude of absolute neutrality, reported Spring Rice, and so was unpleasant to both the Germans and the Allies, particularly Great Britain, in equal portions.[30] He believed that, in spite of the blockade, the American public were sympathetic to the Allied cause, but that sympathy would not be enough to override America's general governing principles, one of which was the right to trade when and where it desired. That attitude caused Spring Rice to believe that the USA was a potential rallying point for other neutrals on the blockade issue. And, more importantly, Britain would have to face the facts that:

> although we are undoubtedly in the right in exercising our right of search we can only exercise it at great inconvenience to neutral nations for the very simple reason that ships are immeasurably larger than they were and the search takes three weeks instead of three hours. There is also unfortunately the added difficulty of doubtful manifests and the absence of any adequate guarantee of the accuracy of ships papers. And if we ask for a Government guarantee we should have to forego our right of search. The inevitable consequence is that a large consignment of harmless goods is held up for fear that a clandestine consignment of contraband may have found its way into the ship. In ordinary times this would perhaps have been a matter of smaller consideration but at the present moment the great difficulty is to find bottoms to carry American products.[31]

The British Ambassador also thought Wilson and Bryan were weak and feeble men, who would be pushed into more drastic action than they would normally take if Britain pressed too hard for the right to detain and seize ships carrying contraband.[32] Spring Rice's view was based on the advice he was receiving from such American sources as former President, Theodore Roosevelt. Roosevelt cautioned Spring Rice to be wary of stretching belligerent rights further than they could be accepted by moderate men in government. If the British pushed too far too fast, then the German lobby in the United States, which was well organised, would be given an opportunity to make their case stronger.[33]

The American entry into the war on Britain's side in the spring of 1917 changed the strategic relationship from one of the possible to one of the real. At the heart of that relationship were the issues of finance and maritime power.[34] Assuming

---

[30]   FO 800/85, The Grey Papers (hereafter Grey Papers), PRO, Kew, London, memo from Spring Rice to Grey, 8 Jan. 1915.

[31]   Ibid.

[32]   Ibid, memo by Spring Rice to Grey, Jan.5, 1915.

[33]   Grey Papers, private telegram from Spring Rice to Grey, Jan.10, 1915.

[34]   See Greg Kennedy, 'Strategy and Supply in the North Atlantic Triangle, 1914–1918' in B.J.C. McKercher and Lawrence Aronsen, eds,, *The North Atlantic Triangle in a Changing World: Anglo-American-Canadian Relations, 1902–1956* (Toronto, 1996), pp. 48–80.

victory and that a normal economic and financial regime would be reinstated in Europe after the war, British War Cabinet members continued to see the financial situation, even in the spring of 1917, as being a manageable problem. Chancellor of the Exchequer, Andrew Bonar Law, foresaw no problem in raising money in the United Kingdom. He acknowledged that indebtedness would double from £4 billion to £8 billion if the war carried on for longer than a year, and that there was some danger that Britain's Allies would not be able to meet their indebtedness to Britain after the war.[35] The involvement of the United States, however, now signalled the opportunity to achieve Britain's primary war aim: to ensure that the British Empire was not weaker in the post-war period.[36] Getting America to take over the financing of the Allies so that 'we should not be the only large creditor of our present Allies' was an important British war aim.[37] While American money was a desirable part of the British war effort, an increased American merchant marine, capable of competing globally with the British merchant fleet, was not. Britain was by far the most important maritime nation in the entire Alliance. While it is arguable that the sudden end of the war may have prevented the American maritime contribution to the war from reaching its full potential, an enormous amount of work still would have been required to enable the United States to match the British output.[38] Therefore, as the war ended, Britain was still in possession of the world's largest merchant marine and a global trading empire that would help it rebuild its economic strength.

That position of inferiority would not be overcome by the United States throughout the inter-war period. Despite war debts, depression and a changing international system, the United States remained a close, but still lesser, rival to Britain's imperial maritime power and its economic strength.[39] When war broke out in Europe once more in the autumn of 1939, no formal alliance between the two nations existed. Once again the British Empire was engaged in a European war with America being neutral. And, once again, the issues of how America's fiscal,

[35]   Minutes of Imperial War Cabinet Meetings, (CAB) 23/40, TNA, Kew, London, Imperial War Cabinet 7, April 3, 1917.

[36]   War Cabinet Memorandum, (CAB) 24/4, TNA, Kew, 'Memorandum on Economic Offensive by Sir Edward Carson' [G156], September 20, 1917; ibid., 'Notes on Sir Edward Carson's Memorandum entitled "Economic Offensive" with some Immediate Practical Suggestions for Action by the President of the Board of Trade', [G 158], October 4, 1917.

[37]   CAB 23/40, War Cabinet minute 7, April 3, 1917.

[38]   S.W. Roskill, *Naval Policy Between the Wars*, Vol.1 (London, 1968), pp. 80–81, 90–91.

[39]   Zara Steiner, *The Lights That Failed: European International History, 1919–1933* (Oxford, 2005); Keith Neilson, *Britain, Soviet Russia and the Collapse of the Versailles Order, 1919–1939* (Cambridge, 2005); Robert Self, *Britain, America and the War Debt Controversy: An Unspecial Relationship (British Politics and Society)* (London, 2006); George C. Peden, *Arms, Economics and British Strategy: From Dreadnoughts to Hydrogen Bombs* (Cambridge, 2007).

economic and maritime power fit into that British war effort required managing. Two of the most significant men involved with the management of that strategic relationship were Philipp Kerr, Lord Lothian, who was Ambassador to the United States from August 1939 until his death in December 1940, and Lord Halifax, who served after Lothian until 1946.

On 30 August 1939, Lothian presented his credentials to President Roosevelt. The occasion gave the two men an opportunity to have initial discussions about the strategic situation facing both the British Empire and the United States. Lothian was struck by the lack of neutrality that Roosevelt displayed, personally, towards the dictator powers. Japan and the Far Eastern situation occupied a good deal of the conversation.[40] The President told Lothian that he thought the Russo-German agreement of that year would cause Japan to seek some sort of negotiated agreement with China, brought about with Britain and America's assistance. If such was the case, Roosevelt said, the two Western powers should be friendly towards the suggestion but show no eagerness. If, however, Japan became more hostile in the future, he would apply further military pressure on that nation by the deployment of aircraft carriers and bombers to the Aleutians, threatening the Japanese mainland, as well as by moving the American main fleet to Hawaii.[41] Roosevelt's views coincided with Lothian's own goals as Ambassador, to ensure the smooth and continued progress of the solid relations his predecessor, Sir Ronald Lindsay, had constructed over Far Eastern security matters. However, it was also clear that Lothian would have to make his own statements about that strategic relationship in the near future and that he would have to be wary of how he portrayed the issue to the American people.

In preparation for that statement, one of the first things Lord Lothian did after this conversation with President Roosevelt was to write to the former First Sea Lord and Minister of Defence, Admiral Lord Chatfield. Lothian outlined his views of the British strategic situation and asked Chatfield to confirm or deny his own interpretation as: 'If I am to have any real effect here it is essential that I should understand thoroughly the British view of the future of the war.'[42] The strategic position, as Lothian saw it, consisted of five key elements. Russia's defection to Germany had eliminated the possibility of a two-front war. This lack of a second front meant that in all likelihood Britain had to be prepared for a long, drawn-out war, much like the First World War. This meant the main strategic weapon for the British, again as in the previous war, was to be a long-distance blockade. As to the other main Powers in the equation, no one knew what Italy was likely to do, nor could Japan's actions be predicted. However, with regard to the latter, Lothian was sure that the Asian power would be certain to exploit British and French difficulties in Europe for its own ends in the Far East. Finally, Americans

---

[40]   FO 371/22815/A5899/98/45, tel. from Lothian to FO, August 31, 1939.

[41]   Ibid.

[42]   CHT [Chatfield Papers, Greenwich Library, Greenwich, London]/6/2, secret, private and personal letter Lothian to Chatfield, September 15, 1939.

were obsessed with trying to ensure that they did not become embroiled in the war in Europe.[43] All of this, Lothian told Chatfield, meant that Britain needed to win at sea and in the industrial arena, the two being inextricably linked. And, 'In the long run the United States of America holds the decisive cards in both respects. Her fleet can make the Pacific, Australia, and Singapore secure, as against Japan. And her machine industry can produce a volume of munitions, especially bombers from a base which cannot be attacked, which will eventually be decisive both against Germany and Italy.'[44] Chatfield replied to Lothian eleven days later, agreeing with most of the points the ambassador had made. In particular, Chatfield was very positive about the situation in the Far East, advising Lothian that he (Chatfield) did not think there would be any big developments in that region in the near future. That stability in the Far East, said Chatfield, was due almost entirely to the restraining influence of the United States and, in particular, its potential to deploy massive power at sea. He believed in the American willingness to help Britain safeguard its interests in the Far East, telling Lothian, 'It always seems to me that is our safest quarter in which to enlist the help of the United States, should it ever be necessary. In fact, I always feel she will volunteer help there *before* we ask for it whenever she thinks the situation is too dangerous, and that I have no doubt you agree with.'[45]

Lord Halifax (then Foreign Secretary) reinforced Chatfield's views on the Far Eastern aspect of Lothian's mission. He was confident that Lothian had entered into his new job fully aware of the true nature of Anglo-Japanese relations, particularly that the Foreign Office was not confident any general agreement that would eliminate the Japanese threat could be arrived at in the near future. Halifax reinforced the point that Lothian was to continue to make, and one that Ronald Lindsay had had to make time and again, that the British Empire would not make a separate deal with Japan concerning the balance of power in the Far East. As for Anglo-American relations and the China question, Halifax told Lothian that it was of the greatest importance for the wider British war efforts that America not be allowed to reproach Britain in any way over such Far Eastern matters.[46] Lothian was aware of the need to tread carefully where Anglo-American relations and the Far Eastern Question were concerned. He was determined not to allow any rekindling of, or addition to, any perceptions that Britain might leave America to hold the ring alone in the Far East, something that had been created by the Simon–Stimson controversy of 1932.[47] As 1939 came to a close, Lothian told *The Times*

---

[43]   Ibid.

[44]   Ibid.

[45]   CHT/6/2, secret and personal letter from Chatfield to Lothian, September 26, 1939.

[46]   FO 800/397, personal and confidential letter from Halifax to Lothian, September 27, 1939.

[47]   Lothian Papers, GD 40-17-387, letter from Lothian to W.A. White, (editor of *Emporia Gazette*, a Kansas newspaper), April 6, 1939; ibid., GD 40-17-398, letter from F.W.

editor Geoffrey Dawson that America was prepared to stand up for its rights in the Far East, and that stance meant indirectly that the USA was protecting British interests as well. The USA would continue to maintain such economic pressures on Japan as the embargoing of war materials and would also provide financial support for the Chinese war effort. Most importantly, Lothian did not believe that America's actions were a danger to the British position globally. He doubted very much that such actions would immediately cause Japan to look southward towards British and Dutch possessions, thereby taxing already stretched British military assets.[48]

Lothian remained undeterred, however, about the willingness, and the reality, of America's now holding the ring or the British Empire in the Pacific. In November 1940 he wrote to the British MP Victor Cazalet, who had mentioned in an earlier letter the anti-American feelings circulating in England. Remembering the sequence of events of the First World War, certain circles were angered that once again that America seemed reluctant to do its proper duty and stand beside England quickly and, instead, seemed to be waiting to obtain more advantage at Britain's expense.[49] Lothian's reply in early November reflected his interpretation of the American actions to date:

> The best answer to the criticism which is being made in England of the United States today is, that the United States is really holding the baby for us in the Pacific. There she has moved into the front line, and so long as she maintains her present policy the British and French interests in the Pacific are secure.[50]

After the fall of France in June 1940, Japanese pressure mounted on Britain to close the Burma Road, the main artery of war materials to China. Lothian's advice to the Foreign Office was to enquire whether there was a possibility of any all-round agreement with the Japanese. His main goals in such a settlement centred around the idea that the European Powers should give access to Japan for oil and rubber concessions in return for a generous settlement with Chiang Kai-shek and a non-fortification agreement which would keep Japan out of the European war and

---

Alexander to Lothian, May 5, 1940. For complete context of the issue that Lothian would have dealt with see Keith Neilson, 'Perception and Posture in Anglo-American Relations: The Legacy of the Simon–Stimson Affair, 1932–1941', *The International History Review*, XXIX (June 2007), pp. 313–37.

[48]   Lothian Papers GD 40 17 400, personal letter, from Lothian to Dawson, personal, December 18, 1939. See also, Lothian Papers, GD 40 17 398, Lothian to W.W. Astor, MP, December 18, 1939.

[49]   Lothian Papers, GD 40/17/399, Victor Cazalet to Lothian, October 2, 1940.

[50]   Lothian Papers, GD 40/17/406 Folder 204–406, 30 April 1940, personal letter from L to Percival Witherby; Lothian Papers, GD 40 17 514, Lothian to Sir Alan Lascelles (Buckingham Palace), private and personal, April 2, 1940; GD 40/17/339, Lothian to Cazalet, November 3, 1940.

Germany out of the Pacific Ocean.[51] While Lothian realised that the United States was watching the Burma Road issue carefully, in order to ascertain if perhaps a now-isolated Britain would concede key aspects of support for China in the face of Japanese pressure, the Ambassador did not grasp the difficulties that any sort of settlement with Japan would entail for the Anglo-American relationship. Nor, according to the Foreign Office, did he appreciate that there was little incentive for the Japanese to be willing to 'play the game' now that Britain was in a vulnerable state.[52] If Britain acquiesced rapidly, or indeed tried to negotiate with the Japanese, American propaganda, particularly the China Lobby, would cry appeasement and betrayal, making any sort of progress in creating a workable Anglo-American deterrence strategy towards Japan even more difficult.[53] Given the delicacy of the Anglo-American relationship at that point, Lothian's handling of the Burma Road issue, therefore, is an instructive example of his strengths and weaknesses as Ambassador to Britain's most important ally.

Lothian placed his trust in the American policymaking elite's being more a factor in American actions in the Far East than public opinion. In early July, he informed the Foreign Office that, while American public opinion might indeed take Britain to task for closing the Burma Road temporarily, he believed that financial and economic pressures on Japan would continue to be applied.[54] This view put him squarely in disagreement with Sir Robert Craigie and many of the Foreign Office officials tasked with overseeing Britain's Far Eastern policy. Much of the Foreign Office's concern was over whether Lothian's assessment of what the Americans really expected from both any closure, or, after such an event, the reopening of the Burma Road was accurate. A lack of clarity in the Ambassador's aims and direction clouded the decision-making process.[55] Lothian believed that a now more educated and aware America would not like the closure, but also could not argue against the realities of the British strategic position due to events in Europe. Overstretched, alone and without the necessary military resources available to contemplate a two-front conflict, Britain's temporary buying of time would be understood, if not liked, by the majority of the American public and policymaking elite.[56]

In light of the predominance of Europe in Anglo-American affairs, Lothian followed the only option available to him. He continued to impress upon the Americans the need for their continued economic pressure on Japan, as well as increased military aid to Britain. The latter, he argued, would allow Britain to recover its military strength more quickly, an act that was not only important for

---

[51]   FO 371/24666/F3544/43/10, tel., Lothian to FO, July 5 1940.

[52]   Ibid., Dening minute, July 7, and Brenan minute, July 8, 1940.

[53]   Ibid., Gage minute July 9, 1940.

[54]   FO 371/24666/F3544/43/10, tel. Lothian to FO, July 9, 1940.

[55]   FO 371/24667/F3568/43/10, Craigie to FO, tel., immediate, July 11, 1940; FO 371/2470/F4489/43/10, 'The Burma Road', memo by Sterndale Bennett, October 1, 1940.

[56]   Ibid.

the welfare of the British situation in Europe, but also a vital necessity if London was to continue to have any effective deterrence capability against Japan. He also called for joint Anglo-American conferences and planning sessions for the Far East, with the intention of sending a strong message of solidarity to Japan.[57] As well, he kept the American Secretary of State, Cordell Hull, and President Franklin Roosevelt informed of the progress of Anglo-Dutch discussions for pooling military resources in order that the American policymakers could have as accurate a picture as possible of the true condition of the military situation in the Far East.[58] In particular, having come to accept the limits of America's willingness to move overtly, Lothian emphasised the particular importance of sustained economic pressure on Japan to Hull. The Ambassador continued throughout October to try and entice the Americans into taking a more open part in Anglo-Dutch naval and defence talks, but to no avail. Still, the very act of continuing to share the most up-to-date information on such activities was important, as the Ambassador continued to create bonds of closeness and confidence with the American policymakers.[59] By mid-October, as the question as to whether or not Britain would reopen the Road became imminent, Lothian's interpretation of the importance of reopening the Road for the continued well-being of confident Anglo-American relations in the Far East had won the day.[60] As the year wore on, Lothian's ability to interpret the American strategic position towards the Far East to London, and to give London's views to Washington, improved, gaining him the much-needed credibility he required to continue to cement Anglo-American strategic relations. His untimely death in December 1940 did not create any substantial disruption in the management of those relations due to the quality of his successor: Lord Halifax.

Halifax had a number of advantages upon his assumption of the post. A key British policymaker for decades, a man at the heart of many foreign policy debates, he was a known figure to the American policymaking elite. In particular, he was a representative that Cordell Hull could relate to quickly, a factor that made the smooth running of strategic relations before the American entry into the war a far easier exercise in foreign policy. Part of this affinity was a product of both men having occupied similar posts (Secretary of State and Foreign Secretary) over the last few years, Hull from 1933 and Halifax from 1938 until 1941. They had formed a professional relationship and shared their view of the world in those capacities. However, Halifax's commitment to eliminating Anglo-American tensions over Far Eastern affairs, manifest in such ways as attempting to end the lingering effects of the Simon–Stimson disagreement allowed him to

---

[57]   *Foreign Relations of the United States* Vol.IV, The Far East, 1940, Sept.16, 1940, P.120, memo of Conversation between Hull and Lothian/Casey.

[58]   Ibid., Sept.30, 1940, P.159, memo of Conversation between Hull and Lothian.

[59]   Ibid., Oct.5, 1940, P.167, memo of conversation, Hull and Lothian.

[60]   FO 371/24670/F4646/43/10, Halifax to Churchill, letter, September 25, 1940.

gain the complete trust and confidence of this valuable ally.[61] Halifax also sought to have India included on the Pacific War Council, in 1942, after the American entry into the war. This was another of his attempts to safeguard Britain's wartime relations with the United States with an eye to the future.[62] More than anyone else, Halifax was aware of the ongoing dislike Americans of all types had for the British rule in India.[63] The question of imperialism and how it could be justified to the Americans in the post-war world was a constant source of anxiety for him, and one in which his efforts were tested to the full. The safeguarding of not only the Anglo-American relationship, but also the British Empire, involved two things that were not mutually supportive. Halifax's enormous knowledge of British foreign and defence policy and his unquestioned ability to understand what impact changes in the Anglo-American dynamic would have on Britain's ability to retain its imperial strength were undoubtedly one of the attributes British Prime Minister, Winston Churchill, an vehement imperialist himself, valued most in his Ambassador.

The shift from peace-time to war-time Ambassador created a number of new conditions for Halifax to consider in relation to how he did business with the American administration. The expansion of the Roosevelt system was a new and important development in itself, with various new characters walking onto the American strategic foreign-policymaking stage. However, it was not only the changes to the American system of doing business that were a challenge. The flood of British special missions and advisers that invaded Washington after 7 December 1941, a trend started by the immediate arrival of Churchill and his entourage for a Christmas conference with Roosevelt and his cabinet, set the new tone for Halifax's role. He was not the only conduit for information and influence in the relationship, even in the traditional diplomatic realm.[64] However, despite the concentration on the Roosevelt–Churchill dynamic of the special relationship on the strategic direction of the war effort, that aspect alone should not be given

---

[61]   See Keith Neilson, 'Perception and Posture in Anglo-American Relations: The Legacy of the Simon-Stimson Affair, 1932–1945', *International History Review*, 29 (June 2007), pp. 313–37; Halifax diary, A7.8.11 17 Sept. 1942; Halifax diary, A7.8.11, 25 Sept. 1942.

[62]   Robert E. Sherwood, *The White House Papers of Harry L. Hopkins*, 2 vols (London, 1948–49), vol.II, pp. 520–21.

[63]   Halifax Diaries, A7.8.8, Wed., March 26, 1941.

[64]   David Reynolds, Warren Kimball and A.O. Chubarian, eds, *Allies at War: the Soviet, American and British Experience, 1939–1945* (New York, 1994); Alex Danchev, *On Specialness: Essays in Anglo-American Relations* (New York, 1998); Alan Dobson, *US Wartime Aid to Britain, 1940–1946* (New York, 1986); William H McNeill, *America, Britain and Russia: Their Co-operation and Conflict, 1941–1946* (Oxford, 1953); Warren F. Kimball ed., *Churchill and Roosevelt: The Complete Correspondence, Vol. I, Alliance Emerging, October 1933–November 1942* (Princeton, 1984); Mark A. Stoler, *The Politics of the Second Front: American Military Planning and Diplomacy in Coalition Warfare, 1941–1943* (Westport, CT, 1977); Randall B. Woods, *A Changing of the Guard: Anglo-American Relations, 1941–1946* (Chapel Hill, NC, 1990).

credit for the overall protection of Britain's imperial interests. Nor should that relationship be only seen through the lens of those special missions and envoys doing 'special' work.[65] Close American confidants, such as Walter Lippman, told Halifax that there was a link between American perceptions of the British in India and the 'criticism about India among the Intellectual classes [that] springs from the old founded sympathy with China'.[66] Indeed, it was in that realm, in his constant and persistent insistence to Hull, Roosevelt and others of the right of the British Empire to expect the war effort to be to its benefit, not its detriment, that his role was most significant.[67]

Halifax realised that it was the peace that was the prize and that setting the context for that settlement should be his main effort. In February 1942 he began to lay the ground work for the peace by working with Dr Buell, the editor of *Fortune* magazine to write and coordinate a series of articles on post-war plans and what the peace was to achieve. Here, Halifax was following a well-established path.[68] Halifax had observed the success of his predecessors, Sir Ronald Lindsay and Lord Lothian in the selective and careful use of the American media to Britain's benefit. Upon the involvement of the United States, Halifax had gone on a tour of parts of the USA, to show the British flag and produce news reports about the heroic British war effort, as well as to discuss issues such as the place of India. It was most important that he got that message out not just to the East Coast press, but into middle-America itself, a place he knew that was very sceptical of British motives in the war.[69] As well, at the same time, he worked with both the American and British intelligence agencies who were monitoring Japanese propaganda efforts aimed at India. These broadcasts had apparently been responsible for an exodus of people from Calcutta, and Halifax viewed such attempts to subvert the Empire's cohesion as most troubling and dangerous to the overall war effort.[70] Halifax coordinated these early efforts to safeguard the Indian issue from any overtly aggressive American media coverage with Harry Hopkins, consulting the

---

[65]   Alex Danchev and Daniel Todman, eds, *War Diaries, 1939–1945: Field Marshal Lord Alanbrooke* (Berkeley, CA, 2001); Alex Danchev, *Very Special Relationship: Field-Marshal Sir John Dill and the Anglo-American Alliance, 1941–1944* (London, 1986); Mark A. Stoler, *Allies and Adversaries: the Joint Chiefs of Staff, the Grand Alliance, and US Strategy in World War II* (Chapel Hill, NC, 2000); Andrew B. Cunningham, *A Sailor's Odyssey: The Autobiography of Admiral of the Fleet Viscount Cunningham of Hyndhope* (New York, 1951); William D. Leahy, *I Was There: The Personal Story of the Chief of Staff to President's Roosevelt and Truman Based on his Notes and Diaries Made at the Time* (New York, 1950).

[66]   Halifax Papers, A7.8.11 Monday, October 19 1942

[67]   Sherwood, *The White House Papers of Harry L. Hopkins*, vol.I, pp. 450–52.

[68]   Halifax Papers, A7.8.10, Friday, February 20, 1942

[69]   Halifax Papers, A7.8.10, Thursday, February 26, 1942.

[70]   Halifax Papers, A7.8.19, 'Most secret' wartime diary, Thursday, March 5, 1942.

American on not only the mood of Roosevelt and other key American decision-makers, but also on the nation's attitude to the issue in general:

> We spent a good deal of time discussing India; the arguments that are being pressed day by day for and against the British Government making some new far-reaching statement. I said I found it difficult to believe any such statement at this juncture would in fact make any favourable difference either to India's military effort or to her industrial effort. It would certainly impress favourably United States opinion. We agreed, however, that the effect, direct or indirect, on the mass of Indian population was the important factor, but pretty difficult to estimate with any certainty. They are very ignorant here about Moslems and princes, and most other things that go to make up the Indian problem. Incidentally a statement on which Winston and Stafford Cripps agree will be in itself no mean achievement.[71]

By September of 1942, despite the use of a combination of published articles and speaking tours by British academics to expound the virtues of India's condition and role in the war, Halifax was very aware of the pressure being applied to the Anglo-American relationship by the matter of India. And, while he and the Heads of the Joint Staff Mission were aware of these tensions, Halifax advised that there was no easy remedy for them and no need to make any spectacular announcements or acts designed to sway American opinion.[72] In early 1944 Halifax himself was still delivering important speeches and lectures to both the media and private audiences on the India issue, knowing full well that his words on the topic could ignite all sorts of post-war difficulties for Anglo-American relations if he misread the situation or made a single misstep in his management of the matter.[73] At a packed Constitution Hall, on 28 January 1944, he lectured to the Washington elite: '... don't think it was at all the kind of thing they expected. I gave them a good deal of history, to make the point of how accidental had been our intrusion into the business of government.'[74]

That 'good deal of history' was taken by such American officials as Sumner Welles, Under-secretary of State from 1937 to 1943, as the declaration of Indian independence. Despite Churchill's violent opposition to any American attempts to prevent the post-war retention of as much of the pre-war Empire as possible, Halifax had argued and won the case that, to ensure the long-term benefits of the wartime Anglo-American relationship, India would have to be given the opportunity for some greater freedom.[75] Hull and Roosevelt had pursued greater Indian autonomy

---

[71]   Ibid., Friday, March 6, 1942.

[72]   Ibid., Saturday, Sept.19, 1942. See also Kevin Smith, *Conflict Over Convoys: Anglo-American Logistics Diplomacy in the Second World War* (Cambridge, 1996).

[73]   Halifax Papers, A7.8.14, Sunday, January 23, 1944.

[74]   Halifax Papers, A7.8.14, Friday, January 28, 1944.

[75]   Sumner Welles, *The Time for Decision* (New York, 1944), pp. 300–302.

even before Pearl Harbor, constantly pressuring both Halifax and Churchill for greater public declarations in favour of increased independence, especially in the interpretation of the Atlantic Charter. By 1944, with victory in both Europe and the Far East appearing more guaranteed by the day, the American administration became even more emboldened over the issue.[76] Aware of this growing sense of dissatisfaction with Britain's handling of India, Halifax gave his speech on 28 January in the hope that he could defuse a situation which he felt could have a disastrous impact on Anglo-American strategic relations, particularly with regard to the Far East. In that speech he told America:

> We hope that India, in what we believe to be her own highest interests, will wish to remain within the British Commonwealth. But if, after the war, her people can establish an agreed constitution and then desire to sever their partnership with us, we have undertaken not to overrule such decision … If India cannot yet agree to move forward as a single whole, we are prepared to see her large component elements move forward separately. We recognize all the objections to a rupture of Indian unity, but we also believe that stability cannot be found through compulsion of the great minorities … This attitude is in complete conformity with the principle of the Atlantic Charter.[77]

One of those vital military topics which he dealt with well, despite his disdain for it as a topic of discussion, was the vital question of shipping allocation.[78]

In conjunction with Harry Hopkins, a key adviser to President Roosevelt, Halifax lobbied the American President and his administration for the creation of at least two million tons of merchant shipping to aid the British war effort. In the face of isolationist press, as well as a growing demand on the American shipbuilding yards created by America's own armament programme, the efforts wrestled free the two million tons by the end of April 1941.[79] By the spring of that year, Halifax's touring of various American cities and regions, as well as his continual collecting of all levels of American opinion of Britain's war effort, led him to believe that the nation was by a large majority in favour of all aid to Britain. That aid included making every effort to provide the tools and transportation necessary for waging a winning war effort, including valuable shipping assets:

> There would seem to be a small opinion that feels we can't win, and that therefore it is hopeless; a much larger opinion that is not yet convinced that the situation is so serious as to warrant their taking every risk, which if they were convinced, they would be willing to do. In this connection, much has been said to me about

---

[76]   Cordell Hull, *The Memoirs of Cordell Hull*, 2 vols (London, 1948), vol.II, pp. 1483–97.

[77]   Welles, *The Time for Decision*, p. 301.

[78]   Halifax Papers, A7.8.8, Tuesday, April 29 1941.

[79]   Ibid., Wednesday, April 30 1941.

the importance of our giving a clear picture of the shipping position. There is a feeling that we have not painted it black enough or as black as it is. As against all this, they all seem to agree when you put it to them that the fundamental facts are clear enough, namely that the United States would be in a bad shape if we were not there to look after the Atlantic and Singapore, and that therefore form their own point of view they are bound once their mind is made up on fundamentals to see the wisdom of throwing everything in.[80]

Halifax's role was that of being a key supporter of the main technical effort being made by the special mission headed up by Arthur Salter to procure this vital shipping. Salter, perhaps the most knowledgeable man in the British administration on matters related to logistics and supply, was a powerful force in terms of technical and detailed argument. And, his barrage on the Americans over what the British needs were and why was as relentless as they were detailed.[81]

In January 1942, Halifax recognised immediately the centrality of the shipping question to the Anglo-American alliance now that America was formally at war. He, along with General Dill, the senior British representative in America, worked with the British and American Chiefs of Staff and various Heads of Missions, for those first six months of 1942, to protect British strategic interests in the shipping allocation decisions.[82] Halifax was also aware of the technical and numerical advantage the new American merchant fleet would have over the British in the post war. In particular the new, fast and large C2 ships were a worry to him, prompting him to note after a visit to a shipyard constructing those vessels: '…I imagine they will be an element in our postwar problems with the Americans'.[83] By the time Salter left in 1944, he and Halifax had created a cooperative and professional environment with regard to shipping allocation and provision. This critical element, if not handled with tact and persistence, had the potential to be a considerable liability to the Anglo-American effort. Halifax must be given a great deal of credit for his efforts in ensuring the protection of British interests while at the same time doing so without unnecessarily antagonising a sensitive and suspicious ally. That tact and toughness in the handling of the shipping issues was an important part of Halifax's work in preparing the groundwork for Anglo-American negotiations over the shape of the peace.

The first critical aspect for Halifax in shaping the post-war peace was to establish the return of a strong British presence in the Far East. Halifax was fortunate to have as a mentor on Far Eastern affairs the FO's most knowledgeable official on the subject. Sir George Sansom, a long-serving member of the Tokyo embassy staff in the 1930s, was in Washington to advise various British missions on conditions

---

[80]   Halifax Papers, A7.8.8, Monday, May 12 1941.

[81]   Halifax Papers, A7.8.8, Tuesday, May 27 1941.

[82]   Halifax Papers, A7.8.10, Sunday, January 11, Friday, March 27, Friday, May 29, all 1942.

[83]   Halifax Papers, A7.8.13, Friday, December 3 1943.

in the Far East. Halifax thought his views and opinions were invaluable, giving greater weight to Sansom's opinions on matters than to those of the former special Governor of Singapore, Duff Cooper.[84] In October, Sansom advised Halifax that China would want to recover Manchukuo, Formosa and Korea after the war and that this would not necessarily make Japan's rebuilding impossible if the British allowed Japan to re-enter the global economic environment again as rapidly as possible.[85] This was also the opinion of former American Ambassador to Japan, Joseph Grew. Halifax saw Grew often to chat about how matters could be resolved in the Far East. Grew recommended a quick economic recovery for Japan would be the solution, but Halifax was attuned to the mood of America by the late 1942 and realised that such aspirations were perhaps too much to hope for:

> He thinks that after the war Japan will clearly have to give up what she has taken fron China, but that we shall all make a great mistake if we do not make it possible for her to have reasonable economic opportunity. This is also Sansom's view. I foresee that American feeling will be about as bitter in this matter as English opinion was about hanging the Kaiser in 1919.[86]

If there was to be a just peace in the Far East, America could not be allowed to construct a Pacific Versailles.

However, Halifax was unable to create a cooperative Anglo-American approach to the management of the Far Eastern campaign. By May 1944 he reported from Washington that American attitudes towards the British efforts in that region were decidedly negative. Americans believed their war effort to be a righteous one, but British efforts to be at all times tainted by the ultimate objective of aiming to return an oppressive imperial system to the Far East. Given Roosevelt's close management of America's China policy, and the lack of a coherent British strategy for a return to the region, Halifax was limited in how much influence he could exert on the American decision-making system.[87] By early 1944 it was clear that America would run Pacific affairs in the postwar, despite the Ambassador's repeated expression of the fact that 'British opinion had the deepest distrust of anything like international control of colonies, though they would be prepared to have any amount of common consultation'.[88] For Halifax the challenge in 1944 and 1945 was to attempt to prevent the Americans dominating any more elements of the Anglo-American post-war world. Having been a integral part of the visit to Washington by the Secretary of State for Foreign Affairs, Anthony Eden, in March 1943, and of Prime Minister Churchill's May trip to Washington, where post-war

---

[84]   Halifax Papers, A7.8.10, Thursday, April 30 1942.

[85]   Halifax Papers, A7.8.11, Tuesday, October 20 1942.

[86]   Ibid, Monday, November 9 1942.

[87]   L. Woodward and M.E. Lambert, *History of the Second World War: British Foreign Policy in the Second World War*, 5 vols (London, 1976), vol.IV, pp. 534–40.

[88]   Halifax Papers, A7.8.14, Tuesday, June 27 1944.

planning had been the key point of the events, Halifax was left to try and manage any momentum or progress established during those exploratory talks.[89]

In 1943 the first administrative organs of the Anglo-American peace-building process were put in place. By May the Allies had concluded a preliminary agreement which would establish the United Nations Relief and Rehabilitation Administration (UNRRA). That organisation was approved by September of the same year and began to operate an international administrative body to distribute relief supplies in the post-war period. Economic issues also were included in this organisation, but would not be resolved until well after the war.[90] At the same time, the European Advisory Commission was set up in London in November 1943. This body was responsible for coordinating the surrender terms for Germany and its allies. And, while other UN-sponsored bodies began to appear after this period, in anticipation of the peace that was to come, it was in the areas of influence and control that Anglo-American wartime diplomacy began to play a bigger role. Who would control operations in the Pacific after the war? Who would be the stronger nation in China? What would the alliance relationship be in the reconstruction of Germany? Who had greater interests in remaining the major power-broker in the Middle East?

Some of these questions were answered by discussions that took place at Cairo in November 1943. Roosevelt pushed the American agenda for the post-war Pacific by helping Chiang Kai-Shek to obtain the Cairo Declaration. That statement promised that Japan would lose all territories conquered by her since 1914, China would be fully restored, and Korea would become an independent state; and plans for the invasion of Japan were begun. This planning, and American insistence on taking primacy of place in Pacific affairs in general, caused very hard feelings not only amongst the British military, but also amongst the Treasury, Foreign Office and Cabinet members who were linked to the British negotiations. They rightly saw that the British dominance in that region now was over and that America would be the future guarantor of security in the Far East. The Tehran Conference in November 1943 only further highlighted how the growth of American military capability was translating into diplomatic leverage. Such was the state of affairs that Churchill himself was the butt of Roosevelt's teasing manner at the conference, as the American President worked to coerce the Soviet leader Joseph Stalin into a shared camaraderie by means of both men poking fun at the English Prime Minister.[91] However, all the powers came together in the

[89]   Woodward and Lambert, *History of the Second World War*, vol.V, pp. 1–70.

[90]   John DeNovo, 'The Culbertson Economic Mission and Anglo-American Tensions in the Middle East, 1944–1945', *Journal of American History*, Vol.63 (March 1977), pp. 913–36.

[91]   Frances Perkins, *The Roosevelt I Knew* (New York, 1946), pp. 81–85; David Dilks, ed., *The Diaries of Sir Alexander Cadogan, 1938–1945* (New York, 1972), pp. 580–85; John Charmley, *Churchill's Grand Alliance: The Anglo-American Special Relationship, 1940–1957* (New York, 1995).

summer of 1944, after the successful beginning of allied operations in western Europe, for the Bretton Woods conference. This gathering was held to ensure that post-war economic and monetary policies allowed for the most efficient and expedient reconstruction of a world suffering its second world war in thirty years. This economic and monetary diplomacy would result in the creation of the International Monetary Fund and an International Bank for Reconstruction and Development (the later would eventually be called The World Bank). Both were established to ensure economic stability, primarily through ensuring the solvency of post-war currencies, the avoidance of restrictive trade practices, and the provision of affordable credit for reconstruction. At almost the same time, 39 nations, either fighting with or favourable to the Allies, convened at Dumbarton Oaks near Washington to discuss what shape the replacement organisation for the failed League of Nations would take. Those diplomatic efforts would result in the United Nations. In all cases, political, economic and military representatives were involved, as were banking, industrial and public groups, in the formulation of proposals, structures and powers.[92] The diplomatic efforts required to achieve any coherent and functional direction from both processes was a testament to the desire on the part of all participants to establish bodies that would truly be able to avoid global warfare in the future.

The Yalta and Potsdam conferences, the last of the big wartime gatherings designed to prepare for the post-war, hammered out the final areas of responsibility and interest for the Americans and the British. Exhausted by the war, facing a new America that was operating the world's most powerful armed forces in the world (backed up by the newly created atomic bomb technology), as well as possessing the world's most powerful economy, the final stages of the war saw Britain concentrating all aspects of Anglo-American diplomatic relations on protecting British interests around the world. The Far East was now America's area of responsibility and, if Britain was to remain a viable power in Europe, then America's support there was paramount. Rebuilding war-torn Europe could not be done by Britain and the reclaimed European nations, especially with the economic heart of Europe, Germany and France, devastated by the war.[93] The enormous diplomatic effort that had been an ongoing element of all levels of administration and coordination for the Anglo-American alliance would have to continue into the peace if the post-war world, so costly in the obtaining, was to fulfill those two nations' dream of a peaceful world order.

---

[92]   Williamson Murray and Allan R. Millett, *A War to be Won: Fighting the Second World War* (Cambridge, MA, 2000); Randall B. Woods, *A Changing of the Guard: Anglo-American Relations, 1941–1946* (Chapel Hill, NC, 1990).

[93]   Terry H. Anderson, *The United States, Great Britain and the Cold War, 1944–1947* (Columbia, MO, 1981); David B. Woolner ed., *The Second Quebec Conference Revisited: Waging War, Formulating Peace: Canada, Great Britain and the United States, 1944–1945* (New York, 1988); Donald Cameron Watt, 'Britain and the Historiography of the Yalta Conference and the Cold War', *Diplomatic History*, Vol.13 (Winter, 1989), pp. 67–98.

Anglo-American diplomacy during the war was a complex, dynamic and constantly challenging reality. There was no certainty that things would work smoothly, that egos at various military and political levels would tolerate insult and challenges of perception and interpretation. Money, the life-blood of both capitalist nations, and how it was translated into military power, as well as how it was distributed not only between the two English-speaking nations but how it was given over to other allies, always held the threat of creating a major disruption to the smooth running of the alliance.

IV

In the creation of Anglo-American strategic relations, with a specific focus on how the British way of warfare utilised America in its strategic considerations, there was a great deal of fertile, common ground for strategic relations to work from: common language, shared history, democracy, capitalism, maritime influences, and open societies that valued individualism over social obedience. Still, such commonalities should not be taken to indicate an inevitableness or pre-ordained passing of the trident from the old English Great Power to the new. French's work is illustrative in showing how the pragmatic strategic needs of Britain, working to protect an empire, found an increasing need for the levers of power possessed by the United States. Throughout the period reviewed Britain's policymakers were aware of the potential of America to surpass it in all areas of trade, commerce and military power, but, it was a matter of scale as to what the differential of the two was to be. A Great British Empire was an equal to America. The fragmentation of that empire following the Second World War was the end of that concept of equality, not any actions prior to that. From 1900 to 1945 the principles of those strategic relations had to work from a position of British supremacy in the areas of maritime, economic and fiscal power, with America in an inferior or ascending but not yet dominant position. That position and those principles changed, but not absolutely, after 1945, but that is a different story. For the purposes of understanding the unique place America had, as a global, maritime, economic ally, the work of David French serves as a superior lens for viewing the British needs from that relationship, than the usual calls for considerations of a 'special relationship'.

Chapter 3
Italy and the British Way in Warfare

G. Bruce Strang

David French's *The British Way in Warfare* has influenced a generation of historians writing about British military and strategic policy. A skilful practitioner of the historian's craft, French presented an argument rich in detail and nuance. He eschewed simplistic assumptions that have often tripped up contemporary observers of British decision-making. French argued that for decades Britain's elite adopted an adaptive and flexible approach, but one with certain identifiable tendencies about military spending and strategy. Successive British leaders maintained the concept that Britain's defences had to fall within certain acceptable costs; a military that drained the Treasury and the nation's resources offered no genuine security. Britain tended to favour spending on the navy rather than the army, seeking to control the sea, especially the approaches to the British Isles, but also overseas trade that underlay Britain's economic strength. Britain accordingly often took an inordinately long time to train its army after the outbreak of a war. Until 1904, British statesmen tried to maintain a certain sense of aloofness from Continental affairs, seeking primarily to maintain a balance of power. After 1904, the rise of Germany and Britain's relative economic decline required that Britain commit to wartime and even peacetime alliances. Nevertheless, the core of French's analysis indicated that these traits were tendencies, not absolute strictures. British leaders adopted a mixed paradigm, committing large numbers of troops to Continental warfare or seeking strong Continental allies where and when necessary.[1]

Benito Mussolini, of course, never had the opportunity to read David French's balanced monograph on the British way in warfare. Too bad for him. Had he done so, the Italian dictator might have avoided some serious mistakes in his own thinking about the strategic situation in the 1930s and might have averted the disaster of Italy's participation in the Second World War. Mussolini adopted a narrow vision of the British way in warfare, largely consistent with one aspect of French's explanation. His thinking was not unlike Basil Liddell Hart's writing during the 1930s. Liddell Hart argued that British strategy worked best when Britain used its force obliquely, emphasisng financial power and manoeuvre, and eschewing brute force and large land armies. Liddell Hart lamented Britain's

I would like to thank the Social Sciences and Humanities Research Council of Canada for the research grants that underwrote much of the research for this project.

[1]   David French, *The British Way in Warfare, 1688–2000* (London, 1990), pp. xi–xvi, 225.

departure from this practice during the Great War, and he regretted the slaughter of Britain's youth owing to its commitment to the Western Front.[2]

Mussolini did not generally think systematically about this issue; in dealing with strategic issues, he was an amateur. As such, he sometimes operated with flair and dynamism and sometimes misread situations owing to his simplistic prejudices. As a result, he did not leave a methodical and clearly articulated record of his thinking. One must seek to determine his views from his writings, therefore, but also from reading his actions. The evidence suggests that, for Mussolini, inherent British weakness owing to its democratic institutions, its demographic decline and its traditional concentration on naval power rather than ground forces meant that Italy was poised to challenge Britain for control of the Mediterranean, a vital region for Mussolini given the Italian need to import large amounts of grain and his hopes to develop Italy's colonies in Africa. Italy's industrial weakness, however, meant that Italy had to develop its own fleet, to work to undermine British Imperial communications, and to recruit potential allies, particularly Germany and Japan. If Mussolini were able to carry out this blend of military construction and diplomacy successfully, he thought, Fascist Italy would be able to seize control of the Mediterranean basin and supplant Britain and France as colonial masters throughout northern Africa, creating a new Roman Empire.

Mussolini, unsurprisingly for someone who had grown to adulthood witnessing the venality of the corrupt parliament in Italy, detested liberal democratic regimes. As a young adult, of course, Mussolini had maintained the belief that the unity and power of the proletariat would destroy the bourgeoisie, but he abandoned his revolutionary syndicalist dreams during the Great War. He adapted Wilfredo Pareto's belief that the only way to break the perpetual cycle of renewal of bourgeois elites was to use proletarian violence, although in Mussolini's case he aimed to harness the energy of the working class through exploiting its nationalist impulses. From Friedrich Nietzsche and social Darwinism Mussolini developed his worship for the martial virtues of heroism, dynamism, and faith in national destiny.[3] He believed that Fascism represented the clear antithesis of democracy, which Mussolini contemptuously dismissed as plutocracy, and that Fascism would be able to deal better with the issues that challenged modern societies, from regional and class division to containing personal ambition within the strictures of state control. Only Fascism could restrain self-interested bourgeois elites from

---

[2]   See, amongst many others, Alex Danchev, 'Liddell Hart and the Indirect Approach', *Journal of Military History* 63.2 (1999), pp. 313–37; *idem*, 'Liddell Hart's Big Idea' *Review of International Studies* 25.1 (1999), pp. 29–48, and French, *British Way*, p. xv.

[3]   Adrian Lyttelton, *Italian Fascisms from Pareto to Gentile* (New York, 1973), pp. 20–22. Eduardo e Duilio Susmel (eds), *Opera Omnia di Benito Mussolini*, 36 volumes (Florence, 1951–63; 8 volumes (Rome, 1978–80) [hereafter *OO*], *I* , 'L'individuel et la social', 14 October 1904, pp. 73–75; 'Intermezzo polemico', 25 April 1908, pp. 127–29.

expropriating the patrimony of the state for their own ends.[4] The Duce tended to associate democracy with pacifism, which in his view was a dangerous vice. Pacifism was 'a cloak for renunciation of struggle and cowardice in the face of sacrifice'.[5] Mussolini's Italy aimed to destroy pacifist, bourgeois values at home, and he thought British pacifism sapped the once proud empire of its dynamism.

Mussolini held particular antipathy for Great Britain. From the early days of the Fascist movement, Mussolini had railed against Britain's control of Gibraltar and Suez, the points of access to the Mediterranean Sea. Accordingly, the Royal Navy imprisoned Italy in the Mediterranean, and Fascism aimed to expand Italian power 'economically and spiritually' in order to challenge the plutodemocratic powers that stood in the way of Italy's destiny.[6] In 1925, he horrified one Foreign Ministry official by speaking openly of war against Great Britain:

> Gibraltar, Malta, Suez, and Cyprus represent a chain that permits England to encircle, to imprison Italy in the Mediterranean. If another link, Albania, were added to [that chain], we would have had to break it with a war. A short war; it would not have lasted more than a few weeks, for Italy today is no longer the Italy of the days of Giolitti.[7]

Mussolini's restless expansionism sought to break Britain's control of the Mediterranean, but Italian military and economic weakness and Mussolini's more careful diplomatic and military advisers suggested extreme caution was in order. In spite of these problems, Mussolini broke with Italy's liberal, colonial past, and he frequently displayed an almost reckless bravado when speaking about a clash against Great Britain that he increasingly saw as inevitable.[8]

Given his contempt for parliamentary democracy, it is unsurprising that Mussolini both resented Great Britain and was inclined to believe in its structural weakness. Mussolini obsessed about population trends, and he believed that

---

[4]   *OO, XXII*, Intervista con Associated Press, 1 August 1926, pp. 187–92. *OO, XLIV*, Intervista con Henri Massis, 26 September 1933, pp. 54–67. Aristotle Kallis, *Fascist Ideology: Territory and Expansionism in Italy and Germany* (London, 2000), pp. 29–33, 36–37.

[5]   *OO, XXIV*, La dottrina del Fascismo, p. 124.

[6]   *OO, XII*, 'Atto del nascita del fascismo', 23 March 1919, pp. 321–7. *OO, XIV*, 'Discorso inaugurale al secondo congresso dei fasci,' 27 December 1919, pp. 216–20. For more on Fascist literature attacking Britain and France, see Tracy H. Koon, *Believe, Obey, Fight: Political Socialization of Youth in Fascist Italy, 1922–1943* (Chapel Hill, NC, 1985), p. 153.

[7]   Mussolini, quoted in MacGregor Knox, *Common Destiny: Dictatorship, Foreign Policy, and War in Fascist Italy and Nazi Germany* (Cambridge, 2000), p. 119.

[8]   Knox, *Common Destiny*, pp. 35–6, 118–21; John Gooch, *Mussolini and His Generals: The Armed Forces and Fascist Foreign Policy, 1922–1940* (Cambridge, 2007), pp. 62, 136–44

Britain's demographic decline spelled disaster for the country. Too many people lived in cities, which tended to have lower birth rates, and British plans to reverse the trend had failed. He condemned those 'false and imbecilic' thinkers who believed that lower population numbers would lead to greater well-being and contrasted British demographic weakness with Italian virility.[9] In the lead-up to the Munich crisis, he heavily marked up a report from the British Ministry of Health that implied that Britain would lose 90 per cent of its population over a hundred-year span if current low birth rates did not increase.[10] For Mussolini, Britain's aging population and higher numbers of females sapped the country's vitality, weakened its imperial resolve and doomed it to inevitable decline.[11]

The Duce mistakenly relied on the advice of fellow Fascist hierarch Dino Grandi, the Italian Ambassador to the Court of St James, who encouraged his leader's views. In a major speech to the Fascist Grand Council in 1937, Grandi elaborated his particular vision of British decadence. In his view, Britain was plagued with pacifism born of 'fifteen years of anti-militarist and anti-patriotic propaganda.' For Grandi, 'the robust imperial impulse that characterized the English people of the nineteenth Century is dead.' The British Empire was 'fossilized and inert,' a 'lion without teeth.' Britain's elite were unprepared to spend British blood in defence of the Empire. Instead, like a sick man, it would beg the aid of others, in this case, the small powers. The British people were the only ones stupid enough to believe in the cause of disarmament and, little by little, pacifist corruption had undermined the British spirit. At the time of the Abyssinian crisis, Grandi argued, British decadence combined with military unpreparedness had meant that Britain could not face up to its resolute Italian foe. In light of Germany's rearmament, the government had abandoned its pacifist rhetoric and was now rearming and preparing for war with Germany. In spite of British rearmament, however, Grandi thought that the British people had little stomach for war. He quoted Mussolini, adding that Britain was prepared to 'fight to the last Frenchman,' as it would not lead another generation of young men to slaughter in the trenches. This line of thinking, representative of Grandi's oft-repeated views, echoed Mussolini's belief that the time was approaching when Italy could challenge British and French power in the Mediterranean.[12]

In spite of Mussolini's views of British weakness, the Italian military situation required caution, as Italy's industrial weakness and the lack of strategic raw

---

[9]   *OO, XXIII*, preface to Dr Richard Korherr, 'Regresso della nascite: morte dei populi', 1 September 1928, pp. 209–16.

[10]   Archivio Storico del Ministero degli Affari Esteri [hereafter ASMAE], Serie Affari Politici [hereafter SAP] – Gran Bretagna, B. 24, Crolla to Ciano, 4 August 1938, 17 August 1938, both seen by Mussolini.

[11]   *Ciano Diary*, 3 September 1937 entry, p. 5; *OO, XXIX, Da Popolo d'Italia*, 30 January 1938, pp. 51–52.

[12]   ASMAE, Carte Grandi, B. 43, fasc. 106, discorso al Gran Consiglio di Fascismo, 1 March 1937.

materials meant that it was difficult for Italy to compete with its potential French and British enemies. At the time of the Abyssinian crisis, for example, when Mussolini threatened war against Britain should it close the Suez Canal or impose an oil sanction, the Duce's military advisers warned him that Italy could not win a war against Britain unless the near impossible occurred and France joined with its new Italian ally against Britain, something that few observers seriously thought possible. Italy had only two battleships available for service, the *Andrea Doria* and *Caio Duilio*. Both of these dated from 1912 and had not yet undergone modernisation. Two other battleships of similar vintage were unavailable as they were refitting. Against this meagre force, Britain could deploy as many as fifteen battleships, all of which carried heavier guns than their Italian counterparts. Britain had sixty cruisers to Italy's thirteen. Italy had no aircraft carriers, meaning Britain would have a considerable tactical edge in deploying air power, in spite of Italy's central location in the Mediterranean. Moreover, Italy's air force had no bombers capable of reaching Britain's bases at Gibraltar or Suez, meaning Italy could undertake no effective strategic offensive. Italy had little effective night fighting capability. Essentially, Italy would have to try to hold the central Mediterranean, and the only potential avenue for an offensive would be to try to impede Britain's use of its base in Malta. Cooperation between the air force and the navy remained limited, and the submarine force was unprepared for war operations. The *Regia Marina* would have therefore little striking power outside of the commitment of so-called '*mezzi insidiosi*', or light guerilla weapons, that Italy did not in fact have available in 1935. Even more seriously, any losses in such an unequal conflict would be far harder for Italy to replace given its limited industrial capacity and difficulties in producing armour plate. In short, Italy could not win a war against England without French help, and the situation as laid out by Mussolini's admirals and generals counselled that it would be extremely unwise even to try.[13]

In order to address these serious deficiencies, Italian naval planners wanted to undertake an ambitious building plan. They proposed an ocean-going fleet that could break out of the confines of the Mediterranean. Ultimately, the so-called escape fleet would consist of up to ten battleships, four aircraft carriers and dozens of modern submarines. Given current Italian industrial capacity, it would take Italy twenty-four years to build this new construction.[14] Mussolini had little choice

---

[13]   Ufficio Storico della Marina Militare [hereafter USMM], DG, 0-N, Operazione B, Cavagnari to Colonial Ministry, 3 July 1935; DG, 1-D, Documento di Guerra L.G. 10 – Piano B, Naval War Plans Office, 16 May 1935; DG, 8-G, Ufficio di Stato Maggiore Generale, processo verbale della riunione del 13 agosto 1935. Giorgio Rochat, *Militari e politici nella preparazioni della Campagna d'Etopia. Studio e documenti, 1932–1936* (Milan, 1971), pp. 226–29. For much more detail, see: Robert Mallett, *The Italian Navy and Fascist Expansionism, 1935–1940* (London, 1998), pp. 11–16, 19–22, 26–34; and Gooch, *Mussolini and His Generals*, pp. 279–96.

[14]   Archivio Centrale dello Stato [hereafter ACS], Ministero della Marina, Gabinetto, B. 195, Studio sul programma navale, 13 January 1936. Mallett, *The Italian Navy*, pp. 48–

but to reject this unrealistic plan, substituting much more modest construction of destroyers, torpedo boats, and submarines.[15] In spite of the strict limits of Italian industrial capacity, however, Mussolini and his admirals did not abandon their hopes of dominating the central Mediterranean. In early 1937, Mussolini approved a plan for re-modernising the remaining two pre-Great War dreadnoughts and new building that would create an imposing fleet of eight battleships. The construction of two additional *Littorio* class vessels above the two already planned would provide four fast, heavily armed battleships that could potentially outmatch their British counterparts; although nominally listed as 35,000 tons in order to comply with treaty obligations, the *Littorio* class actually displaced 42,000 tons, and they carried powerful guns in some ways superior to their British counterparts. If Italy could secure German and Japanese support against the potential British enemy, then Britain's and France's thirty-one battleships would face thirty in the combined fleets of the powers in the anti-Comintern pact. In these circumstances, the *Regia Marina* could hope to secure Italy's coastline and to maintain control over the central Mediterranean, ensuring vital supplies for Italian forces in North Africa, as the British Royal Navy would be compelled to defend against threats in the North Sea and the Far East. The Italian navy could provide sufficient supplies and reinforcements to allow Italian ground forces to seize Egypt and the Suez Canal, given the relatively limited British defences.[16]

Waging war against France and Britain, however, remained a serious risk. Although Mussolini held considerable enmity for both western democracies, British naval power and the fact that most Italians considered France to be Italy's leading historical enemy suggested that Mussolini pursue an oblique approach, at least until he and his diplomats secured tight alliances with Germany and Japan that would draw off sufficient British strength to allow Italy to challenge the Royal Navy in the Mediterranean.[17] Italian policy therefore aimed to condition British strategic choices while awaiting the opportunity for more direct action. If Italy could present a serious enough threat to British Imperial communications and

---

54. Fortunato Minnitti, 'Il problema degli armamenti nella preparazione militare italiana dal 1935 al 1943', *Storia Contemporanea* 9.1 (1978), pp. 42–44.

[15]   ACS, Ministero della Marina, Gabinetto, B. 195, Cavagnari Memorandum, 25 June 1936, and unsigned memorandum, July 1936. Gooch, *Mussolini and His Generals*, pp. 342–48.

[16]   USMM, CN, B. 2729, Cavagnari to Marinarmi, 22 February 1937. USMM, DG, 1-B, Progetti operativi, Cavagnari to Badoglio, 19 November 1937. Mussolini finally approved the building of the final two *Littorio* class battleships late in 1937. *Ciano Diary*, 4 December 1937 entry, p. 32. Ufficio Storico dello Stato Maggiore dell'Esercito [hereafter USSME], I-4, r: 2, c: 2, Riunione presso l'ufficio di S.E. il Capo di Stato Maggiore, 2 December 1937. *Ciano Diary*, 14 February 1938, p. 58. The most complete account in English of Italian naval planning is Mallett, *The Italian Navy*. See also Gooch, *Mussolini and his Generals*, pp. 338–52, 356, 371, 415–18.

[17]   Gooch, *Mussolini and His Generals*, pp. 123–28, 144.

holdings, then British leaders would become more tractable, seeking to appease Italy to reduce the potential threat, and they could become less inclined to support Britain's putative French ally. The British weakness apparent in Mussolini's understanding of the British way in warfare provided an opportunity for Italian diplomacy and military policy to coerce British acquiescence and cooperation in the expansion of Italian power in the Mediterranean.

Italian policy aimed to interfere with Britain's control of its Empire and with British imperial communications in several ways. In 1934, Mussolini established Radio Bari, a propaganda service that broadcast across North Africa and the Middle East. Café owners would often play radio programmes for their customers, and radio typically reached a much wider audience than newspapers in the Arab world. Radio Bari initially aired a mix of Eastern music and news in Arabic, with the latter naturally carrying a pro-Italian slant. In 1935, as the Abyssinian crisis intensified, the tone changed from Italian cultural propaganda to anti-British invective. Radio Bari openly incited the Arab nationalist community, supporting the general strike and urging attacks against British troops occupying Arab lands.[18] This activity continued after the end of Italy's Abyssinian War and the removal of League sanctions against Italy. The Foreign Office compiled a lengthy report on Italian anti-British activities in the Middle East in early 1937. It detailed Italian propaganda in Palestine through Radio Bari, publishing newspapers, and distributing pamphlets. Italian agents provided funding to nationalist groups in an effort to spread rebellion.[19]

Italian agents aimed to create a series of difficulties for Britain in its relations elsewhere in the Arab world. Mussolini famously posed as the Protector of Islam. He did not claim any religious title but aimed merely to show his support for Arab nationalism in its struggle against British imperialism.[20] Mussolini and Ciano courted public and elite opinion, giving moral support to national movements and promising to safeguard the independence of Yemen and Saudi Arabia.[21] Mussolini's press and radio propaganda to support Palestinian grievances against the British Mandatory power sparked unreasonable expectations amongst the Arab population that Italy would steadily increase its support, moving from the realm of propaganda to open advocacy and support of radical change throughout the Arab world.[22] These hopes proved exaggerated, as Mussolini was cautious about

---

[18] Callum A. McDonald, 'Radio Bari: Italian Wireless Propaganda in the Middle East and British Countermeasures, 1934–1938', *Middle Eastern Studies* 13.2 (May 1977), pp. 195–97.

[19] National Archives [hereafter NA], Foreign Office [hereafter FO], 371 20786, E1488/145/65, Warner Memorandum, 13 March 1937.

[20] ASMAE, SAP – Etiopia, B. 166, Quaroni (Kabul) to Ciano, 9 May 1938.

[21] ASAME, SAP – Etiopia, B. 166, Ciano to Quaroni (Kabul) and ten counsulates, 18 April 1938.

[22] ASAME, SAP – Etiopia, B. 166, Mazzolini (Gerusalem) to Ciano, 21, 26 April 1938, 8 May 1938.

precipitating an open breach with Britain, and he certainly placed narrow Italian interests above those of the Arab World. In the negotiations that led to the 1938 Easter Accords, for example, Mussolini had hoped to be able to increase his prestige through securing assurances from Britain regarding the status of Palestine. British negotiators flatly refused to provide any assurances, however, and Italy placed its goal of obtaining British recognition of its empire far above its goals of disrupting British control in the Middle East. Italian diplomats had to make a major effort to placate disappointed Arab leaders.[23]

More directly, Mussolini aimed to threaten British imperial communications through the Red Sea. Ciano sent a Consul, Count Serrafino Mazzolini, to Egypt with the express mission of preparing fifth columns in the event that war broke against Britain. Ciano hoped that Italian nationals in the Canal Zone could create turmoil in the cities and through military sabotage. Given the incendiary nature of these orders should they became public, Ciano insisted that Mazzolini only communicate with Rome personally. Accordingly, little documentary evidence exists about Mazzolini's activity.[24]

Italian agents and diplomats worked with tribes in the Arabian Peninsula in order to increase Italian influence and to diminish Britain's prestige. In spring 1937, Italian agents received a substantial request for arms from Abdul Aziz Ibn Saud, the King of the Hejaz, who controlled much of the Arabian Peninsula. The Saudi Foreign Minister argued that Saudi inclinations were toward friendship with Italy, as Britain was stifling Arab nationalism in Palestine. Ibn Saud wanted Italian friendship and Italian arms in order to strengthen his military control in the region and to limit British interference.[25] Ciano thought it useful to fund the request in spite of opposition from Italian generals who begrudged the expense and the drain on Italy's rearmament programme.[26] After considerable delay due to military stonewalling, Italian diplomats arranged to ship 10,000 rifles, 10,000,000 rounds of ammunition, and ten 75mm artillery pieces plus ammunition. Italy asked for payment for only half of the rifles, providing the remainder of the rifles and the artillery as a gift. Ciano hoped to keep the shipment secret, as he did not want a direct confrontation with Britain over Italian violation of its pledge not to alter the status quo in the region. Ibn Saud declared himself pleased by this sign of Italian generosity.[27]

[23]   ASMAE, SAP – Etiopia, B. 166, Ciano to Quaroni (Kabul) and ten consulates, 19 April 1938, Appunto, 29 April 1938, Ciano to Mazzolini, (Gerusalem), 26 April 1938. *Ciano Diary*, 19 March 1938 entry, p. 91.

[24]   *Ciano Diary*, 3 January 1938 entry, pp. 58–59.

[25]   *I Documenti Diplomatici Italiani* [hereafter *DDI*], *8, VI*, #463, Sillitti (Gedda) to Ciano, 14 April 1937, pp. 579–80.

[26]   *DDI, 8, VI*, #459, Ciano to Sillitti (Gedda), 14 April 1937, p. 576, #360, L'Ufficio di Gabinetto to Ciano, s.d., p. 576.

[27]   ASMAE, Gabinetto [hereafter GAB] 202, Ciano to Thaon di Revel, 12 December 1937, Sillitti (Gedda) to Ciano, 16 December 1937.

Italy also worked to establish influence over Yemeni leaders. An Italian agent negotiated with Sheik Ali el Hamdani to fulfil requests for artillery, rifles, light tanks, and ammunition. Ciano inclined to support the request for political reasons.[28] The military also planned to send a small group of military advisers, under cover in the guise of sanitary workers for the Società Navigazione Eritrea.[29] The chief constraint lay in the difficulty in scraping together sufficient ammunition for the rifles from available stocks in the empire given Italy's commitment in Spain and the continuing insurgency in Abyssinia.[30] The ultimate goal of the supplies and the Italian advisers was to orient Yemeni internal politics in favour of concession of Italian military bases on the east coast of the Red Sea. In all of these cases, Italy did not intend to create a direct conflict with Great Britain. The ultimate goal was to constrict British power and to develop Italy's strategic position. Ciano hoped that in the long term he would be able to establish a military base or bases on the eastern shore of the Red Sea, creating the potential for Italy to strangle British Imperial communications through the Suez Canal. An increased Italian naval and air presence on both sides of the Red Sea would intimidate British leaders and constrain Britain's ability and willingness to interfere with Italian imperial objectives in the Mediterranean. Focusing the resentment of Arab nationalists against British Imperialism and British promises to the Zionist movement regarding Palestine served to increase tensions within the empire and to limit British prestige and power in the region. Mussolini hoped that his diplomacy would convince Britain that it could not afford to block his ambitions.[31]

Mussolini also hoped to be able to constrain British policy through more direct military means. In 1937, Mussolini decided to send reinforcements to Libya, bringing the Italian garrison to two Army Corps. The troops would begin arriving in September, after preparatory exercises in Sicily. As two of the divisions would be mechanised, the move created a potentially serious threat for Britain, as its 1936 Treaty of Friendship and Alliance severely curtailed the size of the British

---

[28]   ASMAE, SAP – Yemen – B. 13, Pariani to Ciano, 1 June 1937, Ciano to Dubbiosi (Sana'a), 7 November 1937.

[29]   ASMAE, SAP – Yemen – B. 16, Pariani to Ciano, Bastianini to Passera (Sana'a), 22 September 1937, signature illegible to Passera (Sana'a), 24 September 1937.

[30]   National Archives and Record Administration [hereafter NARA], Series T586, roll 412, Ciano to Ministero dell'Africa Italiana, 17 February 1938. For research that seeks to minimise the challenge inherent in Italian manoeuvres in the Yemen, see Rosaria Quartararo, 'L'Italia e lo Yemen. Uno studio sulla politica di espansione italiana nel Mar Rosso (1923–1937)', *Storia Contemporanea* X.4/5 (ottobre 1979), pp. 811–72.

[31]   Lawrence Pratt, *East of Malta, West of Suez: Britain's Mediterranean Crisis* (Cambridge, UK, 1975), p. 40. The dominant Italian historiography holds that Mussolini's anti-British activity in the Mediterranean aimed merely to convince Britain to accord Italy parity of rights in the Mediterranean as part of a far-reaching accord. See, for example, Paolo Nello, *Un fedele indisubidiente: Dino Grandi da Palazzo Chigi al 25 luglio* (Bologna, 1993), p. 305. This interpretation is hard to maintain in light of the considerable evidence that suggests that Mussolini's aims went rather further.

garrison in Egypt. Potentially, the Italian mechanised divisions could carry out a rapid strike against Egypt and the Suez Canal before British reinforcements could arrive to protect the region. Mussolini did not necessarily intend to carry out such an attack, but he thought that the threat would constrain British policy and make British leaders more tractable.[32]

Although the move aimed primarily to achieve a diplomatic goal, Italian military planners did not exclude the possibility of a direct attack against Egypt and the Sudan, as Mussolini considered an eventual war with the Western Powers inevitable.[33] General Pariani, Ciano's protégé and the Undersecretary of State at the War Ministry, thought a lightning attack against the Suez Canal could work, although the troops available in Libya needed better supplies, equipment and training. A large indigenous army operating from Italian East Africa would simultaneously attack the Sudan, but this force existed largely on paper. Mussolini liked the idea, as he thought British soldiers would have no stomach for war in the desert. He commented to the German Ambassador that 'the British were undoubtedly splendid sailors, but it was something else to fight in the desert at 50 centigrade'.[34] Pariani's cautious superior, General Badoglio, resisted this idea, however, as he thought British naval and economic power was too great to run the risk of even a single-handed war against Great Britain. For his part, Mussolini continued to treat Britain as a potential enemy, and Italian military planners had to account for that contingency.[35] British military planners and Foreign Office officials well understood the potential military and political threat. They feared that Italy could successfully launch a rapid attack, and even if Mussolini restrained his hand, the troops would give Mussolini the opportunity to present demands that could be akin to blackmail.[36] Mussolini counted on Britain's Imperial overreach

---

[32]   *OO, XLII*, Mussolini to Vittorio Emanuele III, 4 October 1937, pp. 194–95. USSME, H.9, B.2/3, Pariani Promemoria, 14 July 1937. *Ciano Diary*, 18 September 1937 entry, p. 9. Gooch, *Mussolini and His Generals*, pp. 361–62.

[33]   USMM, DG 1, B.1, Situazione politica ed apprestimenti militari, 17 April 1937.

[34]   Mussolini, quoted in *DGFP, D, I*, #792, von Mackenson to von Ribbentrop, 18 July 1938, p. 1152. Lucio Ceva, 'Appunti per una storia dello Stato Maggiore generale fino alla vigilia della "non belligeranza" (giugno 1925–luglio 1939)', *Storia Contemporanea* 10.2 (1976), pp. 233–38.

[35]   USSME, H-6, 12 Pariani Memorandum, 9 February, 1937. Gooch, *Mussolini and His Generals*, pp. 355–57. Robert Mallett, *Mussolini and the Origins of the Second World War, 1933–1940* (Houndmills, 2003), pp. 162–4. *Ciano Diary*, 14 February 1938 entry, p. 58.

[36]   FO 371 21168, R4805/69/22, Sargent & O'Malley Memoranda, 14 July 1937; R3475/69/22, Lt Col. Arnold (War Office) to Nichols (Foreign Office), 20 May 1937, Vansittart Minute, 26 May 1937. FO 371 22430, R321/263/22, Extract from Monthly Intelligence Summary, November 1937, R1258/263/22, Southern Department Memorandum, 10 February 1938. For detail on Britain's relationship with the nominally independent Egypt, see: Steven Morewood, 'Appeasement from Strength: The Making of the Anglo-Egyptian Treaty of Friendship and Alliance of 1936', *Diplomacy & Statecraft* 7.3

and its lack of large ground forces in Egypt as a central element of his diplomatic and strategic planning in the Mediterranean.

In order for this Italian threat to have real teeth, Mussolini needed a strong German ally. He had begun to court German sympathy in early 1936 at the height of the international crisis over his invasion of Ethiopia. He sought to remove one of the major thorns in Italy's relations with Germany by ending Italian sponsorship of Austrian independence. 'If Austria, as a formally quite independent state, were thus in practice to become a German satellite' Mussolini indicated to the astonished German Ambassador, 'he would have no objection'.[37] Mussolini drew closer to Hitler's Germany as a result of the Spanish Civil War. Although he initially resisted involvement, Mussolini ordered the dispatch of a squadron of bombers to help ferry Franco's army from Morocco to Spain. Italy became increasingly involved in the conflict, sending huge stocks of ammunition, armaments and, above all, the largest contingent of foreign soldiers, including five divisions of troops, technicians and specialists, and large numbers of planes and pilots. Italian and German officers, diplomats and intelligence officials coordinated aspects of their mutual interventions, with Italy taking a clear lead, sending larger numbers of troops and amounts of equipment.[38]

Ciano visited Germany in October 1936, arranging German recognition of Italy's conquest of Abyssinia, diplomatic cooperation to prevent discussions leading to a new Locarno, a common understanding regarding Italy's eventual withdrawal from the League of Nations, mutual recognition of Franco's eventual victory in Spain, economic cooperation in south-east Europe, and Italian support for German colonial restoration. Ciano's discussions with various German leaders, including Hitler, focused their vitriol on Great Britain, as Ciano claimed that British leaders sought to encircle Italy.[39] Mussolini publicly highlighted Italy's new relationship with Germany on 1 November 1936, stating that Ciano's visit to Berlin had created 'an Axis around which can cooperate all the European states'. He indirectly warned the British Cabinet that Italy counted the Mediterranean as

---

(1996), pp. 530–62; *idem, The British Defence of Egypt, 1935–1940: Conflict and Crisis in the Eastern Mediterranean* (London, 2005).

[37] Mussolini, quoted in DGFP, C, IV, # 485, von Hassell to the Foreign Ministry, 7 January 1936, pp. 974–77.

[38] For the most detail on the involvement in the civil war, see John F. Coverdale, *Italian Intervention in the Spanish Civil War* (Princeton, 1975). For increasing ties between Italy and Germany as a result of the war, see Mallett, *Mussolini and the Origins of the Second World War*, pp. 86–92; G. Bruce Strang, *On the Fiery March: Mussolini Prepares for War* (Westport, CT, 2003), pp. 56–58.

[39] ASMAE, Ufficio di Coordinamento [hereafter UC] 2, Resconte del primo colloquio Ciano-von Neurath, 21 October 1936, UC 84, Colloquio del Ministero Ciano col Führer, 24 October 1936. *DGFP, C, V*, #572, von Hassell to von Neurath, 6 October 1936, pp. 1041–45, #618, von Neurath Memorandum, 21 October 1936, pp. 1125–30.

a vital interest, while for Britain it was only one road among many.[40] The primary goal of this rapprochement was to intimidate Britain. As Grandi confirmed in a letter to Ciano:

> *If Italy and Germany will show England an increasingly united bloc without cracks, without dead ends, without tendencies to exploit the difficulties of the other, determined to follow a common direction and a united front to the other Powers, British policy will be constrained to come to agreements with Rome and Berlin simultaneously, accepting those conditions that Rome and Berlin together will dictate to London in order to guarantee and maintain in Europe and the world that peace which alone will permit the British Empire to maintain itself laboriously in existence.*[41]

Although the Axis was not an alliance, it did show that the two states had some common aims and shared some common foes. Most particularly, both resented and resisted British meddling in their plans for expansion. In the interim, Mussolini and Ciano hoped to wring concessions from Britain, but they had little desire for friendly relations with the rotting British Empire. Even better, if Italy could also bring Japan into this bilateral arrangement, then it would create 'the gravest danger that has ever threatened the British Empire in the course of its history'.[42]

Accordingly, Mussolini and Ciano courted Japan in the Far East as a centrally important threat to Britain's Empire, although this courtship ultimately proved more difficult to consummate. In the aftermath of the Abyssinian War, they realised that Britain's Imperial defences were stretched extraordinarily thin, and they expected that coordinated pressure from Germany, Italy and Japan could paralyse Britain, constraining its foreign policy and creating the potential for future Italian expansion. As Japan became increasingly embroiled in Manchuria and China, it challenged both the Soviet Union and Britain – two potential enemies for Fascist Italy. Italian and Japanese interests appeared to coincide, creating the opportunity for increased collaboration. Initial discussions centred on improved commercial relations and mutual recognition of their conquests in Manchukuo and Ethiopia, but Italy's leaders clearly hoped to extend the relationship further, as Japanese expansion could serve to diminish Britain's 'power and liberty of action in Europe'.[43] Ambassador Grandi wrote from London:

---

[40]   Eduardo and Duilio Susmel (eds), *Opera Omnia di Benito Mussolini* 8 volumes, *OO, XXVIII*, Discorso a Milano, 1 November 1936, pp. 67–72.

[41]   Emphasis in original. ASMAE, Carte Grandi, B. 40, Grandi to Ciano, 6 November 1936.

[42]   ASMAE, Carte Grandi, B. 40, Grandi to Ciano, 23 November 1936.

[43]   *DDI, 8, IV*, #428, Auriti to Ciano, 4 July 1936, pp. 487–91. Valdo Ferretti, *Il Giappone e la politica estera italiana, 1935–1941* (Milan, 1983), pp. 115–19, 133–40, 237. Valdo Ferretti, 'La politica estera italiana e il Giappone imperiale (gennaio 1934–giugno 1937)', *Storia Contemporanea* 2.3 (1971), pp. 913–18. Reynolds Salerno, *Vital Crossroads:*

The spectre of an Italo-German-Japanese agreement, necessarily and fatally anti-British, is present in the English spirit as a concrete possibility and as the gravest danger that has ever threatened the British Empire in the course of its history. Germany in the North Sea, Italy in the Mediterranean. Japan in the Far East. The three points and the three vital nerve centres simultaneously threatened by the three states that are the youngest, the fiercest, the most heavily armed and the most coldly determined to expand their power.[44]

While Grandi spoke primarily of a diplomatic and political threat, the combined military and naval strength of the three powers was the real peril for Britain, suggesting that expansion through the use of force was also possible.

After the Marco Polo Bridge incident rekindled Japan's war against China in July 1937, Mussolini and Ciano rapidly shifted support from the nationalist Chinese Kuomintang to Japan, shutting down Italian military missions and virtually rupturing diplomatic relations. For his part, Mussolini lauded Japan's 'intrepid resistance' to the League of Nations and its unwarranted interference in Japanese expansion, and he praised Japan's martial prowess. Italian technological superiority in aircraft design offered the opportunity for productive commercial and military relationships with Japan. More importantly, Hirota Kōki, Japan's Foreign Minister in its aggressive new Cabinet, held out the prospect of Italian accession to the anti-Comintern Pact.[45] Although determined eventually to challenge Britain's control of the Mediterranean, Mussolini and Ciano still hoped to secure British recognition of the conquest of Abyssinia and parity of Italian rights in the Mediterranean and the Middle East, so they modulated their policy, alternately offering the hand of friendship and showing Italy's tremendous potential to damage British interests. This twin policy suggested caution in approaching Japan, as too open and close an association could delay or prevent British recognition of Italy's empire. Accordingly, they decided to move with some caution, at least until after

---

Mediterranean Origins of the Second World War, 1935–1940 (Ithaca, NY, 2002), pp. 30–31. Strang, *On the Fiery March*, pp. 58–60.

[44]   ASMAE, Carte Grandi, B. 40, fasc. 93/2, Grandi to Ciano, 23 November 1936.

[45]   ASMAE, SAP – Giappone, B. 18, Auriti to Ciano, 5, 25 May 1937; Chiapparo to Ministero dell'Aeronautica and Ministero degli Affari Esteri, 6 June 1937. ASMAE, GAB 26, Sugimara Appunto per il Duce, 19 July 1937. *DDI, 8, VI*, #689, Auriti to Ciano, 3 June 1937, pp. 892–95; #702, Auriti to Ciano, 7 June 1937, p. 917. ASMAE, UC 53, Hirota to Ciano, 3 July 1937, delivered 31 July 1937. ASMAE, SAP – Cina, B. 61, Ciano to Consulato Shanghai, 26 August 1937. *Ciano Diary*, 23, 27 August 1937, 16 September 1937 entries, pp. 1, 2–3, 9. Michael Godley, 'Fascismo e nazionalismo cinese, 1931–1938. Note preliminari allo studio dei rapporti italo-cinese durante il periodo fascista', *Storia Contemporanea* 4.4 (1973), p. 776.

Great Britain opened the door for League members to recognise the conquest of Abyssinia at the League's meetings in September.[46]

After Mussolini's trip to Berlin in September 1937, his determination to challenge the British Empire grew. Ciano pushed hard for an agreement with the Japanese government. Tokyo delayed, as it was discussing a possible three-way pact with its German partner in the anti-Comintern Pact.[47] Mussolini quickly agreed to this idea, and Italy formally signed the Pact on 6 November 1937.[48] While the pact nominally targeted international communism, Mussolini and Ciano both clearly intended London as its primary target; in Ciano's words, it was 'in reality clearly anti-British'. Nor did Mussolini and Ciano intend the pact merely to apply diplomatic pressure on Britain. Ciano noted that the 'alliance' created an 'unprecedented armed force'[49] He thought it was 'the most formidable political and military combination that has ever existed'. He openly contemplated the three powers fighting together against the decadent British Empire: 'Three nations engaged down the same path, which could lead to war. A necessary fight if we want to break this mold that suffocates the energy and aspirations of young nations.'[50] Although in part, of course, this rhetoric signified the hope that Italian diplomatic and military power could constrain Britain's foreign policy without war, Mussolini and Ciano both contemplated the necessity of war against its potential British enemy for supremacy in the Mediterranean, and Italy's accession to the anti-Comintern Pact was a major step toward achieving Fascism's expansionist goals.[51]

Mussolini and Ciano continued to court Japan in 1938, although still against the backdrop that they hoped to secure British *de jure* recognition of the conquest of Abyssinia. Although they signed the Easter Accords with Great Britain in April 1938, Italian tactical concessions made during the talks meant that the Accords would come into effect only when Italy had withdrawn substantial numbers of its so-called volunteers in Spain. Japanese military and political leaders professed

---

[46]   ASMAE, UC 53, Ciano to Grandi, 2 August 1937, Grandi to Ciano, 5 August 1937. Ferretti, *Il Giappone e la politica estera italiana,* pp. 156–59. Mallett, *Mussolini and the Origins of the Second World War*, pp. 151–52.

[47]   ASMAE, GAB 28, Ciano to Auriti, 3 October 1937. ASMAE, UC 53, Appunto per il Duce, 20 November 1937.

[48]   ASMAE, SAP – Giappone, B. 17, L'accordo italo-nippo-tedesco contro l'internazionale communista, 6 November 1937. ASMAE, UC 53, Appunto per il Duce, 20 October 1937, Colloquio con l'ambasciatore di Giappone, 27 October 1937. *Ciano Diary*, 22 October 1937 entry, pp. 17–18. Ferretti, *Il Giappone e la politica estera italiana,* pp. 166–69.

[49]   *Ciano Diary*, 1, 2 November 1937 entries, p 21. *OO, XLII*, Mussolini to Vittorio Emanule III, 4 October 1937.

[50]   *Ciano Diary*, 6 November 1937 entry, p. 22.

[51]   *OO, XLII*, Mussolini to Vittorio Emanule III, 4 October 1937. ASMAE, UC 84, Colloquio Duce-Ciano-von Ribbentrop, 6 November 1937.

great friendship for Italy and wanted to increase military ties given their potential common enemies. Although the Soviet Union remained the nominal target of the Anti-Comintern Pact, Mussolini and Ciano saw Britain as the main target, as did a faction of the Japanese Kwantung Army, which resented British support for China. In Ciano's words, these common interests and the evidence that Japan had not tied down its entire military strength in Japan meant Japan could fulfill its desired place as a Far Eastern threat to the British Empire.[52]

The situation came to a head in October 1938 after the Czech crisis and Munich. Japanese military and naval attachés presented a three-way Italian-German-Japanese alliance proposal similar to the one that von Ribbentrop had raised at Munich. Ciano, still hoping to secure British *de jure* recognition of the Italian Empire, thought the pact unwise. It would foreclose the possibility of British formal implementation of the Easter Accords. As such, Ciano thought an open alliance premature. Mussolini shared those concerns. An alliance essentially existed already. Why fix it on paper and indicate to Britain, France, the Soviet Union and the United States the open hostility of the three revisionist powers? Why not wait, seeking concessions in the interim until such time as open war became necessary? Although Mussolini clearly accepted the principle of an alliance, he wanted its formal signature delayed.[53] After the British decision to implement the Anglo-Italian Easter Accords, Mussolini indicated that his policy of seeking expansion remained unchanged, and he decided to accept the Japanese proposal for a three-way military alliance directed against Great Britain.[54]

Mussolini's delays in pursuing the signing of a formal alliance ended up costing him dearly. On 31 December, Mussolini informed Ciano that the time was ripe for a written alliance between Italy, Germany and Japan. Mussolini declared that he thought war with Britain and France was inevitable. In the short run, it still could be possible to extort concessions from the West, but an open alliance could put further pressure on British leaders to abandon France to its fate. Finally, the alliance would provide sufficient diplomatic muscle to intimidate Britain, providing cover for Italian forces to occupy Albania with impunity.[55] Both Ciano

---

[52]   *OO*, XXIX, Mussolini to Prince Fulminaro Konoe, 19 March 1938, p. 410. ASMAE, SAP – Giappone, B. 17, Auriti to Ciano, 15 January 1938. ASMAE, UC 53, Ciano to Auriti, 9 April 1938, 6 June 1938, Auriti to Ciano 26 September 1938. *Ciano Diary*, 16 April 1938, 31 May 1938, 1, 21 June 1938 entries, pp. 81, 97, 97–98, 102–3. Ferretti, *Il Giappone e la politica estera italiana,* pp, 212–14.

[53]   ASMAE, UC 53, Giorgio Giorgis (Adetto Navale Tokio) al Sottosegretario di Stato, Ministero della Marina, *Ciano Diary*, 27, 28, 29 October 1938 entries, pp. 148, 148–50, 150.

[54]   ASMAE, UC 6, Ciano to Berlin, 24 November 1938. Ferretti, *Il Giappone e la politica estera italiana,* pp. 221–28. *Ciano Diary*, 16 November 1938, 23 December 1938 entries, pp. 157, 168–69.

[55]   *Ciano Diary*, 1 January 1939 entry, p. 171. ASMAE, GAB 29, Ciano to von Ribbentrop, 2 January 1939. *Ciano Diary*, 2 January 1939 entry, pp. 171–72. For a translated

and von Ribbentrop seemed to assume that a tripartite alliance would be easy to negotiate, in spite of warnings from Japanese diplomats that Japan's military and political elite remained badly divided over the possibility of conflict with Britain. If Italy and Germany intended the tripartite alliance to operate only against the Soviet Union, then the Japanese Cabinet would have little difficulty in signing such a pact. Should Italy and Germany aim the pact primarily against Great Britain, as both countries clearly intended it to do, then the Cabinet would be very reticent to participate, as some factions within the Army and the Gaimushō feared that conflict with Great Britain would immediately draw in the United States. As the Japanese Kwantung Army found itself bogged down in its war in China, that risk seemed too large to ignore. A constitutional crisis in Tokyo in January brought to power a new Cabinet less disposed to challenge Britain and the United States directly.[56]

As the weeks dragged on, Italian diplomats hammered home the difficulties involved in securing Japanese support against Great Britain. Mussolini eventually determined that he might have to accept a bilateral alliance with Germany in the short run, leaving open the possibility of adding Japan as an ally at some future time.[57] Although Mussolini and his more aggressive generals increasingly pushed for an alliance with Germany, von Ribbentrop resisted, as he still hoped to bring Japan into a much preferable tripartite pact. Lengthy discussions in Tokyo within the Japanese Cabinet and amongst senior military leaders failed to change the fundamental position: Japan would sign an alliance only if all parties clearly understood that it would apply against the Soviet Union and not Britain. Those conditions, of course, directly contradicted Mussolini's main reason for wanting the pact in the first place. Ciano indicated to Japanese diplomats that Italy would need to know the Japanese position before his meeting with von Ribbentrop in early May, hinting that Italy would seek to proceed with Germany alone. Italian leaders repeatedly pushed for staff talks with Germany, and the German leadership eventually relented, leading to the desultory staff talks that occurred in 1939.[58]

After it became clear that the alliance including Japan would not materialise, Mussolini and Ciano pushed hard for a bilateral alliance with Germany. The

---

copy from the German files, see *DGFP, D, IV*, #421, pp. 106–9.

[56]   ASMAE, Attolico to Ciano, 21, 25 January 1939, 2, 9 February 1939. *Ciano Diary*, 7 January 1939 entry, p. 174. Ōhata Tokushirō, 'The Anti-Comintern Pact, 1935–1939', in James Morley (ed.), *Deterrent Diplomacy: Japan, Germany, and the USSR, 1935–1940* (New York, 1976), pp. 79–81.

[57]   ASMAE, UC 71, Attolico to Ciano, 6 February 1939, 4 March 1939. *Ciano Diary*, 8 February 1939 entry, 3, 6 March 1939 entries, pp. 187, 195–96, 197.

[58]   ASMAE, UC 71, Ciano to Attolico, 23 February 1939, Attolico to Ciano, 28 February 1939, 2, 4 March 1939. *Ciano Diary*, 25, 27, 28 April 1939 entries, pp. 223, 224, 224–25. For more on the Japanese political situation, see Ōhata, 'The Anti-Comintern Pact, 1935–1939', pp. 85–87. For the Italian-German staff talks, see Strang, *On the Fiery March*, pp. 247–49.

negotiations proceeded quickly, as neither of the Italian principals seemed to care much about the precise details. Mussolini's main concern was that the alliance would cover offensive wars, as he dismissed the possibility that anyone would seek to attack either of the Axis powers. Nevertheless, he recognised to some degree the weakness of Italy's military, and he insisted that Italy would rearm sufficiently only by the end of 1942; only then would Italian forces have pacified Abyssinia and prepared Albania and Libya sufficiently, built and modernised six new battleships, replaced all of their medium and heavy artillery, prepared the economy to deal with a potential Anglo-French blockade, and protected Italian industry against air attack. Once these preparations were complete by 1943, Mussolini indicated, then Italy and Germany could successfully wage a general European war against Britain and France that the Duce saw as inevitable.[59] Significantly, although Ciano and von Ribbentrop agreed during their discussions that neither side would precipitate a general war for three years, such language did not appear in the treaty's text.[60]

Grandi fawningly congratulated Ciano for the negotiations that led to the Pact of Steel. 'The Italo-German military alliance is in fact the greatest blow that could be inflicted [inferto] on the policy of the democracies,' as it exposed the bankruptcy of Anglo-French attempts to wean Italy from the Axis. Although Grandi recognised Britain's war preparations and changed demeanour that had led to the guarantee to Poland, he misread the moral climate; Grandi called it Britain's 'false puritanical make-up', and he believed that Britain would once again go to great lengths to avoid war, backing down repeatedly in the face of the Axis challenge.[61]

For their part, Italian intelligence agents had repeatedly confirmed that Italian policy seemed to be working. They had informed Mussolini that the potential threat of Italy, Germany and Japan terrified the members of the British Committee of Imperial Defence (CID). As the three powers rearmed, and as Italy in the Mediterranean and Japan in the Far East expanded their empires, Britain found it impossible to rearm sufficiently to defend all of its Imperial holdings. The CID, accordingly, pushed hard for an arrangement with Italy, in spite of the objections of Anthony Eden, then Foreign Secretary. Eden had hoped to torpedo any discussions, because he feared that concessions to Italy would merely confirm British weakness. While British generals, Foreign Office officials and Cabinet members granted that Eden might be right, they thought it necessary to try to wean Italy from excessive fealty to the Axis and the anti-Comintern Pact. In effect, intelligence sources confirmed that Mussolini's bellicose conduct was having

---

[59]   ASMAE, UC 7, Notes for discussion with von Ribbentrop, 4 May 1939. See also *Ciano Diary*, 4 May 1939 entry, p. 227.

[60]   ASMAE, UC 85, Colloquio con il Ministero degli affari esteri tedesco von Ribbentrop, 6–7 May 1939. For the German record, see: *DGFP, D, VI*, #341, Unsigned Memorandum, 18 May 1939, pp. 450–52. For the published English-language text, see: *DGFP, D, VI*, #426, pp. 561–64.

[61]   ASMAE, Carte Grandi, B.40, fasc. 93/3, Grandi to Ciano, 20 May 1939.

its desired effect, limiting British strategic options and intimidating Britain's leaders.[62]

Prime Minister Neville Chamberlain and Britain's policy-making elite unwittingly fostered Mussolini's views. One element of Chamberlain's attempts to secure peace for Britain centred on appeasing Italy. As Italian intelligence had indicated, Chamberlain did face strong pressure from military advisers who desperately hoped that Britain could placate the Italian dictator in order to secure Britain's Imperial communications and to prevent the combined threat of three united, revisionist powers: Nazi Germany, Fascist Italy and imperial Japan. Chamberlain believed that Britain could reach an agreement with Italy and that Mussolini would honour it. Even if Mussolini violated any agreement, Chamberlain argued, Britain would have lost little. Its one diplomatic card to play was *de jure* recognition of Italy's conquest of Ethiopia. Chamberlain argued, and most of his diplomats concurred, that the value of recognition would wane over time; it would be best for Britain to get what decrease in tension it could from an agreement with Italy. Chamberlain doggedly pursued an Anglo-Italian arrangement in the Mediterranean, ultimately succeeding in securing the Easter Accords of 1938.[63]

But this agreement did not signal Mussolini's desire for a long-lasting rapprochement with Great Britain. In fact, Mussolini hoped that discussions leading towards an agreement could accomplish three primary goals: to secure British recognition of the conquest of Abyssinia; to split the British Cabinet, detaching Eden from Chamberlain; and to forestall the possibility of an Anglo-French alliance.[64] Mussolini, Ciano and Grandi actively connived with Chamberlain over

---

[62]   NARA, Microfilm Series T586, roll 475, Landini to Luciano, 2 March 1938, ff043521–4.

[63]   An extensive literature exists on this issue. See, among others: Lawrence Pratt, *East of Malta, West of Suez: Britain's Mediterranean Crisis, 1936–1939* (Cambridge, 1975), pp. 63–71; Mallett, *Mussolini and the Origins*, pp. 135–36, 164–66; Salerno, *Vital Crossroads*, pp. 37–41, 47–51; Strang, *On the Fiery March*, pp. 127–36, 139–42. For some centrally important archival evidence that frames the debate, see: University of Birmingham Library [hereafter UBL], Neville Chamberlain Papers 2/24A, 19 February 1938, diary entry. NA, Prime Ministers' Series 1/276, Eden to Chamberlain, enclosing Cranborne memorandum; 4 February 1938, Eden to Chamberlain, 18 February 1938; UBL, Avon Papers 13/1/49N, Eden to Chamberlain, 1 January 1938; FO 371 22403, R1282/23/22, Sargent Minute, 4 February 1938; FO 371 20383, R6149/294/67, Craigie Memorandum, 14 October 1937; notes of 19 February 1938 CAB. FO 371 21160, R5290/1/22, CID D.P. (P), 4th meeting, 23 July 1938; CAB 23/92, CC 6 (38), 19 February 1938, CC 7 (38) & 8 (38), 20 February 1938, plus Hankey Minute of Meeting of Ministers. CAB 24/262, C.P. 165 (36) Eden Memorandum, 11 June 1936. FO 371 20383, R4650/294/67, COS 506, 29 July 1936. FO 371 20412, R6974/226/22, Phillips (Admiralty) to Vansittart, 18 June 1936. FO 371 20381, R3768/294/67, C.P. 174 (36), 18 June 1936.

[64]   ASMAE, US 227, Ciano to Grandi, 3 July 1937; US 231, Grandi colloquio con Chamberlain, 2 August 1937; GAB 29, Ciano to Grandi, 7 February 1938. Strang, *On the Fiery March*, pp. 86–90, 98–99. Mallett, *Mussolini and the Origins*, pp. 149–50, 160.

Eden's dismissal. They used a secret channel through Adrian Dingli, a Maltese-born lawyer at the Inns of Court. He made contact with Sir Joseph Ball, the Head of the Conservative Research Office, who was, more importantly, Neville Chamberlain's confidant. Through Ball, Chamberlain indicated his fervent desire for warmer Anglo-Italian relations, in contrast to the more reticent Eden. Grandi had painted an unflattering picture of Eden, calling him 'an implacable enemy of Fascism and of Italy'. Mussolini's and Ciano's attempt to outmanoeuvre Eden seemed crowned with success when the Foreign Secretary resigned in February 1938.[65]

Mussolini's tactical designs and his disdain for France similarly prevented a genuine rapprochement. From the outset, Mussolini and Ciano explicitly rejected any French association with the talks that led to either the January 1937 Gentlemen's Agreement or the Easter Accords. They hoped that any Anglo-Italian arrangement would serve to isolate France, as Italy's determination to exclude France would emphasise the latter's diplomatic isolation. In spite of his Ambassador's urging that France would pay a significant price for Italian friendship, Ciano rejected the notion; he preferred that 'Paris understands only that our intransigence is absolute'.[66] Continuing negotiations with London aimed to split the two western democracies.[67] During the negotiations that led to the Easter Accords, Ciano held out the hope to British diplomats that Italy would come to a similar arrangement with France, but only after a prior accord with Great Britain. In fact, however, Mussolini could scarcely conceal his disdain for France, and took no steps to reach any durable rapprochement with his Latin neighbour.[68]

When Chamberlain and Halifax visited Rome in January 1939, it proved disastrous. Chamberlain found his hopes for peace confirmed, but Mussolini thought the British leaders tired and weak. The desultory conversations showed no true comity between the two leaders or the two powers. Mussolini defended the Axis and especially Hitler's desire for a 'totalitarian' resolution to the Jewish question. The Duce declared this solution to be just as Germany had suffered greatly at the hands

Robert Mallett, 'Fascist Foreign Policy and Official Italian Views of Anthony Eden in the 1930s', *Historical Journal* 43.1 (2000), pp. 157–87.

[65] ASMAE, GAB 398, Grandi to Ciano, 17, 19, 19, February 1938, Ciano to Segretaria, 20 February 1938, Ciano Appunto, 21 February 1938. Carte Grandi, B. 40, fasc. 93/4, Grandi to Ciano, 20 January 1938. *Ciano Diary*, 20 & 22 February 1938 entries, pp. 77–79. For Chamberlain's words with Grandi after Eden's resignation, see FO 371 22403, R1610/23/22, Cadogan Minute, 21 February 1938. For the Italian record, see ASMAE, SAP – Gran Bretagna, B. 24, Grandi to Ciano, 21 February 1938. For more detail, see: Mallett, 'Official Italian Views', pp. 157–87; Mallett, *Mussolini and the Origins of the Second World War*, pp. 164–68; and Strang, *On the Fiery March*, pp. 126–35.

[66] ASMAE, US 229, Ciano to Cerruti, 6 July 1937, Cerruti to Ciano, 5 July 1937.

[67] ASMAE, UC 89, Ciano to Grandi, 20 June 1937; GAB 28, Ciano to Grandi, 5 July 1937; US 227, Ciano to Grandi 3 July 1937. GAB 29, Ciano to Attolico, 3 April 1938.

[68] ASMAE, GAB 29, Ciano to Attolico, 3 April 1938.

of the Jews after the Great War. The two leaders sparred over France, with Mussolini condemning French leaders and indicating Italy's claims for colonial rectification, although in fact Mussolini's goals were far more extensive than he let on. The Duce rejected the possibility of a general Mediterranean Accord and Chamberlain's pleas for better Anglo-Italian relations found little resonance with him.[69]

As Hitler threatened to invade Poland in August 1939, Mussolini desperately wanted to throw Italy into the fray, in spite of the advice of most of his leading generals and admirals, who outlined the dire straits that faced the Italian military. Mussolini's foreign policy appeared to have achieved little. He had not split Britain and France, rather his actions had helped to bring these two democracies closer together, and he had failed to bring Japan into a grand tripartite alliance. Accordingly, Britain could concentrate a greater proportion of its naval strength in the Mediterranean, as it did not need to send a major fleet to the Pacific in the short term. Mussolini's attempts to coerce Britain in the Mediterranean had largely failed too. In these circumstances, could Italy join the war, even if Germany would provide the main challenge for Anglo-French forces?

Mussolini's thinking in August 1939 shows the unreality of his ideological vision of Britain and its military, and, to a lesser degree, France. Mussolini hoped that Britain's dependence on imported food would make it vulnerable to some form of blockade. He had calculated that Britain would need to import some 70,000,000 quintals of grain, almost four times as much as Italy, as well as 20 tons of other types of food, 17,000,000 tons of minerals, and 12,000,000 tons of petrol. He thought that submarines could implement such a blockade, although it was far from clear how Italy's limited number of ocean-going submarines would operate outside of the Mediterranean through the Strait of Gibraltar. Mussolini also hoped that American neutrality legislation would deprive Britain of access to American resources in the event that the British Empire found itself involved in a general war. The attack from Libya towards the Suez Canal could work, in spite of reports that Britain had begun to reinforce its skeleton garrison there, and in spite of reports that Italian troops in Libya remained short of supplies and relied on extensive shipments from Italy simply to maintain them at peacetime levels. Persistent budgetary problems and industrial limitations continued to constrain Italy's grandiose naval construction plans, tilting the balance against Italy in the Mediterranean, especially as Great Britain had undertaken a substantive building programme of its own.[70] Italian admirals warned that Italy would be unable to

---

[69]   ASMAE, UC 61, Primo colloquio del Duce col Signor Chamberlain, 11 January 1939, dichiarazioni a Chamberlain, no date. For continued British discussions about the strategic situation in the Mediterranean, see FO 371 23981, W4683/108/50, CID SAC 1st meeting, 1 March 1939, Strang Minute, 2 March 1939, Nicholls Minute, 13 March 1939, Cadogan Minute, 16 March 1939. FO 371 22923, C 2751/281/17, Hollis to Strang, sending COS 853, 8 March 1939.

[70]   *DDI, 9, III*, #716, Badoglio to Mussolini, 6 April 1939, p. 618. Gooch, *Mussolini and His Generals*, pp. 401, 439–48, 462–63. Mallett, *The Italian Navy and Fascist*

undertake a strategic offensive and would have a difficult time raising the Libyan army to wartime levels that would enable the attack on Egypt.

The bleak military situation contrasted to Mussolini's optimism and thirst for war created a sense of near panic amongst Mussolini's leading generals and his diplomatic advisors. General Badoglio, his Chief of Staff, for example, sought to discourage the Duce's dreams of military glory. He warned of the dangers of a war waged by Germany and Italy against Britain and France. As Japan's Navy would be on the sidelines, Britain could cover the North Sea while concentrating a substantial part of its fleet against Italy. In these circumstances, the *Regia Marina* would be on the defensive everywhere. It had only two operational modernised battleships, not the eight that it had planned for 1942. Italy would otherwise be hard pressed to defend the central Mediterranean in order to keep supplies flowing to Libya, and in so doing would suffer substantial and largely irreplaceable losses. Only submarines could carry out localised counter-attacks against British and French merchant shipping. In Libya itself, the Italian army was short of supplies, and the Italian army as a whole still needed to replace its antiquated artillery and to bring its equipment up to a war footing. Italy faced critical shortages of raw materials, especially coal and oil. In Badoglio's view, the Italian military found itself in 'total crisis'. For his part, a disappointed Mussolini maintained the vague hope that he could exploit the situation to establish protectorates over Croatia and Greece, but these aspirations proved quixotic. In the end, Italy had little choice but to seek legalistic arguments to evade its obligations under the Pact of Steel; Mussolini could only bluster from the sidelines, declaring that Italy would be a non-belligerent, a term Mussolini coined to reduce the stigma of neutrality.[71]

After Germany's invasion of Poland, the military sought to reinforce Libya, bringing it to a war footing.[72] In spite of substantial reinforcement, though, Badoglio thought it would be a difficult task to carry out an offensive against Egypt. He contemptuously rejected the now-dismissed Pariani's grandiose plans for seizing the Suez Canal, insisting that in future his subordinates develop more realistic objectives. In the meantime, Italy would concentrate on creating an adequate defence of its frontiers, adding to its battleship fleet, and modernising

Expansionism, pp. 115–16, 132–33, 146–47,

[71]   Badoglio to Mussolini, 17, 31 August 1939, in Emelio Faldella, *Revisione e giudizi: L'Italia e la seconda guerra mondiale, 2a edizione* (Bologna, 1960), pp. 132–33, 134. USMM, DG, O-A1, B. 1. Esame del problema strategico in caso di conflitto, 20 August 1939. USSME, I-4, R. 5, f. 13, Direttive di carattere operative, 17 August 1939. ASMAE. UC 9, Attolico to Ciano, 14 August 1939, Ciano to Magistrati, 15 August 1939. Mallett, *The Italian Navy and Fascist Expansionism*, pp. 156–58. Gooch, *Mussolini and His Generals*, pp. 510–13. For more coverage of Mussolini's overpowering desire to join the war and the resistance from his advisers, see Strang, *On the Fiery March*, pp. 307–18.

[72]   Salerno, *Vital Crossroads*, p. 144.

its artillery.[73] Badoglio estimated that it would take until late 1941 or even 1942 to remedy the military's worst deficiencies.[74] In spite of this military counsel of despair, Mussolini still spoke openly of intervention. He thought British and French demographic weakness meant that they lacked the will and the manpower for a decisive ground assault against either Italy or Germany. He argued that Italy had compiled sufficient stocks of raw materials to be able to fight a short war, using its fleet to control the central Mediterranean.[75] Mussolini categorically rejected British attempts to buy off Italy through British provision of coal in exchange for weapons; he reaffirmed his 'firm hostility toward the democracies' and indicated that he would eventually launch a parallel war to his German ally.[76]

Even before Germany's invasion of France, Mussolini spoke frequently about joining the war, although he in part recognised the difficulties that Italy's military would face. Nevertheless, he continued to believe that Anglo-French demographic decline meant that they would not risk a direct assault against Germany or Italy. Accordingly, Italy could participate in a short war emphasising its air power and navy, although Mussolini seemed to see this struggle as more of a moral contest rather than one with specified military goals designed to bring victory. He emphasised that Italy could not remain outside, as to do so would mean Italy would fall from the ranks of the European Great Powers. Italy had no choice but to break out of the Mediterranean prison created by Britain's control of Malta, Gibraltar and Suez. In the Duce's view, this brief war would not drain Italy's otherwise inadequate supplies of petroleum and strategic raw materials. Mussolini's aspirations represented little more than wishful thinking; Italy would have little effective military contribution to make in such a war outside of localised attacks in East Africa and a naval offensive unless Germany were able to smash the French army and drive Britain from the Continent.[77]

As the *Wehrmacht* drove through France, Mussolini finally overcame his military chiefs' caution and brought Italy into the war, although Italian forces had no real prospect of achieving positive results. The situation in Libya remained dire, as troops had inadequate supplies and arms to invade either Egypt or Tunisia.

---

[73]   NARA, microfilm series T-586, roll 405, Minutes of Chiefs of Staff Meeting, 18 November 1939.

[74]   *Ciano Diary*, 10 January 1940 entry, p. 310.

[75]   *Ciano Diary*, 11, 23 January 1939 entries, pp. 310–11, 315. Salerno, *Vital Crossroads*, pp. 181–82.

[76]   *Ciano Diary*, 20 February 1940 entry, p. 322. For more detail on this episode, see Robert Mallett, 'The Anglo-Italian War Trade Negotiations, Contraband Control and the Failure to Appease Mussolini, 1939–1940', *Diplomacy & Statecraft* 8.1 (1997), pp. 137–67. The best account of Italy's foreign policy after the outbreak of war remains MacGregor Knox, *Mussolini Unleashed, 1939–1941: Politics and Strategy in Fascist Italy's Last War* (Cambridge, 1988).

[77]   *DDI, 9, III*, #669, Mussolini to Vittorio Emanuele III, Ciano, Badoglio, Graziani, and Pricolo, 31 March 1940, pp. 576–79.

Mussolini spoke of an aero-naval offensive, but even that task largely proved beyond Italian capabilities despite Germany's crushing victory in France. General Francesco Pricolo, the Chief of the Italian Air Force, wanted to carry out bombing raids against Malta, but Badoglio overruled him, seeking to conserve the air force. Admiral Cavagnari ordered the navy to adopt a defensive posture, above all seeking to avoid virtually irreplaceable losses, although he did indicate that he could send 83 submarines to sea. The navy would seek to hold the central Mediterranean, keeping lines of communication and supply open to Libya. Mussolini eventually accepted this pessimistic advice, although he continued to hope that France's calamity combined with the continued reinforcement of Italy's army in Libya might create the possibility of a successful offensive against Egypt and the Suez Canal in the future.[78]

The situation in 1940 demonstrated the abject failure of Mussolini's foreign and strategic policy. The Duce had hoped to use a combination of diplomacy, bluff and coercion to secure British acknowledgement of Italy's status as a major power in the Mediterranean and to constrain Britain's leaders from interfering with Italian expansionism in Africa and the Middle East. Given the limits of Italian industrial capacity and its paucity of strategic raw materials, Mussolini pursued an oblique approach to realise his otherwise aggressive goals. The Italian Navy could defend Italy and provide sufficient cover for Italian land offensives only against either Britain or France and only with the support of allies. Mussolini tried to secure the support of both Germany and Japan, succeeding in one case and failing in the other, as Japan joined the war only after it was far, far too late for Italy to recover from its disastrous defeats.

Ultimately, Mussolini's tactics failed, and Britain indicated that it would not abandon France to the wolves, at least not to Roman ones. In fact, Mussolini's anti-British actions in the Mediterranean and the Red Sea helped to convince British leaders of the impossibility of satisfying the Axis powers. Even facing this formidable combination, the bellicose Duce showed in early 1940 a desperate need to join the war in spite of military advice that warned of catastrophe for Italy's ill-equipped forces. Mussolini's largely mistaken estimates of British weakness, informed fundamentally by his superficial assessment of British patterns of warfare, led Italy to disaster in the Second World War, as Britain and its belated allies proved sufficiently adept at raising mass armies and adequate naval and air strength to defeat decisively the Italian threat to Britain's Mediterranean Empire.

---

[78]   *DDI*, 9, IV, #642, Riunone presso il Capo del Governo, Mussolini, del Capo di Stato Maggiore Generale, Badoglio, e dei Capi di Stato Maggiore dell'Esercito, Graziani, della Marina, Cavagnari, dell'Aeronautica, Pricolo, 29 May 1940, pp. 495–97. Verbale della riunone dei Capi dei Stato Maggiore, 30 May 1940, and Verbale della riunone dei Capi dei Stato Maggiore tenutasi nell'ufficio del Capo di Stato Maggiore Generale, 5 June 1940, in Faldella, *Revisione e giudizi*, pp. 739–42. Salerno, *Vital Crossroads*, pp. 206–9. Mallett, *The Italian Navy and Fascist Expansionism*, pp. 146–47. Gooch, *Mussolini and His Generals*, pp. 516–17.

Chapter 4

Managing the British Way in Warfare: France and Britain's Continental Commitment, 1904–1918

William Philpott

As the storm gathered over Europe in the late 1930s, Winston Churchill was fond of giving thanks for the French army. Yet between 1914 and 1918, and again in 1939, it was Britain's army which was sent to sustain France. This paradox, of a maritime power engaging in a Continental land war, resolutely if not wholeheartedly, which Michael Howard so cogently analysed in his influential study *The Continental Commitment*, was central to the nature and exercise of British power in the early twentieth century.[1] Within that broad framework there were further paradoxes, paradoxes of practicality as it were: of deployment, employment and commitment.[2] Coalitions such as this are generally analysed from a partial, national perspective, not from that of the partner-adversary which constitutes the other side of any alliance. So it was, until recently, with Britain's Great War coalition with France. Consequently, both then and subsequently it has been represented that this close relationship apparently went against the grain of Britain's traditional strategy, and proved inimical to her own freedom of action, wealth and best interests: such a judgement was indeed central to Basil Liddell Hart's original thesis of a 'British way in warfare'. A large British army on the Continent – and the scale of casualties this entailed when it became engulfed in a static war of attrition (one of whom was Liddell Hart himself) – was presented as an aberration. In fact, if coalition war is one of the paradigms of a British way in warfare as David French posits, it was not the army on the Continent which was problematic – British armies had fought in the Peninsula, the Low Countries and the Crimea in the previous century after all – but the facts that prolonged industrial war was a severe drain on the power of even the world's most potent empire, and that in a military coalition with France Britain was not the senior partner.

---

[1]   M. Howard, *The Continental Commitment: The Dilemma of British Defence Policy in the Era of Two World Wars* (London, 1972).

[2]   W.J. Philpott, 'The General Staff and the Paradoxes of Continental War', in *The British General Staff: Reform and Innovation, 1890–1939*, ed. D. French and B. Holden Reid (London, 2002), pp. 95–111.

The intensifying military relationship between Britain and France which evolved between the signing of the Entente Cordiale in 1904 and their shared victory in 1918 was central to British defence policy. Like all alliances it represented both an accretion to and draw on Britain's own power, and was controversial because it reversed the norms of isolationist British defence policy; not just because France had until the turn of the century been Britain's principal imperial rival, but also because it reshaped Britain's power relationship with the Continent and the Continent's other Great Powers, Germany and Russia in particular. The quid pro quo for security in the world was commitment in Europe; an engagement with European rivalries which penetrated, if never entirely dominated, defence policy and planning in London and the Empire in the ensuing decade.[3] For these reasons the Entente relationship has been assessed and reassessed ever since, in both its diplomatic and defence aspects.[4] It would be fatuous to rehash these complex analyses in this essay. On the other hand, to paraphrase David French, an examination of the way in which France marshalled Britain's resources to protect its security interests will throw light on the changing nature of British power in the era of industrial Great Power conflict, as well as on the nature of the Entente Cordiale itself.[5] How did France perceive British power; how did she try to manage it in her prolonged confrontation with Germany, to maximise it in France's cause; and what impact did this have on the relationship between the two committed yet bickering allies on whose constant union the security and democracy of western Europe depended during Europe's thirty-year crisis?

As Britain's First World War ambassador in France, Lord Bertie, perspicaciously observed in 1916, while Britain was engaged in her greatest continental battle:

> You must not forget that the French judge us purely by our doings on the land, and in France: our mastery of the sea, and all that it involves, is taken as a matter of course, therefore the eye of the public is fixed on our Army and not on the Navy.[6]

The eye of this chapter will be fixed firmly there as well, for it was Britain's military strength, latent and actual, and the British army's performance which preoccupied, even at times obsessed, the French. France faced the same paradox as

---

[3]   As surveyed in J. Gooch, *The Plans of War: The General Staff and British Military Strategy, c. 1900–1916* (London, 1974).

[4]   Key works are S.R. Williamson, *The Politics of Grand Strategy: Britain and France Prepare for War, 1904–1914* (Cambridge MA, 1969), W.J. Philpott, *Anglo-French Relations and Strategy on the Western Front, 1914–1918* (Basingstoke, 1996); and E. Greenhalgh, *Victory Through Coalition: Britain and France during the First World War* (Cambridge, 2005).

[5]   D. French, *The British Way in Warfare* (London, 1990), p. xi.

[6]   Bertie to Lloyd George, 18 August 1916, Lloyd George Papers, Parliamentary Archives, London, E3/14/4.

Britain, for British military support was both an accretion to and draw on France's own resources, especially so once they were engaged in a common campaign on the Western Front against Germany and a wider imperial war with Germany's allies.

As the thorough analysis which accompanied the 2004 centenary of the Anglo-French Entente demonstrated, France's twentieth-century relationship with Britain was a complex one: it was based partly on inter-dependence, partly on respect, partly on fear, and partly on supercilious superiority, leavened with disappointment.[7] All these elements are apparent when France dealt with Britain as a military ally. The central determinants of this fraught relationship were that proud France needed British military support against Germany, did not really like that fact, resented the lack of control she had over that support and disliked the machinations and give-and-take of alliance politics which that entailed. Bossy Marianne wanted to give orders to Britain (or at least to Britain's armed forces), and belligerent John Bull seemed to want to use France to further his own international agenda. 'Fighting to the last Frenchman' was an oft-deployed criticism of an apparent lack of British effort, while on the other hand the heavy blood sacrifice actually being paid by British troops on French soil – heavy in British eyes at least – seemed insufficiently acknowledged. It was ever thus in alliances. Certain individuals rose above this national infighting, and emerged as central figures in the successful Anglo-French war effort. Field Marshal Herbert Kitchener and General Ferdinand Foch stand out on the two sides: the former as the 'architect of victory' who created the new British armies which bore his name; the latter as the generalissimo who led the allied armies to battlefield victory in 1918.[8] Other central figures, such as General Joseph Joffre and Sir Douglas Haig, respectively French and British commanders-in-chief who found themselves fighting together in the crucial 1916 campaign, emerge with less credit.

Foch had been an important figure in the burgeoning pre-war Anglo-French military relationship. It was his contacts with Brigadier-General Sir Henry Wilson in 1909–10, when both headed their nation's staff college, which really initiated the intimate links between the British and French armies which developed before 1914. They subsequently got the blame for the detailed staff talks which drew Britain and France into their shared fate in France and Flanders; fairly in Wilson's case, unjustly in Foch's, for he had little say in French strategic planning.[9] But what did come out of their contacts was a new approach to military cooperation. If a

---

[7]　See the essays in *Cross Channel Currents: 100 Years of the Entente Cordiale*, ed. R. Tombs, D. Johnson and R. Mayne (London, 2004); and *Britain, France and the Entente Cordiale since 1904*, ed. A. Capet (Basingstoke, 2006).

[8]　W.J. Philpott, 'Winning the War: Kitchener and Foch', in *Cross Channel Currents*, pp. 54–61.

[9]　'WF' stood for 'With France', not 'Wilson-Foch', as it was subsequently designated in the official records of pre-1914 British strategic planning. 'Wilson-Foch Scheme – Expeditionary Force to France', The National Archives, Kew, WO 106/49A/2 & 4.

British army was to come to France in the event of a war with Germany – and until war broke out it was always 'if' it should be efficient and able to fit immediately into France's order of battle. As such, it represented a short-term but very real addition to France's strength in the first clash. Wilson has been justly criticised for positing that the six-division British Expeditionary Force (BEF) might be the decisive force in the initial encounter with German armies in northern France, as he did at the infamous 23 August 1911 Committee of Imperial Defence (CID) meeting which discussed the practicality of British intervention in a Continental war seriously for the first time. What lay behind that contention, however, was not merely Wilson's strong Francophilia, but also an acknowledgement that the British army was becoming France's tool.

How did this come about? When asked by Wilson how many troops Britain should send to France on the outbreak of war, Foch famously remarked, 'One single private soldier, and we would take good care that he was killed.'[10] Conversely, the Royal Navy before the First World War was purportedly not worth even this single bayonet to the French.[11] Such was a realistic assessment, for, as Admiral Sir Arthur Wilson had acknowledged early on, 'no action by the navy alone', against German colonies or overseas trade, 'can do France any good'.[12] How to hook and then keep British support on land were the first, peacetime, tasks facing French statesmen and generals; how to manage and maximise it were to be peace- and wartime problems. Staff talks were the hook with which to land the British fish. Begun informally in 1905–6 and resumed in 1935–36, repeated and more intimate as pre-war crises forced common planning, these talks betokened that Britain had not ruled out supporting France on land, and that France might get a British army on the outbreak of war. Arrangements were always conditional and non-binding, but were strengthening by custom and usage.[13] A major element of anti-Continentalist strategic critiques between the wars was that secret staff talks had bound Britain too closely to France. In the absence of any formal British alliance before both 1914 and 1939, military obligation represented a less formal alternative, furnishing a moral commitment to come to France's aid if not a paper one. It was, in 1930s parlance, a limited liability, limited by both contingent and employment, but not no liability at all.[14]

---

[10]   Maj.-Gen. Sir C.E. Callwell, *Field-Marshal Sir Henry Wilson: His Life and Diaries* (London, 2 vols, 1927), i, pp. 78–79.

[11]   Henry Wilson diary, 14 February 1913, cited in ibid., i, p. 122.

[12]   27 June 1905, quoted in Howard, *Continental Commitment*, p. 43.

[13]   The definitive study of the pre-1914 staff talks is S.R. Williamson, *The Politics of Grand Strategy* [previously cited n. 4]. For the significance of the inter-war staff talks see M.S. Alexander and W.J. Philpott, 'The French and the Field Force: Moral Support or Material Contribution?', *The Journal of Military History*, 71 (2007), pp. 743–72.

[14]   T. Wilson, 'Britain's "moral commitment" to France in August 1914', *History*, 64 (1979), pp. 380–90, argues that there was no such commitment on Britain's part. The French nevertheless clearly strove to cultivate one amongst British politicians and soldiers.

Although these staff talks have usually been the focus when analysing the Anglo-French relationship before 1914, the 'military entente' went deeper.[15] In the absence of a formal commitment to send the BEF to the Continent, the French did all they could to develop an informal relationship, based on official missions to Britain and official and unofficial exchanges of officers between the two armies. Senior officers destined to be wartime leaders, as well as junior officers, got to know each other personally, and to understand the structure and ethos of the forces which potentially they were to fight with on the battlefield. Such contacts served three purposes for France. Firstly they allowed her to check on the quality and quantity of British forces which might be deployed to the Continent; secondly they encouraged a 'Continentalist' ethos in the British army which would strengthen the case for intervention; and thirdly they allowed France to induct the BEF in French operational methods so that military cooperation, should it be decided upon, would be as effective as possible.

Having the fish on the hook was the first thing. France also needed to know whether she was landing a whopper or a tiddler. From 1905, when the Entente started to assume a military dimension, France's military attachés and a series of official and unofficial visitors to the British army took pains to assess the size and quality of any likely contingent reinforcement. Liberal war minister Edward Haldane's post-1906 army reforms, which created the BEF and the second-line Territorial Force, were closely monitored by France, whose increasing admiration for the BEF – created they noted from the start 'to permit intervention on the continent and make their influence felt if necessary'[16] – can be traced through pre-war files in the *Archives de l'armée de terre* at Vincennes. What in 1905 had been a rather uninspiring force, disorganised by the succession of military reforms which followed its poor showing in the South African War,[17] had become a genuine asset to France by 1914. The May 1912 annual report on the British army, revised only on points of detail before 1914, was very positive. Its author, Capitaine Le Merre of the *Deuxième bureau* (French military intelligence), judged the British regular army the equal of any other Continental army. Its senior commanders were at the height of their profession; it had excellent infantry, very good cavalry and good artillery; it was well armed and its support services had recently been reorganised. Its *esprit de corps* – 'very combative and confident'

---

[15]   This section draws heavily on an unpublished paper, 'More than "a single private solider": France and the Prospect of British Military Support before 1914', delivered in April 2004 at a conference held at Salford University, 'Refocusing on Europe? Defence and Diplomacy from the Entente Cordiale to the First World War'.

[16]   Huguet to Ministre de la Guerre, 7 January 1907, *Service historique de la defense*, *Archives de l'armée de terre*, Vincennes [AAT] 7N1223.

[17]   'Effectifs que l'Angleterre serait susceptible de mobiliser et de débarquer sur le continent dans le cas d'une guerre entre la France et l'Allemagne', by Huguet, 18 November 1905, AAT, 7N1222/1.

– was perfect.[18] In French judgement the BEF was effective but small. Its potential for expansion was always in their sights.[19] A seventh regular division, cobbled together from colonial garrisons, was a small but carefully monitored immediate addition to the force. Haldane's more ambitious plan to create an Imperial army of 46 divisions was also welcomed. This latent Imperial strength, as Foch's quip implied, was all to the good for France, but it was hard to assess its potential. It was expected to have little immediate impact on the military situation when war broke out.[20] The Territorial Force which, with the colonial forces which Haldane was mustering, was the likely source of further support to France in a longer war, was less promising. Its numbers, training and state of readiness were therefore closely monitored, but not with much confidence.[21] This was a genuine concern for France, for whether the BEF could be sent abroad on the outbreak of war, and whether it could be reinforced in the medium term, depended particularly on the size and efficiency of the Territorial Force and the Special Reserve (the BEF's immediate reinforcing contingent, for replacing front-line losses). Military attaché Victor Huguet was happy to report by the end of 1908, a little over one year into the new reserves scheme, that the Special Reserve was on course to reach full strength during the course of the year, while Territorial Force recruitment was improving.[22] In 1912 Le Merre anticipated that 152,000 additional men of the regular army, reserves and Territorial Force might be sent to France within three months of the outbreak of war. However, the Territorial Force was primarily a home defence militia, and it was thought unlikely that Britain would denude her shores of all her front-line forces at the very beginning of a conflict.[23] Of course, quantitatively, the French would have welcomed conscription (a political hot potato in pre-1914 Britain which the French intelligence service monitored closely); although pragmatically it was recognised that, qualitatively, in the short term such a change would severely disrupt existing arrangements for sending the British army to war and swallow up Britain's small but impressive and professional army. French curiosity was actively encouraged by the British army, strengthening as it did its own growing 'Continentalist' ethos which Wilson and other senior commanders,

[18]   'La cooperation militaire anglaise: hypothèse d'une guerre franco-allemand', by Capitaine Le Merre, 2e Bureau, 15 May 1912, AAT, 7N1227/1, and revised copy, June 1914, AAT, 7N1243.

[19]   Huguet to Ministre de la Guerre, 8 August 1906, AAT, 7N1222/2.

[20]   'Projet de création d'un Etat-Major Général de l'Empire' and 'L'année 1909 en Angleterre au point de vue militaire', by Huguet, 24 February 1909 and 15 January 1910, AAT, 7N1225/1 and 7N1226/1.

[21]   See for example 'L'Armée territoriale anglaise' and 'Au sujet de l'Armée territoriale anglaise', by Panouse, 19 August and 26 October 1912, AAT, 7N1227/2.

[22]   'Rapport general sur l'armée britannique à la date du 1er Octobre 1908', by Huguet, 3 March 1909, AAT, 7N1225/1.

[23]   'La cooperation militaire anglaise', by Le Merre, op. cit. 'Au sujet de l'Armée territoriale anglaise', op. cit., and 'Angleterre, Fevrier 1913', AAT, 7N1243.

notably General Sir John French and Lieutenant-General Sir James Grierson, were actively encouraging as an alternative to traditional maritime strategies.[24]

As the French got to know the British army better they came to like it, but they were well aware that until very recently it had been an imperial police force (and not a particularly good one if its last punitive mission in South Africa was anything to go by), and of its unfamiliarity with Continental ways of war.[25] If it was to be of real support to France the BEF would have to get to France in time to fight, and it would have to understand how France fought. Thus speed and place of deployment and battlefield effectiveness were as vital to France as size. As successive rounds of staff talks made it look increasingly likely that a British deployment to France would be to support the left wing of the French field armies directly – although this was never certain – France put pressure on the British General Staff to speed its deployment so that it could intervene in the first clash. Between 1905 and 1914 the BEF's mobilisation time was reduced from nearly five weeks to just over two.[26] When Sir John French, the arch-Continetalist amongst Britain's senior commanders and a regular guest at French military manoeuvres, was nominated Chief of the Imperial General Staff (CIGS) in 1911, Huguet naturally reported approvingly to Paris his declaration that he intended to get the army ready for war.[27] The Continentalist ethos of the army that had been evident over the past few years was starting to have a real impact.[28] However, the competing pull of Britain's traditional military strategy, amphibious operations on friendly soil or against the enemy's coasts, could not be discounted. Sir John French always had one eye on the Belgian coast,[29] and his ongoing concern with not aligning the British army too closely with the French in the field resurfaced, Huguet was disturbed to report.[30] After French became CIGS, de la Panouse, who had succeeded Huguet as French military attaché in London, confirmed 'notable progress in the British army's preparations with respect to a war on the continent', even if there remained uncertainties about strategic intentions.[31]

---

[24] Philpott, 'Paradoxes of Continental War' and H. Strachan, 'The British Army, its General Staff, and the Continental Commitment, 1904–14', in *The British General Staff*, pp. 75–94.

[25] 'Entrée en fonctions', by Huguet, 1 February 1905, AAT, 7N1222/1.

[26] 'Effectifs que l'Angleterre serait susceptible de mobiliser et de débarquer sur le continent dans le cas d'une guerre entre la France et l'Allemagne', by Huguet, 18 November 1905, AAT, 7N1222/1; 'Memorandum de la conference du 20 Juillet 1911', AAT, 7N1782/2.

[27] Huguet to Ministre de la Guerre, 13 May 1911, AAT, 7N1226/2.

[28] See for example, 'Rapport sur manoeuvres anglaises en 1910', by Le Merre, 5 October 1910, AAT, 7N1243.

[29] W.J. Philpott, 'The Strategic Ideas of Sir John French', *The Journal of Strategic Studies*, 12 (1989), pp. 458–78.

[30] Huguet to Dubail, 18 October 1911, AAT, 7N1782/2.

[31] 'L'armée anglaise pendant l'année 1912', by Panouse, 5 March 1913, AAT, 7N1228/1.

Such preparations owed much to French tutelage. The British army's 'inter-operability' with the French army became an important issue as the likelihood of direct support grew. For example, French observers of the British army's 1909 manoeuvres had returned unimpressed by British higher command. Nevertheless, General Coupillaud concluded, the British army 'would contribute real force and energy to an ally which, taking them into their confidence, knows how to use them', while Huguet at the same time cautioned that their mental preparation would take much longer than their material one.[32] The simplest solution to this would have been to put British divisions under French command, although not surprisingly such a practical solution had proved politically unworkable from the start.[33] Instead, the French army tried to inculcate Continental methods into the British senior officer corps through a series of reciprocal visits to each other's manoeuvres, as suggested by General Durand following his visit to the 1909 manoeuvres.[34] Whether this had any bearing on Foch and Wilson meeting several times over the winter and summer of 1909–10, and Wilson's adoption of some of Foch's methods in British staff training, is impossible to establish.[35] But in future British generals who attended French manoeuvres were attached to French headquarters so that they could get first-hand understanding of the management of divisions and corps in the field. Senior French officers monitored their progress. Foch came to Britain in 1912 to attend the annual manoeuvres, meet senior political and military figures, and even, if Esher's cryptic reference is accurate, attend the CID.[36] Then he reportedly made the odd but prophetic remark to Colonel Jack Seely, British minister of war, that a war of millions was uncontrollable and would bog down, in which case 'your little army, directed by my friend French, with your sea power enabling you to send them where you will, may well prove decisive if ever a conflict comes'.[37] Either he knew nothing of the arrangements made to send the BEF to France, which seems unlikely, or even at that late stage he did not trust the British to send it.[38] General de Castelnau, Joffre's principal strategic adviser, came in 1913, and Joffre himself was to have come over in 1914 had the real thing

[32]   Huguet to Ministre de la Guerre, 29 July 1909, and report by General Coupilluad, August 1909, AAT, 7N1225/2 and 7N1242.

[33]   Philpott, 'Strategic Ideas of French', pp. 462–63.

[34]   'Grands manoeuvres de l'armée britannique en 1909', by Durand, 29 October 1909, AAT, 7N1242.

[35]   Callwell, *Henry Wilson*, i, pp. 77–80.

[36]   Foch to Ministre de la Guerre, 28 October 1912, AAT, 7N1243; 'Mission français aux grandes manoeuvres anglaises', by Panouse, 27 August 1912, AAT, 7N1228; Esher journal, 19 August 1914, in M.V. and O. Brett (eds), *Journals and Letters of Reginald, Viscount Esher* (London, 4 vols, 1934–8), iii, p. 179.

[37]   Rt Hon. J.E.B. Seely, *Adventure* (London, 1930), pp. 150–51.

[38]   It is also possible that Seely was making an oblique post-war criticism of the fact that the BEF was sent to France in 1914, rather than held back for amphibious operations.

not intervened.[39] The French were certainly pleased that the British adopted large-scale manoeuvres in the years before 1914, although despite meeting 'several generals very familiar with our methods and the tendency of our ideas' they judged the 1913 manoeuvres a failure, and that British generals' ability to handle large all-arms formations remained deficient.[40] The process of educating the British senior command was incomplete when war broke out.

As war approached France had to content herself with – seemed to be content with – Britain's modest regular army and limited contingent reinforcements: by 1912 Britain had six efficient ready infantry divisions to send, rather than the three of 1905, with the reserves to sustain them in the field for six months.[41] In that period the French had grown increasingly optimistic about the numbers and quality of the BEF and its reinforcing contingents. It was clear that the British General Staff were doing their utmost to maximise the military support they could offer to their ally, in the absence of formal political instructions to do so.[42] One 1911 report by a visiting French general staff officer, Commandant Stirn, summed up the general French impression of their future ally's army succinctly: 'the six divisions of this force, made up of well led battalions, constitutes a support with real value whose intervention in the European theatre of operations might be a real factor in any success.'[43] This small, well-equipped contingent reinforcement, tactically skilled and of high morale was, however, somewhat lacking in high command aptitude. This immediate assistance was backed by the manpower and financial and industrial potential of the British Empire, and a rather large navy. Recent naval agreements suggested that France could also rely on the Royal Navy in North Sea waters, but this was merely reinsurance, because it was the German army that would invade France, not the Imperial German Navy. From 1912 the Royal Navy could at least get the British army to France, even if it had been unwilling to guarantee such a passage at the CID meeting the previous year. This suggests that the Entente with Britain represented a short-term boost, and a long-term guarantee of French security. What Britain did not offer was a mass conscript army. One would think France might be disappointed, but pragmatism led her to accept Britain's contribution in the form it took. Haldane's system was a remarkably practical military organisation adapted to the characteristics of the British nation, Stirn reported, which in the event of a Continental war would allow her to fulfil any role which her political agenda determined. Besides, if she had

[39]   Panouse to Ministre de la Guerre, 21 July 1914, AAT, 7N1228.

[40]   'Grandes manoeuvres anglaises, 1913', Panouse to Ministre de la Guerre, 13 October 1913 and 'L'armée anglaise pendant l'année 1913', by Panouse, 19 January 1914, AAT, 7N1243, 7N1228/1 and /2.

[41]   'L'armée anglaise pendant l'année 1912', op. cit.

[42]   'La cooperation militaire anglaise', op. cit.

[43]   'Rapport de mission en Angleterre', by Commandant Stirn, 1er Bureau, 23 October 1911, AAT, 7N1243.

twenty army corps of the quality of the BEF, he intimated, then the British army would be the arbiter of Europe's future.[44]

At Mons, on the Marne and at Ypres in 1914 the BEF, together with its short-term contingent reinforcements gave a good account of itself, proving that France's pre-war evaluation was accurate, and faith in its ally's military professionalism justified. But command problems emerged from the start, not simply in terms of operations, but also in matters of Franco-British cooperation. The Tommies fought hard, but their generals would still need to be watched and supervised. Moreover, the 1914 BEF was a short-war force, all but spent by the end of the year, and not the decisive factor as some had speculated; not on the Continent at least. Yet its deployment there would fatefully compromise Foch's – and British maritime strategists' – alternative for a decisive deployment of British force in the long attritional struggle which the Entente was facing by the end of 1914.

Moreover, in August 1914 France unexpectedly found that she had landed a whale (in 1939 it was to be an eel), which brought its own problems. A small effective reinforcement became a vast, rapacious but uncertain swarm which settled in northern France. This was British power that France had not anticipated, and it brought new political problems which detracted from effective military cooperation. That is not to say that France did not want it – quite the opposite – but that when, where and why it was to be committed to battle would be contentious issues.

There was a guiding principle in the management of the Anglo-French alliance: while Britain would never accept French direction in naval matters, the military situation gave France the higher claim to impose her will on Britain.[45] The plain fact was, after Kitchener had taken the decision to recruit a mass army, France was always going to get large British reinforcements. How large and how quickly were still the matters at issue. Differences of opinion manifested themselves early on, when Kitchener met French leaders for the first time on 1 November 1914. The new British armies were a future prospect: but what the French wanted then was effective reinforcement in the short term (the first battle of Ypres was reaching crisis point). To Foch's entreaties Kitchener offered a delaying tactic: 'On July 1st, 1915, you will have one million trained English soldiers in France. Before that date you will get none or practically none.'[46] Thus were the parameters set for the fraught year of preparation, in which for Frenchmen the British were always offering too little too late, and for Kitchener the French were always demanding too much too soon.[47]

[44]   Ibid.

[45]   Esher Journal, 24 May 1916, Viscount Esher papers, Churchill Archives Centre, Cambridge, ESHR 2/16.

[46]   Marshal Ferdinand Foch, *The Memoirs of Marshal Foch*, trans. T. Bentley Mott (London, 1931), p. 184.

[47]   W.J. Philpott, 'Kitchener and the 29th Division: A Study in Anglo-French Strategic Relations, 1914–1915', *The Journal of Strategic Studies*, 16 (1993), pp. 375–407.

Nevertheless, as the military situation developed into attritional stalemate Kitchener was obliged to send reinforcing divisions sooner, and Haig required to commit them earlier, than either would have wished. The consequence was the Somme, notorious in Britain to this day as 'the glory and the graveyard of Kitchener's army'.[48] In Picardy in 1916 British potential was finally harnessed to France's cause – not particularly efficiently attached to the French flywheel at this point it should be acknowledged – and for France it was about time: the French press was full of letters from Deputies and others asking what the British were doing.[49] From then on, whatever the Imperial or exterior excursions championed by more pessimistic spirits in London, and the diversion of forces elsewhere,[50] the British army shared France's burden of defeating the main enemy in the main theatre. It never took the lion's share, as Haig's self-promoting accounts of his command would subsequently suggest,[51] but it was a fair share. And Haig, for all his complaints while working on a day-to-day basis with difficult and demanding allies, knew that fundamentally that was his mission, and that his army could only win the war in concert with that of France.[52] 'In the most literal sense … we are defending England in France', was CIGS Sir William Robertson's straightforward way of reminding his ministerial colleagues exactly what the Western Front was all about.[53]

A huge British army encamped in northern France for four years was not what France was anticipating in August 1914. Of course, when it came down to fundamentals, a huge increase in military manpower, whether Anglo-Saxon or otherwise, was welcomed once German armies also dug in for the duration on French soil. The disruption and confusion Kitchener's expansion of the British army caused in Britain was bad enough, and endorsed pre-1914 French fears; its repercussions for France were serious. The motivation and management of this allied force became an ongoing problem for Joffre and his successors. A small coalition force could, *de facto* if not *de jure*, be tacked onto a wing of the French army and directed as part of the French battle line; an expanding mass army could not, or at least not without much greater effort and difficulty. Personal politics were not easy. Neither Sir John French, the BEF's first commander, nor his successor Haig were particularly easy to get on with. The former was temperamental and

---

[48]   B.H. Liddell Hart, *History of the First World War* (London, 1970), p. 231.

[49]   Esher to Fitzgerald, 26 May 1916, ESHR 2/16.

[50]   B. Millman, *Pessimism and British War Policy, 1916–1918* (London, 2001).

[51]   See for example, G.A.B. Dewar and J.H. Boraston, *Sir Douglas Haig's Command* (London, 2 vols, 1922).

[52]   W.J. Philpott, 'Haig and Britain's European Allies', in *Sir Douglas Haig: A Re-appraisal 70 Years On*, ed. B.J. Bond and N. Cave (Barnsley, 1999).

[53]   'A Paper by the General Staff on the Future Conduct of the War', 16 December 1915, Sir William Robertson papers, Liddell Hart Centre for Military Archives, King's College London, I/15/10.

argumentative, the latter self-important, secretive and mistrustful.[54] Such would not have mattered so much if the armies had been separate, but in a coalition theatre tensions were bound to occur. These command differences, already well explored,[55] were the main problem of the inter-allied relationship. None of France's solutions – strong military missions to manage the BEF, modelled on pre-war supervisory practices; the appointment of a senior general, Foch, to coordinate the allied armies in the field; conferences to coordinate strategy and operations; formal imposition of French command authority on the British; even the suggested amalgamation of British and French armies by divisions under French command – was perfect. By 1918, however, under Foch's supervision as generalissimo of all the allied armies in France and Italy, a system with elements of all these methods ensured a functioning and effective battlefield coalition. In all this a strong element of France's pre-war sense of superiority persisted. As the writer Raymond Recouly suggested to Premier Aristide Briand during one of the periodic crises in Anglo-French relations, the British actually welcomed it when France took a firm hand: 'Collectively the British recognise that someone must direct the war; they also recognise that in every way we are far better prepared to do so than they are.'[56] But as the war went on that balance was to shift. As British power grew, France's relative and absolute strength shrank, and there was a supposition that with this shift went a right to a greater, perhaps a predominant, share in directing the war.[57]

The decision to turn a small professional expeditionary force into a Continental mass army was a wholly British one, taken, perhaps surprisingly, by a man who before 1914 had been in the East and had no part in, or truck with, the Continental reorientation of British military policy. But that same man had tried to give his service to France on the last occasion that Germany had invaded; appreciated the importance of French independence for European security; and, perhaps alone amongst British statesmen and military leaders in August 1914, understood that the new sort of industrialised war about to be waged by Europe's Great Powers required the rejection of old-fashioned pre-industrial methods and mindset in favour of mass mobilisation. As such the raising of the New Armies and the later decision to adopt conscription, contentious though it was, were merely the realisation of pre-1914 trends, not an aberration or deviation from an immutable principle of British warmaking.

---

[54]   W.J. Philpott, 'Britain and France Go to War: Anglo-French Relations on the Western Front', *War in History*, 2 (1995), pp. 43–64.

[55]   Philpott, *Anglo-French Relations and Strategy, passim*, esp. pp. 93–111; Greenhalgh, *Victory through Coalition, passim*.

[56]   'Note sure mon voyage en Angleterre', by Recouly, 11–20 December 1915, *Archives de Affaires Étrangères*, Paris, 537.

[57]   Robertson to Esher, 9 August 1916, in *The Military Correspondence of Field Marshal Sir William Robertson: Chief of the Imperial General Staff, December 1915–February 1918*, ed. D.R. Woodward (London, 1989), p. 80.

Kitchener's insight into the sort of war which Britain had got herself into was admirable. His strategic management, on the other hand, playing a long game and looking to throw British weight into the military balance after the Continental armies had exhausted themselves in their breast-to-breast grapple, was anathema to France's leaders. It was not just that with a mass army Britain might win the peace – naturally this interpretation put on Kitchener's actions by the military correspondent of *The Times*, Charles à Court Repington, was seized upon with alarm by the French: a strong Britain was the last thing France wanted at the end of a gruelling war[58] – but also that until it was committed the Entente could not break the stalemate and win the war that would allow it to dictate that peace. In the meantime Britain might pursue her more traditional strategy, using sea power to nibble on the periphery, not just to strengthen Britain's Imperial grasp of the world, but also the general position of the Alliance in the interim. Not surprisingly Joffre set himself against this: impatient to get on with the liberation of *la patrie*, speed and concentration of British effort in France was of the essence, and any distraction from this was to be checked. It meant that 1915, the year of the Dardanelles campaign, was to be the Entente's most contentious year, one of tension, half-measures, strategic misadventures and military defeats. It helped France that, gripped by the competing pull of Flanders, Britain mismanaged her peripheral strategy hopelessly.[59] From 1916 Joffre's alternative, a Continental deployment of British armies, was to determine British strategy for the rest of the war. This was no aberration. Kitchener had always intended that his armies should go the Continent when ready. But French impatience denied him the luxury of time. In the meantime Germany retained the initiative, strengthening her already solid position, well into 1916.

Then Britain and France struck back. Kitchener did not live to see his shiny new armies bashed about on the Somme, dented but tempered at the same time. France might not be blamed for that, although certainly the pressure put on Britain to launch a relief offensive for Verdun contributed to their commitment prematurely, semi-skilled and not fully equipped, especially in vital heavy artillery. Joffre knew this very well: Haig had pointed it out to him often enough during the first half of 1916. By that point, however, France's need outweighed Britain's interest on both sides. Now some form of sacrifice was needed: a sacrifice of power became a ghastly human sacrifice. To paraphrase the Bible, no greater love has an ally than to lay down lives for one's friend.

The Somme reinforced an old dimension to the Anglo-French military relationship. Here France was to lead and train the British army in the proper methods of trench warfare.[60] What use a big army if it was an impotent one? Its deficiencies were immediately apparent to the French commander-in-chief:

---

[58] Panouse to Ministre de la Guerre, 19 August 1914, AAT, 7N1228.

[59] Philpott, 'Kitchener and the 29th Division', *passim*.

[60] The French verb 'entraîner', used by both Joffre and Foch, has subtle dual meaning.

the reasons for their check are to be found in the poor artillery preparation and
the failure to mop up the enemy trenches passed by the leading waves … thirty
thousand casualties in the British Fourth Army and little to show for them;
by way of contrast in the Sixth French Army good result and few losses. The
English do not yet know 'the way'.[61]

The task of bringing on the raw British army fell once more to Foch, the operational
coordinator of the Somme offensive. The details cannot be examined here, but it
proved an effective if bloody apprenticeship. After 1916 the British army would
fight well and determinedly, with fewer reservations, in France's cause. From then
on the Western Front remained her primary campaign, absorbing two-thirds of the
Empire's military forces.[62]

Was this the point where Britain diverged from her traditional strategy, or
had she sealed her own fate some years before? Both David French and John
Gooch suggest so: 1916 'marked the clearest acceptance ever by the British of
a continental commitment and rejection of the "British way in warfare"'.[63] Both
in the field and in broader realms of strategy and policy, old ways were proving
ineffectual in an era of industrialised mass war. 'Business as usual' in economic
strategy, the volunteer principle in manpower strategy, and 'blue-water' maritime
operations all saw their swan song as the British army marched towards the
Somme. Germany, not France should be blamed for that, but France was certainly
dragging it there.

Rather than pursuing a 'British way in warfare' between 1914 and 1918, it
would appear that the British army became an adjunct to a 'French way in warfare'.
How and why? It resulted from a complex interplay between French and British
self-interest. Between 1905 and 1918 France hoped to maximise British power
in the common cause, which would be decided in France on the principal front.
While France cannot be blamed for all that went wrong with the British Army's
Western Front campaign, and probably deserves more credit than she gets for
what went right, the relationship, certainly fraught, was essentially codependent.
It was the coalition paradigm writ large, in which for the first time the British were
the junior partner, something which then and now Britain was always reluctant
to acknowledge: the world's greatest empire pulled along by a medium-sized
continental power. For often as not the French were pulling, or at least guiding,
their ally along a course perceived to be to their mutual advantage, if not always
to their individual liking.

There was always a certain tension within France as to how she conceived and
wished to use British power. Was it the latent potential of her economy and Empire
which was the attraction? With Britain behind her France would be more secure in

---

[61]   Joffre journal, 2 July 1916, *Journal de marche de Joffre, 1916–1919*, ed.
G. Pédroncini (Vincennes, 1990), p. 32.

[62]   French, *British Way in Warfare*, p. 172.

[63]   Ibid., p. 174.

a long war. Or was it Britain's short-term support on the battlefield which France valued, as a makeweight in the always imminent and potentially decisive clash of arms which would begin, or later end, war with Germany? This dilemma ran through France's pre-war dealings with Britain in the 1910s, and was to reoccur in the 1930s. The latter predominated, because, if the next battle was lost, there was always the possibly that the war would be lost along with it. Thus navy, City and Empire were certainly longer-term security guarantees for France. But even though a small professional army was all that Britain might throw into the land balance on the immediate outbreak of war it attracted more attention, and caused more tension, than naval or economic power.

Even if it had yet to receive Liddell Hart's classic formulation, the basic principles of the British way in warfare were not lost on the French. Foch, the Frenchman who worked most closely with the British field army between 1914 and 1918, was quite aware of the pitfalls of trying to manage the British military commitment to the Continent. As he prepared to direct their greatest common endeavour to date he noted:

> Do not kid oneself that the British will do more than attack with a *limited* object. Very limited, for basically they are still organizing themselves for pursuing a political war (drawn out, blockade, leaving them a strong army and in an advantageous position), in consequence we must use our artillery, economise with our infantry, avoid heavy losses … demand from the British a sustained action.[64]

Admittedly at the time the British were still going through the throes of throwing off 'business as usual', adopting military conscription, and concentrating forces in France after a year of ineffectual campaigning in the Middle East. Foch was probably justified in suspecting British motives on the basis of her performance to date. Kitchener's promises, if not hollow, were starting to intimate that, if not quite 'fighting to the last Frenchman', the French would have to do the hard fighting for another year.

Thus, even as British forces finally arrived in large numbers on the Continent during the spring and summer of 1916, and were engaged in a sustained offensive for the first time, the paradox of alliance persisted. British power was always both sustenance and strain to France, and vice versa: Marianne and John Bull were incubus and succubus. The factors which lay behind this were the pre-war Entente Cordiale itself, evolving under French supervision into a military alliance in fact if not *de jure*; a developing and intensifying (if not always easy) relationship with the French army before and during the conflict; but also a new sort or war requiring total mobilisation, which Kitchener appreciated best of all.

In arguing for a British way in warfare it was not so much the Continental component to which Liddell Hart objected – expeditionary warfare has always

---

[64] Note by Foch, 6 April 1916, Weygand papers, AAT, 1K130/9/6.

been a part of British warfare – but the method and purpose of Kitchener's mass mobilisation which scarred, when it did not kill, the young men of his generation. If for the first time British forces shared the challenge of defeating the main enemy army in the main theatre, the French army always bore the greater burden of defeating Germany, her operationally and tactically more advanced army outnumbering British forces, and her generals directing coalition strategy, as more recent cross-Channel research has demonstrated.[65] For these reasons she deserved to predominate.

Once it was there, come what may the British army could never pull out of France; although in the event of a catastrophe its eyes were on covering its ports, not Paris, another source of ongoing tension. Indeed during more anxious moments even France's atavistic fears that her ally coveted those ports would periodically resurface. Perhaps, however much France needed and manipulated British power, she never entirely trusted it.

Coming at the British way in warfare from the perspective of her principal and closest ally helps one to understand the conditional and contingent nature of power, constantly renegotiated in a fluid international and military situation. Great Britain may have been once, but after 1900 she was no longer great enough to continue in splendid isolation as her security challenges came closer to home, and modern warfare became more material-intensive and costly. It was thus in Britain's interest to sustain the alliance as much as France's: not just thank heaven for the French army, but thank heaven for France. Bombastic, cantankerous and bossy though she might be, Marianne was the best democratic guarantee against a German-dominated Europe, the essential bulwark of both the ephemeral but eternal 'balance of power' and Britain's immediate maritime (and later aerial) security across the narrow seas. For America Britain may have represented an aircraft-carrier off the coast of Europe; for demographically-challenged France she was a reinforcement depot. Those reinforcements were generally keen, if not numerous, well led or skilled enough to replace France's own army in the front line. France therefore appreciated British power, if not those who exercised it. By 1914 she had carefully prepared the ground for a British deployment to the Continent, both through staff talks and a programme of 'induction' into Continental military methods. Command, however, remained the major sticking point throughout these years. France would only maximise British power in her cause if she could control it, either through a unified command system or an *amalgame* of the two armies at the operational level. The latter was always unacceptable but the former Foch eventually managed.

In the first half of the twentieth century Britain's relationship with France was a central relationship, defining Britain's place and power in Europe and a world torn by ideological and imperial rivalries; and also a contentious one, because it

[65]   Philpott, *Anglo-French Relations*, *passim*; Greenhalgh, *Victory Through Coalition*, *passim*; R.A. Doughty, *Pyrrhic Victory: French Strategy and Operations in the Great War* (Cambridge MA, 2005).

represented a surrender of power to the old enemy. British power on the Continent between 1914 and 1918 was never as independent or effective as her military leaders might have liked, or they subsequently pretended to. Her political leaders seemed to better understand that it was France's war which Britain was fighting. Prime Minster David Lloyd George in particular was quite willing to listen to French military advice and had no qualms against subordinating British generals to French authority if it would enhance their shared effort, or rein in British wastefulness.

In any war with the major military power of Continental Europe, Britain would be obliged to take a real share of the fighting, as well as provide money and maritime security. Those who advocated a 'business as usual', 'blue water' or 'peripheral' strategy, or subsequently called for reversion to an 'indirect approach', were arguing from historical precedent rather than contemporary strategic reality. In fact such diversions were not really of concern to France. She had her own strategic doubters, but at the same time could generally rely on the sounder strategic minds to throw out such distracting options. And even if they resented its consequences and the impotence which it reduced them to, notorious critics such as Churchill and Lloyd George generally left their strongest words for post-war memoirs rather than wartime arguments. They were, after all, committed to winning the awful war, responsible for managing that expansive and expensive conflict. Essentially, however, that war was being fought for France, with France, in France. It was always how, more than where and why that war was being fought that was problematic. It was the Western Front experience, of day-to-day combat with France, not participation in Continental war, which skewed perceptions of this factor in Britain's war-fighting tradition. Even today one only has to mention the names Somme and Passchendaele for the British media and public to come out in a cold sweat. This cast its pall over the next Expeditionary Force. 'No more Sommes' Prime Minister Neville Chamberlain was wont to berate his military advisers if they appeared too Continentalist in 1930s strategic meetings. Even if they again approached the problem professionally, having been in the last war his generals were not without some sympathy: 'we had a pretty fair bellyful last time of fighting in the Flanders plain with its mud and slime, no to mention it bad memories', Chief of Staff Major-General Sir Henry Pownall noted when a BEF returned to France in 1939.[66] That expedition was shorter but had its own memorable, if less muddy and bloody, disasters: Dunkirk and a second improvised BEF coming a cropper on that same river Somme in June 1940. One shared victory which is remembered as a disaster;[67] one shared disaster which is celebrated as a

---

[66]   Pownall diary, 18 September 1939, in *Chief of Staff: The Diaries of Lieutenant-General Sir Henry Pownall*, ed. B.J. Bond (London, 1972), p. 235. See also Philpott, 'Paradoxes of Continental War', and J.P. Harris, 'The British General Staff and the Coming of War, 1933–39' in *The British General Staff*, pp. 175–91.

[67]   W.J. Philpott, 'The Anglo-French Victory on the Somme', *Diplomacy and Statecraft*, 17 (2006), pp. 731–51.

victory: is the real difference that from 1914 to 1918 Britain was fighting with and for France, while in 1940 she let France fall and fought on alone in her finest hour?

Too little and too late although British military support might always have seemed, France knew that she was as reliant on it as Britain was reliant on her. John Bull and Marianne's union would endure. After more than a century, the bickering newlyweds have settled into a cosy partnership. Perhaps the facts that Britain has reverted to fighting wars outside Europe with her Anglo-Saxon cousins, while a friendly Germany has removed France's Continental security concerns, have helped.

Chapter 5

British Power and French Security, 1919–1939

Peter Jackson

The central importance of Great Britain to French strategy and diplomacy between the two world wars has long been a central feature of the historiography of this period has been based. As early as 1940 Arnold Wolfers characterised French foreign policy during the inter-war years as 'a continuous struggle to get Britain to pledge her support to France'.[1] This judgement has long served as a cornerstone of the historiography of the origins of the Second World War.[2] And yet, since Wolfers, remarkably little scholarly attention has been paid to the role of Britain in French policy over the entire inter-war period. Even less attention has been paid to the way British power and British policy were understood by permanent officials and policymakers in Paris.[3] Scholars have instead largely been content to

---

[1]   Arnold Wolfers, *Britain and France between Two Wars: Conflicting Strategies of Peace since Versailles* (New York, 1940), 76.

[2]   Key works on Franco-British relations between the wars include: P.M.H. Bell, *France and Britain, 1900–1940: Entente and Estrangement* (London, 1996); Michael Howard, *The Continental Commitment: The Dilemma of British Defence Policy in the Era of the Two World Wars* (London, 1972); Arthur Turner, *The Cost of War: British Policy on French War Debts, 1918–1932* (Brighton, 1998); Nicholas Rostow, *Anglo-French Relations, 1934–1936* (London, 1984); Martin Thomas, *Britain, France and Appeasement: Anglo-French Relations in the Era of the Popular Front* (Oxford, 1996); Michael Dockrill, *British Establishment Perspectives on France, 1936–1940* (London, 1999); and Talbot Imlay, *Facing the Second World War: Strategy, Politics and Economics in Britain and France, 1938–1940* (Oxford, 2003). See also the various essays in N. Waites (ed.), *Troubled Neighbours: Franco-British Relations in the Twentieth Century* (London, 1971); D. Dutton (ed.), *Statecraft and Diplomacy in the Twentieth Century: Essays presented to P.M.H. Bell* (Liverpool, 1995); G. Stone and A. Sharp (eds), *Anglo-French Relations in the Twentieth Century: Rivalry and Cooperation* (London, 2002) and M. Alexander and B. Philpott (eds), *Anglo-French Defence Relations between the Wars* (London, 2002). A vivid overview of political, economic and cultural relations between the two states since the seventeenth century is R. Tombs and I. Tombs, *That Sweet Enemy: the British and the French from the Sun King to the Present* (London, 2006).

[3]   On intelligence and policy towards Great Britain, see Peter Jackson and Joseph Maiolo, 'Strategic Intelligence, Counterintelligence and Alliance Diplomacy in Anglo-

adopt Wolfers' assumption that French policy aimed consistently at a peacetime resurrection of the Franco-British military alliance of 1914–18.[4]

The essay that follows can only begin to address these gaps in the literature. It will examine French military intelligence assessments of British intentions and capabilities as well as the interpretations of British policy and opinion put forward by foreign ministry officials. An examination of French perceptions of British power and policy helps to provide a new perspective on France's pursuit of security during this period. French observers understood that a renewal of the wartime military alliance between France and Britain was opposed by the vast majority of British policy elites and an even greater proportion of British public opinion. This understanding was an important factor in shaping French security policy as it evolved away from a strategy based on alliances and strategic preponderance towards one based on multilateralism and the rule of law.

Interpreting British Power

At first glance, the task of French observers interpreting British attitudes towards war and international relations might seem relatively straightforward. Britain and France were both democratic powers that had forged a remarkably intimate alliance between 1914 and 1918. Yet the barriers to mutual comprehension during the inter-war period were formidable. Although cooperation during the Great War was ultimately successful, it did not eradicate the long-standing mistrust that was a product of centuries of rivalry. Indeed the wartime experience functioned in many ways as an obstacle to effective co-ordination during the post-war years.

On the British side, much has been written about the extreme reluctance of Britain's political and military leadership even to discuss military arrangements of any kind with France between the wars. This stemmed, to a large extent, from vivid memories of the Great War and the profound psychological wounds that it had inflicted on British society. The gains that accrued to Britain seemed paltry in light of the terrible human and material price it had paid for victory over the Central Powers. It was also a product of the widely held conviction that Britain had been drawn into making unnecessary and imprudent commitments for war on the Continent during staff conversations with the French in the years before 1914. This

---

French Relations before the Second World War', *Militärgeschichtliche Zeitschrift*, 65, 2 (2006), 417–61.

[4]   The key exception is of course Bell, *Entente and Estrangement*. There is also some consideration of the issue in the following excellent international histories of the period: Jean Baptiste Duroselle, *Histoire des relations internationales de 1919 à 1945*, 12th edition (Paris, 2001); Sally Marks, *The Ebbing of European Ascendancy*, (London, 2002); *eadem*, *The Illusion of Peace: International Relations in Europe, 1918-1933*, (London, 1976); and Zara Steiner, *The Lights that Failed: European International History, 1919–1933*, (Oxford, 2005).

conviction was only reinforced by the British establishment's largely successful efforts to play down the importance of imperial self-interest in its decision to make war. On the French side, there was a sense of 'Anglo-Saxon betrayal' after both the British and the Americans reneged on pledges given to guarantee French security during the Paris Peace Conference. Differing approaches to the German question in European politics drove French and British governments further apart.[5] There was also the issue of imperial rivalry. Although Britain and France had compatible core strategic aims on the Continent (if very different strategies for achieving these aims), on colonial issues they were usually one another's most bitter rivals.[6] The politics of disarmament, which gathered momentum in the late 1920s and early 1930s, widened the gulf between British and French perspectives. British officials considered the large French continental army a destabilising factor in European politics and put pressure on France both to reduce the size of its army and to agree to modest increases in the size of Germany's armed forces. In sum, there were many sources of tension in Franco-British relations.[7]

The weight of both recent and longer-term history was therefore a powerful factor shaping French perceptions of Britain and British power. Also influential were pervasive cultural stereotypes of the British 'mentality' and 'national character'. Among the most solidly entrenched stereotypes was that British policy was animated primarily by a narrow definition of national self-interest. The national myth of 'perfidious Albion' can be traced back to the medieval period. 'God protect us from the loyalty of an Englishman' was a popular aphorism in France as early as the fifteenth century. The image of a self-serving and ruthless English 'race' was reinforced by a long succession of costly wars.[8] 'Selfishness and egotism' was attributed, in large part, to the 'exclusively mercantilist spirit' which even the *Grande Larousse* dictionary identified as a 'defining characteristic of the English people'.[9] This particular representation of the British national character

---

[5]   On these questions see Wolfers, *Britain and France*; W.M. Jordan, *Great Britain, France and the German Problem, 1918–1939* (New York, 1943); A. Sharp, *The Versailles Settlement: Peacemaking in Paris, 1919* (London, 1991); Bell, *Entente and Estrangement*; 113–53; see also the various essays in Waites (ed.), *Troubled Neighbours*; G. Stone and A. Sharp (eds.), *Anglo-French Relations*; and Alexander and Philpott (eds.), *Anglo-French Defence Relations*.

[6]   Martin Thomas, 'Anglo-French Imperial Relations in the Arab World: Intelligence Liaison and Nationalist Disorder', *Diplomacy & Statecraft*, 17, 1 (2006), 1–28.

[7]   See the excellent discussion in Martin Thomas, *Britain, France and Appeasement* (Oxford, 1996), 6–24; on disarmament, see especially M. Vaïsse, *Sécurité d'abord: la politique française en matière de désarmement, 1930–1934* (Paris, 1981); C. Kitching, *Britain and the Problem of International Disarmament, 1919–1934* (London, 1999) and A. Webster, 'An Argument without End: Britain, France and the Disarmament Process, 1931–1934', in Alexander and Philpott (eds.), *Anglo-French Defence Relations*, 49–72.

[8]   Cited in Cornick, '"Perfidious Albion"', 9 and 10 respectively.

[9]   From the Larousse *Grande Dictionnaire Universel* of 1889, cited in Cornick, '"Perfidious Albion"', 17.

reverberated within French officialdom. Lieutenant Colonel Paul Paillole, a veteran counter-intelligence officer within the French *Deuxième* [intelligence] *bureau* with considerable experience working with his opposite numbers in Britain, underlined this gulf between the apparent self-perception of British officials and the way their actions were understood by others. 'Ah, these English,' he observed in a lecture to aspiring counter-intelligence officers in 1942, 'so very gentlemanly, so very "fair play", but, even when they are one's allies, can one ever know what they really think?'[10]

Stereotypes of greed and selfishness operated in tandem with assumptions of French intellectual superiority. French observers were often disdainful of the empiricism and pragmatism that they identified as central to the British mentality. These characteristics, it was often argued, resulted more often than not in short-sighted policies. Paul Cambon, France's ambassador in London for twenty-one years, lamented the 'lack of foresight which is the true characteristic of this people'.[11] He argued that an excessive concern for facts, combined with a repugnance for long-term planning, were a frustrating impediment to Franco-British cooperation. He concluded that 'it is childish to make long-range policy with people who dislike hypotheses and live only for the present'.[12] This frustration persisted eight years later and inspired foreign ministry mandarin Robert Coulondre to observe that British policy 'remains inspired above all by a desire to extract short-term commercial profits, in this case from the rise of Germany ... even at the expense of long-term security for the rest of Europe'.[13] Assumptions concerning the supposed selfish instincts of British elites, along with their alleged distaste for formulating policy according to long-term priorities, were shared at the highest levels of the decision-making elite. During the Paris Peace Conference in 1919, for example, French premier Georges Clemenceau pointed out repeatedly that the British government tended to urge moderation and concessions to Germany only when its own vital interests were not at stake.[14] This experience reinforced deeply-entrenched stereotypes that helped shape the expectations of most French policy elites for much of the following two decades.

---

[10]   France, Ministère de la Défense, Service Historique de Défense-Département de l'Armée de Terre [hereafter SHD-DAT], 1K 545, *Fonds Paul Paillole*, carton 14, 'Aperçu sur les SR Anglo Saxons', part of a 'conférence' given by Paillole to aspiring counter-intelligence officers on 18 January 1941. This observation, along with the anecdote that inspired it, is also in Paillole's memoirs, *Service Spéciaux (1935–1945)* (Paris, 1975), 118–19.

[11]   P. Cambon, *Correspondence, 1870–1924*, 3 volumes, Vol. II, 44; cited in Bell, *Entente and Estrangement*, 17.

[12]   Cited in A. Adamthwaite, *Grandeur and Misery: France's Bid for Power in Europe, 1914–1940* (London, 1995), 76.

[13]   France, Ministère des Affaires Étrangères [hereafter MAE], PA-AP 217, *Papiers René Massigli*, vol. 96, Coulondre to Massigli, 8 December 1932.

[14]   Bell, *Entente and Estrangement*, 120–25.

In sum, there were formidable cultural and political obstacles to mutual understanding and political co-operation between Britain and France. Even in the warm afterglow of the Locarno agreements of December 1925 Alexis Léger, chief of the foreign minister's personal staff and a future secretary general of the Quai d'Orsay [foreign ministry], remarked on 'how little understanding there was at bottom between England and France … England did not and never would understand France. Nor did France, knowing this, understand England … Indifference and vague mistrust are universal.' Austen Chamberlain, Britain's Francophile foreign secretary, agreed with this pessimistic judgement. 'Too true,' he observed, 'and very sad. Indifference and where not indifference, something more than a "vague mistrust" are the corresponding factors here.[15] This was the atmosphere within which French judgements of British intentions and capabilities were formulated.

Perceptions of British Power and Policy between the Wars

The task of assessing Britain's war potential and military effectiveness fell primarily to the *Deuxième bureaux* of the army, naval and air force general staffs.[16] The foreign ministry assumed chief responsibility for interpreting British foreign policy. In Paris the Quai d'Orsay and the military services tended to work independently of one another. Much of the information upon which their assessments were based, conversely, was the product of the collaborative effort by diplomats and military officials posted to the French embassy in London. As a matter of course the reports prepared by all service attachés and diplomatic personnel in London were forwarded to the ambassador's *cabinet* for approval before being sent to Paris.[17] French ambassadors to Britain between the wars were all officials of vast experience whose views were nearly always taken very seriously in Paris. For the most part, diplomats and soldiers tended to respect one another's areas of expertise. But there were frequent divergences of opinion in the grey area where military planning overlapped with foreign policy in the making of strategic policy.[18]

---

[15]   Great Britain, The National Archives (Kew), FO 371 11270, C2192/112/18, 'French attitude towards ratification of Locarno Treaties', 17 February 1926.

[16]   The French air force was created in 1931. Prior to this date the army *Deuxième bureau* was responsible for crafting estimates of foreign air power. On the structure, functioning and effectiveness of French intelligence between the wars, see Peter Jackson, *France and the Nazi Menace: Intelligence and Policy-making 1933–1939* (Oxford, 2000), and Olivier Forcade, *La République secrète: histoire des services Spéciaux français de 1918–1939* (Paris, 2008), 48–195.

[17]   Jackson, *France and the Nazi Menace*, 26–42.

[18]   Jean-Baptiste Duroselle, *Politique étrangère de la France, 1932–1939: La décadence* (Paris, 1979), 242–89.

At the heart of virtually all French assessments of Britain between the wars was the recognition that it was first and foremost an imperial power with interests and commitments across the globe. The imperial dimension of British power presented both attractions and disadvantages from the French perspective. On the positive side, the military potential of the British Empire had been demonstrated on the battlefields of France between 1914 and 1918. At the same time, imperial considerations imposed powerful constraints on British policy towards Europe and made a resurrection of the wartime alliance a difficult, if not entirely unrealistic, proposition.

A lecture on 'The military potential of Britain and its empire' to the Centre des Hautes Études Militaires, given by a senior army staff officer in 1926, underlines the importance attached to British power by French officials. 'One must recognise', the lecturer began 'that without the military, naval and financial contributions of Britain and its empire France could not have persevered into the fourth year of conflict against the Central Powers.' To refuse to recognise the importance of Britain's contribution, he added, 'would be a grave misunderstanding of the *true* balance of power in Europe'.[19] This was an implicit reference to the central dilemma in the mind of every official responsible for the future security of France: Germany had been defeated but retained the war-making potential to mount another bid for European dominance. The demographic and industrial resources that had underpinned the German war effort for four and a half years remained essentially intact after 1919. These resources were the key factor in the 'true' European power balance. For military officials, in particular, Germany's industrial and demographic superiority was nothing short of an obsession that coloured all objective assessments of the military balance and underpinned a consistent tendency to overestimate the number of fully equipped divisions that Germany could mobilise. Added to inflated perceptions of Germany's ability to wage war was a deep-seated conviction that every German government, along with the vast majority of the German people, was animated by an abiding hatred of the Versailles settlement and determined to overthrow it by force. These 'worst-case' tendencies in French assessments of German intentions and capabilities persisted right up to the eve of war in 1939.[20]

The conviction that Germany continued to pose an existential threat to France underscored the continued importance of Britain and its empire to French security.

---

[19]   SHD-DAT, 2N 264–5 'Le potentiel de guerre de Grande Bretagne et son empire', 8 October 1922, emphasis in original.

[20]   See, for example, SHD-DAT, 2N 5–1, 'Note sur les conditions générales de la mobilisation', March 1920; 2N 5–3, 'Résumé de la situation allemande', 13 December 1920; SHD-DAT, 7N 3530–1, 'Comparison de l'état militaire et naval des diverses puissances pouvant intervenir dans un conflit européen et conclusions qu'il semble possible d'en tirer', 7 July 1922. For French perceptions of Germany's capabilities toward the end of the 1920s and through the 1930s, see Jackson, *France and the Nazi Menace*; and Forcade, *République secrete*, 280–333.

Britain, French officials estimated consistently throughout the inter-war years, controlled more than one-third of the world's trade and was guaranteed access to virtually all of the vital raw materials it required to wage modern war.[21] In 1931 trade with Britain and its Empire accounted for roughly 35 per cent of the total value of French international commerce (compared to 25 per cent with French imperial possessions). British shipping carried approximately 45 per cent of all foreign tonnage to and from France.[22] The French were dependent on Britain for over one-third of its imports of coal, coke and other crucial strategic raw materials – including a growing proportion of imported oil and petroleum. In 1937 the *Secrétariat général* of the *Conseil Supérieur de la Défense Nationale* judged that, without British shipping, France would run out of the carburants it required to wage a continental war in less than four weeks.[23]

And the strategic importance of Britain only increased into the 1930s. The worldwide economic crisis struck the British economy much earlier than that of France. But Britain began to shake off the effects of the depression by the middle of the decade while France remained mired in economic stagnation right up to the end of 1938.[24] By the mid-1930s Britain's defence and defence-related industries, including those involved in the production of aircraft, ships, automobiles and machine tools, had achieved clear superiority over those of France. British steel production at the same juncture was nearly double that of France.[25] In 1937 Britain's 'relative war potential' was two and one-half times greater than that of France.[26] It is worth emphasising, finally, that the particular advantages that Britain offered as a potential ally complemented French national strategy as it evolved from the latter half of the 1920s. This strategy aimed at withstanding an initial German blow, mounting another economic blockade and marshalling French resources for a strategic offensive. An offensive would only be mounted, however, once the staying power and military effectiveness of the Reich had been

[21] SHD-DAT, 7N 2839–3, 'L'Empire britannique', 18 June 1921; 7N 2843, 'Organisation de la défense impériale', 19 September 1923; 7N 2840, 'Généralités sur l'Empire britannique', 11 August 1937; 'Plan de renseignement pour 1935', 6 December 1934; 7N 2825–1; 'Etudes: Empire britannique', December 1938.

[22] SHD-DAT, 2N 156, 'Le commerce britannique et le potentiel de guerre français', 18 May 1931.

[23] SHD-DAT, 6N 330–3, 'Application du plan du ravitaillement en carburants our le temps de guerre', 4 March 1937; see also Robert Young, *Command of France: French foreign policy and military planning, 1933–1940* (Cambridge, MA, 1978), 21–22.

[24] P. Clavin, *The Great Depression in Europe* (London, 2000), 167–97.

[25] SHD-DAT, 2N 156, 'Puissance industrielle et politique de défense en Grande Bretagne', 27 November 1935.

[26] Paul Kennedy, *The Rise and Fall of the Great Powers* (New York, 1988), 200 and 332; see also Young, *Command of France*, 19–23.

weakened sufficiently by the blockade.[27] Such a blockade was only possible with the full participation of the Royal Navy. As Robert Young has observed: 'The United Kingdom was, without a trace of exaggeration, the key to the French vision of the war to come … From coal and oil to aircraft engines, British resources remained absolutely central to French calculations of how to win the next war.'[28]

All of this made the political, military, naval and financial support of Britain and its empire a central requirement for any attempt to contain and, if necessary, to defeat German revisionism. But the imperial character of British power also posed formidable challenges to French policymakers. Virtually from the moment the guns fell silent in 1918, Britain's Dominions, with the partial exception of New Zealand, began to oppose any further commitment to fight again on the Continent and held to this position throughout the inter-war period. Their attitude constituted a powerful constraint on British policy. Added to this were the ever-increasing demands of Imperial defence and security in an era of increasingly well-organised and self-confident movements for colonial independence and at a time when Japan had evolved from an ally to a potential enemy. Scarce resources were thus stretched at a time when the domestic political environment placed pressure on policymakers to scale back defence outlays and balance the national budget. To these considerations must be added the powerful effects of both elite and popular resistance to any idea of a renewed military commitment to France. During the first half of the decade, this resistance was strengthened by growing frustration with French policy towards Germany. There was even suspicion among those British policy-makers least sympathetic to France's security dilemma that French insistence on enforcing the letter of the Treaty of Versailles was in fact a bid for renewed political dominance in Europe. This was probably a minority view, but it is clear nonetheless that the great majority of British policy elites tended to see 'French intransigence as the main threat to European peace'.[29] Sir Warren Fisher, the senior British civil servant, summed up this point of view when he observed in 1923 that '… while I admit that the French between 1870 and 1914 had their tails well down and therefore assumed a veneer of moderation, during the rest of the centuries-old existence, they have played the part of bullies … and they are doing

---

[27]   The classic discussion of this strategy is Robert Young, 'La Guerre de longue durée: some reflections on French strategy and diplomacy in the 1930s', in A. Preston (ed.), *General Staffs and Diplomacy before the Second World War* (London, 1978), 41–64

[28]   Robert Young, *France and the Origins of the Second World War* (London, 1996), 68.

[29]   French, *British Way in Warfare*, 182. On these issues more generally, see ibid., 179–85; and John Ferris, *Men, Money and Diplomacy: The Evolution of British Strategic Policy, 1919–1926* (Cornell, 1989). On the role of the Empire and Dominions, see J. Darwin, 'A Third British Empire? The Dominion Idea in Imperial Politics', and A. Clayton, '"Deceptive Might": Imperial Defence and Security', both in J. Brown and W Roger Louis (eds), *The Oxford History of the British Empire: the Twentieth Century* (Oxford, 1999), 64–87 and 280–305.

so now'.[30] From the very outset, therefore, a renewal of the Franco-British military alliance was all but impossible.

Britain and France's Pursuit Strategic Preponderance, 1919–1923

French security policy at the Paris peace conference had settled on three specific security guarantees: Allied occupation of the Rhineland, restrictions on German military strength and an Anglo-American guarantee of France. While there was a certain ambiguity to French policy at the conference, particularly when it came to the economic dimensions to this policy and to its hopes for the political transformation of Germany, the emphasis remained on countering the German problem with an Allied coalition possessing unchallengeable military superiority and thus the means to impose the treaty by force.[31] The immediate post-war period witnessed a swift and dramatic erosion of these three basic pillars of French security, however. The first, occupation of the Rhineland, was conceived as a temporary measure from the outset to 'guarantee the execution by Germany of the peace treaty'.[32] The effectiveness of the second, German disarmament and the demilitarisation of the German Rhineland, depended either on German compliance or, if necessary, the resolve of the victorious powers to enforce them. The post-war years would be characterised by a distinct lack of both German compliance and Allied resolve. Finally, and perhaps most importantly, the Anglo-American military guarantee evaporated in late 1919 when the American senate refused to ratify the Treaty of Versailles. France would spend most of the next two decades trying to obtain replacement guarantees. The most obvious of such replacements was a renewed British commitment to defend France against unprovoked aggression.

A succession of different governments, from that of Alexandre Millerand in early 1920 to that of Raymond Poincaré through May 1924, adopted divergent policies to achieve security. French strategies lurched from insistence on full German compliance to the letter of the Versailles treaty (which refused to countenance treaty revision), to projects for Franco-German financial and industrial cooperation (which assumed a process of negotiated revision on terms favourable to France)

---

[30]   Dockrill, *British Establishment*, 1.

[31]   Excellent accounts of French policy at the peace conference are David Stevenson, 'French War aims and Peace Planning', G.-H. Soutou, 'The French Peacemakers and Their Home Front', and S. Schuker, 'The Rhineland Question: West European Security at the Paris Peace Conference', both in M. Boemke, G. Feldman and E. Glaser (eds), *The Treaty of Versailles: A Reassessment after 75 Years* (Cambridge, 1998), 69–86, 167–88 and 275–312 respectively. But see also J.-B. Duroselle, *Clemenceau* (Paris, 1988), 720–859.

[32]   Cited from a conversation between Clemenceau and Wilson in March 1919 by David Stevenson, 'France and the German Question in the Era of the First World War', in Stephen Schuker (ed.), *Deutschland un Frankreich Vom Konflikt zur Aussöhnung: Die Gestaltung der westeuropäischen Sicherheit 1914–1963* (Munich, 2000), 15–16.

under premier Aristide Briand, to achieving the disaggregation of Germany and a new balance of power in Europe (which assumed revision on French terms) under Poincaré before assenting, finally, to an internationalisation of Germany's reparations debts at the London Conference in June 1924 (which amounted to revision as a result of multilateral negotiations).[33] The role of British power in these various policy conceptions remained fairly consistent. Britain was to provide France with automatic military assistance in the event of another conflict with Germany. Within the French foreign ministry and military establishment it was considered axiomatic that any future British guarantee to France would be accompanied by staff conversations.

A major problem with this policy was that, as we have seen, this was not how British leaders envisaged a future guarantee. And the powerful currents of resistance to another Continental military commitment that existed in Britain were recognised by French observers from the outset. Marshal Ferdinand Foch, along with other opponents of the Treaty of Versailles in parliament and in the public sphere, pointed out repeatedly that, while the Anglo-American Guarantee extended to France in 1919 was presented as an 'immediate guarantee of military assistance against any unprovoked aggression',[34] there was no intention on the part of the Americans or British to supplement the guarantee with a military convention. Such a convention, they argued, citing the example of the Franco-Russian military accord of 1894 and the staff conversations with British military officials before 1914, was the only means of providing the guarantee with the 'automatic' character that could provide genuine security.[35] After the guarantee collapsed definitively in 1920, Lloyd George assured French officials that it would be replaced with a British guarantee. But the British showed little enthusiasm for following through on this pledge with substantive negotiations. Indeed France and Britain were more often than not at loggerheads in the

---

[33]   For an excellent analysis of French policy during this period as well as the relevant literature, see J. Jacobsen, 'Is There a New International History of the 1920s?', *American Historical Review*, 88, 3 (1983), 617–45; and *idem*, 'Strategies of French foreign policy after World War I', *Journal of Modern History*, 55 (1983), 78–95. On the occupation of the Ruhr see, in addition to the works cited in Jacobsen, S. Jeannesson, *Poincaré, la France et la Ruhr (1922–1924): histoire d'une occupation* (Strasbourg, 1997); and J. Keiger, *Raymond Poincaré* (Cambridge, 1997), 274–311. For a superb overview and analysis, see Steiner, *Lights that Failed*, 182–250.

[34]   Cf. A. Sharp, *The Versailles Settlement: Peacemaking in Paris, 1919* (London, 1991), citing Lloyd George, *The Truth about the Peace Treaties*, 2 vols (London, 1938), vol. I, 403.

[35]   SHD-DAT, (1871–1920), 6N 74, *Fonds Clemenceau*, 'L'opinion de M. le Maréchal Foch et la Conférence', no date but almost certainly April 1919 (expressing support for Foch from the chamber foreign affairs commission); see also MAE, PA-AP 029, *Papiers Léon Bourgeois*, vol. 15, 'Réponses du Président du conseil' 29 July 1919 (to parliamentary criticism of the treaty); see also Jere King, *Foch versus Clemenceau: France and German Dismemberment, 1918–1919* (Cambridge, MA, 1960), 50–72; and Jean-Christophe Nottin, *Foch* (Paris, 2008), 440–88.

immediate post-war period over issues ranging from policy towards Bolshevik Russia to the treatment of Germany to the status of the peace settlement in Asia Minor and the Levant. From London, the French Ambassador Comte Saint-Aulaire underlined the extent of both public and elite opposition in Britain to a renewed military alliance with France. 'Today', Saint-Aulaire warned, such a pact would be opposed 'by both plutocrats and workers'. Meanwhile, France's position on cruisers and submarines at the Washington Naval Conference had reinforced British suspicions of French militarism and imperialism. Jacques Seydoux judged that the stand-off had given rise to a 'paradoxical coalition of the two central opposing forces in the British national character: its economic materialism and its sentimentalist idealism'.[36] A resurrection of the wartime alliance was a very distant prospect.

Briand, premier and foreign minister, was the first senior French statesman of the inter-war period to accept the impossibility of obtaining a military commitment from Britain. During negotiations for a Franco-British guarantee treaty in early 1922, the French premier accepted that such a guarantee would be political and would not be backed up by a military convention. Briand was convinced that a political entente between France and Britain could form the basis for the construction of a wider European security regime in which Germany could be enmeshed and thus constrained.[37] He was willing to accept that such an entente would have to be political rather than military. His vision of French security was opposed by (then president) Millerand and rejected by both parliament and his cabinet colleagues as a reckless strategy that bargained away too much for insufficient security guarantees. Briand's government fell and was replaced by that of Poincaré, who was committed to a more traditional approach to security. Poincaré demanded a full-blown military alliance from Lloyd George. When this was not forthcoming, and Germany defaulted on reparations payments, his government resolved to use force to compel German compliance with the Versailles treaty.[38]

Negotiations for a Franco-British pact sputtered along nonetheless until the acrimony generated by the crisis over Turkey in the summer of 1922 brought an end to all serious discussion of the project.[39] The problem, judged Jacques

---

[36]　MAE, Série Z (Europe 1918–1940), Grande Bretagne, vol. 69, 'Le projet d'alliance franco-britannique et la presse', Saint-Aulaire to Paris, 4 January 1922.

[37]　This is clear from MAE, Série Z, *Grande Bretagne*, vol. 69, 'Notes prises au cours d'une conversation entre M. Lloyd George et M. Briand le Mercredi 21 Décembre 1921'; 'Observations sur la rédaction du projet', 28 December 1921 (Berthelot); 'Note de M. Fromageot', 27 December 1921; 'Alliance', 26 December 1921 (Seydoux) and 'Projet d'alliance franco-anglaise', 28 December 1921.

[38]　For analyses of the evolution of policy from Briand to Poincaré see, among many others, Bariéty, *Relations franco-allemands*, 91–120; Keiger, 'Poincaré and the Ruhr Crisis'; and McDougall, *France's Rhineland Diplomacy*, 178–213. For the domestic political context, see Roussellier, *Parlement de l'éloquence*, 154–62.

[39]　MAE, Série Z, vol. 70, 'Au sujet du Pacte anglo-français', 17 February 1922; and 'Pacte franco-anglais', 2 and 4 March 1922.

Seydoux, a senior official within the foreign ministry, was that Britain had 'returned instinctively to the principle by which it been guided over the ages, which consists of opposing the strongest power in Europe with support for the next strongest power'. Tension between Germany and France served British interests, Seydoux argued, by maintaining a 'state of equilibrium which allows Britain to intervene in European affairs as a mediator'. British policy was therefore opposed, in equal measure, to France imposing the terms of Versailles on Germany and to a policy of close Franco-German cooperation. Both scenarios would threaten Britain's ability to manipulate European politics to its political and economic advantage. 'It is thus essential [for Britain] to maintain sufficient points of friction between France and Germany to make any conversation impossible.' For Seydoux, it was British policy, with its instinctive cynicism and self-interest, that constituted the chief obstacle to European peace and reconstruction.[40]

The immediate post-war era was in sum a period of intense frustration for a series of centre-right French cabinets that pursued security through strategic preponderance. French priorities in Europe were to establish a solid balance of power against Germany by imposing the disarmament and reparations clauses of the Versailles treaty on the one hand and by obtaining a security guarantee from Britain on the other. The problem was that these priorities were fundamentally incompatible. The result was a series of difficult negotiations with the Lloyd George government in which both sides blamed the other for the general failure to achieve political or financial stability. The British considered French insistence on 'integral' treaty enforcement short-sighted and feared that efforts to break German power were the necessary prelude to another bid for French continental hegemony. French leaders, conversely, argued that the Versailles regime would be stillborn as long as Britain refused to stand by France in the face of Germany's refusal to fulfil its obligations.

Franco-British relations came close to collapse during the French occupation of the Ruhr in 1923. The Ruhr occupation was the last French attempt to try to impose the treaty on Germany without British support. It was also a last attempt to strike at the federal bonds that held the Reich together in the hope that the Rhineland could be detached from the rest of Germany to form an autonomous province under French protection.[41] This aim was futile and the bid to break up

---

[40]   MAE, PA-AP 261, *Papiers Jacques Seydoux*, vol. 21, 'Note au sujet de la politique de la France à l'égard de l'Angleterre et de l'Allemagne', 1 August 1921.

[41]   That this was the chief objective of the military is not in doubt. See the rich collection of material in SHD-DAT, 2N 237–1, a dossier entitled 'Projet d'organisation d'un état rhénan'. That it was also the aim of the Poincaré government is clear from the material in MAE, PA-AP 118, *Papiers Alexandre Millerand*, vol. 96, especially president Millerand's 'Notes' of a meeting held at the foreign ministry on 27 November 1922. The best account of French Ruhr policy is Stanislas Jeannesson, *Poincaré, la France et la Ruhr (1922–1924): histoire d'une occupation* (Strasbourg, 1997) which is summarised in his article 'French Policy in the Rhineland', *Diplomacy & Statecraft*, 16, 3 (2005), 475–86.

Germany failed utterly. The occupation strategy as a whole achieved mixed results at best. Germany was brought to heel but the result was the general degradation of France's financial position. This only increased the importance of British (and American) economic power to the project of European reconstruction. A commission of financial experts was appointed to adjudicate the stand-off and an international conference was convened in London in July 1924. The resulting settlement provided for German reparations payments in exchange for French withdrawal from the Ruhr.[42] French efforts to pursue an independent policy for security and reconstruction had only driven home the importance of cooperation with Britain.

Britain and France's Multilateral Strategy for Security, 1924–1934

Mutual interest in economic and political stability pushed the two powers back towards compromise and cooperation beginning with the 1924 London Conference and culminating in Britain's willingness to extend a political guarantee to France's western frontier and to the demilitarised status of the Rhineland with the Locarno Accords of October 1925. Both security policy and policy towards Great Britain evolved in fundamental ways during this period. France moved from an insistence that any security arrangement must include staff conversations (and thus constitute a traditional military alliance) to an acceptance that such an arrangement with Britain was impossible and a willingness to accept a political rather than military guarantee from that country. This opened the way for the Locarno Accords and a period of relative stability through to the end of the 1920s. This evolution illustrated the extent to which French security policy adapted to the new normative conditions of the post-1918 era, which favoured multilateralism and international law over traditional alliance politics and the balance of power. But the course of French policy was not determined solely by international pressures. Important internal developments also played a key role. Chief among these were two mutually reinforcing trends in French domestic politics: the steady growth of pacifism as a

---

[42] Standard sources include Stephen Schuker, *The End of French Predominance in Europe: The Financial Crisis of 1924 and the Adoption of the Dawes Plan* (Chapel Hill, NC, 1977); Charles Maier, *Recasting Bourgeois Europe: Stabilization in France, Germany and Italy in the decade after World War I* (Princeton, 1975); Walter MacDougall, *France's Rhineland Diplomacy, 1914–1924: The Last Bid for a Balance of Power in Europe* (Princeton, 1978); Marc Trachtenberg, *Reparation in World Politics: France and European Economic Diplomacy, 1916–1923* (New York,1980); Bruce Kent, *The Spoils of War: The Politics, Economics and Diplomacy of Reparations, 1918–1932* (Oxford, 1989); John Keiger, *Raymond Poincaré* (Cambridge, 1997); Steiner, *Lights that Failed*, 182–250; and, most recently, Patrick Cohrs, *The Unfinished Peace after World War I, 1919–1932* (Cambridge, 2006), 68–199.

political discourse and the election of the centre-left *Cartel des gauches* coalition led by Edouard Herriot in the national elections of May 1924.

This transformation of French security policy began during Poincaré's tenure as premier and foreign minister from early 1922 to May 1924. Over the course of 1923 French policy towards League of Nations-sponsored proposals for multilateral arms reductions changed in important ways. The obstinate refusal to engage with the issue of arms reductions, which had characterised the French position since 1920, gradually gave way to a strategy of using the politics of disarmament to obtain a security guarantee from Britain. Since the first meetings of the League of Nations the British government had placed increasing pressure on France to participate in a multilateral programme for international disarmament. French delegates in Geneva responded by linking arms reductions to national security. They argued that France could not disarm until it received further guarantees for its security in return (by which they meant chiefly a British continental commitment).[43] This argument was accepted in Geneva and resulted in the Draft Treaty of Mutual Assistance of 1923. Although this treaty was rejected by the Poincaré government in late 1923 (on the grounds that it did not include prearranged agreements for military assistance), it provided a template for the Geneva Protocol negotiated by the new *Cartel des gauches* government in September 1924.

The Protocol marked a revolution in French policy in several ways. First, it envisaged the creation of regional mutual assistance pacts based resting on compulsory arbitration treaties. There was no requirement for prearranged military assistance based on staff conversations. Multilateral political and legal guarantees replaced bilateral military alliances as the central element in French security policy in general and policy towards Britain in particular. These guarantees still aimed at deterrence through the threat of force; but this threat was more latent than had been the case during the pre-1914 period of alliance blocs and secret military conventions. Second, the Protocol recognised that Germany must be involved in the construction of European security and could therefore take part in the envisaged mutual assistance pacts. Third, signatories agreed to negotiations leading to a multilateral arms limitation agreement.[44] The government of premier Edouard Herriot secured parliamentary ratification of the Protocol despite determined opposition from the French military establishment and elements of the foreign ministry.[45] But further adjustment to France's position was necessary.

---

[43]   Peter Jackson, 'France and the Problems of Security and International Disarmament after the First World War', *Journal of Strategic Studies*, 29, 2 (2006), 247–80.

[44]   SHD-DAT, 7N 3532–1, 'Origine du protocole d'arbitrage, de sécurité et de réduction des armements', 7 September 1924; P.J. Noel-Baker, *The Geneva Protocol* (London, 1925), especially 215–24 (text); John Lewis Hogge II, 'Arbitrage, Sécurité, Désarmement: French Security and the League of Nations, 1920–1925', PhD Dissertation, New York University (1994), 358–74.

[45]   Jackson, 'Politics of Disarmament', 476–80; Lora Gibson, 'The Role of International Sanctions in British and French Strategic Policy: A Comparative Perspective, 1925–1935',

The Protocol envisaged security guarantees to Germany's eastern European neighbours. As reporting from the French embassy in London made clear, there was no chance that Britain's newly elected Conservative government would accept such commitments.[46] The Conservative foreign secretary, Austen Chamberlain, perhaps the most Francophile of senior British inter-war political elites, took the lead in the complicated multilateral negotiations leading to the Locarno Accords in October 1925. These accords, which included Britain, France, Belgium, Italy and Germany, provided for mutual assistance based on interlocking arbitration treaties and guaranteed the demilitarised status of the Rhineland. Crucially, however, Locarno was limited to western Europe. Germany refused to guarantee the frontiers of its eastern neighbours. Just as importantly, there were no provisions for staff conversations or military collaboration of any kind.[47] France was forced to accept that such arrangements were anathema in the new international environment of the mid-1920s. Security rested on multilateral legal and political guarantees rather than traditional bilateral alliances and military conventions.

Locarno served as a template for French security policy well into the 1930s. A central objective of French foreign policy in Europe over the next decade remained extending the Locarno system eastward and southward to create a Europe-wide security regime. The overriding aim was to enmesh Germany in a network of commitments that would ensure that any future revision of the Versailles settlement would be limited and peaceful rather than unilateral and violent. The result was a series of projects for an 'eastern Locarno', a 'Mediterranean Pact' and a 'Danubian Pact' championed by France over the next ten years. British support remained vital in all of these schemes. Foreign ministry officials argued consistently that only British participation in the envisaged pacts would provide them with the credibility necessary to ensure their success and durability.[48] To obtain British support and participation French representatives consistently linked international disarmament to the success of these ventures. These efforts all failed, however. In Paris the Locarno Accords constituted a crucial point of departure for the construction of a

---

PhD, Aberystwyth University (2008), 41–58.

[46]   SHD-DAT, 7N 3532–6, 'Note sur les dispositions prédominantes en Angleterre à l'égard du Protocole' (note by the London embassy), 30 January 1925; on the British position, see also John Ferris, *The Evolution of British Strategic Policy* (Ithaca, NY, 1989), 142–49; and Steiner, *Lights that Failed*, 381–82.

[47]   On the Locarno Accords, see the essays (and the works cited) in Gaynor Johnson (ed.), *Locarno Revisited: European Diplomacy, 1920–1929* (London, 2004); see also Steiner, *Lights that Failed*, 387–430.

[48]   The evolution of these projects can be followed in MAE, PA-AP 217, *Papiers Massigli*, vol. 9, 'Conférence pour la réduction des armaments'; vol. 10, 'Limitation des armements et project de pacte aérien'; vol. 11, 'Sécurité en Méditerranée'; and vol. 15, 'Europe Centrale'. See also Piotr Wandycz, *The Twilight of French Eastern Alliances, 1926–1936* (Princeton, 1988), 299–422.

wider system of security based on mutual guarantee. In London, conversely, the agreement marked the absolute limit of Britain's commitments to the Continent.

The significance of the multilateral turn in French policy has not been appreciated sufficiently by historians. There is little or no evidence of French efforts to revive the wartime military entente between in the middle decade of the inter-war years. Between 1924 and early 1935 French security policy was based instead primarily on a multilateral strategy aimed at enmeshing and constraining Germany. It focused on obtaining a tougher international sanctions regime to bolster Article 16 of the League Covenant, on establishing automatic mechanisms for identifying aggressors and the application of sanctions (including military sanctions) and on linking any future disarmament to the negotiation of supplementary regional security pacts.[49] A traditional strategy based on exclusive alliances and strategic preponderance, embodied in France's alliance 'system' in eastern Europe, was giving way to a multilateral approach that would integrate, and thus constrain, Weimar Germany. This new orientation to security policy was reflected in the course of French strategic planning. After 1925 French war plans moved gradually but consistently away from offensive action against Germany towards ever greater emphasis on ensuring the 'inviolability of the national territory'. This new strategic imperative was given material expression with the construction of the Maginot Line.[50] At the same time the French army underwent a radical reorganisation in 1928 which left it thoroughly unsuited to undertake rapid offensive action.[51]

Coordinated allied action to compel German compliance with the Versailles treaty was therefore a distant memory by the beginning of the 1930s. In the aftermath of the Locarno Accords the centre of gravity for French external policy shifted decidedly eastwards to focus on economic cooperation with Germany and, eventually, projects for a federal Europe aimed at cementing the political status quo.[52] The emphasis was on the restraining power of international law and the new norms for state behaviour embodied in the Locarno Accords. The effectiveness

---

[49]   Two important PhD theses have recently examined Franco-British strategic relations during this period: Andrew Webster, 'Anglo-French Relations and the Problems of Security and Disarmament', PhD, University of Cambridge (2001); and Gibson, 'International Sanctions'.

[50]   See especially Judith Hughes, *To the Maginot Line: The politics of French military preparation in the 1920s* (Cambridge, MA, 1971) and Martin Alexander, 'In defence of the Maginot Line: Security policy, Domestic Politics and the Economic Depression in France', in Boyce (ed.), *French Foreign and Defence Policy*, 164–94.

[51]   J. Doise and M. Vaïsse, *Diplomatie et outil militaire 1871–1991* (Paris, 1991), 324–62; Guy Pédroncini, *Pétain: le soldat, 1917–1940* (Paris, 1998), 391–419.

[52]   On Briand's foreign policy during this period, see especially Edward Keeton, *Briand's Locarno Policy: French Economics Politics and Diplomacy, 1925–1929* (New York, 1987); Gérard Unger, *Aristide Briand: le ferme conciliateur* (Paris, 2005), 471–595; Achille Elisha, *Aristide Briand: la paix mondiale et l'Union européenne* (Paris, 1965), 269–390; and, most recently, the essays by Robert Boyce, Andrew Barros, Laurence Badel, Eric Bussière, Sylvain Schirmann, Antoine Fleury, Stephen Schuker, Raphaële Ulrich-Pier,

of this approach depended on the full participation of Great Britain in eastern as well as western Europe. The great problem was that Britain consistently refused to join France in underwriting the envisaged regional security arrangements. As the quotations from Léger and Eyre Crowe cited above illustrate, even in the heady atmosphere engendered by the 'spirit of Locarno', Franco-British relations continued to be characterised by rivalry and mistrust as much as entente and collaboration.[53] Prospects of collaboration deteriorated further with the advent of the second Labour government in 1929. As Ambassador Aimé de Fleuriau observed in mid-1931, 'In the Baldwin-Chamberlain cabinet it was considered fashionable to be Francophile [but] since the arrival of the socialists we are no longer *à la mode*'.[54]

The effects of the great depression further undermined cooperation between the two states. British policymakers resented France's unyielding commitment to the gold standard, which weakened the already devalued pound sterling and undermined efforts to stimulate European economic recovery. The two states became chief sponsors of rival currency and trading groupings: the 'sterling bloc' based around the British pound and the 'gold bloc' based around the French franc.[55] The fiercely competitive character of commercial and financial relations did much to erode the Francophile tendencies of many British conservatives. This was unfortunate because the right in Britain had long tended to be more sympathetic to France than the left. Wrangling over disarmament provided another constant source of tension in Franco-British relations. French leaders were unwilling to entertain Germany's demand for theoretical equality in armaments and made British participation in regional security pacts in eastern Europe and the Mediterranean as a prerequisite to any international armaments agreement. British statesmen, for their part, tended to blame this perceived French intransigence for the failure of the World Disarmament Conference. 'The French in present circumstances', observed foreign secretary Sir John Simon, 'do not want a Disarmament Agreement or indeed any agreement about arms at all. They … hope to surround Germany on the East … and no doubt they calculate that, whether we like it or not, we must stand with them in the end against Germany.'[56] The British Cabinet rejected emphatically any commitments beyond Locarno. The effects of these disagreements were far-reaching. Even after the rise of the Nazi regime in Germany, British policymakers from both sides of

---

Renaud Meltz and Naurice Vaïsse in Jacques Bariéty (ed.), *Aristide Briand, la Société des Nations et l'Europe, 1919–1932* (Strasbourg, 2007).

[53]   Marks, *Illusion of Peace*, 75–107; Bell, *Britain and France*, 154–66; Steiner, *Lights that Failed*, 601–32.

[54]   MAE, Série Z, Grande Bretagne, vol. 288, 'Au sujet des dispositions anti-françaises de beaucoup d'Anglais', de Fleuriau to Briand, 18 November 1931.

[55]   Clavin, *Great Depression*, 128–57; and Kenneth Mouré, *The Gold Standard Illusion* (Oxford, 2002), 180–220.

[56]   Webster, 'Anglo-French Relations and the Problems of Security and Disarmament', 253–54.

the political spectrum opted to contain the German revisionism largely through bi-lateral diplomacy rather than through close collaboration with France.

One of the ironies of this state of affairs was that, although the global dimensions of British power were what made Britain such an attractive potential ally for France, imperial considerations operated almost uniformly to inhibit systematic Franco-British cooperation. French officials tended to consider that India and the Dominions exercised a baleful influence on British policy. Georges Bonnet, head of the French delegation at the London Economic Conference of 1933, remarked that 'Britain is no longer free: its Dominions and in particular Canada, whose prime minister, M. [R.B.] Bennett, is an unusually brutal and violent character, have a predominant influence over its policy to the point of modifying totally its position in the space of a few moments'.[57] This first exposure to dealing with the British left a profound impression on Bonnet. As foreign minister during the Czechoslovak Crisis five years later, he argued consistently that France could not count on Britain for strategic support in an eventual military confrontation with Germany. 'We must face up to the reality', he argued in the aftermath of the Munich Agreement, 'that Britain will not march with us if we decide on a heroic attempt to protect the small states in the east. She has other concerns and attributes greater importance to her interests in the Pacific that to the territorial *status quo* in eastern Europe.'[58]

The Imperial lens deployed by British policymaking elites was only one source of frustration however. Another was their alleged insularity and corresponding tendency to misunderstand the European strategic situation in general and their responsibilities as a European great power in particular. For French observers, the most important barometer of British willingness to accept these responsibilities was the attitude of the British public towards a continental expeditionary force. Through to the late 1930s, however, opposition to such a force in Britain stretched across the political spectrum, from the fiscally conservative right to the disarmament-minded left. One of the more worrying manifestations of the British tendency towards myopia in their strategic assessments was the doctrine of 'limited liability' championed by the influential military commentator Captain Basil Liddell Hart writing primarily in *The Times*. Liddell Hart opposed the idea of preparing another mass British expeditionary force for intervention on the Continent. He argued that such a force was not an efficient or rational deployment

57   France, MAE, *Documents Diplomatiques Français, 1932–1939* (Paris, 1972 et. seq.), [hereafter DDF], 1ère série, vol. III, #470, Bonnet to Paris, 9 July 1933.

58   France, Archives Nationale, in Archives Nationales (Paris) [hereafter AN], série C, Commission des Affaires Étrangères de l'Assemblée Nationale [CAÉAN], 16ème Législature, Bonnet Audition, 6 October 1938. On Bonnet's role in the evolution of French policy during this period, see especially Duroselle, *La décadence*, 16–24 and 333–493; Young, *Command of France*, 192–22 and 241–42 and Imlay, *Facing*, 34–48. Anthony Adamthwaite exaggerates Bonnet's role, particularly in 1939, in *France and the Coming of the Second World War* (London, 1977), 262–358.

of Britain's resources. French observers paid careful attention to Liddell Hart's arguments. From London, Lelong prepared numerous detailed reports on Liddell Hart's views and their influence on British policy and these reports were integrated into the assessments prepared by the *Deuxième bureau*. 'However obvious his errors of judgement may appear to us, we are nonetheless obliged to take into account the influence that [Liddell Hart] can have on British public opinion and in particular within the Conservative party'.[59] To counteract his influence the French general staff mounted a sustained campaign to convince official opinion in Britain that a powerful mechanised force was necessary to protect Britain's vital interests on the Continent. [60] But the prospects for such a campaign were never great. As late as July 1936, Charles Corbin, de Fleuriau's successor as ambassador in London, advised the newly elected Popular Front government in Paris that the word 'alliance' continued to exercise a 'veritable terror' on British minds.[61]

Between 1924 and 1934 French policy for security in Europe aimed at constructing a Europe-wide system of interlocking regional mutual assistance pacts. This approach depended on the power of legal and normative restraints on revisionism rather than the overt threat of force represented by more traditional military alliances of the pre-1914 variety. Britain played a pivotal role in all of these schemes, but not as a potential military ally against Germany. French policy elites by now understood that such an alliance was not obtainable. What they sought instead were political and legal commitments from Britain. These commitments would constitute an essential component of a security system that would *include* Germany. This approach must be juxtaposed with the more traditional strategy of constructing a balance of power *against* Germany that had characterised French policy from 1919 through 1923. Multilateralism had replaced the more traditional methods of alliance politics and the balance of power to such an extent that the first sustained pressure for military conversations between the French and British general staffs since 1923 came from London rather than Paris. The stimulus, rather predictably, was not German revisionism but the threat of war with Italy over Abyssinia in late 1935.[62] This strategy has been criticised with

---

[59]   Cf. SHD-DAT, 7N 2822, 'Article du capitaine Liddell Hart', 23 June 1938. For examples of French military attaché reporting on Liddell Hart's views, see SHD-DAT, 7N 2808, 'Étude du capitaine Liddell Hart sur les mesures prises dans l'armée britannique', 8 February 1935; 7N 2811, 'Articles concernant sur l'organisation future de l'armée', 4 November 1936; 7N 2812, 'Jugement du capitaine Liddell Hart sur l'armée britannique', 24 May 1937; 7N 2815, 'La politique britannique de co-operation et l'isolationisme', 5 July 1938.

[60]   See especially Alexander, *Republic in Danger*, 236–78 and Alexander and Philpott, 'The French and the British Field Force'.

[61]   Cf. Imlay, *Facing*, 28.

[62]   Bell, *Entente and Estrangement*, 184–203 and R.A.C. Parker, 'Great Britain, France and the Ethiopian Crisis, 1935–1936', *English Historical Review*, 89 (1974), 293–332.

some justification for having been dominated by 'illusions of pactomania'.[63] It is true that French hopes to obtain British cooperation for their schemes to extend Locarno were unrealistic. Yet it is difficult to imagine another approach achieving greater success. French multilateralism must be understood as a response to the new normative environment of the post-1918 era, where war, or even the threat of war, was all but ruled out as a tool of policy in Europe.

Britain and the Collapse of French Multilateralism

It was Nazi rearmament, rather than French campaigns to influence public opinion and policymakers in London, that sparked the beginnings of change in British military policy. In 1934, the Defence Requirements Committee identified Germany as Britain's 'ultimate' potential enemy and recommended the construction of a Continental expeditionary force consisting of five mechanised divisions supported by fourteen infantry divisions drawn from the Territorial Army. This policy was emasculated, however, by Cabinet opposition led by Neville Chamberlain (then chancellor of the exchequer) and by a lack of industrial capacity. It was not until mid-1938 that a new mechanisation programme was belatedly introduced.[64] By this time even Liddell Hart was championing the creation of an armoured force of two or three divisions for intervention in Europe.[65] British politicians were reluctant indeed to accept the costs inherent in constructing a force capable of assisting France in a future land war in Europe.

Britain's ongoing reticence was crucial because France's multilateral strategy was in tatters by March 1936. Germany's departure from the League of Nations, combined with a steady flow of intelligence on clandestine rearmament across the Rhine, led France to abandon the Disarmament Conference in April 1934 with the declaration that it would 'place in the forefront of her preoccupations the conditions of her own security'.[66] Two alternative policies were therefore pursued over the following eighteen months. A mutual assistance pact was negotiated with the USSR along with a short-lived and ill-fated military alliance with Italy.

---

[63]   Jean-Baptiste Duroselle, 'The Spirit of Locarno: Illusions of Pactomania', *Foreign Affairs*, 50 (1972), 752–64.

[64]   French, *British Way in Warfare*, 189–92; *idem*, *Raising Churchill's Army* (Oxford, 2000); Bond, *British Military Policy*, 162–90; and Keith Neilson, 'The Defence Requirements Sub-committee, British Strategic Foreign Policy and the Path to Appeasement', *English Historical Review*, 118, 477 (2003), 651–84; B.J.C. McKercher, 'Deterrence and the European Balance of Power: The Field Force and British Grand Strategy', 1934–1938', *English Historical Review*, 123, 500 (2008), 98–131.

[65]   SHD-DAT, 7N 2822, 'Article du capitaine Liddell Hart', 12 January 1938; and 7N 2814 'Considérations sur la collaboration militaire franco-britannique', 23 June 1938.

[66]   Vaïsse, *Sécurité d'abord*, 570–74; and Jackson, *France and the Nazi Menace*, 141–53.

The problem with both alternatives was that neither sat easily alongside close relations with the United Kingdom. British policy elites were deeply suspicious of Franco-Soviet negotiations from the outset. At the heart of these suspicions was a combination of mistrust of Soviet motives and exaggerated estimates of the danger of left-wing revolution inside France.[67] Britain consequently opposed a Franco-Soviet military alliance right up to the summer of 1939. This opposition was useful to officials within the French foreign ministry and army high command who, along with anti-communist premier Pierre Laval, were opposed to a traditional alliance with the USSR. The aim became to link the Franco-Soviet pact to existing schemes for an eastern Locarno. There was no military corollary to the Franco-Soviet mutual assistance pact signed on 2 May 1935. The agreement was full of legal qualifications and linked formally to the League of Nations Covenant.[68] British opposition to a Franco-Soviet alliance therefore complemented existing predispositions within the French policy establishment.

Pressure from London was more decisive in altering the course of Franco-Italian relations. During the first six months of 1935 talks between senior French and Italian army and air force officials had resulted in detailed plans for a military collaboration against Germany. During the crisis over Abyssinia, however, the government of Pierre Laval was forced to choose between the strategic potential offered by Britain and the military relationship that had been established with Fascist Italy in June 1935. Despite enthusiasm for the Italian alliance from within the army general staff, the Laval government reluctantly chose to side with Britain, participated in League-sponsored sanctions against Italy, and in doing so alienated its ally just as Hitler was preparing the aggressive phase of German revisionism. The impact of the Abyssinian Crisis was amplified because it occurred at a time when Germany was preparing a hammer-blow to the Locarno regime. The entry of German troops into the demilitarised zone of the Rhineland marked the final ruin of French multilateralism and an imperative to devise a new strategy for national security. Legal and normative constraints were patently inadequate in constraining Nazi revisionism.

All of this only accentuated the importance of Britain to French security. Although the remilitarisation of the Rhineland had been anticipated for at least eighteen months, French policymakers were slow to develop a new strategy. Their priority in the immediate aftermath of the crisis was to try to use Germany's repudiation of Locarno to leverage a British military commitment.[69] But British policy elites remained as reluctant as ever to extend a substantial military commitment to France. In staff conversations in April 1936 British officials were instructed to

---

[67] Dockrill, *British Establishment*, 45–48; and Jackson and Maiolo, 'Strategic Intelligence', 422–35.

[68] Duroselle, *La décadence*, 89–99 and 139–50; and Jonathan Haslam, *The Soviet Union and the Struggle for Collective Security* (London, 1984), 27–51.

[69] Duroselle, *La décadence*, 164–79 and Stephen Schuker, 'France and the Re-militarisation of the Rhineland, 1936,' *French Historical Studies*, 14 (1986), 299–338.

restrict discussion to narrow technical issues and exchanges of basic information. As a result there was no consideration of a British deployment in the event of war on the Continent. As Martin Alexander has observed, 'Cooperation remained confined to highly circumscribed contingencies and stayed a matter for the discretion of the British government'.[70]

Two months later a Popular Front coalition was voted into power and Léon Blum became France's first socialist premier. The new government pursued a rather incoherent series of policy initiatives that included tentative military conversations with the Soviet Union, even more tentative talks with Nazi officials aimed at moderating German policy through economic appeasement, an ambitious rearmament programme and an ill-fated campaign to rally France's allies in eastern Europe. By late 1937 all of these political initiatives had ended in failure. Meanwhile, the ambitious rearmament programme introduced under the popular front was slowed by the need to modernise France's aircraft and armaments industries. Huge backlogs developed and the modernisation programmes of the army and air force faced crippling delays. Production did not begin to recover until the autumn of 1938.[71] The inevitable result was ever-greater strategic dependence on Great Britain.

All of this made intelligence estimates of British capabilities and intentions crucial to the evolution of French strategic policy. France's intelligence services were clear that the army remained by far the weakest of Britain's armed services. In late 1934, when the first decisions were taken in Whitehall to begin construction of an expeditionary force, the French military attaché in London judged categorically that Britain lacked both the material capability and the political will to intervene in another European land war. Memories of 1914–18 had combined with financial austerity to reduce the army's portion of the yearly defence budget steadily since the onset of the depression. Moreover, the armaments industry necessary to equip a substantial Continental army had been dismantled and the levels of recruitment, training and morale in the standing army had also deteriorated steadily since 1918.[72] The decision to invest in just such a field force had not produced significant results as Europe hovered on the edge of war in the summer of 1938. The *Deuxième bureau* described the British regular army at this stage as 'an unhappy compromise between the army of 1914–1918 ... and a new modernised army whose definitive structures will not be established before 1940'. The army was desperately short of all manner of equipment, from armoured vehicles to heavy artillery to light automatic weapons. It noted that, while the rearmament programme undertaken

---

[70]   Alexander, *Republic in Danger*, 262; see also Young, *Command of France*, 126–28; and Thomas, *Britain, France*, 25–53.

[71]   Thomas, *Britain, France*, 89–228; Nicole Jordan, *The Popular Front and Central Europe: Dilemmas of French Impotence* (Cambridge, 1992), 146–279; and Robert Frankenstein, *Le prix du réarmement français, 1935–1939*, (Paris, 1982), 50–63 and 113–75.

[72]   SHD-DAT, 7N 2806, 'Programme du réarmement britannique', 11 October 1934.

by the War Office in 1936 called for the construction of 1,000 tanks, 1,000 heavy artillery pieces and 10,000 anti-tank guns, '[British] industry, state-owned and private, was in no condition to meet these demands'. As in France, the rearmament effort on land was hamstrung by persistent bottlenecks in the production of all types of weapons and heavy vehicles.[73] There were also problems with recruitment. Britain's army was comprised of permanent volunteers whose numbers had decreased steadily over the past decade. This was attributed to 'the traditional English repugnance towards serving in the land forces'. Not surprisingly, French military observers were dismayed with the British government's unwillingness to introduce conscription.[74] In the spring of 1938 Gamelin's staff warned Edouard Daladier, the French Prime Minister, that, unless Britain's military preparations were accelerated, its ground forces would arrive 'too late and with insufficient force to provide any useful assistance to France'.[75]

All of this meant that, in the event of war with Germany over Czechoslovakia, Britain could offer only two undermanned and poorly equipped divisions to support France on the Continent. It was estimated that this force would grow to five or six divisions after six months, and to twelve divisions after nine months. Britain would field an absolute maximum of 245,000 men nine months after mobilisation. France, by contrast, planned to mobilise more than one million soldiers in six days. The good news was that, when this force finally appeared, it would eventually include substantial contingents of armour and motorised infantry. But the overall conclusion, however, was that Britain was incapable of fielding a modern force suitable for Continental warfare. Even the two-division British Expeditionary Force would not be fully ready until 1940 'at the earliest'.[76] This bleak assessment of the potential contribution of British land power in a future war underpinned the emphasis placed on the reintroduction of military conscription in French policy towards Britain during the final year of peace in Europe.[77]

Britain's situation in the air was better. According to French intelligence, the development of German air power had transformed Britain's strategic situation.

---

[73] SHD-DAT, 7N 2815, 'Etudes: Empire britannique', 12 January 1938; 7N 2815, 'La faiblesse militaire de la Grande-Bretagne', 27 October 1938; AN, *Archives Edouard Daladier*, 496 AP 35, Dr. 3, sdr. b., 'Information du Président: la situation de l'armement britannique', Gamelin (army chief of staff and commander-in-chief designate) to Daladier (premier), 22 November 1938 [also in SHD-DAT, 5N 579–2].

[74] SHAT, 7N 2815, 'Etudes: Empire britannique', 12 January.1938.

[75] AN, *Archives Daladier*, 496 AP 35, 'Note sur la collaboration militaire franco-britannique', 24 April 1938.

[76] SHD-DAT, 7N 2815, 'Études: Empire britannique', 12 January 1938; 7N 2815, 'La faiblesse militaire de la Grande-Bretagne', Lelong (military attaché 1936–40) to Paris, 27 October 1938; AN, *Archives Daladier*, 496 AP 35, Dr. 3, sdr. b., 'Information du Président: la situation de l'armement britannique', Gamelin to Daladier.

[77] Daniel Hucker, 'Franco-British Relations and the Question of Conscription, 1938–1939', *Contemporary European History*, 17, 4 (2008), 437–56.

The air force *Deuxième bureau* stressed that 'For the first time since 1815 the United Kingdom faces a threat to the security of its own national territory'.[78] This menace appeared to have had a salutary effect on British policy. 'Over the past three years [since 1935]', another air intelligence report noted, 'Britain has set about increasing its air power to the level dictated by the requirements of its security.' The 'Home Defence Fleet' had increased from a total of 53 squadrons in May 1935 to 123 squadrons in late 1937. Air intelligence estimated that the number of first-line aircraft in the RAF had grown to 1,560, including 850 bombers and 420 fighters. It added that this was only a stage in the restoration of British air power. The objective of Britain's air rearmament programme was estimated to be a Home Fleet of 1,750 first-line planes and a total strength of 2,600 combat aircraft for the metropole and the Empire.[79] The quality of this new material would be very impressive. British engine design, especially by Bristol and Rolls Royce, was regarded highly by French observers.[80]

The level of training and professionalism in the RAF was rated very high despite its rapid growth since 1935. Air intelligence was less impressed with the evolution of British air doctrine. It was clear that the large proportion of bombers in the RAF was intended to function as a deterrent. This met with the approval of French analysts. At the same time, however, the British air staff was criticised for concentrating on fighter and home defence doctrine while 'Bomber Command' lacked a coherent tactical and operational system. Unfortunately, the reverse was true in France, where the *Armée de l'air* remained more interested in planning strategic bombing offensives than with developing an integrated air defence programme. The consequences of this 'strategic' preoccupation would prove catastrophic in May–June 1940.[81] But there was an undeniable dearth of precise intelligence on the performance specifications of British *matériel*. This may explain why one finds no reference whatsoever to plans for radar in a 153-page report on British air power prepared by the air force *Deuxième bureau* in January

---

[78]   France, Ministère de la Défense, Service Historique de l'Armée de l'air (SHAA), 2B 82, 'Etude sur l'armée de l'air de la Grande Bretagne', 1 January 1938.

[79]   Service Historique de la Défense, Département de l'Armée de l'Air [hereafter SHD-DAA], Series 2B, carton 82, 'L'armée de l'air en Grande Bretagne', 1 January 1937. See also the earlier reports on this programme in 2B 82, 'Forces aériennes britanniques', 15 December 1936; 2B 82, 'Evaluation sommaire des forces aériennes britanniques', 8 March 1937; and SHD-DAT, 7N 2822–2, 'Le réarmement britannique: son ampleur, les réalisations actuelles, les prévisions', 20 October 1936.

[80]   See especially on this issue SHD-DAA, 2B 82, 'Etude sur l'armée de l'air de la Grande Bretagne', 1 January 1938.

[81]   SHD-DAA, Archives Guy La Chambre, Z 19261, 'Forces aériennes britanniques', 1 January 1939; and 2B 82, 'Étude sur l'armée de l'air de la Grande Bretagne', 1 January 1938. On French air doctrine, see Robert Young, 'The Strategic Dream: French Air Doctrine in the Inter-war Period', *Journal of European Studies*, 9 (1972), 41–68; and P. Facon, *L'armée de l'air dans la tourmente* (Paris, 1997), 35–66.

1938.[82] French intelligence remained largely in the dark about many technological developments across the Channel.

For French observers, the most impressive aspect of British air power was Britain's aeronautical industry. Aircraft production in Britain was estimated to be 250–300 military machines per month by early 1938. Air intelligence was particularly impressed with the Shadow Aircraft Industry created in early 1937. It predicted that this programme would both accelerate the pace of the current rearmament programme and prepare the way for rapid industrial mobilisation in wartime. Noting that Britain's air budget had increased threefold since 1935, air intelligence estimated that an RAF of 2,600 first-line planes would be constituted 'in terms of quantity as well as quality' by late 1938 or early 1939, with all of the necessary reserves in place by late 1940 or early 1941.[83] It is worth noting that British progress in these domains stood in stark contrast to the complete collapse of French aircraft production in 1937–38. In the summer of 1938 French factories were producing fewer than 50 aircraft per month and the *armée de l'air* possessed virtually no aircraft comparable to the latest prototypes under mass production in both Britain and Germany.[84] The crisis of French air power made an alliance with Britain all the more important during the late 1930s.

Despite the progress that Britain had made in expanding and modernising its air force, the pillar of British power was unquestionably the Royal Navy. Captain Philippe du Tour, naval attaché in London, in early 1938 described Britain as 'an over-populated nation unable to survive without free commerce and open sea lanes'. He felt the British public understood the importance of maritime power and was 'willing to make all necessary sacrifices to ensure the strength of the Royal Navy'.[85] The only serious challenge to this dominance could come from the United States. But French assessments of the global naval balance tended to assume collusion on the part of the 'Anglo-Saxon' navies to limit the size and strength of the world's other maritime powers.[86] The strength of the Royal Navy

---

[82]   SHD-DAA, 2B 82, 'Etude sur l'armée de l'air de la Grande Bretagne', 1 January 1938.

[83]   SHAA, 2B 82, 'Etude sur l'armée de l'air de la Grande Bretagne', 1 January 1938; 2B 82, 'L'armée de l'air en Grande Bretagne', 1 December 1937.

[84]   Facon, *Armée de l'air dans la tourmente*, 23–39; T. Vivier, *La politique aéronautique militaire de la France, 1933–1939* (Paris, 1997), 451–56.

[85]   France, Ministère de la Défense, Service Historique de la Défense, Département de la Marine [hereafter SHD-DM], series 1BB2, carton 94, 'La Marine Anglaise: Conférence du Capitaine du Tour', 22 February 1938.

[86]   The tendency to underestimate the sources of tension between the USA and Britain can be traced to the First World War but became entrenched in the mindset of French naval officials after the bitter experience of the Washington Naval Conference in 1921–22. See, among other sources on this issue, Contre-Amiral L. de la Monneraye Espagnac de Ravay, *Vingt ans de politique navale, 1919–1939* (Grenoble, 1941), 51–66; H. Kowark, 'Marine française et la conférence de Washington', in H. Coutau-Bégarie (ed.), *Aspects*

remained a central (albeit often unarticulated) factor in French calculations of the strategic balance in Europe throughout the inter-war period. This was not least because French observers anticipated that a future conflict with Germany would once again evolve into a long war of attrition in which economic power would be decisive. The crucial importance of the Royal Navy to this strategy was not always acknowledged explicitly, but it was always a factor in assessments of France's geo-strategic situation. [87]

In January 1938 French naval intelligence estimated the total size of the British fleet to be 1,350,000 tonnes. Of a total of 813,000 tonnes in service, the Home Fleet comprised 312,000 tonnes (38 per cent), 242,000 tonnes (21 per cent) were stationed in the Mediterranean and 110,000 tonnes (12 per cent) in the Far East. The level of training and the quality of the material in service were considered excellent and provided the mobility vital to British Imperial strategy. The one significant problem facing the Royal Navy was an insufficiency of medium and heavy cruisers.[88] Aviation provided a potential means of alleviating this problem. Du Tour reported the 'great interests' the British navy had taken in air power and noted that it intended to build ten aircraft carriers by the mid-1940s. Although he judged that the Admiralty exaggerated the future role of air power at sea, he also suggested that the *Marine* might profit by studying the results of British experimentation in this area.[89] Overall, the combat effectiveness and strategic reach of the British sea power was unrivalled. 'The Royal Navy will maintain its present position,' the naval *Deuxième bureau* predicted, 'and that position is first among the world's navies.'[90] Assessments such as this underpinned the unequivocal advice given to the Laval government during the Abyssinian Crisis that the choice between Britain and Italy was no choice at all: '[I]t is Britain which can assist us most effectively, not only in the long term, as a result of its great imperial potential and control of the sea lanes, but even in the early stages of a conflict. We must above all secure and develop the immediate support of Britain.'[91]

---

du désarmement naval (Paris, 1994), 151–230; *idem, Die französische Marinepolitik und die Washington Konferenz, 1919–1924* (Stuttgart, 1978); and J. Blatt, 'France and the Washington Conference', *Diplomacy & Statecraft*, 4, 3 (1993), 192–219.

[87]   See, for example, SHD-DAT, 2N 52–1, 'Etude sur le blocus,' 23 January 1923; and 'Etude Historique du Blocus pendant la guerre 1914–1918', no date but *c.* 1931.

[88]   SHD-DM, 1BB2 94, 'Bulletin d'Études: les marines allemande, italienne et britannique', February 1938.

[89]   SHD-DM, 1BB2 94, 'La Marine Anglaise: Conférence du Capitaine du Tour', 22 February 1938.

[90]   SHM, 1BB2 94, 'Bulletin d'Études: les marines allemande, italienne et britannique', February 1938.

[91]   SHD-DAT, 2N 19–2, 'Note sur la situation relative des forces allemandes et françaises et sur les conséquences à en tirer aux points de vue national et international', 17 March 1935. On the short-lived alliance with Italy, see Robert Young, 'French Military

In order to maintain this position, the Admiralty had devised a rearmament programme that impressed French naval intelligence, the objective being to construct of fleet of over two million tonnes, including 25 capital ships and 80 to 85 cruisers, by late 1942. French intelligence estimated that 272,000 tonnes of new warships had been laid down by Britain in 1937 (more than that laid down by France over the past five years). Total construction for 1938 would be even greater as Britain's shipbuilding industry was being expanded. This industry size was 'a major factor in the global balance of forces'. Yet the French also considered that the days of British maritime supremacy were coming to an end. Naval intelligence concluded that the rise of American, German, Italian and Japanese naval power would make Britain's Empire increasingly vulnerable.[92]

This judgement prompted a series of flawed analyses of British foreign policy in early and mid-1938. Accurate estimates of Britain's strategic vulnerability were married to the hopeful but misguided judgement that British decision-makers would finally recognise the need for a closer diplomatic and military relationship with France. The French naval staff, for example, pointed out that cooperation with France would greatly strengthen Britain's position in the Mediterranean and release naval squadrons for deployment either in the Atlantic or east of Suez.[93] A common assumption in all three services was that the Abyssinian Crisis in 1935 had opened British eyes to the need for such cooperation. Britain, after all, had been forced to request French assistance in the Mediterranean.[94] In mid-1938 the army *Deuxième bureau* judged, prematurely, that 'the gravity of the German menace, most notably from the economic and aerial points of view, has led the British to progressively fashion a Euro-imperial conception of their defence which unites them more firmly with France'.[95] When the policy of the Chamberlain government did not conform to these expectations over the course of 1938, long-standing stereotypes about Britain's myopia and selfishness were strengthened and frustrations with British policy intensified.

Intelligence and the Franco-Italian Alliance, 1933–1939', *Historical Journal*, 28, 1 (1985), 143–68.

[92] SHD-DM, 1BB2 170–1, 'Le programme de trois ans est nécessaire, même si on peut escompter l'appui de l'Angleterre', 4 May 1937; and SHD-DM, 1BB2 94, 'Bulletin d'Études: les marines allemande, italienne et britannique', February 1938.

[93] SHD-DM, 1BB2 171–1, 'Mesures à prendre pour la Marine à l'égard de la situation internationale présente', Darlan [naval chief of staff] to César Campinchi [minister of the Marine], 10 January 1938; see also SHD-DM, 1BB2 94, 'La Marine anglaise', February 1938.

[94] SHD-DAT, 7N 2822–1, 'Position de l'Angleterre depuis le traité de Locarno: travail demandé par le Général Schweisguth', 20 October 1936; 7N 2815, 'Etudes sur l'Empire britannique', September 1938; see also SHD-DAA 2B 82, 'Etude sur l'armée de l'air de la Grande-Bretagne', January 1938; and SHD-DM, 1BB7 44, 'Conférence sur la Marine britannique', 22 February 1938.

[95] SHD-DAT, 7N 2815–1, 'Etudes: Empire britannique', September 1938.

French observers in London had always been more pessimistic than their colleagues in Paris. In June 1938, with international tensions mounting over the German threat to Czechoslovakia, French military attaché, General Albert Lelong, reported that British public opinion, the City of London and the vast majority of the Conservative elite all favoured concessions to Germany in order to avoid war. 'It would be difficult for the [Chamberlain] government to follow a firm policy under these conditions', the attaché correctly concluded. The British temperament 'with its horror of commitments of any kind' would limit London's role in any crisis to that of 'a peaceful mediator'. 'As for France,' he concluded, '[the British] proclaim the solidarity of their policy with ours, but this is in order to restrain us.'[96]

The absence of a clear British military commitment to uphold the European political order was a crucial factor shaping French policy. This does not mean that French policy was made in London, however. While the British government made strenuous efforts to moderate French policy – particularly with regard to the civil war that raged in Spain from mid-1936 through mid-1939 – the pressure exerted by London was only one factor among several that led the French government to opt for a policy of acquiescence when faced with the *Anschluss* in March 1938 and war over Czechoslovakia in September of that year.[97] Just as important was the clear sense that France was neither materially nor psychologically prepared for war at this juncture. Edouard Daladier, who combined the portfolios of premier and minister of defence during the final eighteen months of peace, was acutely aware of the strains that massive rearmament had placed on France's newly reorganised defence industries. A particularly alarming gap that had opened up between German and French air power. The premier was also aware of the profound divisions in French society over the question of war in 1938. There seemed no hope of leading France united into the lengthy conflict that was expected.[98] British policy was an important element in the making of French appeasement. But it did not dictate this policy.

At the same time, there can be no denying that the military and political situation of France meant that Great Britain had never been more important to French planning than in 1938–39. As tension mounted over Czechoslovakia, the

---

[96]   SHD-DAT, 7N 2822–2, 'L'opinion publique et la crise Tchécoslovaque', 1 June 1938.

[97]   See, among others, Yvon Lacaze, *La France et Munich: étude d'un processus décisionnel en matière des relations internationales* (Berne, 1992); Adamthwaite, *France and the Coming*, 238–51; Duroselle, *La décadence*, 335–66; Young, *In Command of France*, 202–20; Jackson, *France and the Nazi Menace*, 247–97; Martin Thomas, 'France and the Czechoslovak Crisis', *Diplomacy and Statecraft*, 10, 2–3 (1999), 122–59; and *idem*, 'Appeasement in the Late Third Republic', *Diplomacy and Statecraft*, 19, 3 (2008), 566–607.

[98]   See especially Yvon Lacaze, *L'opinion publique française et la crise de Munich* (Berne, 1991); and Young, *France and the Origins*, 83–87 and 114–22.

French premier received a series of dire warnings about the vital importance of British support. 'More than ever,' declared chief of defence staff General Maurice Gamelin to Daladier in late March, 'it is essential that we have Britain with us.'[99] On the eve of his departure for a summit meeting with Chamberlain in April 1938, Daladier received a lengthy analysis of the strategic situation from the secretariat of the French national defence council. Warning of the possibility that Italy would join with Germany in the event of a conflict, 'France cannot resist forces three times as numerous,' the SGDN insisted. Franco-British military cooperation was therefore essential.[100] From Paul Marchandeau at the ministry of finance came repeated warnings that France was dependent on British support to maintain the solvency of the franc.[101] Daladier's personal cabinet summed up the strategic situation with this conclusion: 'France can only defeat Germany in a war if it is assured, in every possible respect, of total British assistance.'[102] The problem was that that assurance was not forthcoming in the summer of 1938. The British government had made it clear the previous November, again in April and again on 8 September that Great Britain would not enter a war 'caused by German aggression against Czechoslovakia'.[103]

Premier Daladier went to Munich with profound misgivings. Since assuming the portfolio of defence minister in June 1936 he had received a steady stream of pessimistic assessments of German intentions. 'The Munich agreement is really only a short respite,' he warned his colleagues several days after the four-power conference, 'Hitler will find a pretext for an armed conflict before he loses his military superiority.'[104] The overriding expectation was that a strengthened Franco-British military relationship would emerge out of the wreckage of the alliance with Czechoslovakia. In the aftermath of Munich, however, the two states were no closer to a military alliance than they had been before the crisis. The French defence establishment was deeply chagrined at the hollow character of conversations held between the French and British military representatives in November 1938, where the British government obstinately refused to enlarge its plans for an expeditionary force of two divisions. All of this brought Franco-British relations to a desperately low ebb in early 1939. Daladier's frustration with the British position boiled over in expressions of antipathy and even contempt. Chamberlain, in his estimation, was a fundamentally weak character, a 'desiccated

---

[99]   DDF, 2ème série, VIII, #432, 14 March; and #445, 15 March 1938.

[100]   MAE, Papiers 1940, *Fonds Daladier*, Volume I, 'Note sur la collaboration militaire franco-britannique,' 24 April 1938.

[101]   Martin Thomas, 'Czechoslovakian Crisis,' 128–46.

[102]   AN, *Archives Daladier*, 496 AP 31, Dr. 5, 'Note sur la mobilisation industrielle,' 5 April 1938.

[103]   For these warnings see, respectively, DDF, 2ème série, vol. VII, document #41; DBFP, 3rd series, vol. I, #164; DDF, 2ème série, vol. XI, #405; and DBFP, 3rd Series, II, #814.

[104]   Cited in Elisabeth du Réau, *Edouard Daladier* (Paris, Fayard, 1993), 294.

stick', the British Empire reduced to little more than 'a frail reed', a completely unreliable alliance partner.[105]

And yet France's strategic options remained as limited as ever in late 1938. The only other potential Great Power ally against Nazi Germany was the USSR. For a host of reasons, many of which (though by no means all) stemmed from ideological hostility to Bolshevism, French policy elites were unwilling to place their trust in Stalin's commitment to collective security.[106] Britain remained the only major power capable of providing the strategic support that would allow France to face the prospect of another European war with confidence. Nor were all assessments of British policy as bleak as those of Daladier in the aftermath of Munich. From London General Lelong lamented the effects of British attitudes but also insisted that there were grounds for optimism:

> It is necessary to struggle constantly against the insularity of the British nation, whose territory has not been invaded since 1066 and who, having long since achieved national unity, is incapable of imagining the situation of less happy peoples … Nonetheless, a certain number of British qualities, a respect for the rights of others, a love of the rule of law based on a certain conception of justice, and, finally and above all, this people's tolerance, ensure that the British people will not shirk their important role in world affairs.[107]

Britain, for all of the flaws in the characteristics of its citizens, remained a vital partner in all projects to contain and if necessary defeat revisionism in Europe.

Britain and France's Decision for War, 1939

The situation of strategic dependence that characterised France's relationship with Britain began to ebb away in the aftermath of the Munich Four Power Conference.

---

[105]   See Orville Bullitt (ed.), *For the President: Personal and Secret: Correspondence between Franklin Roosevelt and William C. Bullitt* (London, 1973), 308–11. See also du Réau, *Daladier*, 299–308; and Young, *In Command of France*, 214–21. See also the bleak report on British military preparedness despatched by the military attaché in London in AN, *Archives Daladier*, 496 AP 11, dr. 2, sdr a, 17 November 1938; and 'Information du Président: conversations franco-britanniques', 22 November 1938.

[106]   Alexander, *Republic in Danger*, 290–305; Young, *Command of France*, 145–50; and Jordan, *Popular Front and Central Europe*, 259–79; Duroselle, *La décadence*, 112–21 and 352–54; for a contending interpretation see J.-J. Becker and Serge Berstein, *Histoire de l'anti-communisme en France, 1917–1940* (Paris, 1987), 237–335; and Michael Carley, 'Prelude to Defeat: Franco-Soviet Relations, 1919–1939', *Historical Reflections*, 22, 1 (1996), 159–88.

[107]   SHD-DAT, 7N 2815, 'La politique britannique de co-operation et l'isolationisme', Lelong report, 5 July 1938.

One important factor was the very different perspective on the international situation adopted by the British and French national leaders. Neville Chamberlain remained optimistic that peace had indeed been saved and adopted a relatively complacent attitude towards the German threat. There was no major diversion of resources to rearmament in Britain in late 1938. The French case was very different. While a significant number of French policy elites advocated a policy of retreat and retrenchment, Daladier pressed forward with a major amplification of France's rearmament effort. Government spending on new armaments more than tripled from 1938 to 1939.[108] These increases were made possible by the dramatic recovery in both industrial production and investor confidence from late 1938 through to the outbreak of war. The bottlenecks that had hamstrung rearmament since 1936 began to disappear in late 1938. Also of crucial importance was a perceptible shift in the national mood. Anti-war sentiment waned during the final year of peace and the outlines of a national consensus over foreign policy emerged. The prospect of war was no longer as divisive and opinion polls indicated the majority of French public opinion was opposed to further concessions to German territorial demands. [109]

Added to improvements in the situation inside France were more optimistic estimates of Britain's ability to wage war on the Continent. According to French estimates, British rearmament had begun to pay dividends in mid-to-late 1938. But great advances in the strengthening of British military power were expected by 1940–41. As a military intelligence assessment noted, the only state to exceed British rearmament expenditure was Nazi Germany and, if one added military spending in the Dominions, 'The British empire already has the largest defence budget in the world'.[110] General staff memoranda on military cooperation emphasised that, while Britain's contribution on land would be almost negligible early in a conflict, the Royal Navy and Air Force could play a decisive role in securing France's maritime lines of communication and especially in improving the glaring imbalance between French and German air power. It was expected that Britain's latent financial strength would once again prove crucial in the anticipated

[108]   AN, *Archives Daladier*, 496 AP 11, Dr. 1, sdr. b, Daladier before senate finance commission, 17 July 1939; Peter Jackson, 'Intelligence and the End of Appeasement', in R. Boyce (ed.), *French Foreign and Defence Policy, 1918–1940* (London, 1998), 234–60; du Réau, *Daladier*, 254–310; Robert Frankenstein, *Le prix du réarmement français* (Paris, 1982), 197–217 and 306.

[109]   See, among many sources on these developments, Michel Margairaz, *L'état, les finances, l'économie. Histoire d'une conversion, 1932–1952*, vol. I (Paris, 1991), 473–85; Robert Frank, *La hantise du déclin: finance, défense et identité nationale, 1920–1960* (Paris, 1994), 180–88; Jean-Louis Crémieux-Brilhac, *Les français de l'an 40*, vol. I, *La guerre: Oui ou non?* (Paris, 1990); Young, *France and the Origins*, 121–29; and Daniel Hucker, 'French Public Attitudes towards the Prospect of War in 1938–1939', *French History*, 21, 4 (2007), 431–49.

[110]   SHD-DAT, 7N 2815–1, 'Etudes: Empire britannique', September 1938.

guerre de longue durée.[111] These considerations were never far from the minds of French civilian and military leaders. They had been important considerations in the decision to appease Germany in 1938 and would play an even more pivotal role in the decision to stand up to German aggression the following summer.

It was at this juncture, moreover, that the balance of influence within Franco-British relations began to shift. British policymakers began to worry that France might abandon resistance altogether and come to an arrangement with Germany that would leave Britain isolated and vulnerable. These anxieties were encouraged by several French officials in a subtle campaign of manipulation aimed at convincing the British of the need to make a concrete military commitment to the Continent resting on joint military planning and the introduction of conscription. This was combined with a deception campaign aimed at reinforcing British government fears of a German attack on Holland and Belgium in late 1938 and early 1939. These efforts succeeded. By mid-January 1939 all three military services were advocating joint military planning with France. Even the Admiralty, by far the most resistant of the services to a closer relationship with France, was arguing that Britain could not risk war without the full cooperation of the French navy. In late January the British cabinet finally approved staff conversations with France based on the hypothesis of war with the Axis powers.[112] France had gained the military commitment it required to adopt a policy firmness in response to further Nazi or Fascist revisionism.

The German occupation of Bohemia and Moravia the following March provided added stimulus to the creation of a Franco-British military alliance. During staff talks that began in April 1939 lessons of the First World War were applied to create not only mechanisms for military collaboration on land, at sea and in the air but also extensive structures for commercial, financial and industrial collaboration. The overriding objective was preparation for industrial war that would play to the strengths of the Entente and the weaknesses of the Axis.[113] The size and armament of the British Expeditionary Force proposed by the British in April 1939 proved a major disappointment to French officials. But French dissatisfaction was at least partially alleviated by the commitment implicit in the introduction of conscription

---

[111]   See, for example, AN, *Archives Daladier*, 496 AP 35, dr. 3, sdr. b, 'Note sur la collaboration militaire franco-britannique', prepared for premier Daladier by Gamelin's staff, 24 April 1938; 'Etude sur la participation de l'Angleterre dans l'éventualité d'"une action commune franco-britannique en cas de guerre', 8 November 1938; and SHD-DAT, 5N 579–2, 'Accords d'Etats-Majors', Gamelin to Daladier, 4 April 1938.

[112]   Talbot Imlay, 'The Making of the Anglo-French Alliance, 1938–1939', in Alexander and Philpott (eds.), *Anglo-French Defence Relations between the Wars* (London, 2002), 101–7.

[113]   Imlay, *Facing*, 48–63 and 96–115; see also Martin Thomas, 'Imperial Defence of Diversionary Attack? Anglo-French Strategic Planning in the Near East, 1936–1939', and Martin Alexander, 'Preparing to Feed Mars: Anglo-French Economic Coordination and the Coming of War, 1937–1939', both in Alexander and Philpott (eds.), *Anglo-French Defence Relations*, 157–85 and 186–208 respectively.

at the end of that month. By the eve of war, moreover, the French and the British were preparing to re-establish the Supreme War Council of 1918 and had also created a framework for the most intimate and extensive 'intelligence alliance' in history – with arrangements for systematic information-sharing, joint assessment and the coordination of intelligence collection.[114]

The significance of these developments is too often ignored in analyses of Franco-British relations that view the pre-war period through the lens of 1940. Also overlooked is the extent to which the French were able to impose their strategic conceptions on the British. If Britain took the initiative in guaranteeing Poland in March 1939, the French were able to insist that similar guarantees be extended to Romania and Greece. It was France that took the lead, moreover, in the ill-fated efforts to negotiate a Franco-British-Soviet alliance in May–August 1939. Finally, in general terms, the long-war strategy adopted by the Entente on the eve of war reflected almost exactly the vision of the French defence establishment as it had evolved since the late 1920s.[115]

Conclusion

In September 1939 British power was central to virtually every aspect of French preparations for war. The Franco-British military alliance was late in emerging and proved inadequate when put to the test in May–June 1940. And there can be no denying that under the surface of newly established alliance machinery lurked nearly twenty years of often sharp and profound disagreement over the most vital questions connected to European security. As one historian has observed of Franco-British relations during this period: 'The capacity of two great nations with essentially common interests to nevertheless to misunderstand each other seemed endless.'[116] This is no doubt true. But it should not obscure the fact that the Franco-British alliance of 1939 constituted the most intimate relationship that had ever existed between two Great Powers in peacetime. Nor should the failure of the two states to make common cause earlier in the decade be attributed to French misunderstanding of to the geo-strategic importance of Britain. French policymaking rested on a generally accurate interpretation of British power. The problem was instead that the generally accurate assessments of British opinion and policymaking provided by observers in London were not always integrated into French strategies for national security. From 1919 through 1923 French

---

[114]   Jackson and Maiolo, 'Strategic Intelligence', 453–60; Alexander and Philpott, 'The French and the British Field Force', 766–70; Hucker, 'Question of Conscription', 449–56; and William Philpott, 'The Supreme War Council and the Higher Management of Coalition War', in Alexander and Philpott (eds.), *Anglo-French Defence Relations*, 209–26.

[115]   This trend is clear in Imlay, *Facing*, 17–127.

[116]   Cf. Anthony Clayton 'The Royal Navy and the Marine Nationale, 1918–1939', in Alexander and Philpott (eds), *Anglo-French Defence Relations*, 44.

statesmen, with the exception of Briand, strove for a British military commitment that was never on the cards. Similarly, from 1924 through to the mid-1930s British willingness to underwrite French projects for a Europe-wide system of mutual assistance pacts was consistently overrated. And yet all of this only serves to illuminate the central role of British power in all formulations of national security policy as it evolved from 1919 through 1939.

That there was considerable variation in this policy between the wars is the other chief conclusion that emerges from this essay. The essentially static image of France's security policy in Wolfers' analysis must be revised. Wolfers' focused overwhelmingly on geo-politics. When one takes into account the influence of both the changed normative environment after 1918 and the impact of domestic politics on French decision-making, a very different picture emerges. From 1919 through 1924 French policymakers in the main sought security through traditional strategies of military alliances and strategic preponderance. A reconstitution of the military entente with Britain was therefore the central element in French policy. From 1924 through 1934, however, French foreign policy aimed at achieving security through the creation of a regime of interlocking mutual assistance guarantees. Britain was important to this strategy not as a traditional alliance partner but instead as a joint-guarantor. Crucially, only British adherence could give the various regional security pacts envisaged by Paris the credibility required to truly constrain Germany or any other state with revisionist ambitions. Britain's refusal to play its allotted role therefore undermined French designs. The strategy began to come apart as Nazi rearmament gathered momentum and was destroyed altogether by the remilitarisation of the Rhineland and the consequent destruction of Locarno in March 1936. French policy then reverted to the earlier strategy of deterrence, aiming to confront Germany with a credible eastern counterweight on the one hand and Franco-British military and diplomatic cooperation on the other. But French policy in eastern Europe foundered. And when Hitler initiated the aggressive phase of his revisionist design, France found itself in a situation of strategic dependence on Britain.

French appeasement was thus an inevitable consequence of the failure of an earlier multilateral and system-building strategy. This fact has been largely ignored in the historiography – which has focused overwhelmingly on British unwillingness to make a Continental military commitment. While Britain's refusal to make common cause with France is a prominent feature in this literature, the changing nature of the commitment desired by France is not. A careful look at the changing role of Britain in French security policy sheds new light on the character of that policy as it evolved from 1919 through 1939. It also illuminates yet another path not taken by British statesmen between the wars.

Chapter 6
Germany, Britain and Warmaking

Dennis Showalter

The editors of this Festschrift proposed two approaches to the contributors. One was to focus on Britain's way of war in the context of relationships with other powers over a period of time. The other was to use case studies to describe specific relationships at specific times. Neither quite worked when Germany, or more accurately Prussia/Germany, was the other half of the dialogue. If nothing else, the subject has been done to death even compared to Anglo-French and Anglo-American interaction – and done to death from a common perspective. Both popular and academic histories tend to present Anglo-German relations in terms of fundamental dichotomies: political, cultural, moral – perhaps psychological.

Even a scholar like Niall Ferguson, who suggests the 'pity' of Britain's Great War with Germany, finds himself at seventh and last confronting the paradox expressed in a familiar aphorism, slightly modified for present purposes: 'a bird and a fish may seek common interests, but where can they come together?' The metaphor seems no less applicable to a tiger and a tiger shark. Enduring alliances are insurance policies against objective dangers, constants transcending any treaty connections. Prussia/Germany developed as a continental edifice that acquired global pretensions. Britain became a world construction with continental imperatives. They had neither a common bond nor a common threat strong enough to bind them in any relationship but one of mutual convenience.[1]

But did that make their conflict inevitable? States and the societies they represent approach war in three contexts. The first involves *intentions*: goals sought and prices willing to pay. Intentions in turn are pursued through *institutions*: systems and structures. What, then, are the relationships between institutions and ways of war? Finally, war is a matter of *instruments*: armed forces able to go somewhere and stay there in the face of significant opposition. David French's seminal monograph, *The British Way in Warfare, 1688–2000*, depicts an approach accepting warmaking as normal but not normative: a way *in* war, shaping state and society without defining them. To turn to Germany, on the other hand, is to confront a way *of* war: a close, comprehensive link between war and the state, war and society – arguably at least, a defining connection. A way in war and a way of

---

[1] Hans W. Koch, "The Anglo-German Alliance Negotiations: Missed Opportunity or Myth?', *History*, 54 (1969), 378–92, specifically addresses the pre-1914 situation but raises solid points on the alliance issue generally.

war came together on the continent of Europe. Over a span of two centuries their interaction was one of history's central defining processes.

Prussia /Germany

Intentions

Early modern Prussia was an archetype of the middle-ranking Central European power, too large to be safely ignored, yet too small to pursue anything like an independent policy vis-à-vis Bourbon France or Habsburg Austria. The state had neither natural frontiers nor internal cohesion. It developed and survived, like so many of its counterparts, as an artificial construction.[2] Not until the end of the seventeenth century did some states become rich enough to define borders by fortress systems, or powerful enough to seek such more or less ephemeral national boundaries as the 'French Hexagon'.

Frederick William, the Great Elector, and his son and successor King Frederick III based their security policies on an army efficient enough to be attractive enough to great powers and grand coalitions that they would pay for its presence on their side and negotiate to keep it from their enemies. Frederick William I (1715–40) sought to replace clientage by conciliation. Believing Prussia's interests best served by a stable international situation, he took pains to alienate no one, consistently deferring on diplomatic issues to Austria in particular. Doubling the size of Prussia's army was not a challenge but an insurance policy.[3]

Frederick II's departure from that pattern reflected his conviction that the network of treaties underpinning the Pragmatic Sanction, the right of Maria Theresa to succeed Charles VI on the throne of Austria, could not survive Charles's death. Austria was certain to be challenged, perhaps dismembered, no matter what Prussia did or did not do. Frederick saw his choice as whether to be hammer or anvil, windshield or bug. Unlike its rivals and counterparts on the Continent, Prussia had no imperial pretensions – no dreams of wealth from overseas colonies, no visions of being a Third Rome, no heritage of crusade against the heathen Turk. Prussia's essential interest, in the mind of its King, lay in securing a position at the gaming table. And the best way of achieving this was by the rational application of force for limited ends.

Frederick intended to create a one-time fait accompli, overrunning Silesia and then negotiating a permanent settlement. Instead Prussia faced fifteen years of war and preparation for war that left the state on the edge of ruin. The King's response

---

[2]   Christopher Clark, *Iron Kingdom: The Rise and Downfall of Prussia, 1600–1947* (Cambridge, MA, 2006), is particularly good for the early years.

[3]   Cf. Gerhard Oestrich, *Friedrich Wilhelm I: Preussischewn Absolutismus, Merkantilismus, Militarismus* (Goettingen, 1977); and Keinz Kathe, *Der "Soldatenkoenig": Friedrich Wilhelm I, 1688–1740: Eine Biographie* (Koeln, 1981).

was to rebuild, rearm, and re-establish Prussia's position as a prop of stability: aggrandising itself within limits accepted by an international consensus reluctant to challenge the formidable Prussian army.[4]

The combination worked for a quarter-century after Frederick's death. Its eventual failure reflected neither the decay of Prussia's army nor the ineffectiveness of its diplomacy as much as the mushrooming of Napoleon's unfocused imperial ambitions. Diplomacy for the Emperor was no more than the waging of war by other means. What seemed the limitless capacity of the French Revolutionary army to sustain his pretensions escalated the stakes of those wars beyond anything a multi-polar European system could sustain.[5]

Prussia's response to the new German order differed essentially from that of the mediatising elites elsewhere in 'middle Germany'. Reformers and conservatives found particular common ground in a sense of unique victimisation. Between 1806 and 1815 an increasing body of emotion insisted Prussia was suffering tribulations that merited special recognition. The legends that grew up around Frederick the Great had already generated a sense that Prussia was special, different from both the universalist Austrian Empire and the parish-pump principalities of the west and south

That did not mean Prussia sought hegemony, or even primacy, in Germany during and after the Wars of Liberation. The common thread of policy recommendations involved Prussia developing as a European power in a German context – in other words, recovering the status won by Frederick the Great, only with a new foundation based on a common German identity. De facto Austro-Prussian dualism, implemented through the German Confederation, was seen as the best way to sustain the 'German centre' against both France and a Russia whose messianic Emperor Alexander I seemed to have no more sense of boundaries than Napoleon possessed.[6]

After Waterloo, Prussia consciously and consistently assumed a facilitator's role in the Concert of Europe, the Holy Alliance of the three eastern empires, and

---

[4]   This argument is developed in Dennis E. Showalter, *The Wars of Frederick the Great* (New York, 1996). Cf. for a general framework James M. Sofka. "The Eighteenth Century International System: Parity or Primacy?" *Review of International Studies*, 27 (2002), 147–63.

[5]   Paul Schroeder's characterisation of "Napoleon's Foreign Policy: A Criminal Enterpriese", *The Journal of Military History*, 54 (1990), 147–62, is a central theme of his *The Transformation of European Politics, 1763–1848* (New York, 1994). David A. Bell, *The First Total War: Napoleon's Europe and the Birth of Warfare as We Know It* (New York, 2007), presents Napoleon as the central figure in a developing European mentality affirming war's apocalyptic, redemptive character.

[6]   Philip Dwyer, 'The Two Faces of Prussian Foreign Policy: Karl August von Hardenberg as Minister for Foreign Affairs, 1804–1815', in *'Freier Gebrauch der Kraefte' Eine Bestandsaufnahme der Hardenberg-Forschung*, ed. T. Stamm-Kuhlmann (Munich, 2001), pp. 75–91.

the German Confederation. It required a second European revolution in 1849/49, the re-emergence of a French Empire and a near-tectonic shift in Austria's German policy, to redefine that role. Even then the dynamic initiatives of Chancellor Otto von Bismarck and Chief of Staff Helmuth von Moltke sought limited ends. However revolutionary the results of these conflicts appeared to observers and historians, the German Revolution of 1866–70 was more turnout than turnover, involving Austria's expulsion and France's exclusion as much as Prussia's expansion.[7]

Bismarck was convinced Germany had fought under near-optimal military and diplomatic conditions.[8] He remained correspondingly unsusceptible to 'victory disease': the temptation to overrate German capacity to shape events in Europe by direct intervention. Instead he presented the new Reich as a sated power, the fulcrum of Europe, with himself the honest broker – or more pragmatically the honest croupier. Between 1872 and 1887 Bismarck succeeded in bringing the Great Powers into a complex network of treaties whose common denominator was that no one could count on support for aggressive behaviour as defined by the others. That structure depended, however, on a level of commitment to the status quo beyond any statesman's ability to guarantee, and beyond Germany's capacity to control.[9]

The effect of Bismarck's dismissal in 1890 by the new Kaiser Wilhelm II is too often exaggerated. Bismarck was seventy-five, with a spectacularly unhealthy lifestyle; his active years were limited. Friedrich von Holstein, new *eminence grise* of the Foreign Office, and front man Bernhard von Buelow, who became Chancellor in 1900, initially sought with fair success to present Germany as the mechanic of Europe, relieving stress points, lubricating frictions and collecting a reasonable percentage for services rendered.[10] Initial successes at that level encouraged the overstretch of *Weltpolitik*.

Weltpolitik was anything but a coherent programme of economic or political imperialism. It is better described as the globalisation of the post-Bismarckian approach to international relations. So far as an aim existed, it was to confirm Germany's position not as hegemon, but as primary power, of Europe. German civilian and military leaders, however, were inexperienced in the nuances of world power politics. Theirs was the heritage of Prussia, a regional power with direct limited interests beyond its immediate frontiers. The result too often resembled

---

[7]   Dennis E. Showalter, *The Wars of German Unification* (London, 2004).

[8]   Eberhard Kolb, *Der Weg aus dem Krieg. Bismarcks Politik in Krieg und die Friedensanbahnung, 1870/71* (Munich, 1989).

[9]   Konrad Canis, *Bismarcks Aussenpolitik 1870 bis 1890: Aufstieg und Gefaehrdung* (Paderborn, 2004), is the best recent survey Still remarkably useful for its narrative of the Mediterranean Agreements is Joseph V. Fuller, *Bismarck's Diplomacy at its Zenith* (New York, 1922). Karl Otmar Arentin, *Bismarcks Aussenpolitik und der Berliner Kongress* (Wiesbaden, 1978), is a case study of the Chancellor's approach.

[10]   Norman Rich, *Friedrich von Holstein: Politics and Diplomacy in the Age of Bismarck*, Vol. II (Princeton, 1965).

Prussian policy between the death of Frederick II and the Battle of Jena: a search for cheap success at low risk. Nor did the Second Reich have statesmen able to play second-best hands into winners at an international poker table against reasonably competent rivals. What began around the turn of the century as a general sense that Britain stood in Germany's way led to an equally general sense of *Einkreisung*, encirclement, which in turn mushroomed from the vague nightmare of 1900 to the grim reality of 1914.[11]

Germany's behaviour in 1914 has been described in terms ranging from a deliberate war for hegemony, through a calculated risk, to a leap in the dark. But however malevolent the Reich's diplomatic intentions, they were for all practical purposes unaccompanied by preparations for utilising the victories the government expected the army to win. Germany fought the Great War without a purpose. Its aims were cobbled together on a constantly changing improvisational basis. Its strategy was a succession of increments. Its tactics were epitomised by Ludendorff's famous aphorism of 1918 – punch a hole and let the rest follow. The combination was a predictable recipe for disaster.[12]

From Frederick to Bismarck, Prussian grand strategy had been must successful when it accepted the axiom that victory depends on a definition of ends. Germany wanted normalcy in the years after 1918, but was unwilling to achieve it at the price of abandoning the illusions and delusions of the Great War.[13] The turn to Nazism that began in the late 1920s represented a 'flight forward', an effort to escape that cognitive dissonance, as much as a belief in the Nazis' promises to make things better. The Nazi Party has been compared by scholars to almost every possible human organisation, even medieval feudalism. The one adjective that cannot be applied is 'patriarchal'. Hitler's public persona was that of a leader, an elder brother, perhaps even an erotic symbol, but never a father. Change was the movement's flywheel: 'we march though we don't know where we are going'.[14]

That mantra moved German intention after 1918 steadily into what Heinrich Heine called the airy empire of dreams – or nightmares. If Germany's First World War lacked purpose, its Second World War was literally aimless; a product of Hitler's conviction that conflict was the iron law of history, and war was a total process to be waged ruthlessly and fanatically. Even the most blinkered British diplomats of the 1930s, the most desperate during the summer of 1940, understood viscerally that there was no room for negotiation of alliance with Hitler's Reich

---

[11]   Cf. Peter Winzen, *Buelows Weltmachtkonzept. Untersuchungen zur Fruehphase seiner Aussenpolitik* (Boppard, 1977); and the contributions to *Escape into War?: The Foreign Policy of Imperial Germany*, ed. Gregor Schoellgen (New York, 1990).

[12]   The best recent overview is Holger Herwig, *The First World War: Germany and Austria, 1914–1918* (London, 1997).

[13]   See Stephen Bruendel, *Volksgemeinschaft oder Volksstaat: Die "Ideen von 1914" und die Neuordnung von Deutschland im Ersten Weltkrieg* (Berlin, 2003).

[14]   Ian Kershaw, *The Hitler Myth: Image and Reality in the Third Reich* (Oxford, 1987).

except on temporary, instrumental bases. There was no room for reason, no room for calculation, because for Hitler there was only endless sacrifice in the ultimate arena, where individuals and races strove to the death in order that humanity might progress. By 1945 Germany had been effectively atomised. Its old orders were destroyed, displaced, discredited. The defeat of Nazism left only fragments, some to be discarded and others restored.[15]

Institutions

German institutions in the period under consideration developed by a process of integration through administration. The principalities of early modern Europe were frequently amalgams of otherwise discrete territories, under princes whose patents of sovereignty were too new or too questionable to bear close scrutiny.[16] A 'well ordered police state' was a major step up from ad hoc improvisations like those of Frederick William I, whose royal cane directly chastised Prussia's slackers and wrongdoers between 1715 and 1740.[17]

The Prussian state justified itself not by divine right in the manner of Louis XIV, or on prescriptive grounds of the kind later articulated by Edmund Burke, but in instrumental terms, with protection and stability being exchanged for loyalty and obedience. It was a contract no less firm for being unwritten, the Prussian kingdom was at pains even during the worst stages of the Seven Years War to affirm its side of the agreement. Once the war ended Frederick the Great bent every effort towards reconstruction as soon as possible and maintaining peace through deterrence.[18]

Social contract theory has been sufficiently intellectualised that it is easy to overlook the fact that all state systems, even in a twentieth century characterised by ideologies calling for unlimited commitment, depend fundamentally on some form of an if-then relationship based on the exchange of protection for service. The French Revolution nevertheless fundamentally challenged Prussia's contract paradigm. Contemporary critics suggested armies were inseparable from their social values. Reformers called for nurturing a sense of commitment that would actualise the latent loyalty Prussians felt for state and crown. The king's subjects would be transformed into Prussian citizens by a network of top-down reforms based on universal military service epitomising membership in the political

---

[15]   Ian Kershaw, *Hitler 1936–1945: Nemesis* (New York, 2000).

[16]   Peter Burke, *The Fabrication of Louis XIV* (New Haven, CT, 1992), is an excellent case study of the process of legitimating rule.

[17]   This concept is developed in Marc Raeff, *The Well-Ordered Police State: Social and Institutional Change through Law in the Germanies and Russia, 1600–1800* (New Haven, CT, 1983).

[18]   See T.C.W. Blanning, "Frederick the Great and Enlightened Absolutism", in *Enlightened Absolutism: Reform and Reformers in Later Eighteenth Century Europe*, ed. H.M. Scott (Ann Arbor, MI, 1990), pp. 265–88.

community. The reform movement remained significantly incomplete. But the army it created, operating within a coalition held together by the low common denominator of defeating Napoleon, was at the top of the list in fighting spirit.[19]

Integration again defined the military reforms of the 1860s. The Prussian parliament shared in general the government's position that significant military reform was necessary for Prussia to maintain its status (and for the increasing number of German nationalists, play a role in unifying Germany) in the face of Austrian and French hostility. Details of structure and service only defined the duelling ground. The crucial question was who would control the purse strings: Crown or Landtag. This was the wedge issue that escalated into a constitutional crisis that, for all its sound and fury, remained limited by mutual decision, and ended in compromise after the Battle of Koeniggraetz.[20]

The Bismarck/Moltke friction during the Wars of Unification is similarly best understood in a sound-and-fury context. Both men saw themselves in a collegial relationship: members of a cabinet system headed by the King, with any institutional superiority of one office over the other as being adjustable – or better said, subject to modification. Certainly Moltke did not regard Bismarck in the same way a French general of the Third Republic regarded the premier. A more appropriate parallel would be the tensions between the Departments of State and Defense in the US Cabinets during the Vietnam Wars, or after 9/11.[21]

Under the conditions of Bismarck's Reich no significant element of German society, whether defined in economic, political, or ethnic terms, felt itself sufficiently excluded or sufficiently victimised to reject its chances in the system. Bismarck's demonstrated virtuosity at manipulating interest groups and creating new ones, usually described in negative terms, offered hope as well. The middle classes had for decades been pushing into the foci of status and power – a process understood not as selling out but as buying in. Jews embraced the Reich with an enthusiasm that denied an anti-Semitism whose influence up to 1914 was in any case limited enough to seem trivial in retrospect. An embryonic working class had almost to be driven out of the Imperial consensus by the anti-Socialist legislation of the 1880s. Parliament's right to approve or disprove the military budget thus

---

[19] Dierk Walter, *Preussische Heeresreformen 1807–1870. Militaerische Innovation und der Mythos der "Roonischen Reform"* (Paderborn, 2003), pp. 143–66, 235–324, is state of the art in scholarship and reasoning on the first Era of Reform. Dennis E. Showalter, 'The Prussian Landwehr and its Critics, 1813–1819', *Central European History*, 4 (1971), 3–33, remains useful.

[20] Dieter Langewiesche, "Reich, Nation und Staat", *Historische Zeitschrift*, 254 (1992), 341–81; and L. Haupts, "Die liberale Regierung in Preussen in der Zeit der 'Neuen Aera,'" *Historische Zeitschrift*, 227 (1978), 45–85. Rolf Helfert, *Der preussische Liberalismus und die Heeresreform von 1860* (Bonn, 1989), and "Die Taktik preussischer Liberaler von 1858 bis 1862," *Militaergeschichtliche Mitteilungen*, 53 (1994), pp. 33–48, are the most detailed on the politics of reform.

[21] A point developed in Showalter, *Wars of German Unification*, p. 146 *passim*.

gave it a corresponding leverage impossible to ignore. The Second Reich may not have been a parliamentary state, but the political parties' increasingly sophisticated pursuit of tactical advantage through negotiation and manoeuvre was arguably moving Germany towards a de facto parliamentary system – if only as a short-term means of brokering the decisions finessed or postponed since 1871.[22]

Characteristic at this stage of the governments generated by democracy, nationalism and industrialisation since the 1780s was that no one was really sure how to run them effectively.[23] The United States had nearly self-destructed over an issue – slavery – which proved ultimately unsusceptible of compromise in the context of a federal system. For decades afterwards reunification was a manifestation of force majeure as well as mutual consent. That Bismarck's domestic political machine leaked oil did not make it worth trading in for a new one.

The events of 1866 and 1870–71 demonstrated beyond reasonable challenge the collective advantages of a state-of-the-art military system. Moreover, in a Second Reich lacking obvious common symbols of integration, after 1871 association with the military experience became central to German self-identification. The army never became the school of the nation and the hammer of socialism envisioned by right-wing idealists. For the mass of men in the ranks, however, military service did play a major role in certifying and affirming adulthood. The dramatic changes in German society since the 1790s had invalidated or marginalised many traditional male rites of passage. Once completed, military service increasingly defined maturity. Marriage, permanent employment, a place at the men's table in *Kneipe* or *Gasthaus* – all were associated, directly or indirectly, with a certificate of demobilisation.[24]

Integration through administration persisted throughout the Great War – and afterwards – under stresses even the most apocalyptic patrioteers had not expected. Wilhelm Deist describes the final collapse as a 'camouflaged strike', with the 'proletariat' of the war machine downing tools.[25] The emotions of most of the disaffected soldiers were better expressed in a joke created by American GIs in the Second World War. A suitably edited version is: 'When I get home, first I'll have a beer. Then I'll make love to my wife. Then I'll take off my pack.' The Revolution

---

[22]   Cf. Margaret Lavina Anderson, *Practicing Democracy. Elections and Political Culture in Imperial Germany* (Princeton, 2000); Jonathan Sperber, *The Kaiser's Voters: Electors and Elections in Inperial Germany* (Cambridge, 1997; and Wolfgang J. Mommsen, "A Delaying Compromise: the Division of Authority in the German Constitution of 1871", in *Imperial Germany 1867–1918*, trans. R. Deveson (London, 1995), pp. 20–40.

[23]   Mommsen, "Society and State in Europe in the Age of Liberalism, 1870–1890" in *Imperial Germany 1867–1918*, pp. 57–74.

[24]   Ute Frevert, *A Nation in Barracks: Modern Germany, Military Conscription, and Civil Society*, trans. A. Boreham and D. Brueckenhaus (New York, 2004),

[25]   Wilhelm Deist, "Verdeckter Militaerstreik im Jahre 1918?" in *Krieg des kleinen Mannes. Eine Militaergeschichte von unten*, ed. W. Wette (Munich, 1992). pp. 146–67

of 1918 was 'incomplete' only in a Marxist context.[26] A political revolution, a turnout rather than a turnover, it was at bottom a response to the Second Reich's breach of contract.

Political reconfiguration seemed a reasonable means for achieving social and economic change on a compromise basis in the context of a national unity whose alleged violation by the Versailles Treaty remained among the Weimar Republic's deeply festered grievances. When one reconstruction failed, a second seemed perfectly rational. Never have a people fought better in a worse cause than did the Germans between 1939 and 1946. A primary reason was National Socialism's promise, from its inception to its destruction, not merely to resolve but to transcend the divisions that seemed to defy Republican, and by extension democratic, solution. [27] Hitler, after all, promised change: 'give me ten years and you will not recognise Germany'. It took twelve, but he kept his word.

Instruments

Operational implementation of the German way of war, reduced to its essence, involves applying total force in limited contexts for limited objectives. Failure to comprehend this point reflects a tendency, particularly in the Anglo-American intellectual community, to equate limited war with limited force and – particularly since Vietnam – with open-ended commitments. In principle the German way of war kept these poles widely separated. However extreme might be the use of means, the ends remained circumscribed and subject to negotiation. And the means themselves were calculated, again at least in principle, to restrict the demands made on society as a whole.[28]

The Soviets considered war a science. To Americans it is a management problem; to the French an intellectual exercise. The Germans understood war as an art form. Though requiring basic craft skills, war defied reduction to rules and principles. Its mastery demanded study and reflection, but depended ultimately on two virtually untranslatable concepts: *Fingerspitzengefuehl* and *Tuchfuehling*. The closest English equivalent is the more sterile phrase 'situational awareness'. The German concept incorporates as well the sense of panache – the difference, in horseman's language, between a hunter and a hack – or in contemporary terms, the difference between a family saloon and a high-performance sports car.

---

[26]   Dietrich Orlow, "1918/19: A German Revolution," *German Studies Review*, 5 (1982), 187–203.

[27]   See Ruediger Graf, *Die Zukunft der Weimarer Republik: Krisen und Zukunftsneigungen in Deutschland, 1918–1933* (Munich, 2008). Useful as well are William Brustein, *The Logic of Evil: The Social Origins of the Nazi Party, 1925–1933* (New Haven, 1996); and Juergen W. Falter, *Hitlers Waehler* (Munich, 1991).

[28]   Dennis E. Showalter, "Total War for Limited Objectives: An Interpretation of German Grand Strategy", in *Grand Strategies in War and Peace*, ed. Paul Kennedy (New Haven, 1991), pp.105–23.

The German way of war was rooted in a Prussian state located in the centre of Europe, ringed by potential enemies, lacking both natural boundaries and natural resources. Frederick the Great systematised and codified a century's hard-bought experience: Prussia must fight short, decisive wars – partly to conserve assets, partly to convince the losers to make peace and keep it; partly to deter other potential challenges. This meant developing a forward-loaded military system, an army able to go to war from a standing start with its effectiveness highest in the beginning. It meant that nothing should be wasted on secondary concerns. That wasted time – the one thing above all Prussia did not possess. It meant not merely seeking battle, but holding nothing back once the fighting started while simultaneously minimising the randomness of combat.

These requirements encouraged a tactical orientation. That stands in direct contrast to the United States, whose fundamental military problems since at least the Mexican War have been on the level of strategy and grand strategy: where to go and how to sustain the effort. Actual fighting has been a secondary concern – which is why so many of America's first battles have been disasters.[29] Prussia, on the other hand, was unlikely to recover from an initial defeat. This was the lesson and the legacy of Frederick the Great.[30]

Its reverse side was the sterility of victories won in vacuums. Prussia by the end of the Seven Years War was on the point of conquering itself to death. Napoleon's career as general and emperor offered an even clearer example of war without purpose that became war without end. In response, by the 1820s, Carl von Clausewitz argued that limited conflicts were not merely a manifestation of friction, the inevitable grit in any machine run by humans. Limited war occurred instead because of the protagonists' intentions and wills. Far from being the modification of an ideal, limited war was as valid on its own terms as absolute war. Each specific conflict must be shaped by its motives. Violence expressed diplomacy; it did not replace it.[31]

In that context, Prussian theorists, commanders and policymakers began developing a second, higher level of warmaking: the operational. 'Operational art' is usually defined in general terms as the handling of large forces in the context of a theatre of war. The German approach emphasised speed and daring: 'war of movement.' This involved manoeuvring to strike as hard a blow as possible,

---

[29]   The underlying theme of *America's First Battles, 1776–1965*, ed. C.E. Heller and W.A. Stoft (Lawrence, KS, 1986).

[30]   These points are developed in the author's *The Wars of Frederick the Great*; and in Christopher Duffy, *Frederick the Great: A Military Life* (London, 1985).

[31]   See Peter Paret, *Clausewitz and the State*, rev. edn (Princeton, 1985); Martin van Creveld, "The Eternal Clausewitz", *The Journal of Strategic Studies* 9 (1986), *Special Issue on Clausewitz and Modern Strategy*, ed. M. Handel, pp. 35–50, is another perceptive overview. Raymond Aron's *Penser la guerre: Clausewitz*, 2 vols (Paris, 1976), concedes Clausewitz's acceptance of limited war as a *Ding an sich*, but the speculative, metaphysical nature of the work as a whole nevertheless invites the reader into realms of the absolute.

from a direction as unexpected as possible. It depended on, and in turn fostered, particular institutional characteristics: a flexible command system, high levels of aggressiveness, an officer corps with a common perspective on warmaking. The whole was epitomised by military writer Friedrich von Bernhardi in 1912 – win a victory as rapidly as possible by concentrating decisive force at the decisive spot, then exploit it with the utmost energy.[32]

The Second Reich had not been founded in adversity. Bismarck had not promised blood, toil, tears and sweat. The army had delivered unification at relatively low cost. No one could be quite certain how Germany's citizens would react to the demands of 'hard war', to say nothing of total war. Moltke, who remained Chief of Staff until 1888, increasingly described the best practical method of waging modern war as prophylactic: keeping conflicts short by a combination of quick victory and prompt negotiation.[33]

The army in turn accepted the deteriorating international position defined by civil political authority as a given, and accepted the task of preparing for a war that its own calculations suggested might well be unpredictable, uncontrollable and ultimately unwinnable Stig Foerster describes the German army as marching 'fully conscious into catastrophe'. It is more accurate to say that the German army marched fully conscious into high risk, with no end-game in prospect. When War Minister Erich von Falkenhayn allegedly declared 'even if we go under, it was a good run', he aphorised a shift in the German way of war that implied a redefinition of the concept.[34] As industrialisation and bureaucratisation enabled increasing armies' size, as technology facilitated their concentration in the theatre of war, the new German Empire kept pace. In 1914 its armies took the field without a hitch. At the other end of the military spectrum, Germany boasted Europe's best-trained infantry and its most effective artillery. What it lacked from start to finish was the mobility necessary to complete strategic movements like the great sweep through Belgium, and to develop the tactical victories won on the battlefield.

That dimension was added as a response to a Versailles Treaty designed to prevent Germany from ever again waging war effectively. Instead, under Hans von Seeckt, Germany began developing an army able to fight outnumbered and win. The Reichswehr, Seeckt insisted, must dictate the conditions of battle by taking the initiative. It was on the offensive that the superiority of troops and commanders achieved the greatest relative effect. The leader's responsibility was above all to maintain pace and tempo. Boldness was the first rule; flexibility the second. Doctrine and training alike emphasised encounter battles: two forces

---

[32]   Robert Citino, *The German Way of War, From the Thirty Years War to the Third Reich* (Lawrence, KS, 2005), develops this theme brilliantly.

[33]   Stig Foerster, 'Facing "People's War:" Moltke the Elder and Germany's Military Options after 1871', *Journal of Strategic Studies*, 10 (1987), 209–30.

[34]   Cf. Stig Foerster, "Der deutsche Generalstab und die Illusion des Kurzen Krieges, 1871–1914", *Militaergeschichtliche Mitteilungen*, 51 (1995), pp 61–96; and Terence Zuber, *Inventing the Schlieffen Plan: German War Planning 1871–1914* (New York, 2002).

meeting unexpectedly and engaging in what amounted to a melee – a melee in which training and flexibility had a chance to compensate for numerical and material inferiority.

By 1939 massed formations of tanks working in close cooperation with aircraft not only proved able to break open enemy positions; they could break out as well, moving forward more than a hundred miles a day, linking up far behind enemy lines in battles of encirclement that, taken on their own terms, remain among history's great military achievements. It is correspondingly ironic that the mobility that made the victories possible encouraged the intellectual and operational overstretch that confirmed the military's enmeshment in a Third Reich which insisted nothing was impossible. Therefore no limits were necessary.[35]

Britain

Intentions

The base dates for the Anglo/British and Prussian/German concepts of war relate to the same phenomenon: the shrinking of Europe. It was 1640 when Frederick William became the head of a state previously tucked safely away from the tides of full-scale war and now ravaged to the point of dissolution, It was 1688 when England experienced its last successful invasion after five centuries of back and forth across the English Channel and the Scottish border. Strategically England was at best a 'demi-island'. The Channel offered nothing like 'free security'. It could readily be crossed in force. Nor was England alone on its 'sceptered isle'. Far from the 'Celtic fringe' of later historical myth, Scotland was a consistent major threat, Ireland a persistent running sore, and both unconquerable in practical terms.[36]

English policy from at least the time of the Tudors correspondingly accepted – albeit not always willingly – that England's first line of defence lay across the choke point of the Low Countries: Flanders and the emerging Dutch Republic. It was from that region's ports that a prospective invasion was most threatening – and most readily deterred, or in the best case prevented entirely.

The best means of keeping those ports in friendly hands was a forward policy on the Continent. The glacis sought was initially modest: on the scale of that 'Calais' Queen Mary declared was written on her heart. The expanding scale of European warfare, however, called increasingly for its expansion. It was increasingly clear

---

[35]   See Dennis E. Showalter, *Hitler's Panzers: The Lightning Attacks that Revolutionized Warfare* (New York, 2009); Azar Gat, *British Armour Theory and the Panzer Arm; Revising the Revisionists* (London, 2000); and James S. Corum, *The Roots of Blitzkrieg* (Lawrence, KS, 1992).

[36]   *The Civil Wars: A Military History of England, Scotland, and Ireland 1638–1660*, ed. J.P. Kenyon, J.H Ohlmeyer and J.S. Morrell (Oxford, 1998).

that the long-term security of the Low Countries depended on stability in northern and western Germany, from which Flanders could readily be enveloped and overrun. Directly securing and maintaining this kind of forward position required permanent levels of naval and military force no British administration could cajole or compel, even after the 1703 Act of Union reduced to a shadow the historic threat from Scotland. The alternative was not Continental *commitment* but Continental *involvement* on a continuing basis.[37]

For much of the eighteenth century Britain's preferred partner was Austria, and Britain's preferred policies were oriented towards sustaining Habsburg power in the Holy Roman Empire.[38] Upsetting the balance of power in Germany was the first step to placing Britain's Continental position, then the island itself, in mortal danger.

Particular imperatives of its alliance policies led Britain ever further afield; to the Mediterranean, the Baltic,and the Balkans. The complex juggling involved in pursuing objectives that could easily become mutually exclusive required insight, ruthlessness and luck. Britain had all three from 1688 to 1763 – plus a restraining consciousness of the limits of British power.[39] The War of the League of Augsburg, the Wars of the Spanish and Austrian Succession, and the Seven Years War each involved leading and sustaining international coalitions against France. Britain's primary cause of success was the common understanding that close, continued attention to the European balance of power was the linchpin of British security and liberty.

At the same time, Britain strove to maintain and strengthen the cohesion of an external empire that, while a policy end in itself, also provided the means to sustain successful Continental involvement, both directly and as a drive belt of Britain's banking system. Increasingly France reacted negatively to growing frictions in North America and India. Austria sought to distance itself from a Britain appearing to take its Habsburg connection for granted. Britain carried water on both shoulders, until the Diplomatic Revolution of 1756 removed both buckets.

An alliance with Fredrick the Great proved a poor substitute – not least because Frederick had too many diplomatic and military troubles of his own.[40] The German theatre of the Seven Years War amounted to a dead end. On the other hand, where Britain stood alone, from Plassey to Quebec Britain prospered. It was more than isolationism and hubris that led Britain to turn away from Continental involvement

---

[37]   The theme of Brendan Simms' seminal *Three Victories and a Defeat. The Rise and Fall of the First British Empire* (London, 2007).

[38]   Derek Mc Kay, *Allies of Convenience: Diplomatic Relations between Great Britain and Austria, 1714–1719* (New York, 1986), despite its limited time-frame, establishes the highly contingent nature of the relationship on both sides.

[39]   Simms, *Three Victories and a Defeat*, p. 673.

[40]   Karl W. Schweitzer, *Frederick the Great, William Pitt, and Lord Bute: Anglo-Prussian Relations, 1756–1763* (New York, 1991).

– until the American Revolution found the kingdom not merely isolated, but confronting a Europe with old scores to pay. The result was what Brendan Sims calls 'the greatest and most irrevocable strategic disaster in British history'.[41]

These are strong words. There is a correspondingly strong case that no amount of domestic mobilisation, no increase in naval or military effectiveness, not even greater financial leverage, would have averted the catastrophe American independence represented for the First British Empire. While their motives may be debated, British ministers turned their back on Europe; Europe not only left them to their fate but greased the skids.[42]

Britain's recovery depended in part on reorganising its global position; at first informally by re-establishing the new United States as a major commercial partner, then by conquest and governance elsewhere, beginning at the turn of the century. The Second British Empire constructed in the nineteenth century was, however, more expensive, less strategically relevant and less profitable than its predecessor. While not exactly acquired in Sir John Seely's 'fit of absent-mindedness', forestalling actual, potential and imaginary rivals did play a significant role in specific cases. So did 'magpieing' – picking up a piece of territory for no obvious reason beyond its availability.[43]

In contrast Britain sustained its Continental involvement during the Revolutionary/Napoleonic Wars as though its existence were at stake – which was in fact the case. Britain was the diplomatic and financial lodestone of coalition after coalition. The Iberian Peninsula may have been the only region of Europe where Britain could deploy and support more than token forces over a long period of time. But the Peninsular War was significant by draining French resources, proving the French were not invincible, and not least showing British good faith, in convincing Austria, Russia and Prussia, to defy the Emperor even in high-risk circumstances.[44] As for the Hundred Days, one can do no better than to quote the Duke of Wellington: 'I don't think it would have done had I not been there.'

British intentions regarding the Continent did not change after 1815. A Continental glacis remained a fundamental interest – perhaps *the* fundamental interest. The reconfigured European political order called, however, for a different approach. The Congress of Vienna, by creating the Kingdom of the Netherlands, did much of Britain's work for it; the Concert of Europe was expected to facilitate the rest. Belgium's breakaway in 1830 removed one of the props, but though the treaties guaranteeing the neutrality of the new state of Belgium were not optimal, they were workable. Diplomacy backed by money and force filled the

---

[41]   Simms, *Three Victories and a Defeat*, p. 664.

[42]   R.W. Tucker and D.C. Hendrickson, *The Fall of the First British Empire: Origins of the War of American Independence* (Baltimore, 1983).

[43]   John P. Halstead, *The Second British Empire: Trade, Philanthropy, and Good Government, 1820–1890* (New York, 1983), explains much in its title alone.

[44]   Cf. Rory Muir, *Britain and the Defeat of Napoleon* (New Haven, 1996); and Charles Esdaile. *The Peninsular War: A New History* (London, 2002).

gap reasonably. In an age of growing communication within states, warships (Palmerston to the contrary) could send messages as well as soldiers. Bankers could be the best messengers of all.[45]

They were a plausible alternative in a context of Continental armies that increased exponentially in size after 1816, and exponentially in mobility with the midcentury development of railway networks. Initially the Prussian aspects of the 'German Question' were of secondary interest to Whitehall.[46] Successive British foreign secretaries might have reason to question Bismarck's insistence that the new Germany wanted only peace and stability in Europe. The successes of the German army, however, acted as a deterrent to expressing doubt by challenge.[47] The 1871 proto-technothriller *The Battle of Dorking*, with its depiction of a near-future Britain prostrate before a German invasion, drew loud protests from critics who described the scenario impossible as long as the Royal Navy kept the seas, and some complaint as well from land-warfare specialists who declared that large-scale invasion under modern conditions was by no means as easy as *Dorking* implied.[48] What was obvious was the impossibility of reversing the scenario: projecting British land power onto the Continent in the face of a hostile Germany, on even the scale of the Napoleonic Wars, without making precisely the kind of foreign commitments successive British governments were determined to avoid – or without developing an army sized and equipped beyond any feasible political or fiscal possibilities. In short, however deep might run underlying Anglo-German antagonisms, common sense dictated underplaying, indeed submerging, them in diplomatic contexts for the foreseeable future.[49]

That approach held well into the beginning of the twentieth century. The development of the Anglo-French–Russian entente reflected to a degree Britain's concern for directly securing its imperial interests, as opposed to structuring a

---

[45]   Best on the Concert's heyday is the last third of Paul W. Schroeder's magisterial *The Transformation of European Politics, 1762–1848* (Oxford, 1994). And Niall Ferguson, *The Cash Nexus: Money and Power in the Modern World, 1700–2000* (New York, 2001), almost makes international banking fun.

[46]   Anselm Doering Manteuffel, *Vom Wiener Kongress zur Pariser Konferenz: England, die deutscheFrage, und das Maechtesystem, 1815–1856* (Goettingen, 1991).

[47]   Cf. Klaus Hildebrand, "Grossbritannien und die deutsche Reichsgruendung", in *Europa und die Reichsgruendung*, ed. E. Kolb, *Historische Zeitschrift, Beiheft* 6 (Munich, 1980), 9–62; Peter Peel, *British Public Opinion and the Wars of German Unification, 1864–1871* (College Park, MD, 1981); and Michael Pratt, "A Fallen Idol: The Impact of the Franco-Prussian War on the Perception of Germany by British Intellectuals", *International History Review*, 7 (1985), 543–75.

[48]   I.F. Clarke, *Voices Prophesying War*, rev. edn (Oxford, 1992), pp. 27ff.

[49]   Paul Kennedy, *The Rise of the Anglo-German Antagonism, 1860–1914* (London, 1980).

future confrontation with Germany.[50] British consideration of a near-future Continental war saw Britain's primary roles as financial and economic. For Germany to expect British neutrality in the face of a German invasion of Belgium was a bigger gamble than the Schlieffen Plan itself. And yet, Britain did take its own good time to clarify its intentions. As late as 3 August 1914, one Liberal MP declared himself unwilling to support a European war because of a few German regiments in a corner of Belgian territory.[51]

The wisdom of Britain's decision has been challenged ever since, most recently and persuasively by Niall Ferguson. In *The Pity of War*, he eloquently describes a victorious Germany presiding benevolently over a peaceful, prosperous Continent much like today's European Union, relating harmoniously with a Britain spared the hecatombs of the trenches and their consequences.[52] Apart from the familiar observations that the Second Reich was nothing like the Federal Republic, and Kaiser Wilhelm and Helmut Kohl resembled each other only in waistlines, Ferguson's point highlights the centrality of Continental involvement to the British way in war. From 1914 to 1918 Britain indeed 'put it to the touch / to win or lose it all' – in the seventeenth-century words of the Marquis of Montrose.

In the inter-war years British policy followed a pattern of maintaining the glacis by any feasible means, from working through the League of Nations to signing a naval treaty with Nazi Germany.[53] And in the end the last great Imperialist, Winston Churchill, sacrificed the Empire rather than abandon Europe – or, better said, rather than abandon Britain to the fate awaiting it without the European connection.

Institutions

Britain's modern way in war was built around two institutions, parliament and banks, and the synergies between them. 'Parliament' stands here as much for a state of mind as a way of government. British society as it developed from the early modern era was voluntary. English, Scots and Irish, its 'little platoons' defied absorption into a Hobbesian Leviathan or its Continental simulacra.[54] Successive central governments learned that lesson or paid a price that could be capital. In particular the execution of Charles I was a seismic shock and a seismic warning: governing in the British Isles required special talents.

---

[50]   Keith Wilson, *The Policy of the Entente: Essays on the Determination of British Foreign Policy 1904–1914* (Cambridge, 1985).

[51]   Trevor Wilson, *The Myriad Faces of War* (Cambridge, 1986), pp. 33–34.

[52]   Niall Ferguson, *The Pity of War* (London, 1999).

[53]   Gustav Schmidt, *The Politics and Economics of Appeasement: British Foreign Policy in the 1930s*, trans. J. Bennett-Rutte (Leamington Spa, 1986), is a detailed treatment of a familiar subject by an excellent German scholar.

[54]   See the case studies in *An Ungovernable People? The English and their Law in the Seventeenth and Eighteenth Centuries*, ed. J. Brewer and J.A. Styles (New Brunswick, NJ, 1980).

Charles II and William of Orange each understood this in his own way. James II learned the lesson in exile. English triumphalists discovered as well – albeit more slowly – that the Act of Union and the Treaty of Limerick depended for implementation on compromise – the kind of compromise where the Scots eventually provided the brains, the English provided the character, and the Irish the muscle.[55]

That is more than a bar-room aphorism. The British Isles were by Continental standards about as difficult as the Balkans to govern at everyday levels. One of the major factors in the Royal Navy's tactical successes in the later Age of Sail was the sheer ferocity of its boarding parties.[56] The charge was no less significant than the volley in the Peninsula and at Waterloo.

Cooperation trumped confrontation in Westminster as well. Without engaging in detail the still-growing body of specialist literature, it is reasonable to general that the 'interests' developing in an increasingly complex society overlapped and interfaced with each other, and with the political parties, the administration, and the courts. Patronage and preferment, grants and bribes, greased the wheels. Ideas were important as rallying points and foci for debate. Their power and appeal were, however, checked because – as in Germany a century later – no significant group was sufficiently unhappy with the game's rules to stand aside and risk being dealt out.[57]

This pattern of cooperation in turn made possible the banking system that financed Britain's Empire and its wars. The problem facing Continental governments was less the lack of money than the capacity to raise money. In a pre-industrial, pre-Marxist era, the serious sources of funding were taxes and loans. Both require participation for anything but minimum results. Participation requires trust. The Bank of England was founded as an emergency measure to facilitate government borrowing. But regular repayment of principal and interest facilitated a climate of confidence that in turn encouraged a general climate of credit. In that context war could literally be good business, sometimes in defeat as well as victory.[58]

Britain's developing finance system enabled making loans and paying subsidies to Continental states less economically fortunate or more militarily threatened – a forerunner in many ways of the Second World War lend-lease programme. Its underpinnings of voluntarism and confidence underwrote the Royal Navy. N.A.M. Rodger makes a convincing argument that its construction and maintenance was so complicated and so comprehensive it could only be accomplished by consensus:

---

[55]   For a far more sophisticated treatment see Linda Colley, *Britons: Forging the Nation, 1707–1837* (London, 1992).

[56]   A point established in Roy Adkins, *Trafalgar – The Biography of a Battle* (London, 2005).

[57]   Clyve Jones, *Parties and Management in Parliament, 1660–1784* (Leicester, 1984), is a workmanlike survey.

[58]   Still standard on the subject is John Brewer, *The Sinews of Power: War, Money, and the English State, 1688–1783* (London, 1988).

voting taxes, lending money, offering skills. A state could raise an army. It took a society to support a navy.[59] And British society was likely to support a navy because ships of the line could not be put on wheels, while soldiers could be marched anywhere. Thus the army's budget had to be authorised annually – an unmistakable thumb on its jugular.

With all that, Continental involvement was probably the most consistent source of strain between parliament and administration, perhaps even between government and people, in the period covered by this essay. Public interest might favor a glacis; private affinity tended towards isolation and imperialism. The 'Hanoverian question' created when George I assumed the throne in 1714 was a bone in the throat of successive governments for three-quarters of a century.[60] Britain was not an immediate participant in the coalitions against Revolutionary France, and the Peninsular commitment was never deeply popular. From Wellington's point of view at least, it appeared at times as though the Whig opposition was willing to surrender de facto to Napoleon if they could retain their property.

In that context money and profit were the o-rings of British policy. Guineas supplied on favourable terms replaced gunpowder whenever possible.[61] Global trade and domestic industrialisation boosted national income to a point where sometimes, even total war could seem good business. In fact for the century after Waterloo, cooler – or more pragmatic – perspectives prevailed. In European contexts, diplomacy became the conduct of war by other means – particularly as the post-Napoleonic Empire's profit ratios were too low to underwrite military power on a continental scale. Sustaining the glacis directly, through alliance systems underwritten by a potential military presence, gave way to sustaining it by leverage: the Concert of Europe underwritten by industry and finance.

When the Concert devolved into a jazz orchestra, Britain played along – sometimes stepping out for a solo, as in the case of the South African War of 1898–1902, but more often as part of the ensemble. The Congress of Berlin and the Mediterranean Agreements indicate that what was called 'splendid isolation' for public consumption resembled more the jazzman's understanding that harmony depends on cooperation. Britain's European policy in the second half of the nineteenth century was in practice far more bipartisan than some of the more spirited Parliamentary debates on specifics might suggest.[62] The familiar turn-of-the-century image of Britain as a 'weary titan' seeking surcease from global burdens similarly invites reconsideration. The efforts to strengthen formal

---

[59]   N.A.M. Rodger, *The Safeguard of the Sea* (London, 1997), pp. 430ff.

[60]   Jeremy Black, *The Continental Commitment: Britain, Hanover, and Interventionism, 1714–1793* (London, 2003).

[61]   John Sherwig, *Guineas and Gunpowder: British Foreign Aid in the Wars with Francem, 1793–1815* (Cambridge, MA, 1969).

[62]   See particularly E. David Steele, *Lord Salisbury: A Political Biography* (London, 2001). Also useful is Joerg Femers, *Deutsch-Britische Optionen. Untersuchungen zur internationalen Politik in der spaeten Bismaeck-Aera (1879–1890)* (Trier, 2006).

ties to the 'settlement colonies', the Dreadnought revolution in naval affairs, the fundamental Haldane Reforms of the army, alike enjoyed levels of political and public support that indicate a high degree of commitment to European affairs and European balances.

Any doubts about the issue are best dissipated by considering Britain's casualty lists in the Great War – and those of Canada, Australia and New Zealand and India as well. The economically minded might address Britain's transformation to a net debtor nation, and its broad social and psychological ramifications. Students of political history can study a negative: the absence of serious discussion – arguably, indeed, any discussion at all – in House or Cabinet of a negotiated peace, a separate peace, or any of the other behaviours the rest of Europe was prone to ascribe to 'perfidious Albion'.[63]

The inter-war years reflected Britain's continued commitment to maintaining a Continental glacis. The League of Nations replaced the Concert of Europe as the preferred instrument.[64] But concern for de facto French primacy was manifested in a sympathetic approach to Mussolini's Italy despite its overt Mediterranean ambitions. It showed during the 1920s in public and political arguments for bringing Weimar Germany into the European community, and during the 1930s in a consistent, persistent policy of negotiation and conciliation towards the Third Reich.[65] The major difference was financial. It was not pacifism that restricted British security spending with the Ten Year Rule and its equivalents. It was inability to fund anything resembling convincing armed diplomacy in face of the absolute threats mounted by fascism.[66]

The Second World War completed the circle. More than at any time since Marlborough's day, Britain's focus was across the Channel. Only this time there was no Empire, no banking system, to fund resistance beyond a few months. The solution came in the form of a Special Relationship with the United States. Ironically, America assumed Britain's traditional role by financing and equipping an increasing percentage of the joint war effort. By 1945 more US than British tanks were in the army's front-line service. The Royal Naval Air Service was essentially dependent on US aircraft (and, in passing, New Zealand crews).

---

[63] See above all David French's trilogy: *British Economic and Strategic Planning, 1905–1915* (London, 1982); *British Strategy and War Aims, 1914–1915* (London, 1988); and *The Strategy of the Lloyd George Coalition, 1916–1918* (London, 1995). Adrian Gregory, *The Last Great War: British Society and the First World War* (Cambridge, 2008), is an excellent starting point from a home-front perspective.

[64] George W. Egerton, *Great Britain and the Creation of the League of Nations: Strategy, Politics, and International Organization, 1914–1919* (Chapel Hill, NC, 1978).

[65] On this see most recently Ian Kershaw, *Making Friends with Hitler: Lord Londonderry, the Nazis, and the Road to War* (New York, 2004).

[66] But for an alternate perspective, see David Edgerton's chapter 'The Military-Industrial Complex in the Interwar Years', in his *Warfare State: Britain, 1920–1970* (Cambridge, 2006), pp. 15–58.

The USA paralleled Britain in the Napoleonic Era and the Great War as well by deploying relatively late to the fighting fronts even after Pearl Harbor.

The most significant point for purposes of this essay, however, is the fundamental Anglo-American agreement: not merely 'Europe first' but 'Continental priority'. The principle of invasion was never seriously questioned in London – only the nature and the timing. And much of that debate is best understood as involving tactics and leverage.[67] The vestigial imperialism and unsustainable globalism of the immediate post-war years do not hide the numbers. For a half-century Britain's primary military presence has been on the Continent; its primary weapons systems designed for European deployment. Discussions, even in the heyday of Duncan Sandys's term as Minister of Defence, have involved percentages rather than principles.

Institutions

The British army has so often been characterised as a projectile fired by the Royal Navy that its actual modern origins have become obscured. The army as it developed in the Age of Marlborough was essentially an instrument for projecting power into 'near Europe': the glacis of the Low Countries.[68] That was the only possibility for a large-scale, sustained forward military policy. Not until the middle of the eighteenth century did the number of ships available for troop movements, and their carrying capacities, increase to the point where European-style land forces could be sustained in anything but limited numbers. Such commitment also required significantly developed infrastructures at the far end: something on the scale of Britain's North American colonies, without the disease and climate factors that kept Caribbean garrisons in balance the hard way. Even in India, for most of the eighteenth century British troops, Crown's or Company's, were far outnumbered by locally raised sepoys.[69]

Operationally British cavalry and infantry stood at the top of Europe's lists in the Low Countries and along the Rhine during the Age of Marlborough. British logistics were state of the art, with the Duke setting an example of concern for administration. In secondary theatres as well, particularly an Iberian Peninsula where small armies were beaten and large ones starved, British expeditionary forces managed to strike a balance between performance and sustainability, especially during the War of the Spanish Succession.[70]

---

[67] A fresh perspective on a familiar topic is Andrew Roberts, *Masters and Commanders: How Roosevelt, Churchill, Marshall and Alanbrooke Won the War in the West* (London, 2008).

[68] Roger B. Manning, *An Apprenticeship in Arms: The Origins of the British Army 1585–1702* (New York, 2006).

[69] For a fresh perspective, see D.P. Ramachandran, *Empire's First Soldiers* (New Delhi, 2008).

[70] David Chandler, *The Art of Warfare in the Age of Marlborough* (London, 1976).

The issue was not operational effectiveness but cost-effectiveness. Armies raised and sustained by British methods were significantly more expensive than their Continental counterparts. The growing scale of war, numerically and geographically, made keeping up directly a politically and economically questionable process. Committing small forces ad hoc had less and less effect. 'Descents' – for example, putting landing parties of a few hundred men ashore somewhere on the French coast – became so vulnerable to local defences and countermeasures that the technique was abandoned. Maintaining an effective British presence in western Germany during the Seven Years War ratcheted the budget ever higher to no better end than a continuing stalemate.[71]

Even before the lure of India and the demands of North America drew down available forces in the third quarter of the eighteenth century, it seemed the better part of wisdom to avoid or minimise the commitment of British ground troops in Europe. That policy seemed justified by the embarrassing performance of the British contingents in the Low Countries in 1793–94.[72] The Coruna campaign of 1809 was a heroic disaster. The occupation of Walcheren Island in the same year was an epidemiological one: for the rest of the Napoleonic Wars the regiments unfortunate enough to have been sent there suffered collectively debilitated health.[73]

The British army that fought in Spain was at the opposite end from Prussia of the military reform movements generated by the Revolutionary/Napoleonic Wars. The British response to the French challenge might best be described as a comprehensive overhaul, maximising the positive qualities and advantages of an eighteenth-century-model long-service professional force without essentially changing its matrix. The results were good enough to decide the Battle of Waterloo. They were fundamentally out of step with the much larger, conscription-based, forces that emerged in Congress Europe – and the much larger budgets that sustained them.

Keeping pace directly with the new Continental order involved social, political, and economic costs unthinkable in the emerging Britain of Bright and Cobden, Jeremy Bentham and John Stuart Mill. In Wellington's phrase, the next best solution was to put the soldiers out of sight in a burgeoning second British Empire. There they remained until the Crimean War highlighted the consequences. Militarily the Crimean campaign is actually better understood in traditional Imperial rather than modern European contexts. A substantial expeditionary force landed in the middle of nowhere was likely to need more than steamships and telegraphs. It would

---

[71] Reginald Savory, *His Britannic Majesty's Army in Germany during the Seven years' War* (Oxford, 1966).

[72] G.J. Evelyn, "'I learned what one ought not to do": The British Army in Flanders and Holland, 1793–95', in *The Road to Waterloo. The British Army and the Struggle Against Revolutionary France, 1793–1815*, ed. A.J. Guy (London, 1990), pp. 16–22.

[73] Gordon Bond, *The Grand Expedition: The British Invasion of Holland, 1809* (Athens, GA, 1979).

have to bring its own infrastructure – or develop it in a hurry, under pressure. The British learning curve was higher than is generally understood or accepted.[74] The damage, however, was done in the first months. For a half-century considerations of direct military involvement on the Continental glacis were haunted by memories of Scutari's hospitals and Balaklava's harbour.

The changing demands of Empire contributed as well to changing the nature and disposition of Britain's army. Above all the experiences of 1857–58 in India called for a massive increase in the size of the subcontinent's British garrison. Combined with related colonial expansion in Egypt and South Africa, the result was to make the British army, for the first time in its history, a genuine Imperial force, configured for internal security and power projection in a global context. The home establishment was bits and pieces, able to produce little more than an army corps for field service and much of that improvised. That pattern persisted with the Haldane reforms. Service was voluntary; cost per man was the highest in Europe. The Territorial Force was intended for home defence; the six divisions of the Expeditionary Force were projected as deployable anywhere in the world – or the Empire – they might be needed.[75] Recent research has suggested a similar pattern developing in the Royal Navy, with home defence eventually based on light forces and submarines, with the major surface units, successors to Sir John Fisher's original battle cruisers, playing a world role.[76]

In that context the reshaping of the British Army within four years into the mass, Continent-oriented force of 1918 must count as one of history's greatest military revolutions in every sense of that much-abused term. Its success owed much to a fundamental pragmatism that defined doctrine in terms of what works.[77] But in a general context it is not amiss to suggest that the British army's learning curve was structured and sustained by Continental experience more than two centuries old. The links from Uncle Toby and Corporal Trim to Old Bill and Young Bert were close and comprehensive. Even the terrain was familiar.

On one hand the Great War seemed to have demonstrated beyond question that Britain's survival as a Great Power, perhaps its survival at all, depended on its overseas connections. The mandate system, especially Palestine and Iraq, provided unfamiliar challenges. Even on familiar ground like India, the British army found more demanding responsibilities. The requirements of Empire diverged from those of modern war to such a degree that an increasing body of professional literature advocated specialisation. This solution was, however, consistently rejected by a

---

[74]   See Hew Strachan, *Wellington's Legacy: the Reform of the British Army, 1830–54* (Manchester, 1984).

[75]   E.M. Spiers, *Haldane: An Army Reformer* (Edinburgh, 1980).

[76]   Nicholas Lambert, *Sir John Fisher's Naval Revolution* (Columbia, SC, 1989).

[77]   Albert Palazzo, *Seeking Victory on the Western Front: the British Army and Chemical Warfare in World War I* (Lincoln, NE, 2000), uses is specific subject to develop admirably the relationship of doctrine and pragmatism.

War Office and a senior officer corps that never lost sight of the essential nature of Britain's Continental involvement.[78]

The result, which persisted through the Second World War, was a general-purpose army: one that lacked virtuosity, did nothing particularly well – and fought itself to exhaustion during 1944/45 in order to re-establish the Continental glacis [79] A force of 'good plain cooks' it may have been. But the British Army delivered the basics of British strategy – in cooperation with a Royal Navy that by May 1945 was almost as much a brown-water force as a blue-water one in the Western hemisphere. It continues to do so in the casernes and on the manoeuvre grounds of Germany to the present day.

Conclusion

Comparing the British way in war and the German way of war appears to leave no doubts about the superior approach. When they were put head to head, whose flag went up over whose capital city – twice? In war, winning may not be everything, but losing isn't anything.

Similarly, the 'why' of the outcome offers a comforting answer: democracy triumphing over authoritarianism, 'Dad's Army' prevailing against the Waffen SS, at least metaphorically. Yet David French notes that British policymakers throughout this period have been reluctant to provide the public with 'more than the barest minimum of information' about their decisions.[80] And in terms of public morale there was little to choose between Britain and Germany in their great confrontations.

What about focus? It is as much mantra as cliché that, in war, strategy must drive tactics. Certainly the British experience reflects understanding of that concept, if not always its articulation. Loss of focus in the late eighteenth century gave way to sustaining the Continental involvement deemed vital to the nation's security and existence, even at barely sustainable cost. Germany for its part abandoned the focus that was its Prussian heritage, and fought two world wars with what amounted to no strategy at all. Whether the differences reflected situations; Britain had to decide to fight in a Continental context; Germany had no choice, or decisions: excessive military influence and the illusions caused by 'victory disease, the result was the same.

But let us consider a fourth possibility, involving social/political contracts. In 1918 the Germans in effect sued the government for breach of contract. In 1933 they willingly concluded another – this one designed without options. From

---

[78]   On this see particularly Harold R Winton, *To Change an Army: General Sir John Burnett-Stuart and British Armored Doctrine, 1927–1938* (Lawrence, KS, 1988).

[79]   A good overview is David French, *Raising Churchill's Army: The British Army and the War against Germany, 1919–1945* (New York, 2001).

[80]   David French, *The British Way in Warfare, 1688–2000* (London, 1990), p. 239.

1688 to 1945 the British had a full share of hard graft, but never downed tools. French again credits British policymakers with being 'consistently adaptive'.[81] Prussian/German policy, in contrast, shifted from adaptive to inflexible – certainly after 1890, arguably before. Might Britain's way *in* war have provided a level of flexibility among intentions, institutions, and instruments, while Germany's way *of* war eventually fused into rigidity sustainable only at the cost of losing the war itself?

The generalisation is easier to present than to prove – but David French is also known for leaving readers with material for further reflection.

---

[81]   Ibid., 233.

Chapter 7

The Territorial Army and National Defence

Hew Strachan

On 10 May 1940, men of the Oxfordshire and Buckinghamshire Light Infantry, who had arrived in France in January 1940 and had spent the spring building anti-tank ditches and repairing roads, were pushed forward into Belgium. Acting in conformity with Plan D, the Anglo-French scheme to check a German attack on the Low Countries by advancing to the line of the River Dyle, they encountered little initial opposition. On 12 May they found themselves skirmishing with German infantry in the vicinity of Waterloo. In June 1815, the last time that they – or rather their antecedents – had met Germans at Waterloo, they had been on the same side. But that is not the distinction that is important to this story. The unit which had fought alongside the Prussians in the Waterloo campaign, the 52nd Light Infantry, which became 2nd Battalion, the Oxfordshire and Buckinghamshire Light Infantry in 1881, was a regular regiment; the unit which now found itself swept up in the Allied retreat as the Wehrmacht overran Belgium and France, the 1st Bucks Battalion, was part of the Territorial Army.

Like other elements of the British Expeditionary Force as it fell back to Dunkirk, the 1st Bucks Battalion struggled to keep its cohesion, being deprived of one company and finding itself separated from its transport and support weapons. The commanding officer collapsed from the strain. Major B.K. Heyworth, a solicitor from Beaconsfield, succeeded him and organised the defence of Hazebrouck, where the battalion arrived on 25 May. On 27 and 28 May, with its companies scattered around the perimeter and only intermittently in touch with battalion headquarters, 1st Bucks Battalion held Hazebrouck against a German Panzer division. It was an action, according to a German broadcast, 'truly worthy of the highest traditions of the British Army'.[1] Heyworth and the battalion's adjutant were killed. Of the 600 men with which the battalion began the action, 100 died or were reported missing, between 200 and 250 were wounded, and about 210 escaped.

Major Elliot Viney, who had taken over the command from Heyworth, was not one of them: he was captured when the battalion headquarters was cut off by the German breakthrough in the evening of 27 May. Viney was awarded the DSO.

This essay began its life as the inaugural Elliot Viney Memorial Lecture, given at the invitation of the Lord Lieutenant of Buckinghamshire, Sir Nigel Mobbs, and delivered at Stowe School on 4 February 2004.

[1]   Ian Beckett, *Call to Arms: Buckinghamshire's Citizen Soldiers* (Buckingham, 1985), 115.

A director of the printing firm Hazell, Watson and Viney, based in Buckingham, he had found himself commanding an infantry battalion in a major action on foreign soil and received a decoration reserved for commissioned officers who have performed meritorious service under fire. What was he doing there? An easy answer would be paternal influence. His father Oscar, who had been wounded in the First World War while serving with the same regiment on the Somme, was commanding the battalion in 1932, the year in which Elliot had joined it. In 1939, his younger brother, Laurence, was similarly commissioned into the 1st Bucks Battalion, and, although wounded in 1940, escaped. Family influences were important in explaining who joined the Territorial Army and why they did so. But the question is more general: what was the Territorial Army, of which Elliot Viney and the 1st Bucks Battalion, were part, designed to do?

Another scion of a famous Buckinghamshire family, the Verneys, gave one answer. John Verney joined the North Somerset Yeomanry, then still mounted, in 1937. He explained his motivations for doing so in *Going to the Wars*, his marvellous volume of wartime memoirs:

> I had no obvious leanings towards militarism; on the contrary. I soon found, as I had suspected, that the outward forms of army life were totally uncongenial. I disliked from the start marching in step, calling people 'sir', and being called 'sir', saluting and being saluted …
>
> Wars and rumours of wars, I fancy now, cast only a faint shadow over my life then. Shadows there were, but they came rather from an inherent melancholy. Quite simply, the prospect of a fortnight's riding in camp every year had probably more to do with my joining. Introspective, shy, tormented with most of the inhibitions of that age, I was passing through a period of various self-imposed ordeals, imposed for the good of my 'soul', and of these riding, which frightened me, was one.[2]

John Verney was not alone. Cavalry might have lost its role on the battlefield by the 1930s, but service in the yeomanry was popular and its regiments could have long waiting lists. Laurence Viney's school friend Michael Strachan joined the cavalry squadron of the Cambridge University Officers Training Corps on going up to Corpus Christi College in 1938 precisely because it meant that, at a time when he was struggling with the other expenses of university life, he could ride free of charge. Much to his chagrin the squadron was mechanised the very same year. That was one image of the Territorial Army: outdoor recreation, a convivial and bucolic social life, at the taxpayer's expense.

The founder of the Territorial Army, Richard Burdon Haldane, had much grander objectives when he was appointed secretary of state for war in December 1905. He spoke of creating a 'Hegelian army', a description which in isolation

---

[2]   John Verney, *Going to the Wars: A Journey in Various Directions* (Harmondsworth, 1958; first pub. 1955), 19–20.

probably did not leave the inhabitants of the War Office, and especially the officers of the newly created general staff, much the wiser, but which he explained and developed in a sequence of memoranda written between January and April 1906:

> The problem, as it presents itself to my mind, is how to reorganise the military forces of this country in such a fashion as to give the whole nation what is really a National Army, not separated from itself by artificial barriers of caste and class, but regarded by the people as something that is their very own. It is the essence of such a conception that an army fulfilling these requirements should have its roots within the people themselves, and should be developed into that perfection of organization which can only come to be regarded as an organic whole, existing for the whole purpose of protecting British interests, no matter where in the world those interests are threatened.[3]

In 1906 those interests were most obviously threatened – or so it seemed – on the North-West Frontier of India. Haldane set about fashioning from Britain's regular army a British Expeditionary Force to go not to Europe, as it would do in 1914, but to south Asia to meet a Russian invasion advancing through Afghanistan. The problem that then emerged was that, if the regular army was halfway across the world, it would be unable to protect Britain itself from invasion. The National Service League, formed in 1902 and presided over from 1905 by Britain's best loved general, the diminutive and white-moustached Lord Roberts, argued that Britain needed conscription on European lines precisely for that reason – for home defence.[4] The case for conscription in Britain advanced by the National Service League became the public justification for the Territorial Force (as the Territorial Army was called from its inception in 1908 until 1920). The military correspondent of *The Times*, Colonel Charles à Court Repington, writing in June 1907, declared that 'the primary use of the Territorial Army is for home defence in the absence of the Regular Army abroad. It is, as Mr Ramsay Macdonald [*sic*] has well said, the hearth and home idea which is at the root idea of this new force.'[5]

Repington's mention of Ramsay MacDonald was significant. Most parliamentary supporters of the National Service League were to be found in the ranks of the Conservative party. MacDonald was the leader of the Independent Labour Party, and a vehement opponent of conscription. He accepted, however, that, if there were any justification for military service, it resided in a form which

[3]   Haldane's 4th memorandum, 25 April 1906, Haldane papers, National Library of Scotland MS 5918, ff.44–45, as quoted by Peter Dennis, *The Territorial Army 1907–1940* (Woodbridge, 1987), 10. I have relied heavily on Dennis in what follows. See also Edward Spiers, *Haldane: An Army Reformer* (Edinburgh, 1980).

[4]   R.J.Q. Adams and Philip Poirier, *The Conscription Controversy in Great Britain 1900–18* (Basingstoke, 1987), 1–32.

[5]   The military correspondent of *The Times* [Charles Repington], 'The First and Second Lines', first pub. 1907, *The Foundations of Reform* (London, 1908), 376.

predisposed the nation to use force solely for the purpose of its own defence. These were the ideas promoted by his friend, the French socialist Jean Jaurès, in *L'armée nouvelle*, a book first published in 1910. Its arguments rested on an idealised form of military service, linked to notions of citizenship, promulgated through the political philosophy of the Enlightenment, and made reality (at least in Jaurès's account) by the *levée en masse* of the French Revolution.[6] If the state gave the individual civic rights, then the individual also incurred an obligation to defend those rights through military service.[7]

By 1907, conscription in countries of continental Europe like France had therefore acquired another role: its purpose was not just strategic, not just the defence of the nation, but also social – to integrate the armed forces and society, to make the army the embodiment of the nation, and to educate society to think nationally. In short, the aim was a Hegelian army. Haldane hoped to do the same but in terms acceptable to British institutions and traditions. Thus enlistment in the Territorial Force was to be voluntary, not compulsory. Its organisation and administration were to be local, in the hands of county associations chaired by the Lord Lieutenants, not those of the War Office (although the latter set the training standards). Finally, the Territorial Force, through the Officers Training Corps to be established in universities and schools, was to extend its reach into education itself.

The social case for the Territorial Force was weakened by the disparity between Haldane's ambition and the reality. Haldane had hoped to enlist 314,000 men, and in 1906 the War Office's Director of Military Training, Major-General Douglas Haig, spoke of raising 900,000.[8] In practice roughly 250,000 joined, and the Territorial Force struggled to retain even those. Its claim to be the link between army and society, to be the basis for a national army, looked thin when most of the nation and most of society did not want to be a part of it. The division of labour in defence still retained the unfairness inherent in any system of voluntary enlistment: the burden was borne unequally by the willing.

Equally, if not more, serious was the issue of strategy. France had long and exposed land frontiers, with an inveterate enemy in the shape of Germany to the east: its defensive needs demanded a mass army. Those of Britain, being an island, did not. The Royal Navy, not least because of its determination to secure its primacy in the defence budget, was adamant that it could prevent any invasion of the United Kingdom. The strategic argument, whether for conscription or for a Territorial Army designed for home defence, was accordingly contentious, a matter

---

[6]   Thomas Hippler, *Soldats et citoyens: naissance du service militaire en France et en Prusse* (Paris, 2006).

[7]   For the application, or inapplicability, of these arguments in Britain, see Hew Strachan, 'Liberalism and conscription 1789–1919', in Strachan (ed), *The British Army, Manpower and Society into the 21st Century* (London, 2000), 3–15.

[8]   Peter Simkins, *Kitchener's Army: The Raising of the New Armies, 1914–16* (Manchester, 1988), 11.

of inter-service rivalry at one extreme and national identity at another. Repington had continued his article of June 1907 by exclaiming, 'What folly it then is for statesmen to ask the people to create this force [the Territorial Army], and, at the same time, to tell them that this country can never be invaded!'[9] Both the Committee of Imperial Defence, a cabinet committee responsible for the coordination of military and naval planning, and Haldane himself, anxious to justify the creation of the Territorial Force, wrung from the navy the concession that a hostile force of 70,000 might just manage to slip past its patrols and get ashore. And so the War Office asserted, conveniently and predictably, that the 250,000 men of the Territorial Force would be enough to swamp such an invasion.

Haldane was attacked from both sides – by those who said that an invasion in force was a real threat and therefore wanted conscription to counter it, and by those who said the fear of invasion was fantasy. The latter argued that the Territorial Force was militarily inefficient, and that the money it received would be better spent on the Royal Navy. Haldane's problem was that, in responding, he could not be entirely honest. The underlying justification for the Territorial Force was in fact not home defence but the need to provide a reserve for the regular army. Designed primarily for colonial war, the British army was, at least by the standards then prevailing in Europe, tiny. On mobilisation in 1914, each of the French, German and Russian armies would expand to totals approaching three million men; the British Expeditionary Force sent to France in August only just exceeded 100,000 men. Confronted by such a contingency, the regular army had no large-scale reserve. Of those who trudged from Mons to the Marne at the end of August 1914, 60 per cent were reservists who had served as regulars and had been recalled; but a small army generated fewer reservists compared with a big army, and a long-service army also tended to have only older (and therefore less fit) men to call upon.

So the second strategic argument for the Territorial Force was that it should be the means of expanding the regular army. In other words, in the event of war it would not stay at home, but would go abroad. This was very different from Continental models of military service, which could assume that the defence of the nation, narrowly conceived and applied with geographic precision, was sufficient justification for a citizen army. For France, conscription, reserve service and home defence were united; for Britain, they were not. The most likely area of operations for the Territorial Force was continental Europe, not the south coast of England. Home defence had to be interpreted as forward defence: better to protect home and hearth on somebody else's territory, given all the damage and destruction that war causes, than fight a war on one's own.

Many members of Haldane's own party, the Liberals, were deeply alarmed by such thinking. Opposed to any treaty obligation to France, they rejected the notion of a Continental commitment. Moreover, the Liberal government became increasingly reliant on Labour support, a dependence inaugurated by the 'Lib-Lab'

---

9 [Repington], *Foundations of Reform*, 376.

pact of 1903; after 1910 the Liberals could only command a majority in the House of Commons by dint of Labour votes. For the latter, a Territorial Force, if it were conceived of not as a citizen army but as a reserve for the regular army, smacked of militarism – not constitutional propriety. The historic function of the regular army at home, at least in the eyes of the Left, was not defence against invasion but aid to the civil power. The Territorials would become strike-breakers, just as their antecedents in the yeomanry had ridden down the protesters at Peterloo in 1819 or had been called out to counter the Chartists in the early 1840s. Sir Ian Hamilton, the Adjutant General, who went on to command Territorials at Gallipoli in 1915, was asked to pen a reply to the arguments of the National Service League and to justify the Haldane reforms. His words, published in 1910, were not likely to assuage the fears of the Left:

> In the Territorials there is hardly a man who has not joined for the express object
> of having a good fight if any fighting happens to come his way. There is hardly
> a Territorial, I believe, who does not, at the bottom of his heart, hope to go into
> one historic battle in his existence.[10]

As Hamilton put it, the Territorial Force would tap into the inherent bellicosity of those who did not care too much whom they fought – foreign invader, enemy abroad, or trade unionist – or where they did so – Britain, France or Russia. All that motivated them was an inherent enthusiasm for the military life and a chance of combat. The opposition of the government's own supporters proved decisive. The concerns of the Labour party and, even more, of left-leaning Liberals meant that the Territorial Force did not in the event have any formal commitment to overseas service. This was its besetting problem when the First World War broke out.

Lord Kitchener, hastily recalled by the prime minister after he had boarded the boat at Dover en route for Egypt, became secretary of state for war on 5 August 1914. Britain's war with Germany was only one day old. No serious fighting had yet occurred, and, although the British general staff knew that its regular army was still better designed for colonial conflict than for Continental war, Britain's military thinkers could only glimmer what that might mean for the mobilisation and organisation of Britain's military effort. Nonetheless, Kitchener, like Roberts, did not allow the fact that he had gained his own reputation fighting outside Europe to obscure his vision of the army required by war within Europe. He set about the formation of a mass army intended to fight a war that would last at least three years.

By the end of 1915 Kitchener had raised over two million men by voluntary enlistment. It was a staggering achievement, but in doing so he largely bypassed the Territorial Force and its accompanying organisations as bequeathed him by Haldane. It was an affront that has dogged the history of the Territorial Army ever

---

[10]   Ian Hamilton, *Compulsory Service: A Study of the Question in the Light of Experience* (2nd edn, London, 1911, first pub. 1910), 120–21.

since. The Territorial Army's advocates, beginning with Haldane himself, accused Kitchener of not using an existing and established machinery at a time of national crisis; the Territorial Army's critics suggested that Kitchener's actions provided a clear indication of the false premises and unresolved tensions upon which the Territorial Army was founded.

Kitchener was no friend to the Territorial Force, a 'town clerks' army' as he called it.[11] In this he was like many other regular soldiers, then and since. But in 1937 another regular, Major-General Sir Frederick Maurice, who ended his career as Director of Military Operations in 1918, took him to task, writing in the official biography of Haldane:

> There is not to-day any one acquainted with the problem who is not convinced that if Kitchener had used Haldane's system as it was meant to be used, and if the same assistance in the provision of regular officers and non-commissioned officers had been given to the Territorial Army as was given to the Kitchener army, the expansion of our military forces would have been far more orderly and more rapid than was the case.[12]

Kitchener was more right than Maurice allowed, but as with so many of the decisions that Kitchener reached in his first few days in the War Office, his reasons for being right were either wrong or opaque. Kitchener himself did not explain his thinking, allowing others to impute to him gut reactions based on his earlier experiences, in this case service with volunteers in the French army in 1871.[13] Three reasons for Kitchener's rejection of the Territorial Force as the basis for the expansion of the British army in 1914 are self-evident from what has already been said. First, it was not fully recruited. Second, it was not obliged to go overseas: by July 1914 only 18,683 of its 268,777 members had accepted a liability to go abroad in the event of mobilisation.[14] Third, there were no plans for its expansion to the size that Kitchener (rightly) deemed appropriate for the war in hand. This was perhaps the most important obstacle of all, since it related to a fourth and fundamental consideration. The county associations were charged with responsibility for the Territorial Force. Run by rural magnates, predominantly civilians susceptible to local and family pressures, they were understaffed and seemed unlikely to rise to the challenges of mass mobilisation, which itself demanded central coordination. Fifthly and finally, the Territorial Force had a pre-existing strategic function, which the deployment of the British Expeditionary Force to France had only served to bring into sharper relief. The task of home defence seemed more, not

---

[11]   Ian F.W. Beckett, *The Amateur Military Tradition 1558–1945* (Manchester, 1993), 226.

[12]   Frederick Maurice, *Haldane: The Life of Viscount Haldane of Cloan KT, OM* (2 vols, London, 1937–39), I, 361.

[13]   George H. Cassar, *Kitchener: Architect of Victory* (London, 1977), 22, 198.

[14]   Simkins, *Kitchener's Army*, 18.

less, urgent as the German army overran Belgium and threatened the Channel ports. In November 1914, the depredations wrought in the Pacific by the German navy's East Asiatic Squadron would prompt the Admiralty to despatch the battle cruisers of the Grand Fleet to the south Atlantic, leaving the North Sea deprived of direct defences: Kitchener found himself more reliant on the Territorials to ward off the danger of invasion than was comfortable, particularly given his doubts about their military capabilities.

The Territorials' grievances with Kitchener, and the disputes that they generated, have – somewhat ironically – served to obscure the Territorial Force's very real achievements in the First World War. Despite the pre-war reluctance to enter into the Imperial service obligation, it was able to send formed battalions abroad faster than the New Armies. From 21 August 1914, units in which 80 per cent volunteered to go overseas were allowed to complete to establishment. As a result the London Scottish (1/14th London Regiment) arrived in France in September and in November became the first Territorial battalion to see action, at Messines in the first battle of Ypres. Sir John French, the commander-in-chief of the British Expeditionary Force in France, said that he could not have got through 1915 without the Territorial Force. By February he had 48 Territorial infantry battalions under his command, and during the course of the year the pre-war Territorial divisions formed through Haldane's reorganisation entered the field army's order of battle. By the time of the battle of Loos in October, the first New Army battalions were in the line, but the Territorial Force put two self-contained divisions, the 46th (North Midland) and 47th (London), into the battle. The training levels of the Territorial Force may have been low when compared with those of the regular army, but its members still started the war from a higher base point than a raw recruit, a point which many regulars came increasingly to recognise.

The New Armies may have been the public face of the army's expansion before the introduction of conscription in 1916, but the Territorial Force's own contribution was almost comparable. As each Territorial battalion went overseas, it was able to raise a fresh second-line battalion to replace the first. By the end of the war the Territorial Force consisted of 692 infantry battalions, compared with 267 regular or reserve battalions and 557 New Army battalions. Many of the Territorial battalions remained in the United Kingdom, committed both to home defence and (as fears of socialism, war weariness and even revolution grew from 1917) to supporting the civil power. Nonetheless, 318 went abroad. The New Armies' contribution to overseas service – at 404 battalions – was higher, but not as high as received wisdom seems sometimes to suggest.[15]

In 1914–15 the War Office struggled to cope with the numbers presenting themselves for enlistment, and in August 1914 itself some recruiting offices had to shut their doors. The nationwide network of Territorial Force drill halls was able to take up the slack. Regular infantry battalions had adopted a four-company structure just before the outbreak of the war, but the Territorial Force had retained

---

[15]   Beckett, *Amateur Military Tradition*, 228–29.

the old eight-company organisation. This had ensured a local footprint, enabling every town, and in some cases villages, to have a drill hall, so providing a strong military presence in rural areas. In absolute numbers, the bulk of recruits who enlisted in 1914–15 came from the large cities, but by the same token, as full employment took hold in war-related industries, the proportion of those enlisting – if expressed as a percentage of the male workforce of military age – declined. For the United Kingdom as a whole, those coming forward in rural areas were fewer, not only in overall numbers but also proportionally.[16] But this was not true in Scotland, whose recruiting in relation to its population base outstripped that of England, a reversal of the pre-war norm. In the rural north of Scotland, those who enlisted did so disproportionately through the Territorial Force. Between August 1914 and May 1915, of those who enlisted at Fort George 80 percent joined the Territorials, at Inverness 83 per cent and at Aberdeen 66.42 per cent. Of course they may have done so in order to take advantage of the Territorials' commitment to home service, but that argument is somewhat offset by the fact that in Scotland the percentage joining the army via the Territorials rose – from 35 per cent of Scots recruits in 1914 to 41 per cent in 1915 – just as increasing numbers of Territorial battalions were going abroad. Indeed, in 1915 a Territorial must have seemed likely to get to the front faster than a New Army recruit.[17]

After the First World War the potential contribution to the defence of the nation by the Territorial Army (as it had now become) was unclear. The lack of any obvious invasion threat militated against home defence as a rationale. By the same token the military exhaustion of Europe removed the need for a second-line force to support the regulars on the Continent. Haldane's vision of a 'Hegelian army', a citizen force representative of the nation as a whole, proved unsustainable. Recruiting realities were at odds with its image. Its other ranks were heavily reliant on the working class (as its antecedents, the Rifle Volunteers, had been after the initial rush of middle class enthusiasm on their formation in 1859).[18] On the other hand, its officers, not least because of the financial burden of commissioned service, were associated with Conservatism; by 1936 some members were linked to the British Union of Fascists. The opposition of the Labour Party to the Territorial Army was continuous throughout the inter-war years, and only increased after the General Strike in 1926. Formally speaking the Territorial Army was not liable to be used in aid of the civil power, but Winston Churchill, not for the first time, demanded that it be called out. Once embodied, its members would have been under the same

---

[16]   P.E. Dewey, 'Military Recruiting and the British Labour Force during the First World War', *Historical Journal*, 27 (1984), 199–223.

[17]   Derek Rutherford Young, 'Voluntary Recruitment in Scotland', Glasgow University PhD thesis, 2001.

[18]   David French, *Raising Churchill's Army: The British Army and the War against Germany 1919–1945* (Oxford, 2000), 53; on the Volunteers, see Hugh Cunningham, *The Volunteer Force* (London, 1975); Ian F.W. Beckett, *Riflemen Form: A Study of the Rifle Volunteer Movement 1859–1908* (Aldershot, 1982).

obligations to break strikes as the regulars. In seeming confirmation of Labour suspicions, although Churchill's request was resisted, the units employed instead in 1926, the newly formed special constables, used the Territorials' organisation and buildings.[19]

As fraught were the Territorial Army's relations with the regular army. In January 1920, the secretary of state for war, Churchill, himself a former Oxfordshire Hussar, assured the county associations that, in the event of another major European war, the country would not again follow the precedent set by Kitchener but would use the Territorial Army as the basis for the army's expansion.[20] But he was also therefore persuaded that 'it would be best frankly and plainly to ask would-be recruits to accept Imperial and Oversea obligations and tell them that if, for instance, Germany appeared again on the Rhine, or Russia was advancing on India, they would have to proceed overseas'.[21] In promoting the principle of general (rather than home) service in the event of national emergency, Churchill stressed that the Territorials would go abroad as self-contained units, and that they would form their own brigades and divisions. He thus consolidated the Territorial Army's own image of how it could best function as a reserve, that was as 'a self-contained, second line Army'.[22] But ambiguity persisted. The Regular Army needed two other sorts of reservists – those 'needed to make up strengths of units from peace to war establishment on mobilization' and those 'to provide reinforcements to replace casualties as soon as the campaign starts'.[23] In the eyes of the regulars, the value of the Territorial Army lay in its potential to provide it with drafts in the event of a limited war; but the Territorial Army itself was determined that if it was to be used it would be so only in formed units. This tension was not resolved by 1934, when the War Office's *Training Regulations* stated that 'the role of the Territorial Army, in addition to that of providing *the sole means of expansion to form a national army*, includes the liability of supporting the Regular Army overseas in the event of war'.[24] And there was a second tension. The corollary of the 1920 reorganisation was that the Territorial Army would be the main force in a prolonged and major war, while the regular army would bear the brunt in lesser conflicts: which should therefore have priority in terms of equipment? Financial retrenchment, and its concomitant, increasing competition for scarce resources,

---

[19]   Beckett, *Amateur Military Tradition*, 251–52; Peter Dennis, 'The reconstitution of the Territorial Force 1918–1920', in Adrian Preston and Peter Dennis (eds), *Swords and Covenants: Essays in Honour of the Centennial of the Royal Military College of Canada 1876–1976* (London, 1976), 208–11.

[20]   French, *Raising Churchill's Army*, 53.

[21]   Martin Gilbert, *Winston S. Churchill*, companion volume IV (2 parts, London, 1977), 1018

[22]   Dennis, 'The reconstitution of the Territorial Force 1918–1920', 207.

[23]   B.C. Dening, *The Future of the British Army: The Problem of Its Duties, Cost and Composition* (London, 1928), 170–71.

[24]   J.R. Kennedy, *This, Our Army* (London, 1935), 180.

only deepened the tensions between regulars and Territorials. In January 1922 the general staff reported to the committee of national expenditure:

> The General Staff have already pointed out the whole *raison d'être* of the Territorial Army has been definitely ruled out by the Cabinet's decision that a great war was out of the question for 10 years or more. This wipes out any chance of invasion. The Territorial Army cannot find out overseas garrisons, it cannot provide drafts, it cannot furnish reinforcements for an Eastern campaign, and it cannot be used for the preservation of internal order. It therefore fulfils none of the essential tasks which the maintenance of the British Empire demands. On the contrary, it is absorbing money to find which regular units are to be abolished. It is therefore impossible to justify the retention of the Territorial Army in its present form on military grounds.[25]

The Territorial Army was not abolished, but by 1930 it was in a parlous state. It recovered because in the 1930s the defence of the Empire slipped from being the first call on Britain's military capability to being the third. Home defence, the original justification for the Territorial Army, moved back into first place, and reinforcement of the regular army in a European war into second.

In the 1930s Britain did not face invasion from the sea, but it did confront the possibility of attack from the air. In 1928 Sir Hugh Trenchard, the chief of the air staff, declared air defence to be impossible, and argued that the best response to the threat of aerial attack was itself a bomber offensive. But that had not been the view taken by the Army Council in 1923, when it allocated two of the Territorial Army's fourteen divisions for anti-aircraft duties. As the fear of the bomber grew, so did the Territorials' responsibility for home defence. In 1936, Air Commodore L.E.O. Charlton published *War over England*, a mixture of history (with accounts of German air attacks on Britain in the First World War) and apocalyptic warning. Its essential message was unchanged from that of Trenchard: it saw expenditure on fighters as a waste of resources and believed that reprisals using Britain's own bomber force should be the core of the United Kingdom's defence, This paean to air-mindedness sketched a future in which regimental identities were obliterated and 'the old Army ... was faded into nothingness'. Significantly, however, Charlton exempted the Territorials. In his account of the future, they 'were converted *en bloc* into anti-aircraft troops for the service of guns, searchlights, and listening-posts', becoming 'a *corps d'élite* of fine physique and perfect discipline, indistinguishable from the regulars'.[26] By January 1939, five Territorial divisions were earmarked for anti-aircraft duties, a total of 87,000 men, who were to serve locally in defence of their own regions. In March 1939, the secretary of state for war increased the number of Territorial Army anti-aircraft divisions to seven.[27]

---

[25] The National Archives, CAB 24/132, quoted in Dennis, *Territorial Army*, 94–95.
[26] L.E.O. Charlton, *War over England* (London, 1936), 256.
[27] Dennis, *Territorial Army*, 237.

At the same time the Regular Army, as it began to confront once more the imminence of European war, turned increasingly to the Territorial Army. In February 1933, Sir Archibald Montgomery-Massingberd, the Adjutant General and to become Chief of the Imperial General Staff later that year, said that the Territorial Army was vital if the regular army was to be supported in the field. The county associations, for so long accustomed to seeing the army's general staff as their enemy, began to realise that the two bodies shared converging, if not exactly common, interests. In November 1935 the Defence Requirements Committee proposed the formation of a field force for Europe made up of five regular divisions, to be reinforced by twelve Territorial Army divisions after eight months. In the committee's view £26 million was required to modernise the Territorial divisions, a proposal endorsed by Duff Cooper, the secretary of state for war, in December 1936.[28] Once again, therefore, the Territorial Army was being used to offset Britain's reluctance to embrace national service in peacetime. If there were to be a major war in Europe, Britain would need a mass army, but its regular army was too small and too reliant on long service in peacetime to generate its own reservists. As the general staff girded its loins for the eventuality of a new Continental commitment, it looked askance at the adaptation of the Territorial Army for home defence: just when it needed the Territorials to become tactically mobile they were being tied to a stationary role; just when they needed them to be expeditionary, they were being geared for duties in Britain; and just when the regulars needed fresh equipment, priority was being given to anti-aircraft guns for use by these same Territorials.

Confronted by Duff Cooper's demands, Neville Chamberlain, as chancellor of the exchequer, voiced another worry. To ready the Territorial Army for deployment to Europe as a surrogate for the mass army that Britain did not possess would be to reopen the wounds of the First World War. Chamberlain's espousal of the policy of limited liability may have married financial prudence to strategic sense, but he couched it in terms which exploited the emotions generated by the Somme and Passchendaele: he told the Cabinet that he doubted 'whether we were right in equipping the Territorial Force for the trenches'.[29]

Chamberlain's implied concern that the public would not tolerate another war in and for France was not reflected by the pattern of Territorial Army recruitment in 1938 and 1939. Once again it fulfilled its 'Hegelian' role, linking army and nation. In 1938 the yeomanry was permitted to recruit to 30 per cent over its establishment, and infantry battalions to 10 per cent above. In March 1939, the government decided to double the Territorial Army to 340,000. In the following month, Chamberlain, now prime minister, was persuaded to introduce conscription although Britain was still at peace. One of his reasons for doing so was the flood of highly qualified, skilled and well-motivated men who had joined the Territorial Army over the preceding months, many of whom, as they would be in reserved

---

[28]   Brian Bond, *British Military Policy between the Wars* (Oxford, 1980), 221, 237.
[29]   TNA, CAB 23/86/75 (36), 3, quoted by Bond, *British Military Policy*, 238.

occupations, would have to be withdrawn if the Territorials were mobilised and sent overseas. Herein lay the incompatibility between the ideal version of the Hegelian army and the regulars' need for a reserve army prepared for overseas service.

Also at odds were the creation of an army for war in Europe and the maintenance of an army for home defence. Peacetime voluntary soldiering made for long service; war, and particularly a war whose operations would be characterised by high mobility, demanded youth and fitness. In March 1940, 55 per cent of Territorial commanding officers were found to be unfit for command, despite the fact that many of them had notched up twenty years' service. In the first half of 1939 home defence also created a more immediate tension. The Territorials were being required to hone their skills as anti-aircraft gunners during a deteriorating international situation while simultaneously carrying on their normal peacetime jobs. The introduction of conscription, although it circumvented the absurdity of denying those employed on aerial defence any sleep for months on end, created another challenge for the Territorial Army. Having been reassured that it would be the means to expand the army in time of national emergency, it now confronted a situation in which that no longer necessarily pertained. On mobilisation, the 48th Territorial Division lost half its strength, as those who were over-age, unfit or in reserved occupations were removed; their places were taken by conscripts. Territorial divisions were incorporated a new 'national' army.[30] Symptomatic of ruffled sensitivities was the fiat that the Territorials should no longer wear the letter 'T' on their uniforms. At once a recognition of their equal status and an insult to their Territorial Army heritage, the change neatly encapsulated an ambivalence that went to the heart of the Territorial Army's existence.

In the approach of the Second World War, many of these difficulties, and the strains and confusions that they caused, were submerged for those who responded to the needs of the moment. Both Elliot Viney and John Verney reflected a public commitment to defence, which owed less to a memory of the First World War as futile and more to a sense of continuing obligation to the values in whose name it had been fought. John Verney wrote later, although he confessed to being somewhat suspicious of himself as he did so:

> In the autumn of 1936 when I applied for my territorial commission, the Italo-Abyssinian War was recently over, the Spanish Civil War had recently begun. Even a self-absorbed and politically half-baked young man could not fail to be aware that world catastrophe was impending. To join the Territorial Army was the easiest and most obvious course open to anyone who felt he should make some effort to avert it.[31]

---

[30]   Peter Caddick-Adams, 'Phoney war and Blitzkrieg: the Territorial Army in 1939–40', *Journal of the Royal United Services Institute for Defence Studies*, April 1998, 68–69.

[31]   Verney, *Going to the Wars*, 19.

Elliot Viney's battalion was part of the eight Territorial Army divisions sent to France between January and April 1940. Most of the British 'national army', which was caught up in the German invasion of the west and retreated to Dunkirk, was nominally a Territorial army. But it was of course an army that had expanded so rapidly in 1938–39 that neither its equipment nor its training had kept pace. In 1939, 65 per cent of Territorials had served for less than a year, and half of them for less than six months. By November 1939 the first-line Territorial divisions had received only 25 per cent of their equipment.[32] Some of the Territorial Army's units and some of its men, like Elliot Viney, fought magnificently; others did not. Elliot Viney's own account tells the tale, but also reveals his own ability to grip the situation. He found that he just had to be tough with his men:

> Some just wanted to leave, they were lost ... they didn't know what was happening, they knew the Germans were all around them. Some good NCOs who had the personality to gather them together – some wonderful stories of chaps who did that and formed those ambulance drivers and all sorts into wonderful units. But some of them, on their own, just didn't know what was happening and were ready to throw their hands in. But if you could get hold of them and – there wasn't much time – say who you are ... report to the sergeant major and muck in. That's in effect what one was trying to do.[33]

After Dunkirk, the regular army looked round for scapegoats. One was the Royal Air Force, seemingly more conspicuous by its absence than its presence; the other, once again, was the Territorial Army. Major-General Sir John C. Kennedy, who had commanded the 44th (Territorial Army) Division in 1932–34, had written to Basil Liddell Hart in August 1938:

> Territorial training is largely a veneer – which the rough usage of war destroys almost at once – unless it is carefully preserved until war experience gradually produces the real fighting soldier, a man who reacts instinctively to any situation, and is not dismayed by the unexpected.[34]

Between 1940 and 1944 most of the British army spent most of the war in the United Kingdom preparing for the invasion of Europe. The slower pace of preparation, training and deployment meant that for those Territorial Army units that survived the fall of France Kennedy's requirements had a greater chance of being met. The experience of both the build-up to D-Day and then, after June 1944,

---

[32]   Caddick-Adams, 'Phoney war and Blitzkrieg', 68.

[33]   Imperial War Museum Sound Archive, 6806/2, E.M. Viney, quoted in Mark Connelly and Walter Miller, 'The BEF and the Issue of Surrender on the Western Front in 1940', *War in History*, 11 (2004), 431–32.

[34]   Kennedy to Liddell Hart, 28 August 1938, quoted by Dennis, *Territorial Army*, 253.

battle meant that by 1945 the distinction between regulars and Territorials was increasingly artificial. Nonetheless it was still one which could rankle. Territorials believed that their civilian skills made them more flexible and adaptive than the regulars: in 1940 Elliot Viney was sure that the Territorial private soldier was more intelligent than a regular non-commissioned officer.[35] If regulars were given command of Territorial units, or if regular units were accorded roles which implied that they were more combat effective, the raw nerve of perceived inferiority was soon exposed. And that remained the principal problem after 1945, throughout the Cold War and into the twenty-first century. For the Territorial Army its biggest problem was the suspicion with which it was viewed by the regulars. They were its fiercest critics, showing a scepticism with regard to its capabilities which harked back to Dunkirk.

There was a fundamental paradox here. After 1945, the role of the Territorial Army stood a chance of being clarified in a way that had not applied between 1908 and 1945. In the era of the two world wars, the Territorial Army was caught between three roles: the 'Hegelian' army, in which the Territorials were the link between the regular army and society; home defence; and the reserve for the regulars. In 1946, neither the first nor the second of these functions seemed important. Between 1945 and 1960 conscription ensured that the army and society were linked without the Territorial Army acting as an intermediary. In July 1946, 60 per cent of the total strength of the armed forces were national servicemen. Nor was home defence a Territorial Army task. Plans for a Territorial Army of between eight and ten divisions, adumbrated in October 1946, were confirmed in 1949 when the report of a committee chaired by Sir Edmund Harwood on the future size and shape of the armed forces settled on the higher figure. The report itself proposed that five of the ten divisions should be earmarked for home defence and internal security, but the chiefs of staff then rejected the civil defence role.[36] Field Marshal Viscount Montgomery, as Chief of the Imperial General Staff, had already set about converting the Territorial Army into a proper reserve army by drafting time-expired national servicemen into it for a further three and half years' part-time service.[37] Thus, for the first time in its existence, the Territorials' function was simple and singular: they were the second-line army, ready to reinforce the regulars in the event of war.

In practice the confusion about the role of the Territorial Army had not been resolved. The incorporation of national servicemen was delayed in its implementation and unsatisfactory in its effects: the voluntary, long-term service which characterised the Territorial sat uneasily alongside the compulsory short service of the conscript. By 1955, only two Territorial divisions were available

---

[35]   Connelly and Miller, 'The BEF and the Issue of Surrender', 427.

[36]   L.V. Scott, *Conscription and the Attlee Governments: The Politics and Policy of National Service 1945–1951* (Oxford, 1993), 225–34.

[37]   Gregory Blaxland, *The Regiments Depart: A History of the British Army 1945–1970* (London, 1971), 13–14.

to reinforce NATO in Europe, and they were then allocated, like the rest of the Territorial Army, to home defence, a function that became more important as the salience of the nuclear threat also grew.[38] With the Duncan Sandys Defence White Paper of 1957, the abolition of conscription and the shift from a mass army to a policy of deterrence, the United Kingdom no longer needed a reserve for its field army and put even less weight on the notion that the Territorial Army was a 'Hegelian' force. However, this did not mean that the tensions between the Territorial Army's identity and its strategic functions were resolved. The Chief of the Imperial General Staff was not happy with the reduction in military manpower, and could not be persuaded that Britain's land commitment to the defence of Europe could be restricted to a 'tripwire' force, designed to trigger massive nuclear retaliation as its ultimate sanction.

In 1965, the Deputy Chief of the Imperial General Staff, Lieutenant-General Sir John Hackett, and the Director of Army Staff Duties, Major-General Michael Carver, set about a major and deeply unpopular reorganisation of the Territorial Army. Like their forebears in the late 1930s, they were concerned that the mobilisation, training and equipping of the Territorials would take too long for them to be of value in a battle in Europe. In Carver's own words:

> The Sandys reforms had relegated most of the Territorial Army to home defence, but had not fundamentally reformed it or the other forms of reserve. The liability of National Servicemen to be called up into the Territorial Army after the end of their service, although never implemented, had helped to preserve a far larger number of units than could be manned at a viable strength by volunteers or could be adequately equipped. The concept of a separate army, which could not be ready for operations until after mobilization and training, was irrelevant to current NATO strategy; nor did defence against troops landed in the United Kingdom from the air or sea make sense in that context.[39]

'Hackett and Carver' (their names played into the hands of their critics) were also anxious to reduce the massive overheads generated by the Territorial Army's network of drill halls – its regional footprint. They argued that the Territorial Army's younger members were attracted by the idea of fewer units but ones which would be fully manned and could therefore train effectively, even if they had to travel further to do so. Their solution (or rather the solution of Lieutenant-Colonel Hugh Beach, who worked for Carver, having just completed a tour as commanding officer of the Cambridge University Officers Training Corps) was to merge the Territorial Army, which was designed to produce formed units to supplement those of the regular army, and the Army Emergency Reserve, which provided skilled individuals, into one body, the Territorial and Army Volunteer Reserve (T & AVR

---

[38]   Ibid., 338.

[39]   Michael Carver, *Tightrope Walking: British Defence Policy since 1945* (London, 1992), 90–91.

in the new acronym). The aim, in Carver's words again, was 'not to produce a separate volunteer army, as the TA traditionally had sought to be, but to bring the regular army from a peace to a war footing'.[40] Paradoxically this ambition also brought a reduction in establishment from 120,000 to 50,000.

Regimental identities, lost through amalgamations and disbandments, went to the heart of regional loyalties, even more so in the case of Territorial units than of regular, and the opposition to the reforms on the part of the county associations was deep. They were supported by the Conservative party, now in opposition, and sustained by the argument that it was illogical to base Britain's defence on the centrality of nuclear deterrence while reducing a force designed in part to combat 'the devastation of a nuclear attack' and already – by virtue of its existing structure – 'spread all over Britain ready to play a part of most crucial importance if the ghastly need arose'.[41] These arguments – those of home defence – were sufficiently strong to persuade the government to add a third tier to the T & AVR structure, described by one of the 'old and bold' as 'the only section having an affinity with the old Territorial Army'.[42] T & AVR I, the 'ever readies', consisted of 8,600 specialists liable to call up without a national emergency, while the bulk of the new force, 42,000 in all, were contained in T & AVR II, to be called out when warlike operations were in preparation or progress. T & AVR III consisted of 23,000 troops for home defence only: poorly equipped and generally neglected, this sop to the county associations and old regimental loyalties, despite many of them being hallowed by combat experience in the Second World War, soon withered.

By 1970, therefore, the Territorial Army was fit for only one task – to provide individuals and units to fill gaps in the regular army. It had no obvious role in home defence or internal security. In the event of major war one-third of Britain's defence strength was meant to come from the reserves, and the concept that drove the restructuring – like that of the 'national army' of 1939–40 – was that of 'one army', in which the regulars provided the commanding officers, adjutants and permanent staff instructors for the Territorials. The home defence role re-emerged fitfully after the Conservative return to power in 1979. Sustained by the desire to enhance conventional defence and so raise the threshold for the resort to nuclear weapons in the defence of western Europe, the 1981 Defence White Paper set out to strengthen the Territorial Army specifically for the protection of the United Kingdom, and proposed an expansion to 86,000 men. In practice, at the end of the Cold War its establishment was the same as it has been a decade earlier, 76,000, and its primary role remained, in the words of the 1988 Defence Estimates, to 'provide more than 50,000 troops to BAOR [the British Army of the Rhine]

---

[40] Michael Carver, *Out of Step: The Memoirs of Field Marshal Lord Carver* (London, 1989), 343–44.

[41] Blaxland, *The Regiments Depart*, 468.

[42] Geoffrey Cousins, *The Defenders: A History of the British Volunteer* (London, 1968), 203.

including two infantry brigades as part of I Br[itish] Corps'. The sole response to the 1981 White Paper had been the formation of a Home Service Force of 3,000 men, which, together with the elements of the Territorial Army which would not have been deployed to Germany in the event of war, would have left 29,000 in all for home defence.[43]

The end of the Cold War confirmed the expeditionary trajectory of the Territorial Army, and consolidated its function as a subordinate and supporting element of the regular army. Britain no longer aspired, or was able, to field a mass army for a major war, and so the alternative reservist concept underpinning the Territorial Army, that of a second-line but semi-autonomous force designed to generate the main army to sustain a Continental commitment, was removed. The implicit ambiguity created by the Territorial Army in the era of the two world wars – that the regulars set the standards but the Territorials provided the staying power and so would actually bear the brunt of the fighting – ended. As a result the tensions between the regulars and the Territorials were eased.

By 1989 it was clear that 'The TA's attempt to be the Regular Army in disguise has failed', as its terms and conditions of service, and its training time and facilities, were not equal to the task.[44] The caricatures of Territorial officers – as 'frustrated regulars' who were more overtly enthusiastic about the kit of soldiering than would be good form in the regular, as too keen on the social side of the job, and as overwhelmingly 'middle-ranking and middle-aged'[45] – provided the background to battles for resources in the defence reviews after the end of the Cold War. The Territorial Army was cut, and shrank successively to being a half and then less than one third of the regulars' strength. But as it fell in size it threatened the regular army less and supported it more. The Defence White Paper of 2003 characterised it as 'a part-time but professional force', and continued that 'whereas the Regular Army and the TA were formerly two separate organisations, they are now regularly used in concert'. The latter could no longer put formed units in the field, but paradoxically found itself more exposed to active service than at any time since 1945. Reservists provided 10 per cent to 14 per cent of the United Kingdom's manpower in operations in the former Yugoslavia and up to 20 per cent in Iraq. The Territorial Army's purpose became solely to provide individuals to 'back-fill' regular units in the field, and their indispensability in operations in Iraq and Afghanistan forged a respect that had been absent hitherto.

But there were opportunity costs. Most striking was the loss of the Territorial Army's contribution to home defence. The 1998 Strategic Defence Review and its successor documents put the weight on the ability to project forces overseas so that the United Kingdom could act pre-emptively and preventively. After the 9/11 attacks in the United States in 2001, and the 7/7 attacks in London in 2005, domestic security became an important element in the defence agenda. The

---

[43]   Michael Yardley and Dennis Sewell, *A New Model Army* (London, 1989), 135.

[44]   Ibid., 142.

[45]   Antony Beevor, *Inside the British Army* (London, 1990), 341–42.

integrated relationship between the actions of armed forces abroad and responses at home was one of the features of war that was genuinely 'new' in an era of so-called 'new wars'. And yet the 2003 Defence White Paper stated that:

> The safety and security of the population of the UK is the responsibility of the Home Office and similar bodies and devolved administrations, delivered through the Police, the other emergency services, HM Customs and Excise, port authorities and local authorities.

The White Paper went on to spell out the specific aid that the Ministry of Defence could give, but the only contribution to be made by the Territorial Army was through the Civil Contingencies Reaction Force, created in 2002 as a result of the 'New Chapter' of the Strategic Defence Review, and based on existing Territorial infantry battalions. Its task was to provide assistance in the event of terrorist attack, accident or national disaster, but its network of fourteen regional units was unevenly distributed, none appears to have been up to its established strength of 500 by 2006, and the total was reduced to thirteen in April 2007.

The Territorial Army not only no longer contributed significantly to home defence, it also ceased to provide a link between the army and society. This was the key debate during the drafting of the 1998 Strategic Defence Review. Further cuts to the Territorials rendered them invisible at the local level; drill halls were closed, and units were scattered over such a wide area that they forfeited any cohesive regional identity. To take one example: the 52nd Lowland Volunteers, the single surviving Territorial infantry battalion for all southern and central Scotland, became effectively an administrative and training organisation only, as it would never be deployed as a formed battalion. Other units, representing other military specialisms, were dispersed over a similar – or even wider – area, with the result that, although still collectively quite strong, all lacked standing or salience in their own localities. The case for regional specialisation, so that a recognisable city, town or rural community might have responsibility for, and a sense of ownership of, its 'own' unit (for example an infantry battalion in Glasgow and a field hospital in Dumfries) went by the board, seemingly a victim of the intransigence of the Territorials' 'old and bold' on the one hand and the lack of sensitivity to local identity in Whitehall on the other. This was unfortunate. The function of the Territorial Army in linking the armed forces to British society through regional links became more important, not less, in a society where those who had performed national service were grandfathers and where the regular army had become too small to be itself integrated with society in any meaningful way.

Throughout its hundred-year history the Territorial Army has been caught between its three roles. Political constraints meant that in 1908 Haldane could not be explicit about what he saw as the most important of the three, the need to act as a second line for the British Expeditionary Force. By 1940, as Elliot Viney himself showed, that had become the Territorials' principal function, and by the beginning of the twenty-first century it had elbowed out the other two completely.

But after the end of the Cold War that narrowing of focus was achieved in order to fight limited wars at great distances from the United Kingdom, and in which the legitimacy of British national interests was hotly debated. Using the Territorials in wars that were domestically divisive was hardly likely to ensure the long-term health of a national army.

Employers who once supported their employees in their membership of the reserves found their loyalty tested to the limit when their workers were called up for wars that were not deemed to be national emergencies and whose duration could seem infinite. In July 2008, the Chief of the Defence Staff, Air Marshal Sir Jock Stirrup, said that everyone in the TA should be prepared to serve because 'they are an integral part of our force structure', and went on, 'If you join the TA you're joining the military and you take on the responsibilities the military assumes'. The stresses were felt not just in the relationship between the Territorial Army and its parent society, but also within the reserve forces themselves. The Reserve Forces Act of 1976, which stipulates that no Territorial should be called out to serve more than twelve months in every three years, was breached by the need to sustain strengths in theatre. There were two consequences. The first was to undermine recruiting and retention. Despite an establishment of only 30,000, lower than it had ever previously been, the Territorial Army's actual strength in 2008, at only just over 21,000, was almost 30 per cent below that. Secondly, a two-tier force was the result. Between 2003 and 2008, 2,400 soldiers undertook two or three six-month tours in Iraq and Afghanistan, while the bulk of the force, 18,600 members, accounted for only 11,000 tours in all.[46]

In this context the ambiguities and inconsistencies with which the Territorial Army had had to live in the past began to look more attractive. Preparation for home defence was compatible with long service, the pursuit of a civilian job and a (near) normal domestic life. Haldane's 'Hegelian' army legitimated the personal sacrifices made by the part-time soldier not only to his nearest and dearest but also to his (or her) community, whether defined in local terms or national. As it celebrated its centenary, the Territorial Army, by submerging its own historic identity to help the regular army confront its responsibilities, was in danger of losing its own distinctive strategic roles – roles which were themselves of national importance.

---

[46]   Ian Bruce, 'MoD Waives Rules on TA Repeat Service to Bolster Front-line Troops', *The Herald* (Glasgow), 16 July 2008.

Chapter 8

The British Army and Anglo-American Military Relations in the Second World War

Niall Barr

Britain and the United States of America have a relationship that stretches back to the first attempts of English colonisation on the continent of North America.[1] The relationship between their respective armies is also a long and complex one, particularly as the United States Army was born in battle fighting against the redcoats of the British Army. However, as David Dimbleby and David Reynolds put it, the Second World War brought 'Britain and America closer than ever before, or ever again'[2] and there is little doubt that the most significant and intimate relations were established between the two armies during this war when they fought alongside each other as allies rather than as enemies.

The sheer depth, scale and scope of the alliance between Britain and the United States during the Second World War is hard to comprehend even now. General George Marshall, the Chief of Staff of the US Army rightly called it, 'the most complete unification of military effort ever achieved by two Allied nations'.[3] As such, the cooperation between the two armies was only ever a portion, albeit a significant one, of the combined effort of the two powers.

Once the United States became committed to the war in Europe, the two allies cooperated in an unprecedented way. While the relationship between Prime Minister Winston Churchill and President Franklin D. Roosevelt has come to personify the cooperation and friction of the wartime alliance, the level of military cooperation was 'like many other aspects of the direction of the War … something which had not been attempted previously in history as between Allies'.[4] The formation of the Combined Chiefs of Staff, in which strategic objectives could be debated and arguments resolved, represented a new departure in the management of vast military forces deployed all over the globe. This is not to say that the well-known strategic disagreements between the allies were not serious or, on occasion,

---

[1]   See Kathleen Burk, *Old World New World: The Story of Britain and America* (London, 2007).

[2]   David Dimbleby and David Reynolds, *An Ocean Apart: The Relationship between Britain and America in the Twentieth Century* (London, 1988), p. 115.

[3]   H. Duncan Hall, *North American Supply* (London, 1955), p. 353.

[4]   Historical Record, British Army Staff Part II: Operations, Plans and Intelligence, p. 7, WO202/917, The National Archives of the United Kingdom (TNA).

did not threaten the cohesion of the alliance but what was remarkable was that such diverging views were aired frankly within an organisation that gave equal representation to both partners.[5] From November 1942, British and American forces were deployed together on operations in North Africa and subsequently saw service together in Sicily, Italy, France and Germany. General George Marshall and General Sir Alan Brooke, as the respective chiefs of their armies, oversaw the raising, training and deployment of two enormous armies in multiple theatres of war. The strategic position of the British Isles led to the influx of more than one million GIs during 1943–44 as part of the preparation for Operation Overlord, the invasion of occupied Europe. This led to a level of contact between British people and American soldiers, sailors and airmen that could not have been envisaged before the war.[6] The fact that the alliance held together and reached a successful conclusion in 1945 was proof of its overall effectiveness.

Nonetheless, there were numerous points of friction between the allies and frequent instances of members of both armies becoming frustrated by the inefficiency of having to work with a partner rather than act simply as an independent national army. This essay aims to provide a brief survey of some aspects of the complicated relationship which existed between the US and British Armies during the fluctuating fortunes of the war against Hitler.

The British Army was well used to working within alliances when war broke out between Britain, France and Germany in September 1939. The compromises necessary to maintain alliance cohesion and the resulting frustrations were equally well understood, if not readily accepted, by British officers. Marlborough had cooperated brilliantly with Prince Eugene of the Netherlands during his campaigns in the early eighteenth century. Wellington's victory in the Peninsula during the Napoleonic Wars was only made possible through the integration of Portuguese units into British divisions and the constant assistance, if not coordination, of Spanish armies and guerrillas. However, the 'natural' working partner of the British Army in 1939 was the French, not the American, Army. During the Great War, the British Army had fought alongside the French Army for four years in a not always happy but consistently effective alliance.[7]

Throughout the First World War, the British and French had struggled to develop an efficient method of cooperation and indeed only properly achieved this in the last few months of the war. After the crisis of the German Spring offensive in March 1918, General Douglas Haig, the commander of the BEF, had finally agreed to place his troops under French supreme command. Ferdinand Foch performed in fine style as the Generalissimo of the Allied Armies during the final

---

[5]   See Mark Stoler, *The Politics of the Second Front: American Military Planning and Diplomacy in Coalition Warfare, 1941–1943* (Westport CT, 1977).

[6]   See David Reynolds, *Rich Relations: The American Occupation of Britain 1942–1945* (London, 1996).

[7]   See Elizabeth Greenhalgh, *Victory through Coalition: Britain and France during the First World War* (Cambridge, 2005).

offensives of 1918. The idea of a Supreme Allied Council was revived in 1939 on the outbreak of war, but the actual functioning of the Anglo-French War Council in 1939–40 was a stark warning of the problems that would later rear their heads in the Anglo-American alliance. After the collapse of France in the summer of 1940, the British reviewed this unexpectedly short-lived alliance and admitted that their attitude could be summed up as 'we must run this war, and the French must come to heel and conform to our ideas'. This meant that the British 'thought things out, worked out everything and then presented the French with a *fait accompli* for their concurrence'. It was then speculated that, if Britain ever had an ally of 'fully equal standing' again, that ally would have to be represented at a joint war headquarters – which of course would be in London – and that the ally must be 'capable of dove-tailing … intimately with the British machinery for the conduct of war'.[8]

When the United States entered the war in December 1941, the British experience of alliance warfare was put to good use. The machinery and organisation for a Combined Chiefs of Staff (which might be described as the Anglo-American equivalent of the Anglo-French War Council) was quickly developed and became an essential part of the Allied war machine. But the United States was not an ally of 'fully equal standing' to Great Britain. Even in the winter of 1941, the United States, although still scrambling to mobilise its strength, was set to become a military and industrial giant of far greater power than the United Kingdom. The respective weight of the allies was reflected in the fact that it was decided that the Combined Chiefs of Staff sat in Washington, not London. On hearing that they would be based in Washington, Brooke spluttered that the British had sold their 'birthright'. The Anglo-American alliance as it developed did not become a British show with a walk-on part for latecomers. The British did indeed attempt to 'run this war' and presented the Americans with a number *of faits accomplis* but ultimately, it was the Americans that forced the British to 'come to heel'.[9]

In many respects, the experience of the Great War remained central to the relationship between the British and American armies during the second war. While the British Army had worked within numerous alliances and often with multiple partners, the same was not true of the US Army. Throughout its history, the latter had served as an independent national army, providing defence against the British and Canadians during the early part of the nineteenth century, fighting an offensive war against Mexico in the 1840s. Its longest running task had been its service as a frontier force, protecting settlers and waging war against the indigenous Amerindians. However, the central and defining experience of the US Army during the nineteenth century had been the American Civil War when North and South had fought against one another in a bloody fraternal conflict. The war against Spain in the 1890s had seen the US Army take on the role of a colonial police force, but, in all of these roles, the US Army had acted as a national army achieving the objectives of its government and untrammelled by considerations of

---

[8]   'Anglo-French War Collaboration 1939–40', CAB122/27, TNA.
[9]   Ibid.

allies.[10] Perhaps the only exception to this rule occurred in China during the Boxer rebellion when troops from many Western nations were forced together during the crisis. This meant that the US Army's first real introduction to the complexities and frictions of coalition warfare began when the United States joined the Great War as a 'co-belligerent' rather than as an ally of Britain and France.

When the US Army arrived in France in 1917, the reality of coalition warfare proved equally frustrating for its commander, General John 'Black Jack' Pershing even though the AEF fought as a 'co-belligerent' rather than as an ally. Pershing became a role model for almost every American commander of the Second World War through his insistence that US soldiers would only fight as part of a strong, independent national army.[11]

Just as the British Army had developed a strong working relationship with the French Army, so too did the AEF. Indeed, during its service in France, the AEF was influenced more strongly by the French Army than by the British. American units were largely supplied with French armaments and equipments, and fought alongside the French more frequently than the British. Meanwhile, many British officers developed a faintly disdainful attitude to the enthusiasm and inexperience of the 'doughboys' that came across the Atlantic.[12] British assessments and criticisms of the US Army as unprepared and inexperienced in 1918 were long remembered and coloured British opinions of the US Army in 1941. The sharp divergence of experience for the British and Americans on the Western Front of the First World War had a powerful influence on the soldiers who later commanded armies in the Second World War.

This contrast between the two armies in the Great War can be highlighted by the startling difference in the combat experience of two of the great military rivals of the second war. George S. Patton became the US Army's leading tank expert on the strength of his service in the US cavalry and his staff work for General Pershing. Never having seen a tank, he elected to join the infant US tank force and then successfully organised a tank training school. He then led the first US tank battalion, equipped with French Renault tanks, into action in September 1918. After two days in combat, Patton was seriously wounded but his reputation as the 'Hero of the Tanks' was secure. Patton would not command troops in combat again until he landed in Morocco as a Task Force commander for Operation Torch in November 1942.[13]

Bernard L. Montgomery's experience of combat in the Great War was similar to many British officers of his generation. He first saw combat at Le Cateau in August 1914 and was severely wounded at the first battle of Ypres in November

---

[10]   See Russell F. Weigley, *History of the United States Army* (New York, 1967).

[11]   John Terraine, *To Win a War: 1918, The Year of Victory* (London, 1978), pp. 132–33.

[12]   John Toland, *No Man's Land: The Story of 1918* (London, 1980), p. 244

[13]   Carlo D'Este, *A Genius for War: A Life of General George S. Patton* (London, 1995), pp. 199–267.

1914. After recovery from his wounds, Montgomery served throughout the war on the Western Front, ultimately as the Chief of Staff of the 47th (London) Division. He then saw extensive service in the Irish Civil War, Egypt and the Arab revolt in Palestine.[14]

While the contrast in military experience between Montgomery and Patton was extreme, the same could not be said of their military talents. Both were highly dedicated, professional military officers, each convinced of his own ability to lead armies in the field. Ironically, it was this same dedication and conviction which led to their pronounced rivalry when they did command armies during the war. At the same time, there were a number of American commanders of the Second World War who gained solid reputations during the First. George C. Marshall, the Chief of Staff of the United States Army from 1936–1946, had risen to prominence through his service as Pershing's Chief of Staff while Troy H. Middleton, who saw service in Sicily, Italy and North West Europe, was noted as the finest regimental commander in the AEF during 1918.[15] Nonetheless, as Lucian Truscott admitted:

> My career prior to World War II was not unlike that of many other Regular Army officers of my own age group and background. … I was about as well trained and prepared as any … However, I had had no actual battle experience. I had never heard a shot fired in anger.[16]

This gulf in experience was mirrored by a dearth of contact between the two armies during the inter-war years. The isolationist stance of successive American governments, as well as the trade and naval rivalry which flared up between Britain and America, ensured that there were only very limited opportunities for British and American officers to meet during the 1920s and '30s. While British officers were busy dealing with the problems of Imperial policing, American officers served either at home or on duty in the very different surroundings of Cuba and the Philippines. The British maintained military contact and liaison with the French throughout the 1920s and '30s but there were very few meaningful exchanges between the British and American armies for nearly twenty years. One British Army history trenchantly commented that 'the abysmal ignorance of the American Army on British Army methods was only equalled by the ignorance of the British Army on US methods and problems'.[17]

---

[14]   Nigel Hamilton, *Monty: The Making of a General 1887–1942* (London, 1981), pp. 69–307.

[15]   Forrest C. Pogue, *George C. Marshall: Education of a General 1880–1939* (London, 1964), pp. 164–209; J.D. Morelock, *Generals of the Ardennes: American Leadership in the Battle of the Bulge* (Washington, DC, 1994), pp. 229–32.

[16]   L.K. Truscott, *Command Missions: A Personal Story* (Novato, CA, 1990), p. 532.

[17]   Historical Record, British Army Staff, Part III, Staff Duties, Training and Arms Branches, p. 9, WO202/918, TNA.

As Greg Kennedy has shown, American and British naval cooperation had begun as early as 1936 with attempts to find a joint solution to diplomatic and naval problems in the Pacific.[18] However, during the early period of the war, there were few points of contact where cooperation was actually possible or useful between the two armies. Not only was the US Army still wedded to a strategy of hemispheric defence, but its forces were woefully inadequate to take on any other task.[19] In the secret August 1940 staff talks held in London, and nicknamed somewhat disparagingly as 'Buffalo Bill' by the British, the British participants realised with disappointment that that the US Army would not be ready for combat operations for some considerable time. It was noted that:

(a)   The US could not at present put an Expeditionary Force into the field.

(b)   In 3 months *given sufficient notice* a small force of 3 divisions could be made available.

(c)   In 6 months this might be doubled.

(d)   In 12 months a considerable force of 9 Regular, 4 or 5 National Guard, 2 Armoured and 1 or 2 Cavalry.

(e)   The present US policy is to create a large Army of 1,200,000 men as soon as possible (Target date is July 1942 but it is not likely to be realized) and not a smaller force in a shorter time. This policy would have to be reversed to make (b) and possibly (c) a practical proposition.

(f)   Entry of US in to the war would increase the figure of (d) and possibly of (c).[20]

Their assessment that the US Army would not be ready for combat operations before the summer of 1942 proved remarkably prescient, and indeed the first major commitment of US troops to the European theatre did not take place until Operation Torch began on 8 November of that year. In this situation, it was not surprising that the first assistance the US Army was able to provide was to take over the garrisoning of Iceland during the summer of 1941, and once in the war, the first US troops to reach Britain's shores were sent to garrison Northern Ireland.

By 1941, the lack of contact between the two armies was recognised as a serious problem. General Wemyss, the head of the British Army Staff Mission in Washington informed London that:

---

[18]   See Greg Kennedy, *Imperial Crossroads: Anglo-American Strategic Relations and the Far East, 1933–1939* (London, 2002).

[19]   Mark Stoler, *Allies and Adversaries: The Joint Chiefs of Staff, the Grand Alliance, and US Strategy in World War II* (Chapel Hill, NC, 2000), pp. 1–40.

[20]   Staff Conversations, 27 June 40–12 Dec 41, WO 193/305, TNA.

> I believe that our knowledge of the US Army and its ways is probably more
> meagre than in the case of European Armies. This is the result of lack of
> opportunities for direct contacts and the interchange of officers which elsewhere
> has been so helpful. We may shortly have the Americans as our Allies, when it
> will be to our mutual advantage to have officers with practical experience of
> their Army.[21]

This situation meant that, once Roosevelt and Churchill had agreed to focus upon
the defeat of Germany first, many of the meetings between British and American
officers in 1942 were the first introduction not only to a foreign army but to a
different culture and society. The first American officers who arrived in Britain in
early 1942 found much to perplex them. Britain was still a country under siege,
with the evidence of the blitz in every major city. Its people looked care-worn and
shabby and the general mood was one of grim resignation. This contrasted sharply
with the peacetime atmosphere that still prevailed back home in America. Life in
Britain, with its strict rationing and strictly observed black-out, was their first real
experience of wartime conditions.

The startling realisation grew amongst many American officers that their British
allies were indeed very different. Many British officers regarded the enthusiasm
and brash forcefulness of their American counterparts as mere inexperience and
boorishness. British experience was easily mistaken for arrogance; but much of
the British impatience with inexperienced American officers and units had its roots
in the experience of the Great War. British officers who survived the experience of
warfare on the Western Front often showed impatience with *any* display of what
they regarded as inefficiency or incompetence. Many British officers had seen
too much action, most of it in difficult, if not impossible, situations against the
Germans. It might be said that some had had their enthusiasm and optimism beaten
out of them. In that sense at least, British arrogance was not always 'personal' and
not necessarily connected with any real sense of 'anti-Americanism'.[22]

At the same time, American officers were taken aback by the snobbishness
and social rigidity displayed by many British officers, while their arrogance born
of greater experience also grated. British officers usually impressed Americans as
being both supercilious and conceited. The British Army seemed dry and stuffy,
overcautious and too ready to find reasons not to act and American officers often
just as firmly believed that they had nothing to learn from an army that had been
beaten over and over again.

American officers also found real challenges in working with the British staff
system. The lack of previous contact between the two armies during the inter-

---

[21]   Lieutenant General H.C.B Wemyss, British Army Staff, British Joint Staff Mission
to VCIGS, War Office, 1 July 1941, Military Mission to USA, WO32/9464, TNA.

[22]   See Brian Holden Reid, 'Tensions in the Supreme Command: Anti-Americanism
in the British Army, 1939–1945', in Brian Holden Reid and John White (eds), *American
Studies: Essays in Honour of Marcus Cunliffe* (Basingstoke, 1991).

war years meant that their systems, methods, procedures and terminology had all developed organically with no attempt to make them compatible or understandable by each other. This meant that the very helpful guide to British forces prepared by the American G3 Operations ETOUSA in August 1943 had a six-page glossary of British military terms with a further twenty-three pages of British abbreviations and acronyms.[23] The British also recognised the problem in ensuring that British and American staffs could work efficiently. The War Office 'Notes from the Theatres of War' written after the Tunisian campaign noted:

> It has been shown that when staffs are composed of more than one nationality, or when troops of one nation are fighting under a formation commander of another nationality, difficulties are likely to arise unless higher commanders and staffs possess a knowledge, not only of the organization and staff methods of their allies, but also of the organization and general principles of the tactical employment of allied subordinate formations.[24]

This emerged as a serious problem since the need for the two staff systems to mesh together was important from the very beginning of the alliance.

The British staff system was idiosyncratic and highly confusing for American officers. It was still based upon divisions of responsibility that would have been recognisable to Wellington's staff officers.[25] In essence, the traditional binary system which divided responsibility between the Adjutant General's branch, or 'A' staff which looked after general administration, and the Quartermaster General's branch, or 'Q' staff which concerned itself with supply, had been overlaid, during the reforms following the Boer War, with a General staff branch which performed operational and intelligence functions. The system did not utilise a chief of staff and instead the senior general staff officer (usually a Brigadier General Staff or BGS in the case of an army staff) was supposed to act as 'a first amongst equals'. Not only was the system different but the British terminology for staff officers was confusing as it mixed archaic and modern terms which could be bewildering. It was later noted that: 'For those who have been taught staff functioning according to the United States system, one of the most confusing features of the British system is the terminology of organization as well as personnel'.[26] The British label for general staff officers of GSO 1, 2 or 3 meant very little to the Americans,

---

[23]   'Notes on British Forces', G3 Operations, ETOUSA, August 1943, United States, Army, European Theatre of Operations, United States Army Military History Institute (USAMHI).

[24]   'Notes from the Theatres of War', No. 16 North Africa, November 1942–May 1943, War Office 1943, USAMHI.

[25]   See S.G.P. Ward, *Wellington's Headquarters: A Study of the Administrative Problems* (Oxford, 1957).

[26]   J.D. Hittle, *The Military Staff: Its History and Development* (Harrisburg, PA, 1961), p. 159.

while terms such as 'Deputy Assistant Quartermaster General' which was then abbreviated to 'DAQMG' gave American officers no real indication of their role. When such staff terms were rattled off by British officers who were utterly familiar with their form and functions, it is no surprise that the British system appeared opaque to their American opposite numbers.

The American staff system had been developed under very different influences to the British. Prior to the deployment of the AEF in 1917, the American Army had lacked a properly organised modern staff system. As part of the preparation for the deployment of the AEF, General Pershing had selected groups of officers to study both the French and British systems as used in 1917. Although there was a trace of British influence, in that the Americans adopted the British custom of referring to members of the general staff branch as 'Gs', the dominating influence upon the AEF's staff system was French. This was entirely logical as the AEF had to maintain close coordination and liaison with higher and adjacent French staffs, but meant that the AEF adopted the French 'bureau system' of dividing the staff into five sections, with each section under an assistant chief of staff as well as a special staff group of technical advisers.[27] The AEF also adopted the French system of organising the staff under the control of a Chief of Staff who was to manage the staff and support the commander. Indeed, the AEF adopted French methods to the extent that the 'US staff system was fundamentally the same as the French'.[28]

When British and American staff officers came to work together, it took time for these two very different staff systems to be made to work together efficiently. John P. Downing, an American officer who worked in a British headquarters during the Tunisian campaign, experienced many of the initial problems. He later recalled his first briefing in the new and unfamiliar environment of a British headquarters: 'Tosh explained the map to me. The units were designated just the opposite from American custom: friendly units were in red pencil and the enemy in blue.'[29] Such seemingly small and amusing differences could and did have serious consequences during battle. Downing's found his first introduction to a British officers' mess even more disorientating when the talk turned to what should be served at the forthcoming mess Christmas dinner: 'The whole business seemed extraneous to me, like living in another world. An attack was coming up and yet the main conversation was about the price of the goose and how it would get cooked.'[30]

The perils for new American officers working with the British could be very real. Lucian K. Truscott, who later became one of the US Army's best fighting commanders of the war, very nearly found that his wartime career was over before it had properly begun. After attending a planning meeting concerning Operation Roundup, the projected emergency Allied invasion of France in 1942, Truscott wrote a personal memo about the discussion and left it on his desk. This was an

---

[27] Ibid., p. 211.

[28] Ibid., p. 212.

[29] John P. Downing, *At War with the British* (Daytona Beach, FL, 1980), p. 138.

[30] Ibid., p. 141.

innocent example of the lax security that the British suspected was rife within the American services. American officers, used to living and working in peacetime conditions, initially often failed to appreciate the overwhelming importance of security in wartime. However, when Truscott arrived in his office the next day, he found his British superior coldly handing his memo back to him – it had blown off his desk, flown out of the window, and landed in the courtyard outside. Had he been a British officer, Truscott would have been sacked immediately and his British superior imperiously informed him that it was only due to the 'considerations of Anglo-American relations' that allowed his mistake to be overlooked.[31] Truscott's experience reveals some of the difficulties and tense 'office politics' that could emerge in every Allied headquarters during the war.

We can however, gain a glimpse of successful staff working in the correspondence of Colonel William P. Jones. He served as an American officer in Force 141 which became Alexander's 15th Army Group Headquarters during the Mediterranean campaign. He later wrote:

> the British G Staff fit pretty well with our G1 and G2, and so did at least the corresponding parts of the Engineer and other Special Staff sections, but the A and Q Staffs (Administrative and Quartermaster = G4) were so far different from ours that there had to be practically separate American and British staffs in these fields. … In spite of these problems, I think the headquarters functioned surprisingly well.[32]

It can be difficult to gain a full sense of the various and conflicting views of each other that were held by British and American officers. Yet from their first meeting, thousands of British and Americans were developing opinions on the qualities and flaws of the other. Two middle-ranking officers of very different backgrounds can give us a glimpse into some of these attitudes and perhaps some of their consequences. Major General John P. Lucas first met British officers while he was serving as an observer for the War Department within Patton's newly activated Seventh Army during the invasion of Sicily. Lucas, who had served as an artillery battery commander in the First World War, seems to have taken a jaundiced view of his British counterparts. Acknowledging that there was 'a very profound and fundamental difference between the professional officer of the British Army and his American brother, a difference that is little understood by either individual',[33] Lucas clearly ascribed a great deal of weight to some of the suspicions current in the US Army that the war in the Mediterranean was being fought to preserve and extend the British Empire. Lucas continued:

---

[31] Truscott, *Command Missions*, pp. 34.

[32] William P. Jones to Dr B.F. Cooling, 2 July 1981, Allied Inter-Operability Study, Box No 3, USAMHI.

[33] 'From Algiers to Anzio', p. 6, The John P Lucas Papers, Box 1, USAMHI.

The officer of the British Army is only secondarily a military man. He is primarily 'Empire Conscious' and, with the sea and its lanes kept open by a justly famed and powerful Navy, the British Army has built the Empire. This has required force at times and diplomacy always. These men are, from their extreme youth, trained to think in terms of Empire safety and advancement and every action they take is coloured by a long-term policy which is, in many cases, only dimly understood by their Allies.[34]

Such views would have shocked his British counterparts who would not have subscribed to such opinions. If there was a long-term policy held by the British government concerning the Empire, then it was only dimly understood by most British officers who also would be unlikely to describe themselves as professionals. It is clear from Lucas's private diary that he was indeed suspicious of British motives in the Mediterranean campaign. In his capacity as an observer during Operation Husky, Lucas began to develop decided opinions on British performance:

The British are rather surprisingly slow. Two reasons, I think: (1) Strong opposition and (2) Montgomery is notorious for the meticulous care with which he prepares for his operations … Patton has done a splendid job in this operation but neither Eisenhower nor Alexander have mentioned that fact as yet. Alexander, in particular, has taken advantage of small incidents to embarrass him.[35]

These suspicions and mistrust certainly did not help Lucas when he took command of the Anglo-American 6th Corps at Anzio in March 1944. His relations with his British subordinates during the desperate fighting in the Anzio beachhead were never cordial and, indeed, the lack of mutual confidence between them was certainly a factor in his eventual removal from command[36].

An equal and opposite example of misunderstanding can be found in Lieutenant General Sir Frederick Morgan's enthusiastic account of his trip to the United States in the autumn of 1943. At this point, Morgan held the post of COSSAC (Chief of Staff, Supreme Allied Commander) for the projected Allied invasion of France but there remained no formal declaration of who the commander for the operation would be. Nonetheless, it was widely assumed that General George Marshall, the US Chief of Staff, would eventually be nominated to the position. Morgan visited the United States in the hopes of getting to know his future commander and beginning the work of finalising the details for the invasion.[37]

---

[34]   Ibid., pp. 6–7.

[35]   Ibid., p. 66.

[36]   Carlo D'Este, *Fatal Decision: Anzio and the Battle for Rome* (London, 1991), pp. 220, 403.

[37]   'Diary of Visit to USA', October 1943, Lt General Sir Frederick Morgan, 02/49/1, Imperial War Museum.

In common with many British visitors to the American capital, Morgan made the mistake of generalising about the American character from the sights and sounds of Washington. After visiting Arlington and George Washington's Mount Vernon Estate, he reflected:

> What is really most remarkable is to realize how, in spite of everything that is said to the contrary or in qualification, the real roots of this country lie in England. Another great fact which impressed itself on me is the extreme youth of this country as a country. It is, in fact, only some thirty years older than I am, myself. This is no exaggeration, since one can well date the birth of the national spirit of the United States from the termination of the Civil War.[38]

Just as British officers would have been shocked by Lucas's opinions, so most American officers would have been appalled to find that a senior British General could have such a mistaken view of America. Morgan's impressions certainly fitted the pattern of wider British assumptions concerning American 'youthfulness' and 'brashness' and that thus, the British acting as an older 'brother' should restrain and guide their more exuberant American 'cousins'. Such attitudes were at the root of much of the American infuriation with the British during some of the key episodes of the war.

Opinions and attitudes could divide and so could language. American officers, accustomed to hearing a Southern drawl or a broad Midwestern accent, were suddenly confronted with the 'received pronunciation' of the English upper classes. Truscott was perplexed by his first committee meeting in Britain. He found that the British officers 'spoke with astonishing rapidity, practically through closed teeth and little action of the lips. All this made it very difficult for me to understand English "as she is spoke"'.[39] The English mode of speech was easily parodied by amused Americans:

> So the General called for his battle map
> And figured a plan to escape the trap
> He jumped in his jeep and buckled his strap
> But his batman placed a tray in his lap
> And his Adjutant said, 'I say old chap,
> You cawn't do it now, it's tea time.'[40]

However, the differing vocabulary, terminology and meaning of expressions could have serious consequences on the battlefield.

---

[38]   Ibid.

[39]   Truscott, Command Missions, p. 32.

[40]   'Vignettes of Military History', US Army Military History Institute, March 30 1981, No. 172, USAMHI.

The first real contact between British and American soldiers occurred in the Tunisian campaign following the landings in French North Africa on 8 November 1942. There had been no time or opportunity to ensure that units from both armies knew how to work with one another and this meant that much of the cooperation which emerged between the Americans and British in the Tunisian campaign was of a highly improvised nature. Further, as the 'race to Tunis' developed in December 1942, British and American units were often thrown together at very short notice. The 17th/21st Lancers, as part of Blade Force, was directed to secure a road junction to the south of Mateur. In the heavy fighting that followed the Lancers worked alongside the 1st Battalion of the 1st US Armoured Regiment, equipped with Honey tanks. At one point the Lancers commanding officer was ordered 'to help the Americans by any means'. At the end of the fierce action, the British judged that the 'Americans had done well', having destroyed eight tanks for the loss of fifteen Honeys which were decisively out-gunned by their German opponents.[41] However, during this fierce fighting, the British and Americans had fought alongside one another rather than cooperated fully.

Not all of the improvised cooperation in Tunisia worked as well. On the night of 22–23 December 1942, the 2nd Battalion Coldstream Guards was ordered to assault the last major hill on the road to Tunis. Once 'Longstop Hill' was taken, the defences of the Tunisian capital would be wide open. The Coldstream mounted a vigorous attack which cleared off the German defenders. The only reserve in the area was the 18th US Regimental Combat Team which was then ordered to relieve the British battalion. The relief turned into a disaster. In heavy rain and pitch darkness, the different procedures each army used for conducting a relief in place led to confusion. All of the attempts at 'liaison' and 'co-ordination' (which were conducted very differently in both armies) ultimately meant that the American soldiers dug-in on the lower slopes of the hill rather than on the tactically vital crest. The Coldstream began their march back to a rest camp and had trudged fifteen miles when news came that the Americans had been counter-attacked and the hill reclaimed by the Germans. The weary British soldiers had to march all the way back and mount another attack to retake the hill. The episode caused considerable bitterness between the two allies even though the subsequent Coldstream report on the fighting noted diplomatically that, 'although the British and Americans speak the same language, cooperation at the battalion level in battle is very difficult on account of the differences in organization and terminology'.[42] The experience of the Tunisian campaign meant that cooperation at the tactical level between the two armies was generally approached with more care and preparation in subsequent campaigns.

---

[41]   R.L.V. Ffrench Blake, *A History of the 17th/21st Lancers 1922–1959* (London, 1962), pp. 93–96.

[42]   E.R. Hill, 'The Coldstream at Longstop Hill', *Army Quarterly and Defence Journal*, July 1944, p. 175.

In fact, such strains, tensions and misunderstandings have been common throughout military history whenever two or more armies have to work together in an alliance. It was not surprising that there were frictions and problems between the two armies given their initial lack of knowledge of one another. What remains surprising is that both armies took unprecedented steps to integrate their staff work and to cooperate in such an intimate way.

One of the most important innovations in full cooperation was the brainchild of George C. Marshall. The concept of a supreme commander flowed from his experience of working within the awkward command arrangements of 1917–18 and his assessment of the success of Foch in the role of Generalissimo of the Allied Armies[43]. The Supreme Allied Commander was meant to provide an essential link between the strategic concerns of the two nations and the operational dilemmas of the commanders in the field. There was great debate during 1942 as to who this person should actually be. General Dwight D. Eisenhower, with his wide grin and quick temper, soon became a soldier of international fame and significance but reached his exalted position almost by accident, or at least it seemed that way to the British. In fact, George Marshall had long had his eye on Eisenhower and had recognised his potential.[44] Once selected as the Allied Commander for the Tunisian campaign, Eisenhower became the one soldier who developed the experience, as well as possessing the skills of diplomacy and tact, to be the right man for the job. Ultimately, Eisenhower was selected as Supreme Allied Commander for each subsequent operation, through Sicily, Italy, D-Day and on into the final campaign in Germany. Brooke engineered General Sir Harold Alexander's appointment as Eisenhower's deputy for the Tunisian campaign. He purred that Alexander's appointment: 'could not help flattering and pleasing the Americans in so far as we were placing our senior and experienced commander to function under their commander who had no war experience. We were pushing Eisenhower up in to the stratosphere and rarefied atmosphere of a Supreme Commander.'[45] Brooke might well have added that that was where Eisenhower could do no harm and could exercise little real control over the campaign.

In fact, Eisenhower became an indispensable part of the Allied military machine although he soon realised just what a difficult task he had been given. He described his post thus: 'I am a cross between a one-time soldier, a pseudo-statesman, a jack-legged politician and a crooked diplomat. I walk a soapy tight-rope in a rain storm with a blazing furnace on one side and a pack of ravenous tigers on the other'.[46]

---

[43]   Alfred D. Chandler, *The Papers of Dwight David Eisenhower: The War Years*, No. 23, Volume 1 (Baltimore, 1970).

[44]   Carlo D'Este, *Eisenhower: Allied Supreme Commander* (London, 2002), pp. 284–92.

[45]   Alex Danchev and Daniel Todman, *War Diaries, 1939–1945: Field Marshal Lord Alanbrooke* (London, 2001), p. 365.

[46]   Stephen E. Ambrose, *The Supreme Commander: The War Years of Dwight D. Eisenhower* (Jackson, MS, 1999), p. 144.

Eisenhower's insistence on scrupulously fair dealings between the Allies became legendary. On one occasion, he demoted an American officer and sent him home for calling a colleague 'a son of a bitch'. The British officer went to Eisenhower to plead the American's case but Eisenhower insisted: 'I am informed that he called you a British son of a bitch. That is quite different. My ruling stands.'[47] American commanders were soon accusing their Supreme Commander of having 'become British'. Yet Eisenhower held firm to his original conception of the role throughout the war. He later commented to Brooke (who eventually came to appreciate Eisenhower's real value) that:

> My objective was always to promote a practical basis of co-operation founded
> upon mutual respect, understanding and complete frankness. In this I always had
> the warmest support from every officer, British and American with whom I was
> associated. That purpose continues, in my estimation, to be important.[48]

Eisenhower's insistence on cooperation and integration meant that the Allied armies in the field were supported by integrated and combined staffs which included officers and personnel from both armies, and worked efficiently and effectively together. The rivalries, arguments and tensions remained very real and important but the integrated staffs of Allied Forces Headquarters in Tunisia and Italy, and later the Supreme Headquarters Allied Expeditionary Force in Northwest Europe, were the essential glue that held the armies and their efforts together.

One aspect of this cement which bound the two armies together which has been long overlooked is the work of the British Army Staff in the United States. This was only one of a number of important missions which the British sent across the Atlantic to connect British and American government departments in their war work. However, the British Army Staff developed in a haphazard fashion which resulted in overlapping functions and not a little confusion amongst the members of the Missions and the Americans that had to deal with them. It was in the desperate days of July 1940 that the members of the British Tank Mission to America, under the chairmanship of Michael Dewar of the British Ministry of Supply, first arrived in Washington to an uncertain welcome. Its members were made only too aware that the general opinion in the American capital was that 'Britain would be defeated in the near future'.[49] Although the Mission was unsuccessful in its task of persuading the Americans to build British tank designs in American factories, it did eventually place large orders for American tanks which saw service as the M3 and M4 Medium Tanks.

---

[47]   Ibid., p. 81.

[48]   General Dwight D. Eisenhower to Field Marshal Alan Brooke, 4 March 1946, Eisenhower papers, Pre-Presidential Files, Box 3, Eisenhower Library, Abilene, Kansas.

[49]   'Recommended Changes to the Mediurm Tank Programme', 27 March 1942, AVIA38/137, TNA.

The War Office sent out a further Mission in August 1940 under Major General R.P. Pakenham-Walsh with a wider brief which included tanks and artillery. A proposal to equip the equivalent of ten British divisions with a full complement of American munitions and equipment saw further representatives required in Washington, and by January 1941, the nine representatives were brought together into No. 200 Military Advisory Mission to the British Purchasing Commission. Then, in April 1941, No. 29 Military Mission under Lieutenant-General Sir Colville Wemyss went to Washington to coordinate contact with American intelligence organisations. In June that year, No. 208 Military Mission was activated to act as the Quartermaster General's liaison on matters of military stores. This confusing situation was finally regularised in July that year when the various Missions, comprising 65 officers and 230 other ranks, were amalgamated into the British Army Staff. Once America joined the war, the Staff were able to operate openly as a liaison body between two allies and its work expanded dramatically. Its main functions involved supporting the Combined Chiefs of Staff in Washington, exchanging intelligence and information between the War Office and the US War Department, and organising the movement of equipment and supplies from America to British forces in the field. Even a simple listing of all of the various tasks and functions undertaken by the British Army Staff would give little indication of the vast array of work and responsibilities discharged. Yet, by the end of 1944, the British Army Staff in America had grown to encompass 400 officers, 500 other ranks including 300 ATS, and 1,000 civilians based in 45 stations across the United States.[50] This unsung organisation ensured that one important cog in the great machine of the Alliance ran smoothly.

The cooperation between the American and British armies may well have been profound during the Second World War but the end of the war also saw the abrupt termination of that relationship. Just as Lend Lease was terminated on the day after VJ Day so the United States Army was not able to cooperate with an ally in peacetime as it had in wartime and most of the organs which had enabled that relationship, such as the Combined Chiefs of Staff and the British Army Staff, quickly withered away.

In July 1946, the American and British Chiefs of Staff discussed the formation of a 'Fellowship of US-British Comrades'. This membership association was designed to 'perpetuate, develop and extend the spirit and practice of British-US cooperation which began in the combined and integrated headquarters and staffs of the Combined Commands, in each of which US and British men and women, serving under a single commander, worked together in the cause of freedom'. All agreed that this was a noble and admirable idea but money was required from each of the three services to kick-start the scheme. The US Armed Forces quickly allotted $10,000 but the British failed to come up with the required £2,500 to make

---

[50]   Historical Record, British Army Staff Part I: Historical Outline, p. 13, WO202/916, TNA.

the proposal a reality. The Fellowship died a rapid and quiet death.[51] This long-forgotten episode was an apt demonstration of the reality that Anglo-American military cooperation, while close during the war, was actually often only skin-deep. The close relationship between the two armies would only have existed in the memories of those who served were it not for the emergence of a new threat which required large-scale military cooperation. Yet that cooperation, important though it was, was never quite the same again.

---

[51] CAB122/1036, TNA.

Chapter 9

Cooperation in the Anglo-Canadian Armies, 1939–1945

Douglas E. Delaney

… Andy McNaughton came to see me about the misuse of the Canadian Corps during last week's exercise!! (I had been forced, owing to the situation which occurred in the exercise, to split the Canadian Corps and employ one of its divisions in another corps). Not according to the 'Convention'. However with a little talk we settled the matter amicably and all is now well. However, the 'Constitution' does not make things easier and renders the use of Dominion troops even more difficult than that of allies.

General Sir Alan Brooke, Commander-in-Chief Home Forces, following a meeting with Lieutenant-General A.G.L. McNaughton, Commander Canadian Corps, 31 January 1941[1]

Both McNaughton and Brooke heard harbingers in this incident they did not like. McNaughton worried that the splitting up of the Canadian Corps during Exercise Victor (22–25 January 1941) betrayed a British desire to carve up the Canadian contingent without consultation, treat it like any British formation, and dilute the Canadian profile in the war effort. Brooke grumbled, then and later, that McNaughton, and perhaps other Dominion commanders, would 'sooner … [risk] losing the war than [agree] to splitting the Dominion forces'.[2] Their concerns were understandable. A number of factors worked against smooth cooperation between the British and Canadian armies. The constitutional and legislative arrangements were cumbersome. A growing sense of Canadian nationalism found expression in Canada's political and military leaders of the Second World War. And the Great War experience, which had fuelled that Canadian sense of nationalism, had set significant precedents and shaped the Canadian Army's senior leadership of the Second World War. As might have been expected, these factors led to difficulties – difficulties that have preoccupied several historians, particularly Canadian historians, for some time.[3] And why not? The problems that arose between senior

---

[1] Alex Danchev and Daniel Todman, eds, *War Diaries, 1939–1945*: *Field Marshal Lord Alanbrooke* (London, 2001), p. 137 (entry for 31 January 1941).

[2] Ibid., p. 432 (entry for 21 July 1943).

[3] On the troubled McNaughton-Brooke relationship, see for example J.L. Granatstein, *The Generals: The Canadian Army's Senior Leaders in the Second World War* (Toronto, 1993), pp. 66–79; Captain John Nelson Rickard, 'McNaughton's Dagger: the Raising,

Canadian and British generals were real and they make for engaging reading. But, real though those troubles may have been, they belie the fact that cooperation in the Anglo-Canadian armies was really quite good. British military authorities very reasonably accommodated Canadian desires as to where, when and how Canadian troops would fight. And, in spite of numerous personality clashes, Canadian senior commanders did not allow national politics to interfere with the fighting of the war. Canadian formations served under British command and British units fought in Canadian formations often and effectively. In many ways, they were interchangeable. There was simply too much at stake and too much common ground in terms of training, doctrine, experience and outlook for the situation to have been otherwise. This chapter seeks both to analyse the difficulties of the relationship between the Canadian Army's senior leadership and the British high command and to explain why those difficulties had a negligible affect on the ability of the British and Canadian armies to work together.

The complex framework for the command and control of Canadian forces overseas 1939–45 had its roots in the precedent of the Great War, an event that accelerated Canada's move towards full autonomy. Canada may have been a self-governing Dominion since 1867, and the Canadian Militia Act of 1904 may have permitted that the senior army post in Canada could be held by a Canadian, but the country did not have a Canadian as Chief of the General Staff until 1908, and even that did not mean much.[4] When Canada mobilised the First Canadian Division in 1914, it promptly and properly placed the formation under the command of a British Army officer, Major-General Edwin Alderson. Canada simply did not have anyone with the requisite military experience and training to fight a division in 1914. Not until June 1917, when Canadian Lieutenant-General Sir Arthur Currie succeeded General Sir Julian Byng as commander of the Canadian Corps, did Canada have a general competent enough to take full responsibility for the

---

Training and Employment of the Canadian Army, 1939–1945' (Unpublished PhD Dissertation, University of New Brunswick, 2006); John Swettenham, *McNaughton, Volume 2, 1939–1943* (Toronto, 1969); and Terry Copp, 'Examining a General's Dismissal: Army Part 16', *Legion* (May–June 1997), http://www.legionmagazine.com/en/index.php/1997/05/examining-a-general%E2%80%99s-dismissal/. On Crerar's clashes with Montgomery, see Paul Douglas Dickson, *A Thoroughly Canadian General: A Biography of H.D.G. Crerar* (Toronto, 2007), pp. 326–36; Douglas E. Delaney, 'When Harry Met Monty: Canadian National Politics and the Crerar-Montgomery Relationship', in *The Canadian Way of War: Serving the National Interest*, ed. Bernd Horn (Toronto, 2006), pp. 213–34; Stephen Ashley Hart, *Montgomery and 'Colossal Cracks': The 21st Army Group in Northwest Europe, 1944–45* (Westport, CT, 2000), pp. 155–83; Granatstein, *The Generals*, pp. 108–15; and Nigel Hamilton, *Monty: The Field Marshal 1944–1976* (London, 1986), pp. 34–36.

   [4]   On the development of Canada's military forces between 1867 and 1914, see George F.G. Stanley, *Canada's Soldiers: The Military History of an Unmilitary People* (Toronto, 1974), pp. 233–305, J.L. Granatstein, *Canada's Army: Waging War and Keeping the Peace* (Toronto, 2002), pp. 24–52.; and Stephen J. Harris, *Canadian Brass: The Making of a Professional Army, 1860–1939* (Toronto, 1988), pp. 11–100.

nation's military forces in the field. Currie still had to rely on a number of British staff officers in key positions throughout the corps to make things work, but the appointment to corps command was an important step. The timing was right. It coincided with a growing sense of national identity throughout the corps and the Canadian government's desire to have a greater say in the direction of the war. Prime Minister Sir Robert Borden had just joined the newly-formed Imperial War Cabinet and he intended that Canada would have a say in how the war was fought. Appalled by the carnage of the Passchendaele offensive in the autumn of 1917, he reportedly told the British Prime Minister, David Lloyd George, 'If there is ever a repetition of the battle of Passchendaele, not a Canadian soldier will leave the shores of Canada as long as the Canadian people entrust the government of their country to my hands.'[5] His position, and that of his government, amounted to a veto for Currie, who had the 'right of referral' to the Canadian government on any matter concerning the employment and organisation of Canadian military forces overseas.

Currie took full advantage of his unique position in the British Expeditionary Forces (BEF). He maintained complete control over the composition and employment of the Canadian Corps's four divisions and its supporting troops. As an example, he resisted a BEF-wide reorganisation of infantry brigades from four battalions to three, opting instead to maintain four-battalion brigades because he believed the reduction in combat power would be detrimental to the fighting ability of his subordinate formations.[6] By 1918, not only did Currie's divisions outnumber their British counterparts 21,000 troops to 15,000 troops, he also had three times as many engineers and two more artillery brigades than any British corps commander in France or Flanders.[7] By its strength and its capability, the corps bought Currie credibility and influence. He could even determine under which army his Canadians would fight. At Passchendaele, he told the BEF Commander, Field Marshal Sir Douglas Haig that the Canadian Corps 'would not fight under [General Hubert] Gough', the commander of the British Fifth Army in whom Currie had little confidence.[8] Haig gave in, allowing Currie to fight under General Sir Herbert Plumer's Second Army. Currie exploited his 'veto' to get what he believed his corps needed, and yet he still did everything asked of him by the British chain of command. He fought the battle of Passchendaele to its agonising

---

[5]   Quoted in Robert Craig Brown, *Robert Laird Borden: A Biography, Volume II*, (Toronto, 1980), pp. 137–38.

[6]   Shane B. Schreiber, *Shock Army of the British Empire: The Canadian Corps in the Last 100 Days of the Great War* (Westport, Connecticut: Praeger, 1997), pp. 19–20.

[7]   Library and Archives Canada (LAC), RG 9, III, D2, Vol. 4809, File 196, 'Principal Differences Between Canadian Corps and British Corps'. (n.d.)

[8]   Sir Arthur Currie to Frank Underhill, 17 September 1920. Quoted in A.M.J. Hyatt, 'The Military Career of Sir Arthur Currie' (PhD Dissertation, Duke University, 1965), p. 131. See also Daniel G. Dancocks, *Sir Arthur Currie: A Biography* (Toronto, 1985), pp. 110–12.

conclusion, despite his well-voiced misgivings about the futility of the offensive,[9] and he later pounded his corps through six major offensive operations, during the last 100 days of the war, sustaining 45,830 casualties in the process.[10] Currie confirmed Canada's military autonomy while accumulating an impressive record of success on the battlefield. His influence on the generation of senior Canadian officers that followed him cannot be overstated.

The most significant of all those officers was Andy McNaughton. No one had more influence on the relationship between the British and Canadian armies in the Second World War. Having started the Great War as a battery commander, having earned a reputation as a highly-skilled artillery officer and counter-battery expert, and having risen to the rank of Brigadier-General in command of the Canadian Corps Heavy Artillery, McNaughton was both product and proponent of the 'strongly national atmosphere of the Canadian Corps of 1915–1918'.[11] Only 31 years old when the war ended, McNaughton was at the front of his pack of peers who stayed in the Canadian Permanent Force. In 1921, he attended the British Army Staff College at Camberley, where he received an exceptional confidential report.[12] Shortly after his return from Camberley, McNaughton became the Vice Chief of the General Staff, a post he held for four years. He attended the Imperial Defence College (IDC) in 1927, and became the Chief of the General Staff in 1929. McNaughton retired from the army, for the first time, in 1935 to become President of the National Research Council, a post that suited his considerable skill as a scientist.

His politics and his strategic outlook were both anchored in 1918. While attending the IDC, McNaughton produced a service paper entitled *The Principles of Imperial Defence: A Canadian Aspect*, in which he argued that the Great War had demonstrated that there was no going back to the deferential days of Canada's colonial past. In the next war, McNaughton argued, Canada would be more British ally than British subordinate. Future commanders of Canadian forces, in dealing with British military authorities, would have relationships analogous to the one that Haig had with Marshal Ferdinand Foch in 1918, 'which though in theory amounted to unity of command, was in fact nothing of the sort. The actual instructions to Sir Douglas Haig show that he had in no sense been relieved of his constitutional responsibility and that, for his actions, even in compliance with

---

[9]   Dancocks, *Sir Arthur* Currie, p. 111; and Hyatt, 'The Military Career of Sir Arthur Currie', pp. 130–32.

[10]   Colonel G.W.L. Nicholson, *Canadian Expeditionary Force, 1914–1919* (Ottawa, 1962), pp. 548.

[11]   C.P Stacey, *Arms, Men and Governments: The War Policies of Canada, 1939–1945* (Ottawa, 1970), p. 205. On McNaughton's Great War career, see John Swettenham, *McNaughton: Volume 1, 1887–1939* (Toronto, 1968), pp. 30–166.

[12]   Swettenham, *McNaughton*, Vol. 1, p. 193.

Foch's *instructions*, he would still be accountable to the British Government'.[13] McNaughton was arguing a Canadian case from a British point of reference. He might just as well have substituted Currie for Haig and Haig for Foch, but the analogy was clear enough. Not since 1917 could the British high command simply tell Canadian commanders what they were to do. McNaughton intended that it would remain that way.

While CGS and Canada's senior soldier, McNaughton immersed himself in Imperial-Dominion relations. In 1931, with the Statute of Westminster formally recognising the independence of the Dominions, he suggested an interdepartmental committee look at new legislation to delineate the legal relationship between the forces of Canada and the United Kingdom.[14] The result was the reciprocal Visiting Forces Acts of 1933.[15] The Canadian and British acts, nearly identical, defined the key terms that would be used to define relationships in the Anglo-Canadian armies during the Second World War: *serving together* and *in combination*. *Serving together* defined a relationship in which the forces of each nation shared little more than location, whereas *in combination* denoted a relationship in which the forces of one nation had been placed under the control of a commander from the other. Canadian troops were *in combination* when placed under British higher command in one of the active theatres of war, or when specifically assigned to a British formation, as was the case when the Canadian Corps acted as the Reserve for General Headquarters (GHQ) Home Forces from July 1940 to November 1941.[16] The Acts also included an important caveat: 'For the purposes of this section, forces shall be deemed to be *serving together* or acting *in combination* if and only if they are declared to be so serving or so acting by order of the Governor in Council ....'[17] Placing the authority for designating forces as either *serving together* or acting *in combination* with the Government of Canada ensured the 'right of referral' that had existed since Currie's time, a right that McNaughton held very dear. As his biographer has noted, 'he knew very well what this legislation meant for Canada and he refused to surrender a particle of it thereafter'.[18]

---

[13]   LAC, MG 30 E 133, Papers of General A.G.L. McNaughton (McNaughton Papers), Vol. 109, *The Principles of Imperial Defence: A Canadian Aspect*, p. 27.

[14]   See Swettenham, *McNaughton*, Vol. 1, pp. 249–52.

[15]   On the arrangements for the command and control of Australian and New Zealand forces, see Nicholas Mansergh, *A Survey of British and Commonwealth Affairs: Problems of Wartime Co-operation and Post-War Change, 1939–1952* (London, 1958), pp. 104–5.

[16]   In July 1940, McNaughton took command of the newly-formed 7th Corps, which included 1st Canadian Division, some British corps troops and, eventually, 2nd Canadian Division. The 7th Corps was redesignated the Canadian Corps on Christmas Day 1940.

[17]   House of Commons of Canada, *An Act Respecting the Visiting Forces of His Majesty, and the exercise of command, discipline and attachments of Commonwealth Forces when serving together* (Ottawa, 1933), pp. 5–6.

[18]   Swettenham, *McNaughton*, Vol. 1, p. 252.

Plucked from the presidency of the National Research Council by Prime Minister William Lyon Mackenzie King to lead the Canadian Army contingent overseas in 1939, McNaughton came back to the army with somewhat of a Messiah complex. Taking his role as Currie's heir seriously, he soon set about consolidating as much power and influence as possible.[19] Before he accepted the appointment as GOC 1st Canadian Division, he tangled with the Minister of National Defence, Norman Rogers, arguing that a fully equipped division was the minimum the Canadian public would accept as a fighting force and that any government that 'did not satisfy this desire would have difficulty remaining in office'.[20] McNaughton felt safe making that veiled threat. He knew he had a well-established reputation throughout Canada as a gifted soldier-scientist and his opposition to compulsory military service sat well with Prime Minister King, who thought McNaughton 'the best equipped man for the purpose'.[21] An order in council of 2 November 1939, provided that the 'appropriate Canadian service authorities' – meaning the Senior Combatant Officer (McNaughton) or the Senior Officer of Canadian Military Headquarters (CMHQ) – could designate portions of the Canadian forces 'in combination' if the situation demanded it.[22] McNaughton used that authority, promulgating eight 'orders in detail' for a variety of *in combination*-deployments between February 1940 and June 1943.[23]

However, McNaughton was not always wise about how he exercised his authority. In April 1940, for example, he agreed to a War Office request for a Canadian brigade to participate in an attack on Trondheim, Norway – but he failed to inform the Canadian government for more than 30 hours.[24] McNaughton undoubtedly felt a certain sense of urgency in the Trondheim request, and he was within his legal authority in accepting it, but the Canadian government, especially the Department of External Affairs, was miffed at the slow notice, and McNaughton seemed oddly surprised. He also seemed entirely put out when his Minister of National Defence, J.L. Ralston, later assured the Canadian House of Commons, 'the decision as to the employment of troops outside the United Kingdom is a matter for the Canadian government ... the appropriate Canadian service authority

[19]   As the Senior Combatant Officer overseas, McNaughton commanded 1st Canadian Division (August 1939–July 1940), 7th Corps (July 1940–December 1940), 1st Canadian Corps (December 1940–April 1942, and First Canadian Army (April 1942–December 1943).

[20]   Queen's University Archive (QUA), Norman Rogers Papers, Conversations with Major-General McNaughton regarding his acceptance of Command, 4 October 1939. Quoted in Granatstein, *The Generals*, p. 62.

[21]   LAC, William Lyon Mackenzie King Diaries (King Diaries), 6 October 1939.

[22]   *Proclamations and Orders in Council passed under the Authority of the War Measures Act, I,* pp. 165–166. Cited in Colonel C.P. Stacey, *Six Years of War: The Army in Canada, Britain and the Pacific* (Ottawa, 1966), pp. 255–56.

[23]   See Appendix G, Stacey, *Arms, Men and Governments*, p. 560.

[24]   Granatstein, *The Generals*, p.63.

[under the Visiting Forces Act] cannot authorize the embarkation of Canadian Forces from the United Kingdom without the authority of the Minister of National Defence.'[25] Piqued, McNaughton later told Prime Minister King that he 'would not accept censure and [Ralston] should be very certain he was right before he gave it'.[26] It was preposterous for McNaughton to take exception to his Minister's comments, but totally in character.

Incredibly, even after the Trondheim incident, he still managed to wring more powers from the Canadian Cabinet War Committee. On 31 July 1941, the Committee approved a small Canadian expedition to Spitsbergen. Owing to a high level of secrecy, it did so with only an outline plan of the operation and without knowledge of the objective location. But, in granting its approval, the Committee stipulated two conditions: that the operation should have 'the approval of the U.K government' and that 'General McNaughton be authorized to act, in this regard, on his own judgment, having regard to the prospects of success, and the risks involved.'[27] McNaughton played the secrecy card well and continued to play it well. As raiding operations increased in 1941, and as the need for secrecy remained extremely high, he convinced the War Committee to extend the provision of its Spitsbergen decision to other 'minor operations'. In effect, the Canadian Cabinet delegated to McNaughton the approving authority for anything short of a major raid. And even that restriction soon disappeared. In April 1942, when considering the possibility of a divisional raid on Dieppe, McNaughton requested that the term 'minor' be deleted from the authority granted him nine months earlier. And the Cabinet War Committee complied.[28]

With that much authority granted him, McNaughton felt obliged to defend Canadian military autonomy vigilantly with British military authorities. In January 1941, he wrote to Brooke that he was 'most anxious, on grounds both of military advantage and of constitutional propriety, that the Canadian Corps should be kept together' although he did recognize that he might consent 'for valid reason our Divisions might be detached.'[29] Brooke accepted McNaughton's position and forwarded the Canadian's letter to the commanders of the Southern and Southeastern armies, under whom the Canadian Corps might serve.[30] In July 1942, McNaughton told the Chief of Combined Operations, Vice Admiral Lord Louis Mountbatten, that all detailed proposals for Operation Jubilee, the raid on Dieppe, 'would be subject to my approval in the same way as C-in-C Home Forces and Chiefs of Staff Committee had approval for operations of British Troops' and he arranged, with the Commander-in-Chief Home Forces, General Sir Bernard Paget,

---

[25]   Stacey, *Six Years of War*, p. 263.

[26]   Ibid.

[27]   LAC, RG 2, 7C, Vol. 5, Cabinet War Committee, Minutes 31 July 1941.

[28]   LAC, RG 2, 7C, Vol. 9, Cabinet War Committee, Minutes 1 May 1942; and Stacey, *Arms, Men and Governments*, p. 209.

[29]   LAC, McNaughton Papers, Vol. 252, McNaughton to Brooke, 1 Feb 1941.

[30]   Ibid., Brooke to McNaughton, 5 February 1941.

for Lieutenant-General Harry Crerar, Commander 1st Canadian Corps, to act as the 'responsible military officer' for Canada.[31] Most British senior commanders accepted McNaughton's restrictions. General Sir Bernard Law Montgomery was an exception. In July 1943, McNaughton insisted on visiting Canadian troops in Sicily during the earliest stages of Operation Husky. But Montgomery, as Commander of Eighth Army, with 1st Canadian Division and 1st Canadian Army Tank Brigade acting *in combination*, objected to the disruption this would cause the green Canadian formations, both fighting their first actions of the war.[32] On his return from the Mediterranean, an incensed McNaughton – once again – took his concerns to Brooke, who by this time was Chief of the Imperial General Staff (CIGS). McNaughton considered it 'a matter of principle that there should be no doubt that representatives of the Cdn Army would have access to our troops at all times in their discretion'.[33] Brooke, who found McNaughton 'livid with rage' and 'spent 1¼ hours pacifying him', acknowledged 'failings in personalities' on both sides:

> it was typical of Monty to try and stop McNaughton for no valid reason, and to fail to realize, from a Commonwealth point of view, [the] need for McNaughton to visit the Canadians under his orders the first time they had been committed to action … [I]t was typical of McNaughton's ultra political outlook always to look for some slight to his position as a servant of the Canadian government. The troubles we had did not, I am sure, emanate from Canada, but were born in McNaughton's brain.[34]

Brooke was right in that the issue meant way more to McNaughton than it did to anyone in the Canadian government. Ralston later told McNaughton that the Canadian Prime Minister had expressed 'annoyance' over the incident, but 'not nearly the resentment that might have been expected'.[35]

McNaughton did take his 'ultra political outlook' too far. He thought he knew better than his own government when it came to matters of policy. His asserted his view that First Canadian Army not be divided with the British military authorities – and the Canadian government. By 1943, he was completely out of sync with his political masters. The Canadian Prime Minister may have entered the war wanting

---

[31]   Ibid., Memorandum Operation Jubilee, 25 July 1942; Memorandum Operation Jubilee, 20 July 1942.

[32]   On the 'Sicily Incident', see Rickard, 'McNaughton's Dagger,' 239–65; and Stacey, *Arms, Men and Governments*, pp. 224–28.

[33]   LAC, McNaughton Papers, Vol. 250, Memorandum of a Conversation with General Sir Alan Brooke at the War Office, Wednesday, 21 July 1943 (dated 23 July 1943).

[34]   Danchev and Todman, eds, *Alanbrooke War Diaries*, p. 432 (entry for 21 July 1943).

[35]   LAC, McNaughton Papers, Vol. 250, Memorandum of Discussion Hon. J.L. Ralston, Lt-Gen McNaughton, Lt-Gen K. Stuart, at HQ First Canadian Army, 29 July 1943.

only a small army contingent and a desire to avoid Great War-scale casualties (which he believed would invariably lead to another conscription crisis and a national split on linguistic lines) but, by 1942, public demand in English-speaking Canada for military action, had forced him to reconsider his position.[36] King could count votes, but he also understood McNaughton's inveterate opposition to any division of First Canadian Army – so the government side-stepped its senior general. In October 1942, Ralston and the Chief of the General Staff, Ken Stuart, travelled to London where they met with Prime Minister Winston Churchill and Brooke to convey two points of policy: first, the Canadian government's desire to see its troops in action during 1943, and second, that the Canadian Army did not have to be employed as a whole.[37] This came as a bit of a surprise to British military authorities who had been operating under the assumption that the 1st Canadian Corps and, after April 1942, the First Canadian Army were indivisible. Brooke remarked that it was also '[n]ot an easy matter to lock them into any of our planned offensives' because of what it entailed in terms of shipping changes and tasks already assigned to other formations.[38] But, in March 1943, King appealed personally to Churchill, and, after considerable administrative wrangling, in April, the 1st Canadian Division replaced the 3rd Division for the upcoming invasion of Sicily, much to the consternation of everyone in 3rd Division. McNaughton made his objections to the deployment known, but he learned to live with the decision. He became far more concerned in August 1943 when he learned of plans to send 5th Canadian Armoured Division and 1st Canadian Corps Headquarters to Italy. McNaughton, who could see the possibility of First Canadian Army, and his command of it, disappearing, confronted Ralston over the issue and threatened resignation, stating that if 'dispersal [of First Canadian Army] was decided on [Ralston] should let someone else carry on in command'.[39]

It was a foolish move because, by this time, McNaughton had very little support anywhere. King, who liked McNaughton for his anti-conscription stand, was going with the political flow. Ralston was tired of McNaughton's opposition to Mediterranean operations. Vincent Massey, the Canadian High Commissioner in London felt the same way and resented McNaughton's political meddling. But most of all, his Canadian and British military colleagues came to doubt his abilities as a field commander, none more so than Brooke. He had known McNaughton

[36]   J.L. Granatstein, *Canada's War: The Politics of the Mackenzie King Government, 1939–1945* (Toronto, 1975.); and Adrian Preston, 'Canada and the Higher Direction of the Second World War, 1939–1945', *Royal United Service Institute Journal*, 110 (637) (1965): 28–44.

[37]   Danchev and Todman, , eds. *Alanbrooke War Diaries*, pp. 327, 329 (entries for 6 and 15 October 1942).

[38]   Ibid., p. 329 (entry for 15 October 1942).

[39]   LAC, MG 27 IIIB11, James Layton Ralston Papers (Ralston Papers), Vol. 66, Notes on Meeting Ralston, Stuart, McNaughton, 5 Thursday August 5, 1943. See also LAC, William Lyon Mackenzie King Diaries (King Diaries), 10 August 1943.

since they had both served in the Canadian Corps Counter Battery Office during 1917–18 and he considered McNaughton a friend.[40] But Brooke had doubts as to McNaughton's ability to command a formation in the field, doubts which had begun to surface as early as June 1941: 'The more I saw of the Canadian Corps at that time the more convinced I became that Andy McNaughton had not got the required abilities to make a success of commanding the Corps.'[41] His impressions did not improve. Brooke visited First Canadian Army during the Home Forces exercise Spartan in March 1943, where he watched McNaughton try unsuccessfully to pass one corps through another. It confirmed his 'worst fears that he [McNaughton] is quite incompetent to command an army! He does not know how to begin the job and was tying up his forces into the most awful muddle.'[42] McNaughton's Canadian subordinates shared the same doubts. Even his protégé Harry Crerar turned on him. Within three weeks of Exercise Spartan, Crerar was lunching with the CIGS and discussing the 'best method of having McNaughton called back to Canada to avoid his commanding a Canadian Army'.[43] Crerar understood that, politically, any attempt to remove McNaughton could not look like a British initiative, so he advised Brooke to raise his concerns discreetly with Ralston and CGS Kenneth Stuart, which Brooke did during the Trident Conference at Washington in May 1943.[44] During a July visit to London, Stuart, who had been tasked to investigate the matter, found that Paget also shared Brooke's opinion; they both believed that, while McNaughton was a brilliant scientist with a talent for research and development, he was definitely 'not suited to command an army in the field'.[45] The machinations that followed were delicate and detailed accounts of McNaughton's removal have been told elsewhere.[46] Suffice it here to say that all the discussions and investigations led to a meeting on 8 November 1943, when Ralston and Stuart

---

[40]   Danchev and Todman, eds, *Alanbrooke War Diaries*, p. 536 (entry for 29 March 1944).

[41]   Ibid., p. 164 (entry for 15 June 1941).

[42]   Ibid., p. 388 (entry for 7 March 1943). For a more detailed account of McNaughton's performance on Exercise Spartan, see John Nelson Rickard, 'The Test of Command: McNaughton and Exercise SPARTAN, 4–12 March 1943,' *Canadian Military History*, Vol. 8, No. 3 (Summer 1999): 22–38.

[43]   Danchev and Todman, eds, *Alanbrooke War Diaries*, p. 391 (entry for 7 March 1943).

[44]   Dickson, *Thoroughly Canadian General*, p. 218–25.

[45]   Stuart to Ralston, 12 Nov 1943. Cited in Stacey, *Arms, Men and Governments*, p. 232.

[46]   Paul Dickson, 'The Hand that Wields the Dagger: Harry Crerar, First Canadian Army, Command and National army', *War & Society*, Vol. 13, No. 2 (1995): 113–41; Stacey, *Arms, Men and Governments*, 231–47; Swettenham, *McNaughton*, Vol. 2, pp. 721–350; and Granatstein, *The Generals*, pp. 72–82.

advised McNaughton that he would be relieved.[47] Not surprisingly, the soldier-scientist did not take it well and undertook to fight the decision. The problem was that all doors were closed to him. He cabled the Prime Minister on 10 November, but King, although he was sympathetic to McNaughton, did not back him. Brooke and Paget held their ground. And Stuart was even ready to support the dissolution of the First Canadian Army if it meant getting rid of McNaughton. McNaughton had little choice but to step aside, and the government announced his removal from command 'for medical reasons' on 28 December 1943.

Even though it ended unpleasantly, the period of McNaughton's tenure as Senior Combatant Officer illustrates very well how reasonably the British high command, and the government of the United Kingdom, accommodated Canadian desires concerning the employment of Canadian troops. In the spring of 1940, the requests for Canadian troop commitments to the Trondheim operation and the Second British Expeditionary Force went through the proper channels – from the War Office to CMHQ and then to McNaughton. Brooke accepted McNaughton's restrictions on detaching elements of the 1st Canadian Corps and, later, the First Canadian Army. In 1942, Montgomery relented and allowed McNaughton to insert Crerar into the operational chain of command for the 2nd Canadian Division raid on Dieppe as the 'responsible military officer' to the government of Canada. In 1943, when Canadian political authorities had a change of policy and requested the deployment of a division and an Army Tank Brigade to the Mediterranean theatre – to gain battle experience and to pacify Canadian domestic demand for action – Churchill agreed, and Brooke made room for the Canadians, bouncing a British division that had already been training for the operation. Later that year, when the Canadians decided they wanted to ameliorate their Mediterranean commitment with an armoured division and a corps headquarters, Brooke made it work over the objections of Montgomery and General Sir Harold Alexander, Commander 15th Army Group, who protested that 'we already have as much armour in the Mediterranean as we can usefully employ in Italy' and who did 'not want another Corps Headquarters at this stage'.[48] And when the time came to remove McNaughton from command, the CIGS suggested it to the Canadian Minister of National Defence, who, with the Chief of the General Staff, conducted his own very thorough investigation and took the necessary action. Even on the related issues of what to do with the First Canadian Army Headquarters, and who should command if it remained in existence, British military authorities, Brooke in particular, proved accommodating. Although both he and Stuart had thought it might be best to eliminate the First Canadian Army and carry on with two independent Canadian corps in two separate theatres, the Canadian government

---

[47]   LAC, Ralston Papers, Vol. 66, Notes on Monday November 8, 1943; and LAC, McNaughton Papers, Vol. 250, Memorandum of Discussions with Colonel Ralston (Minister of National Defence) and Lt-Gen K. Stuart (CGS), dated 10 November 1943.

[48]   The National Archives (TNA), WO 214/55, Papers of Field Marshal Earl Alexander of Tunis (Alexander Papers), Alexander to Brooke, 16 October 1943.

favoured the retention of the First Canadian Army. So, Brooke and Paget had agreed to fill out the First Canadian Army with a British corps under command, some British staff officers for the army headquarters, and line of communications troops.[49] And, while there had been talk of placing the Canadian army under the command of an experienced British general, Brooke accepted that, for political reasons, the post had to go to a Canadian.

Of course, British willingness to accommodate the Canadians was also tied to need and self-interest. Manpower was a persistent concern. In May 1941, the Field Force Committee promulgated its plan for a field force of forty-seven infantry divisions, ten armoured divisions and eight tank brigades.[50] The British Army was nowhere near capable of furnishing that many formations. In fact, to meet those projections the Dominions, India and exiled allies would have to be tapped for a combined total of 20 infantry divisions, two armoured divisions and one independent tank brigade. The number of divisions mattered because it affected British diplomacy. In November 1943, on the eve of the Tehran Conference with American President Franklin Delano Roosevelt and Soviet General Secretary Joseph Stalin, Churchill had twelve divisions (including three Canadian divisions) committed to Overlord while the Americans had already earmarked fifteen for the same purpose. Churchill needed a substantial field force to leverage his position with the Americans; so he insisted that the Secretary of State for War assign a further three divisions to Overlord because, as he wrote: 'I should like to be able to tell [the Americans], "We will match you man for man and gun for gun on the battlefront".'[51] Given what Churchill needed for diplomatic purposes, and given the unrelenting manpower problems of the field force, a Canadian Army of three infantry divisions, two armoured divisions, and two independent tank brigades was surely worth a compromise or two. Churchill understood that. So did Brooke.

After McNaughton's departure such compromises had to be made with Harry Crerar. Only one year younger than McNaughton, Crerar was similarly schooled and equally well connected in the Canadian and British armies. He had entered the Great War in 1914 as an artillery captain and finished it as a lieutenant-colonel commanding an artillery brigade.[52] While working in the Corps Counter-Battery Cell, he made friends of both McNaughton and Brooke, eventually succeeding Brooke as Staff Officer Royal Artillery. He attended Camberley in 1923, where

[49]   LAC, Ralston Papers, Vol. 66, Interview with Gen. Brooke, CIGS, Saturday, November 6, 1943; and Vol. 45, Substance of Conversation Between the Minister, General Paget, and General Stuart on Monday, Nov. 8, 1943.

[50]   David French, *Raising Churchill's Army: The British Army and the War Against Germany, 1919–1945* (Oxford, 2000), p. 186.

[51]   TNA WO 259/77, Churchill to Grigg, 6 November 1943; and David French, 'Invading Europe: The British Army and its Preparations for the Normandy Campaign, 1942–44', *Diplomacy and Statecraft*, 14 (2003): 278.

[52]   The definitive work on Crerar is Dickson, *A Thoroughly Canadian General*. For a concise synopsis of Crerar's career, see Granatstein, *The Generals*, pp. 83–115.

Brooke was one of his Directing Staff, and he stayed in England after the course to take a staff position under Archibald Wavell in the War Office. In 1929, when McNaughton became CGS, Crerar happily joined his mentor's staff at National Defence Headquarters in Ottawa, where he served until attending Imperial Defence College in 1934. In August 1939, Brigadier Crerar left the Royal Military College, where he had been Commandant, to set up the CMHQ in London and assume the responsibilities of Senior Officer CMHQ. In mid-1940, he left London for Ottawa and the appointment of CGS. During his eighteen months as CGS, the bureaucratically-adroit Crerar was unquestionably 'the catalyst' in getting a reluctant government to approve the creation of a Canadian field army.[53] Crerar returned to the United Kingdom in November 1941 to take temporary command of 1st Canadian Corps while McNaughton was ill and on sick leave. Like McNaughton, Crerar was a very proud Canadian, the main difference between the two being in how they intended to use the army to enhance Canadian autonomy and prestige.

Whereas McNaughton wanted to keep First Canadian Army intact and save it for a high-profile, Hundred Days-type drive against Hitler's armies, Crerar believed that Canadian credibility demanded some sort of combat action now. Shortly after taking temporary command of the Canadian Corps in December 1941, he let Brooke know that he was 'all out to play to the utmost', and his actions spoke to his sincerity in this regard.[54] He lobbied hard for Canadian participation in raiding operations, eventually securing the August 1942 Dieppe mission for 2nd Canadian Division.[55] In contrast to McNaughton, who tended to reject the input of British umpires and senior commanders out of hand,[56] Crerar invited Montgomery to give guidance on training and senior command appointments in the Canadian Corps, and he went along with nearly all of Monty's suggestions. Not surprisingly, this pleased Montgomery, who later told Crerar that he was 'well satisfied with the [1st Canadian] Corps' and that the Canadian general had done 'splendidly' during Exercise Tiger in May 1942.[57] Brooke too thought Crerar had improved the corps

---

[53]   Paul Dickson, 'The Politics of Army Expansion: General H.D.G. Crerar and the Creation of First Canadian Army, 1941', *Journal of Military History*, 60 (April 1996): 278.

[54]   Imperial War Museum (IWM), Papers of Field Marshal Viscount Montgomery of Alamein (BLM) 20/5, Brooke to Montgomery, 8 Jan 1942.

[55]   Stacey, *Six Years of War*, pp. 308–9; and Dickson, *A Thoroughly Canadian General*, pp. 198–203.

[56]   As just one example, see McNaughton's response to criticisms of Spartan, which he considered 'a quite inadequate test', LAC, MG 30 E 133, McNaughton Papers, Vol. 250. Memorandum of a Discussion Hon. J.L. Ralston, Lt-Gen McNaughton, Lt-Gen K. Stuart at HQ First Canadian Army 29 July 1943 (dated 2 August 1943).

[57]   LAC, MG 30 E 157, Papers of General H.D.G. Crerar (Crerar Papers), Vol. 2, Montgomery to Crerar, 30 May 1942. See also John A. English, *The Canadian Army and*

'out of all recognition' to what it had been under McNaughton.[58] Crerar was also fully supportive of the Canadian government's desire to see Canadians fighting in the Mediterranean, a point of view he saw fit to share with Brooke, Massey and Ralston.[59] Still, in spite of his more flexible approach to the employment and training of Canadian forces, Crerar took the business of Canadian military autonomy very seriously. In many ways, he was as drawn to national politics and grand strategy as McNaughton. He had served with alacrity on the interdepartmental committee that made recommendations to the Government of Canada on the Visiting Forces Acts of 1933.[60] He also wrote and spoke a lot on the 'important military problems which … we in Canada have urgent need to face'.[61] To Crerar, that meant strengthening Canadian defences at home and realising that the defence of Canada extended beyond Canadian borders and was connected with that of Great Britain and the other Dominions. Crerar was not shy about treading beyond the limits of strictly military affairs. His concern for Canada's autonomous position within the Empire, and within Imperial military coalitions, was strong, and would remain strong until the end of his life.

That penchant for politics did not endear him – at all – to Montgomery. In fact, it was the primary irritant in their relationship.[62] Montgomery believed that anyone who so concerned himself with political issues could not possibly be a field commander.[63] Immediately prior to assuming command of 21st Army Group, he wrote to the CIGS that Crerar was 'quite unfit to command an army in the field at present', recommending instead Lieutenant-General Sir Miles

---

the *Normandy Campaign: A Study of Failure in High Command* (Westport, CT, 1991), pp. 125–42.

[58]   Danchev and Todman, eds, *Alanbrooke War Diaries*, p. 388 (entry for 7 March 1943).

[59]   Ibid., p. 381 (entry for 10 February); LAC, Ralston Papers, Vol. 66, Notes on Meeting with Ralston, Crerar, Montague, 30 July 1943; University of Toronto Archives (UTA), Vincent Massey Papers, Box 311, Diary May 12th, 1943

[60]   LAC, Crerar Papers, Vol. 11, 'The Statute of Westminster and its Bearing on the Armed Forces of the Crown' (drafted by Lt-Col H.D.G Crerar) 1st Dec 1931; 'Second Interim Report Submitted by the Interdepartmental Commiteee to Study Certain Questions of Defence and Discipline of the Armed Forces, which were Raised at the Imperial Conference 1930' (dated November 17, 31); and 'Second Interim Report Submitted by the Interdepartmental Commitee to Study Certain Questions of Defence and Discipline of the Armed Forces, which were Raised at the Imperial Conference 1930' (n.d.).

[61]   LAC, Crerar Papers, Vol. 11, 'Address to the Canadian Institute for International Affairs (also Given to the Canadian Institute on Economics and Politics, Geneva Park, 11 August 1936)' (n.d.); 'Problems of Canadian Defence' (1925); and 'The Development of Closer Relations Between the Military Forces of the Empire'.

[62]   Delaney, 'When Harry Met Monty', pp. 213–34.

[63]   On Montgomery's negative view of Crerar's political tendencies and how it affected his assessment of Crerar's generalship, see Hart, *Montgomery and 'Colossal Cracks'*, pp. 168–75.

Dempsey for command of First Canadian Army.[64] Crerar's insistence that he have an oversight role for 3rd Canadian Division's Overlord preparations, as he had done for the 2nd Canadian Division raid on Dieppe two years earlier, only soured Montgomery's opinion of him. Indeed, particularly with regard to Overlord, Montgomery did his best to exclude Crerar from any operational responsibilities, while 3rd Canadian Division was 'serving temporarily in another army'.[65] During a visit of the Canadian Prime Minister on 18 May 1944, Montgomery even tried unsuccessfully to secure King's concurrence in this regard. Crerar continued to assert his right to be consulted on all matters pertaining to the employment of Canadian troops; and this, combined with his support for Major-General Rod Keller, the egregious commander of the 3rd Canadian Division, only deepened Montgomery's conviction that he was 'very definitely not a commander'.[66] A month after the start of Operation Overlord, Montgomery advised Brooke that he was 'keeping [Crerar] out of it as long as I can'.[67] This did not sit well with the CIGS. He dealt daily with the issues of Alliance diplomacy, Commonwealth cooperation, industrial mobilisation and manpower shortages; so he understood and accepted 'the true position of Canadian Forces, and conditions connected with their employment'.[68] He could also read Montgomery's intentions. Getting rid of McNaughton had been difficult enough; getting rid of Crerar was out of the question: 'I want you to make the best possible use of Crerar, he must be retained in Command of the Canadian Army, and he must be given his Canadians under his command at the earliest possible moment. You can keep his army small and give him the less important role, and you will have to teach him.'[69] Montgomery relented and First Canadian Army Headquarters became operational on 23 July, but Crerar sensed the slight. It heightened his already-high sensibilities to doubts about his ability to command an army in battle. When Lieutenant-General John Crocker, Commander 1st Corps, objected to Crerar's plan for a limited attack to expand the bridgehead eastward, Crerar took it that Crocker 'resented being placed under my command and receiving directions from me … I do not know whether this attitude is personal, or because of the fact that I am a Canadian – but it certainly showed itself'.[70] Crerar's insecurities led him astray here. Crocker had a long reputation for being direct and honest when in disagreement with superiors, so this was nothing new for him; but Crerar did not know that in July 1944, and the timing of the dispute, coming as it did on the heels of Montgomery's obvious efforts to keep him

---

[64]   Liddell Hart Center for Military Archives (LHCMA), Papers of Field Marshal Viscount Alanbrooke of Brookeborough (Alanbrooke Papers), 6/2/23, Montgomery to Brooke, 28 December 1943.

[65]   IWM, BLM 73, diary 26 May 1944.

[66]   IWM, BLM126/9, Montgomery to Brooke 7 July 1944.

[67]   Ibid.

[68]   TNA, WO 214/55, Alexander Papers, Brooke to Alexander, 22 July 1944.

[69]   IWM, BLM 126/12, Brooke to Montgomery, 14 July 1944.

[70]   LAC Crerar Papers, Vol. 8, Crerar to Montgomery, 24 July 1944.

out of the battle, did not help matters.[71] Montgomery arbitrated in the affair, and Crerar and Crocker eventually got down to business, but the incident did nothing to raise Crerar's stock in the army group commander's estimation.

Their spats continued, mostly because Montgomery refused to acknowledge that Crerar could not be treated as any other British army commander. He fumed when Crerar missed a 3 September conference, ostensibly to attend a memorial service commemorating the losses of the 1942 Dieppe raid at the newly liberated port. In this case, Montgomery was the touchy one. He railed that the absence was inexcusable and told Crerar that their 'ways must part'.[72] This time, however, Crerar refused to accept the dressing-down, snapping back that he had responsibilities both to the government of Canada and to the soldiers of the 2nd Canadian Division, particularly the survivors of the 1942 raid, and he let it be known that he intended to raise the issue with his government. He even took the step of recommending to the Canadian CGS that the Canadian government change the relationship of First Canadian Army and 21st Army Group from 'in combination' to 'serving together'.[73] Montgomery was caught. He could not get rid of Crerar. Even Brooke could not get rid of Crerar, not easily anyway. Within a few days, Montgomery apologised, grudgingly, but his opinion remained unchanged. He tried again to keep Crerar out of action when the Canadian fell ill with dysentery during battles of the Scheldt Estuary in October, even trying to enlist the support of the Canadian Minister of National Defence at one point to thwart Crerar's return, but to no avail.[74] Crerar recovered and returned to battle by the end of October, and Montgomery still had his doubts, but Crerar performed satisfactorily for the rest of the war. He directed the gruelling Operation Veritable to a successful conclusion in February–March 1945, as an example; and the relationship between the two generals did eventually settle into something workable.[75]

But lost beneath the din of their clashes is the fact that Canadian and British formations worked well together. It is too easy to forget the obvious evidence that this was the case. While Montgomery and Crerar fumed over the Dieppe incident, 1st Corps (under First Canadian Army Command) was preparing to assault Le Havre, 3rd Canadian Division was closing in on Boulogne and Calais, 2nd Canadian Division was surrounding Dunkirk, and 4th Canadian Armoured Division was driving to Bruges and the Leopold Canal. Quite simply, while Montgomery

---

[71]   Douglas E. Delaney, 'A Quiet Man of Influence: General Sir John Crocker,' *Journal of the Society for Army Historical Research*, 85 (Autumn 2007): 185–207.

[72]   LAC, Crerar Papers, Vol. 7, Notes on Situation 2–3 September 1944. On the Dieppe ceremony incident, see J.L. Granatstein, *The Generals*, 112–13; and Dickson, *A Thoroughly Canadian General*, pp. 329–34.

[73]   LAC, Crerar Papers, Vol. 4, Crerar to Stuart, 5 September 1944.

[74]   Dickson, *Thoroughly Canadian General*, p. 358.

[75]   Montgomery did look into the possibility of having Dempsey's Second Army clear the west bank of the Rhine instead of Crerar's army, but that proved impracticable. Hart, *Montgomery and 'Colossal Cracks'*, pp. 176–78.

and Crerar bickered, their staffs and subordinates got on with the business of fighting the war. And they did so throughout the campaigns in Northwest Europe and the Mediterranean. First Canadian Army fought effectively under 21st Army Group for nearly ten months.[76] In Normandy, 3rd Canadian Division fought under John Crocker's 1st Corps for a solid month, then, near the end of July, Crocker's corps came under Crerar's command, where it remained until March 1945. Guy Simonds fought his 2nd Canadian Corps under Dempsey's Second Army during Operations Atlantic (Goodwood) and Spring, and, for the latter operation, he had 7th Armoured and Guards Armoured Divisions under command. Later, during Operation Totalize, Major-General T.G. Rennie's 51st (Highland) Division and the 33rd Armoured Brigade formed one of two armoured/mounted infantry columns for the assault.[77] John Crocker was delighted with the support he received from the 1st Canadian Armoured Personnel Carrier Squadron when he laid siege to Le Havre in September, and he was similarly pleased with the performance of 4th Canadian Armoured Division in Operation Suitcase north of Antwerp in October.[78] For Operation Infatuate in the Scheldt Estuary, the 52nd (Lowland) Division, the 4th Special Service Brigade and No. 4 Commando all served under Simonds – and this at the lowest point of the Montgomery–Crerar relationship. Brian Horrocks was 'impressed' with 2nd and 3rd Canadian Divisions, which formed part of his 200,000-man 30th Corps for the first phase of Operation Veritable.[79] He also described the mammoth administrative preparations as 'smooth' and Crerar as being both 'full of common sense' and 'underrated'.[80] In Operation Plunder, the crossing of the Rhine in March 1945, 2nd Canadian Corps again came under command of Second Army, with the exception of 3rd Canadian Division, which joined 30th Corps, and 9th Canadian Infantry Brigade, which fought as part of 51st (Highland) Division. In Sicily, during July and August 1943, Simonds had gained his first battle experience as GOC 1st Canadian Division, under Lieutenant-General Sir

[76]   Terry Copp's recent study of First Canadian Army operations in Northwest Europe argues that Crerar's resource-starved formations accomplished a great deal in the autumn of 1944, given the circumstances. Terry Copp, *Cinderella Army: The Canadians in Northwest Europe, 1944* (Toronto, 2006), pp. 57–83. And Montgomery did later admit to having made a 'bad mistake' in not assigning enough resources to clearing the Scheldt Estuary and the approaches to Antwerp. Field-Marshal Viscount Montgomery of Alamein, *Memoirs* (London, 1958), p. 297.

[77]   On Operation Totalize, see the very detailed study by Brian A. Reid, *No Holding Back: Operation Totalize, Normandy, August 1944* (Toronto, 2004).

[78]   C.P. Stacey, *The Victory Campaign: The Operations in Northwest Europe, 1944–1945* (Ottawa: Queen's Printer, 1966), pp. 334–35, 390–91.

[79]   Lieut-General Sir Brian Horrocks, *A Full Life* (London, 1960), pp. 243–55.

[80]   Sir Brian Horrocks, with Eversley Belfield and Major-General H. Essame, *Corps Commander* (New York, 1977), p. 182.

Oliver Leese's 30th Corps.[81] Later, despite personal problems that arose between Leese and Lieutenant-General E.L.M. Burns, 1st Canadian Corps fought its way, quite effectively, through the Hitler Line (May 1944) and the Gothic Line (August/ September 1944) as an Eighth Army formation. In the former operation, the 1st Canadian Armoured Brigade supported the 8th Indian Division in its crossings of the Gari and Rapido Rivers and, in the latter, the 21st Tank Brigade helped 1st Canadian Division break through the Gothic Line defences. And this is not a comprehensive catalogue of Anglo-Canadian land operations by any means. So the question begs asking: why did the friction that existed between high-ranking personalities in both armies have so little impact on the battlefield?

For a start, commanders and staffs in both armies spoke the same language – the language of common staff training, organisation and doctrine. The language of Camberley and Quetta permeated the senior officer ranks of both armies. [82] This was no accident. The War Office and the India Office took care to ensure common entrance examinations, similar curricula, continuous exchanges of Directing Staff and students, and adequate vacancies for Dominion officers.[83] Between 1919 and 1939, Canada sent 63 of its officers for two years of staff training at either Camberley or Quetta.[84] Forty-eight of them were still serving in 1939; and while that does not sound like a lot, it represented more than 10 per cent of all Canadian Permanent Force officers at the outset of war. All Canadian staff college graduates had connections, friends or acquaintances in the British or Indian Armies. Most rose to prominent rank. Even after Camberley and Quetta discontinued their year-long courses in the autumn of 1939 and converted to a series of abbreviated war staff courses, Commonwealth commanders and staffs continued to be infused with

---

[81]   On the rough relationship between Burns and Leese, see Douglas E. Delaney, *The Soldiers' General: Bert Hoffmeister at War* (Vancouver, 2005), pp. 154–56; and Granatstein, *The Generals*, pp. 133–43.

[82]   This had been the case since long before the Great War. See Richard A. Preston, "The Military Structures of the Old Commonwealth", *International Journal*, Vol . 17, No. 2 (Spring 1962): 98–121.

[83]   See the extensive correspondence between the India Office and the War Office on the 1938 reorganisation of Staff College Camberely into a Junior Wing at Camberley and a Senior Wing at Minley Manor, and how that affected the programme at Quetta. British Library (BL), India Office Records (IOR)/L/MIL/7/3203. This correspondence includes discussion on vacancies for Indian Army officers at both Camberely and Minley Manor, vacancies for British Services officers at Quetta, and positions reserved for Dominion officers at both Colleges. On common entrance examinations see, as just one example, *Report on the Examination for Admission to Staff Colleges at Camberley and Quetta held in February–March 1925* (London, 1925).

[84]   See Appendix II to John A. Macdonald, 'In Search of Veritable: Training the Canadian Army Staff Officer, 1899–1945' (Unpublished MA Thesis, Royal Military College of Canada, 1992).

a common method of doing business.[85] In 10–18 weeks, depending on the course, the stripped-down curricula of the war staff courses gave the students what they needed to be staff officers in formation headquarters – tactics, army organisations and weapons, staff duties, administration, and training. Some Canadian officers attended the British war staff courses in 1939 and 1940, but it was not enough to accommodate the rapid expansion of the Canadian Army. So, in the autumn of 1940, McNaughton had Guy Simonds establish a Canadian War Staff Course, which Simonds did largely based on the curriculum of the 17-week course at Camberley. The language stayed the same. Even after the Canadian War Staff Course relocated to the Royal Military College at Kingston, Ontario, in mid-1941, roughly one-third of the Directing Staff on any given course came from the British Army.[86] This level of common training and cross-pollination meant that staffs and commanders in the British and Canadian armies understood each other: they wrote their orders in the same formats; their staffs were much the same in terms of organisation and function; their divisions, brigades and battalions were nearly identical; and staff officers knew who to contact for what in the other nation's formations. A survey of war diaries for British and Canadian army formations in 1944 reveals remarkable commonality in orders formats, appreciations, letters, map markings, and fire-plans. The 3rd Division and the 3rd Canadian Division had more in common than a name.[87] Crerar certainly saw the value in common staff training. In spite of his strong national sentiment, he was against decentralised staff colleges for the British Commonwealth, something he felt certain would erode interoperability.[88] If there were difficulties, such as those that occurred between Crocker and Crerar in July 1944, they owed more to matters of personality or tactical opinion; it was not because the disputing parties did not understand each other. In fact, for Dempsey or even for Crocker, dealing with the 2nd Tactical Air Force in Normandy proved much more trying than any Canadian formation they commanded.[89] The Canadian and British Armies had so much in common it should come as no surprise that their units and formations were practically interchangeable.

Common battle doctrine also helped. The British Army, as David French has pointed out, may have been doctrine resistant, but, after late-1942, Montgomery

---

[85]   See Joint Services Command and Staff College (JSCSC), Staff College War Course, 1939–45 Senior Officers War Course SD/INT/A/Q Precis; BL, IOR/L/MIL/7/3203 Creedy to Under Secretary of State, India Office, 28 September 1939; Wartime Reorganization of the Staff College Quetta, 20 October 1939.

[86]   Macdonald, 'In Search of Veritable', Appendix IV.

[87]   See, for example, the War Diaries for Operation Charnwood, 7–9 July 1944. WO 171/410, War Diary (WD) 3rd Division; and LAC, RG 24 Vol. 13766, WD 3rd Canadian Division.

[88]   LAC, Crerar Papers, Vol.11, 'The Development of Closer Relations Between the Military Forces of the Empire'.

[89]   Terry Copp, *Fields of Fire: The Canadians in Normandy* (Toronto, 2003), pp. 92–97.

did successfully 'impose a single interpretation of doctrine on his subordinates',[90] and the Canadians had plenty of exposure to him – in the Southeastern Army, in the Eighth Army, and in the 21st Army Group. It was not just a combination of Montgomery and common training that disposed the Canadians to accept operational and tactical methods that favoured the carefully orchestrated application of firepower, the wearing down of the enemy, and neutralisation of his weapons as prerequisites to manoeuvre.[91] There were strategic considerations as well. Manpower problems imposed constraints on how the British and the Canadians fought. Whereas full mobilisation had exhausted British human resources and made manpower-conservation a principle of British doctrine, the spectre of conscription did the same for the Canadians. The Canadian government, the Prime Minister in particular, desperately wanted to avoid conscription as a means of replacing Canadian casualties.[92] Conscription in 1917 had led to outrage among French Canadians and riots in the province of Quebec; and the results of an April 1942 plebiscite on compulsory military service had shown that Canada was still completely divided on the issue – 83 per cent of English Canadians being in favour, 72.9 per cent of French Canadians being opposed.[93] With the government resisting conscription and with the prospect of a reinforcement shortfall, particularly for infantry, Canadian commanders had to be careful about how they spent their soldiers. Not surprisingly, the Canadians showed the same predilection for firepower as their British counterparts – better to spend shells than lives. A few examples of offensive operations make the point. When the Eighth Army started the assault for Operation Diadem in May 1944, it did so behind the earth-shaking fire of 1,060 guns, each firing an average of 420 rounds in the first 12 hours alone.[94] For Operation Charnwood, John Crocker's 1st Corps had for its attack on Caen the support of 467 heavy bombers dropping 2,562 tons of bombs, 632 guns, plus the naval gunfire of a battleship a monitor and two cruisers.[95] Ten days later, Lieutenant-General Sir Richard O'Connor had heavy bombers plaster five different targets with a combined total of 5,008 tons of bombs to pave a way for his three attacking armoured divisions.[96] For the first phase of Operation Totalize, Guy Simonds arranged for 1,020 bombers to strike selected targets with

---

[90]   French, *Raising Churchill's Army*, p. 281.

[91]   Shelford Bidwell and Dominick Graham, *Firepower: The British Army Weapons and Theories of War* (Barnsley, S. Yorkshire, 2004), pp. 282–97.

[92]   J.L Granatstein and J.M Hitsman, *Broken Promises: A History of Conscription in Canada* (Toronto, 1977), pp. 185–244.

[93]   Ibid., p. 171.

[94]   Lt-Col. G.W.L. Nicholson, *The Canadians in Italy, 1943–1945* (Ottawa, 1966), p. 401; and Brigadier C.J.C Molony, *The Mediterranean and the Middle East, Volume VI, Part I* (Uckfield, East Sussex, 2004), p. 99.

[95]   TNA WO 171/258, WD 1st Corps (July 1944), Operation Charnwood 1 Corps OO No. 3, 5 July 1944.

[96]   TNA CAB 106/959, The Goodwood Meeting, 18–21 July 1944.

3,462 tons of ordnance, then his armoured and infantry columns advanced behind a moving barrage fired by 360 guns.[97] Between Crerar, Horrocks and their staffs, they coordinated the fire of five Army Groups Royal Artillery (AGsRA), and seven divisional artilleries for a preliminary bombardment that delivered an average of 9 tons of shell onto each of 268 targets, during the first 24 hours of Operation Veritable.[98] This is not to say that commanders in both armies applied template solutions to tactical problems – far from it. All of the operations cited above were unique in terms of enemy, terrain, the application of fire, and manouevre. But the fundamental assumption common to all was this: it is unwise to move unless you are able to neutralise whatever can hurt you. The stakes were too high and neither the British nor the Canadians could afford excessive casualties.

After considerable study, one scholar of military cooperation in the British Commonwealth came to this conclusion: 'No theorist would have devised it. It posed difficult problems to which solutions had to be found. But it worked.'[99] It worked indeed. The system was thorny and complex at times; no commander relishes arrangements in which subordinate commanders have rights of referral to their own governments. But, in the Anglo-Canadian case, the acknowledged right of referral accommodated a growing desire for autonomy – with the Canadian Army, with the Canadian government, and with the Canadian people. This was critical to sustaining Canada's war effort. So, whatever the inconveniences for the British high command, they were worth it for the five divisions and two brigades the Canadians brought to battle, especially in light of Britain's chronic manpower problems. There were difficulties, especially for those dealing most intimately with the awkward apparatus for Anglo-Canadian cooperation. McNaughton was unquestionably touchy and highly strung, but he still wanted to fight, and fight in what he considered the most significant way: with a big Canadian Army in Northwest Europe. Crerar was touchy too, but, in the end, he fought his army reasonably well, and did everything asked of him by 21st Army Group. Montgomery had no time for national politics, or for people who disagreed with him, but even he gave way whenever he had to do so. And Brooke had the unpleasant task of keeping all the egos under control, something that was never easy. Personality clashes did not help – no question – but neither did they derail what decades of common training, doctrine and experience had put on track.

---

[97] Stacey, *Victory Campaign*, p. 218.

[98] TNA CAB 106/991, Operation Veritable: Clearing the Area Between the R. Maas and the R. Rhine 8 February–10 March 1945, p. 51; and Stacey, *Victory Campaign*, p. 467.

[99] Mansergh, *Survey of British Commonwealth Affairs*, p. 107.

Chapter 10

The Naval War Course, *Some Principles of Maritime Strategy* and the Origins of 'The British Way in Warfare'

Andrew Lambert

Any study of the 'British Way in Warfare' must begin with Sir Julian Corbett's elegant, deceptive book of 1911, *Some Principles of Maritime Strategy*.[1] While many have noted its intellectual origins, the message it imparts and even the role it played in contemporary policy debates, few recognise that it had been developed to serve the educational needs of senior officers, and reflected eight years' experience teaching senior officers. Furthermore, the nature and significance of that teaching has been seriously underestimated ever since Arthur Marder's pioneering treatment in 1961.[2] In reality the War Course prompted the development of *Some Principles*, an educational text developed for senior naval officers. The War Course and the book were classic examples of British practice, informal, unplanned and slightly amorphous, which would be at once the key to their success, and the occasion for their obscurity.

Sir Julian Corbett (1854–1922)

The 'British way' was created by a remarkable man. As befits an Edwardian gentleman of leisure, Julian Corbett found his calling late in life. Despite obtaining a good degree and qualifying for the Bar, he spent his days travelling, fishing, and writing novels and plays before a chance commission introduced him to naval history. Joining the field at a peculiarly stimulating point, just as naval educational need and academic professionalism began to interact, his early works broke the mould of contemporary naval history. While the influence of Professors John Knox Laughton and Samuel Rawson Gardiner was obvious in his handling of evidence,

---

[1]   J.S. Corbett. *Some Principles of Maritime Strategy*. London 1911.

[2]   A.J. Marder. *From the Dreadnought to Scapa Flow: Volume 1. The Road to War, 1904–1914 (FDSF I)*. Oxford 1961. Basing his analysis on published memoirs and a few first-hand reminiscences Marder ignored the relevant archives, did not conduct a systematic analysis of the aims and objectives of the programme, or even a basic head count of how many officers attended.

Corbett's intellectual approach was original. He placed the study of naval affairs in the broad context of national policy, locating dramatic passages of combat in the development of national aims. The ability to draw out the larger patterns and ideas that informed past events would be his greatest asset. With forensic skill Corbett fashioned coherent, persuasive strategic studies from fragmentary evidence. While some details of his work have been modified over time, the larger patterns remain unaltered.

From the start Corbett avoided the Whiggish habit of using the past to set up the present. For him *Drake and the Tudor Navy* was not the dawn of the great empire he lived in, but a first faltering step toward a national strategy that could serve the vital interests of keeping Europe from falling under the dominion of a single, over-mighty, power while ensuring the defence of the British Islands. He made it clear that sea power was not a decisive instrument, especially in the days of Queen Elizabeth. At this stage he shared Mahan's tendency to dismiss the strategic impact of commerce destruction, despite finding good evidence that English naval operations had seriously affected the ability of the Spanish government to function.[3] Instead he stressed how often English aims had been thwarted by the lack of a professional army, and the failure of combined operations, linking history with contemporary writings by soldiers and journalists.[4] He stressed that British strategy was 'maritime', and not 'naval', emphasising the interdependence of the two services.[5]

The message was more clearly delineated in *The Successors of Drake*, where Corbett emphasised that this period taught 'the limitation of maritime power', not its strength, and that the 'real importance of maritime power' was its 'influence on military operations'.[6] He condemned the tendency to study naval and military history in isolation. These two books set out his life's work, the use of history to trace the evolution of an English/British strategy through historical case studies and strategic theory. However, there remained a missing dimension: he had no obvious audience, and therefore little stimulus to develop.

In 1900, Corbett began publishing in the new *Monthly Review*, edited by his friend Henry Newbolt (author of 'Drake's Drum' and other salty rhymes!). A Liberal/Imperial concern for Britain's status as a Great Power informed his writing, and he shared the platform with noted defence analysts Spenser Wilkinson, John Colomb, H.W Wilson and Colonel Frederick Maude. In 1902, he produced three articles on naval education, using information supplied by naval friends, notably

---

    3   J.S. Corbett. *Drake and the Tudor Navy*. 2 vols. London 1898 vol. II pp. 368–69; D.M. Schurman. 'Civilian Historian: Sir Julian Corbett' in *The Education of a Navy: The Development of British Naval Strategic Thought 1867–1914*. London 1965 pp. 154–55.

    4   J.S. Corbett. *The Successors of Drake*. London, 1900 pp. 407–9. G.S. Clarke and J. Thursfield. *The Navy and the Nation*. London 1897.

    5   The title of Corbett's key strategic primer of 1911.

    6   Corbett, *Successors* Preface pp. vi & vii.

Commander Herbert Richmond.[7] Corbett supported the reforms introduced by
Second Sea Lord Admiral Fisher, including a new entry scheme and curriculum
for the College at Dartmouth. This was not surprising; the key ideas used by Fisher
were Richmond's.[8] However, Corbett's impressive advocacy helped secure public
acceptance of radical change and opened the way to his life's work. He was 47.

Corbett's teaching career began in 1903, over the next eleven years he lectured
on the bi-annual Naval War Course, providing between ten and twelve lectures
a session, often repeated for officers unable to attend the full course. This was
his only teaching experience. He never held a university post, and rarely spoke
to civilian audiences. Every book Corbett wrote after 1902 was informed by the
specific nature of his audience – naval officers, educators and policymakers. He
was not, in the modern sense, a historian.

Corbett's Liberal/Imperialist politics informed the development of his strategic
ideas. He sought the security and stability of the Empire through adequate strength
and effective preparation. Over time Corbett responded to a variety of security
challenges, from the Continental delusions of the British Army to the naval dreams
of the Kaiser. That experience, reflected in the constantly changing syllabus of
the War Course, the opinions of those he taught and the intentions of the course
directors shaped his book, while the particular challenges of 1911 determined the
content and the style of *Some Principles*.

That his strategic concepts survived such temporary aberrations as the latter
stages of the First World War and the longer, if less bloody, age of the Cold War, to
reappear in the twenty-first century as the basis of British strategy should come as
no surprise. Corbett developed his ideas from a broad analysis of British strategic
experience, linking historical evidence, strategic theory and Clausewitzian
analysis. His purpose was to develop a theoretical understanding of the unique
character of British strategy.

The Origins of the Naval War Course

The opportunity for Corbett's work came with the creation of a War Course for
senior officers. While Fisher claimed the credit, he had been pushing at an open
door.[9] Admiral Philip Colomb had given six lectures a year at the Royal Naval
College Greenwich (RNC) between 1887 and 1895. These lectures formed the basis
of his 1891 book *Naval Warfare: Its Ruling Principles and Practice Historically*

---

[7]   B. Hunt. *Sailor-Scholar Admiral Sir Herbert Richmond, 1871–1946.* Waterloo,
Ontario, 1982.

[8]   D. Schurman. *Julian S. Corbett, 1854-1922. Historian of British Maritime Policy
from Drake to Jellicoe.* London 1981 pp. 29–30.

[9]   R. Mackay. *Fisher of Kilverstone.* Oxford 1973 p. 259. Fisher to Selborne 29.7.1901:
A. Marder (ed.). *Fear God and Dread Nought: The Correspondence of Admiral of the Fleet
Lord Fisher of Kilverstone: Volume I (FGDN 1).* London 1952 pp. 202–4.

Treated.[10] From 1898, College Captain Henry May delivered the lectures. In June 1900, the Admiralty directed the Admiral President of Greenwich to arrange 'for the formation of a Naval Strategy course at the RNC, on the general lines suggested in your memo and that of the Director of Naval Intelligence (DNI)'. This innovation followed an embarrassing question in the House of Commons, which elicited the inaccurate information that no attempt had been made to teach strategy to naval officers.[11] Henry May devised the initial Course, from an approved model: 'The broad lines on which the course was started were those of the American Naval War College but altered to suit the different conditions under which the work was to be carried out.'[12] The DNI agreed: 'when the course of strategy is in full operation … the RNC will be doing good work for the education of the senior officers of the Service.'[13]

In reality the War Course was founded by the DNI, Fisher's old friend Rear Admiral Reginald Custance, a serious student of strategy and tactics. Custance used his term as DNI (1899–1901) to raise the profile of his Department in Admiralty policymaking. The War Course was a logical development, and Custance probably discussed the subject with Fisher while they were colleagues at the Admiralty in the mid-1890s. They fell out spectacularly in 1901 over the issue of Mediterranean reinforcements.[14] Unlike Fisher Custance was not given to bragging, being more concerned with results.[15]

In September 1900, the Admiralty outlined the agreed elements of the War Course:

1. Prepare a plan of operations under existing conditions
2. Attack and defence of fortified places
3. Lines of communication, coal supplies in operations
4. British and Foreign Trade Routes
5. Tactical questions
6. Naval history 'one or more naval campaigns being selected for special study'
7. International Law

Students would also study steam, navigation, naval architecture and languages.

---

[10]   A work of similar purpose to Mahan's better known *Influence of Sea Power* of 1890. Like any serious naval educator, Colomb created his system as a synthesis between naval history and strategic ideas.

[11]   A.J. Marder. *The Anatomy of British Sea Power*. London 1940 p. 389.

[12]   Slade to Corbett RNC Greenwich 20.5.1906: CBT 13/2/1 Slade's Notes on the origins of the Course.

[13]   Admiralty to President RNC Greenwich 2.6.1900: ADM 203/64

[14]   Mackay, *Fisher* p. 237.

[15]   Custance to Bridge 17.10.1901; BRI1/15 in Mackay, *Fisher* at p. 238.

Just in case anyone thought these were mere training exercises: 'The results of the work of the class in the subjects under 1, 2, 3 & 5 of the War Course are to be forwarded for the information of their Lordships at the end of the session.' From the start the War Course provided analysis and advice that would otherwise have required the creation of a large staff on the German model. Little wonder no foreign officers were admitted. Two days later fundamental changes were promulgated affecting the work, and working conditions for captains attending the course. First, 'naval strategy and other technical subjects connected therewith will be compulsory', a development influenced by foreign experience with strategy courses which had 'hitherto not formed part of the usual curriculum'. With Treasury consent the course qualified for full pay, at a cost of £2,400 per annum, for 25 Captains and Commanders: now officers could be ordered to attend [16]

Initially Henry May taught the eight-month course alongside the demanding task of College Captain.[17] The original scheme proved to be overly compressed, allowing little or no time for the essential element of 'self-education', and conflated training and technical elements with intellectual work. Once this classic service education failing was regonised, such 'practical' elements as navigation and naval architecture were soon dropped.

The new programme required a public launch, which *The Times* provided in early 1902. The author, probably naval correspondent James Thursfield, linked the course with Mahan and the United States Naval War College at Newport, before developing a scathing critique of the intellectual failure of the Greenwich College to meet the aims of its founders in 1873, a failure he attributed to the dominance of mathematics. Like the American institution, the new Course would challenge hidebound ideas, and promote fresh thinking. Bitter experience and the absence of a British Mahan had persuaded the Admiralty to prefer a War Course to a College:

> Our own experience of colleges has been so pitiful that we prefer development along the lines of a naval war course, in which the students are the equals of the lecturer, as together they explore, with the aid of Intelligence Department reports and other publications, the lessons of history, commerce, and strategy.

Due regard was paid to the German origins of modern military education, citing Moltke's definition of strategy as 'the art of applying the available means to the desired end'. Britain was lagging behind all the 'great maritime nations' in such theoretical study. Clearly based on information provided by the DNI, the article complimented the current Admiralty Board for making a start and concluded with

---

[16]   Admiralty to Admiral President RNC Greenwich 20 & 22.9.1900: ADM 203/64.
[17]   Schurman, *Corbett* pp. 32–34.

a dire warning from the French army in 1870, reinforcing familiar lessons from the Boer War.[18]

May's handling of the second War Course impressed Captain Reginald Bacon. While Bacon recognised the underlying intellectual problems caused by changing technology and limited hands-on experience, the main lesson he took from the Course was the inevitability of a line-ahead formation in future fleet battles. However:

> These early war courses were chiefly useful in causing senior officers to 'think', and to bring them face to face with an appreciation of the vastness of the problems that war would create. … sudden inspiration could not be relied on to solve war problems, and he was made to realise the need for constant study and thought if he was to acquit himself with credit in the Great Ordeal. The appreciation of these facts was of even greater value to the individual than the actual instruction provided by the course.[19]

Such intellectual stimulus would be a major objective of this, and indeed any serious course of further education. Nor was it accidental: Corbett's 1903 lecture notes stressed 'object of course to direct and assist private study', because the 'practical advantage of historical study is the chief value of a method of studying strategy'.[20]

The Navy had taken a decisive step towards sustained educational improvement, but May needed help. While he handled the core naval subjects civilian experts and junior officers delivered the rest of the programme. May had been quick to pick out a talented student, Captain Reginald Tupper lately of the DNI's department, to lecture on the Spanish American War of 1898 and direct war games on the first two courses.[21] After the first course, supported by a random agglomeration of naval historians, May invited Corbett to contribute. Like most military educators May wanted something up to date:

> Within reason I would prefer that you should choose your subject. It ought however to be so far modern that some lessons applicable to present day warfare should be deducible from it.
>
>   Again I think a short course of lectures such as I am suggesting it might be desirable to treat either the tactics or strategy of the period as apart from other considerations.

---

[18]   'The War Training of the Navy. VII. The Naval War Course.' *The Times* 25.1.1902: p. 6 col. A.

[19]   R. Bacon. *From 1900 Onwards.* London 1940 pp. 30–35, at p. 32–33

[20]   Corbett, 'War Course Lecture notes October 1903': Corbett Lectures, Liddell-Hart Archives Centre (LHAC).

[21]   Reginald Tupper to Corbett 26.10.1906: CBT 13/3/69. R. Tupper. *Reminiscences.* London n.d. pp. 112–15. Tupper served at the Naval Intelligence Division in 1896.

However, it might appear with the benefit of hindsight that May knew little more about Corbett than that he had 'made a study of naval history' and showed no evidence of having read *Drake* or *Successors*.[22] Once again the connection may have been Custance. Not only did he believe that history was the key to the underlying principles of naval warfare, but he and Corbett, Councillors of the Navy Records Society, the unofficial Naval Historical Section, were working together to reissue eighteenth-century tactical instructions to the fleet.[23] Society publications, heavily influenced by the NID, were key texts for the War Course. Corbett would integrate historical material into an educational system dedicated to altogether more present-minded, practical attainments. The critical influence of the Navy Record Society on the War Course was recognised in 1903, when May joined the Council. After his death in May 1904 the new Course Director took his place *ex officio*.[24]

Corbett agreed within the week, and May began to refine his concept:

> With regard to the subject we had last year a series of lectures on tactics from Mr Hannay[25] bringing in the galley period & they may probably be repeated with some modifications this autumn – so that I should prefer that you should take up a subject in which strategy came in more. As Mahan has so well shewn politics will greatly affect any future struggle for sea power & it is distinctly necessary to remind naval officers that expediency and strategy are not always in accordance. An Admiral may have the force on the spot but may be restrained by political considerations from striking at the right time and place. Generally speaking the faults, failures & decadence of nations & their commanders are insufficiently considered, so that the difficulties likely to beset one in the present day are minimised.[26]

May's brief, which Corbett summarised as 'the deflection of strategy by politics', would dominate his teaching and writing for the next decade.[27]

---

[22] Henry May to Corbett 19.9.1902 RNC Greenwich: CBT 13/3/50: May offered £5 each for between four and eight one-hour lectures.

[23] A.D. Lambert. *The Foundations of Naval History: John Knox Laughton, the Royal Navy and the Historical Profession*. London 1998 pp. 200–201, 235–37. In *The Navy From Within* (London, 1939) at pp. 134 & 137, K.G.B. Dewar noted using these books to study tactics. He ignored Corbett, the editor of the material, following the bitter post-war feud over Jutland.

[24] For a list of Councillors 1893–1915 see: Lambert *Foundations* pp. 235–37.

[25] David Hannay, journalist and naval writer; his cursory, present-minded approach to naval history was an anathema to the new professionals, who took their lead from Laughton. Lambert, *Foundations* pp. 152, 161, 164.

[26] H.J. May to Corbett 27.8.1902 RNC: CBT 13/3/51

[27] J.S. Corbett. 'The Teaching of Naval and Military History' *History* April 1916, pp. 12–24.

After hearing his first lectures in late October, May considered Corbett had 'in a sense joined the Greenwich Staff' and should pay his respects to the Second Sea Lord, whose brief included Greenwich. The meeting between Fisher and Corbett would be postponed, but only briefly.[28] Not that Corbett lacked naval contacts. In November 1903 he dined at the Athenaeum with the DNI, Prince Louis of Battenberg, Sir James Thursfield, his art historian friend Sir William Richmond and his son Captain Herbert Richmond RN, the Directors of Naval Construction, William White, and of Naval Education, James A Ewing.[29] Personal, social and professional connections between Corbett, the Navy and the War Course meant it was but a small step from his social world into naval service.

The War Course at Greenwich

In early 1904, May devised a short course on strategy and fleet tactics for Admirals, asking Corbett to lecture on the American Revolution: 'the question is can we draw any useful lessons from the failures'. By this stage Corbett had become a core contributor to the Course, working with May to define and deploy the concept of 'Command of the Sea'. While May jokingly advised Corbett that his lectures were only laid on 'because naval officers needed keeping awake', he secured Treasury consent to put those officers attending on full pay.[30]

The War Course emerged just as key British policymakers, Prime Minister Balfour, John Fisher and navalist soldier Sir George Clarke, Secretary of the newly established Committee of Imperial Defence (CID), were beginning to develop a national or 'Imperial' strategy. Clarke tried to make the CID the central planning organisation of the British Empire, overseeing a joint-service maritime strategy that avoided the twin dangers of 'blue water navalism' and conscriptionist homeland defence.[31]

Clarke's intellectual influence on Corbett was obvious, notably in 1900 when he wrote: 'The real importance of maritime power is its influence on military operations.'[32] In 1902, Clarke advised him to focus on grand strategy, not naval operations: Corbett addressed England's strategic impact in the Mediterranean in the seventeenth century in his Naval War Course lectures, repeated as the Ford Lectures at Oxford in 1903. When they appeared in print as *England in the Mediterranean* Corbett credited Clarke with the key idea of showing how the Navy had exerted influence in a major theatre across a long period, neatly combining the twin strands of his career – historical scholarship and higher education. This

[28]   H.J. May to Corbett 30.10.1902 & 2.11.1902 RNC: CBT 13/3/54–5
[29]   Dinner at the Athenaeum 7.11.1903 signed menu: CBT 13/3–4
[30]   May to Corbett 20.1.1904: CBT 13/3/56–57: Admiralty to Pres RNC 4.5.1903: ADM 203/9
[31]   Schurman, *Corbett* pp. 21, 26 & 34.
[32]   Corbett, *Successors* p. vii.

ability to place his material in two distinct intellectual environments demonstrated considerable skill – skill consciously employed to bridge the potential divide between history and naval education. It would be a feature of everything he wrote thereafter. *England in the Mediterranean* stressed how a relatively small naval presence had exerted an influence far greater than mere numbers, or battles, would suggest.

Clarke's aim had been to prompt a public debate, secure closer cooperation between the services and thereby enhance the power of his office. In this he was doomed to disappointment. However, he continued to feed Corbett information to be deployed in the *Monthly Review*, 'preaching the gospel of Greenwich and Geo. Clarke – which they both want crammed in – that all our mistakes are due to neglecting to treat Naval and Military strategy as one'.[33]

Revising the Course

In June 1903, May reported that the second War Course – October 1902–June 1903 – had been attended by 29 officers, 32 having taken the previous course. However, only ten officers completed the eight-month course, five more had attended for seven months and another six remained at Greenwich long enough to gain some benefit. The programme needed to be reconsidered. The rapidly expanding Edwardian Navy needed many more officers of all ranks, so the best men were frequently withdrawn for command and shore posts. May proposed cutting the course by reducing language-teaching. The programme included lectures on the cooperation of naval and military forces by Lieutenant Colonel E.S. May RA (Professor of Military Art and History at Camberley); his namesake told him he could hardly pitch his lectures too low as naval officers knew virtually nothing about strategy.[34] May was pleased with the naval history lectures provided by Corbett, and Captains Anson and Tupper. He hoped more officers would volunteer. He recognised the need to study trade and commerce in war, hoping the Camperdown Committee would help to find lecturers. Tupper served as Secretary of the Committee, and devoted much of his career to trade issues.[35] To reflect current strategic concerns the War Game was set in the Mediterranean. The three-week course for Admirals was 'mainly intended to initiate these officers into the methods of studying strategy and tactics in use at Greenwich'. They also had the benefit of three lectures on International Law and Corbett's naval history course. May received very positive reports from all those who attended.

The Admiral Superintendent praised May's 'care and skill', suggested the Admiralty ensure the full course of 24 officers attended, and that the outside lecturers should be accessible to other officers. DNI Prince Louis of Battenberg

---

[33]   Corbett to Newbolt 15.6.1904 & 17.6.1904: CBT 13/2/25& 27.

[34]   B.J. Bond. *The Victorian Army and the Staff College, 1854–1914*. London 1972 pp. 197–98.

[35]   Tupper, *Reminiscences* pp. 143–4 at RNC and then Camperdown Committee.

minuted that attendance would be 'practically obligatory' while First Sea Lord, Admiral Lord Walter Kerr, directed May to provide reports for promotion and appointments. He concurred that the course should be divided into two shorter blocs, to improve the completion rate.

The new session saw two four-and-a-half-month courses replace the long course. This would require additional lecturers, and the Admiral President was to report on the cost implications.[36] May quickly reorganised the course, but the extra dozen naval history lectures required Treasury sanction, as they raised the cost from £400 to £550.[37] The intervention of Kerr, Battenberg and the First Lord, Lord Selborne, reflected the Navy's high-level commitment to further education. Treasury sanction indicated Cabinet-level concurrence. If the War Course had become a fixture it remained a fluid, dynamic programme.[38]

The Admiralty advised tightening up the curriculum for the short course, by dropping practical subjects, languages and navigation. Admiralty Secretary W. Graham Greene streamlined reporting procedures, requiring the Director to classify officers within each rank. These reports would be used by the First Lord's Private Office. On 21 August the Admiralty publicised the fact that there would now be two courses per year in the usual newspapers, and asked for volunteers.[39]

Slade, Corbett and Fisher

Henry May's sudden death in May 1904 was a shock, but he left a well-established programme in place for his successor, course graduate Captain Edmond Slade (1859–1928). An unusually well-read officer, Slade took a serious interest in the Franco-Prussian War and German military thinking, he would be the ideal foil for Corbett in developing 'the British Way'. He was also entering a minefield, for in October the new First Sea Lord Admiral, Sir John Fisher, embarked on a radical reform programme that would hasten the process of change.

Under Fisher's stewardship Slade was given two naval assistants and funds for extra outside lecturers.[40] Slade wanted to spread the word beyond the Course, advertising lectures by such luminaries as Corbett and Custance in *The Times* and the service clubs.[41] However, Fisher had different concerns: he wanted the Course to inform the development of naval policy, war plans and strategy. It would

---

[36]   Admiralty to Pres RNC 16.7.1903: ADM 203/9.

[37]   Report on the 2nd War Course 1902–1903, Submitted by R-Adm H.J. May 23.6.1903 with minutes. H.J. May to Admiral President RNC 25.7.1903. Admiralty to Treasury 19.8.1903 & reply 21.8.1903: ADM 1/7713.

[38]   R.H. Harris. *From Naval Cadet to Admiral*. London 1913 pp. 408–9. Harris was President at Greenwich 1903–6.

[39]   Admiralty to Admiral President 21.8.1903: ADM 1/7713.

[40]   Admiralty to Pres RNC 1.3.1905: ADM 302/9.

[41]   Capt of War College to Pres RNC 13.3.1905: ADM 203/9.

provide intelligent analysis of pressing issues, many of which related to the shift of strategic focus from France to Germany.

Having established himself as the key civilian contributor to the Course, Corbett was drawn into Fisher's orbit. Highly impressed by the *Monthly Review* articles on educational reform, Fisher had invited him to Portsmouth in 1903, to be briefed on other aspects of his incendiary reform agenda.[42] In May, he asked Corbett to comment on draft plans, and received 'a long and strong letter ... concerning the condition of strategical study in the Navy as revealed by the amateurish rubbish that appeared in official Admiralty papers. It ended in my being instructed to try to teach sea strategy at the War College.' Far from being annoyed Fisher applauded Corbett's honesty.[43] This initiative was supported by new DNI Captain Charles Ottley, another exponent of a combined maritime strategy.

Corbett became an unofficial member of Fisher's inner planning group just as the War Course took a turn towards 'staff and planning' functions, the DNI being overworked with routine business. This suited Fisher, who preferred to run at least two independent strategic planning units. It should be stressed that the lectures requested by Fisher and Ottley did not deal with strategic theory, they were historical case studies. Course Director Slade lectured on strategy, and helped Corbett produce a guide to the strategic terms used in the history lectures, the first draft of *Some Principles*. The additional lectures increased Corbett's role in the War Course at a pivotal moment in his intellectual development. A growing mastery of British naval history provided a rich collection of source material from which to develop strategic 'lessons', while his recent introduction to the strategic writings of Carl von Clausewitz provided the theoretical tools and structural framework needed to organise this material into a coherent system. While Corbett claimed the work was not easy, nor the audience appreciative, it would unwise to take his ironic self-deprecatory remarks at face value.

In reality Corbett addressed the anti-intellectual tendencies of the contemporary naval mind head-on, opening his guide to strategic terms – later known as the 'Green Pamphlet' – with an argument for theory. That battle won he turned to Clausewitz, especially his concept of limited and unlimited war.[44] The main lines of his strategic ideas were obvious from the outset, and appeared in print six years later, refined and developed by teaching and further historical study. Constant audience feedback refined Corbett's delivery, while the preparation of two major books and numerous lecture courses tested key issues raised by the strategic problem of Great Britain in historical terms. This originality was vital, old

---

[42]   Fisher to Corbett 6.7.1903: FISR 3/26 3722 FG I pp. 274–75.

[43]   Corbett minute attached to Fisher to Corbett 24.5.1905 & Fisher to Corbett 22.4.5.1905: FISR 1/4/166–8.

[44]   C. Bassford. *Clausewitz in English: The Reception of Clausewitz in Britain and America 1815–1945*. Oxford 1994 p. 97.

research reflects old circumstances – and old questions. Only a fresh examination of the evidence can hope to produce contemporary insight.[45]

An effective grand strategy would require improved links with the Army; Battenberg approved Slade's idea of a student exchange between Camberley and the War Course, if the Treasury would sanction the cost.[46] 'The more we can instil sound ideas on naval war and the practical possibilities of joint action between the two Services into the minds of rising military men, the better.'[47] It was highly significant that Slade invited Corbett, and not a naval officer, to lecture at Camberley. 'I think it very important that sound ideas should be inculcated in the Staff College. They are quite ready to receive them.'[48] Student exchanges and links between the War Course and Camberley were already in hand. Commandant Colonel Henry Rawlinson proposed Corbett's lectures should examine 'the Function of the Army in relation to gaining command of the sea, and in bringing war with a Continental Power to a successful conclusion'. The November 1905 course examined 'how we can confine enemy's strategy if we are acting with an ally as in 7 Years War'.[49] Influenced by G.F.R. Henderson's posthumously published essays, which may have introduced him Clausewitz, Corbett lectured on combined operations at Camberley and Aldershot in 1905, 1906 and 1907. Henderson's statement that the primary object of British combined operations was naval dominance provided a useful opening. While Rawlinson accepted this fundamental tenet of the 'British Way' he argued that, once command of the sea had been secured, an army would be needed 'to bring our opponent, whoever he may be, to complete submission'. But Rawlinson saw no need for these armies to be 'wholly composed of British troops'.[50] Both men took their inspiration from the Seven Years War and Corbett opened his lecture with an explicit statement: 'Combined Operations are the characteristic expression of the British method of making war, as opposed to the Continental method.'[51] Despite this promising start the Army lost interest in maritime strategy, it preferred to cooperate with the French rather than the Royal Navy.

That said, the new opportunities had an immediate impact on Corbett's work. The 1905 naval and military courses were published in 1907 with a telling sub-

---

[45]   A.D. Lambert. 'The Principal Source of Understanding: Navies and the Educational Role of the Past' in P. Hore (ed.). *The Hudson Papers Volume 1*. London 2001 pp. 35–66.

[46]   Admiralty to Pres. RNC 15.5.1905: Adm 203/9.

[47]   Battenberg Minute 16.11.1904: ADM 1/7859 cited in N. d'Ombrain. *War Machinery and High Policy: Defence Administration in Peacetime Britain 1902–1914*. Oxford 1973 p. 76.

[48]   Slade to Corbett 22 August 1905 (Royal Naval College): Corbett Lectures, LHAC.

[49]   Rawlinson to Corbett 25 August 1905 & Corbett notes on: Rawlinson to Corbett, 30 August 1905: Corbett Lectures, LHAC.

[50]   Rawlinson to Corbett 2.10.1905: Corbett Lectures, LHAC

[51]   'Combined Operations' Lecture 1. p1. Corbett Lectures, LHAC.

title: *England in the Seven Years' War: A Study of Combined Strategy*. His analysis of Britain's most successful maritime conflict was novel: 'history on the large scale with military principles guiding the selection'.[52] This Clausewitzian study of 'the British Way' at its zenith consciously harmonised political, diplomatic, naval and military elements as a template for contemporary strategy. Little wonder Fisher loved Corbett's 'luminous' book.

Corbett's initial idea, to write a book about strategy, had foundered on the very obvious rock of his legal training. Increasingly aware that the practical application of strategy turned on small details, he discovered that many 'standard' authorities were factually unreliable. Consequently the book evolved into a marriage of historical narrative and strategic commentary, giving due emphasis to the effective balance between naval, military and diplomatic effort, rather than focusing on any one arm.[53] He stressed that the Prussian alliance and the neutrality of Belgium had been critical.

To produce a modern teaching text for senior officers, a case study of British strategy in action, Corbett deliberately bent history to serve the didactic purpose: the dictates of Clausewitzian theory forced 'events into a posthumously conceived historical pattern'.[54] He did this with such skill that few historians have ever noticed.[55] He was a lawyer by training, an advocate of considerable literary power. The exercise proved successful: within a year he found the students using his ideas in exercises.[56]

The War College at Portsmouth

By this stage the Course had left Greenwich, and in January 1906 Corbett was lecturing at Devonport. 'We are much better installed than at Greenwich – "with every modern convenience." Round me is raging a most interesting war game to test what we could do in case of having to take up arms with France – but this in confidence. We are fast becoming something like a general staff.'[57]

This odd arrangement was no accident. Fisher opposed the establishment of a formal naval staff, he wanted a quasi-official body, under his control, to deal with the politico-strategic problems thrown up by his bitter rivalry with the Staff-led Army or with Admiral Sir Charles Beresford. In May he enquired if Corbett was interested in his 'scheme for the extension of the Naval War College at Portsmouth'.[58] Although he disclaimed any such purpose, Fisher wanted Corbett

---

52 Schurman, *Education* p. 164.
53 Schurman, *Corbett* p. 61
54 Ibid. p. 167.
55 Ibid. pp. 44–45, and discussions with Professor Baugh.
56 Schurman, *Corbett* p. 47.
57 Corbett to Newbolt 30.1.1906: CBT 3/44.
58 Fisher to Corbett 12.5.1906: FISR 1 /4 201: FG pp. 81–82.

to write a suitable press article. He need not have worried; Corbett took the bait because he saw the basis for an effective war-planning system:

> You will have no difficulty in interesting me in your scheme of extending the War College. My mouth waters already. For three years I have devoted all my energies to it, and nothing, not even your combined training, seems to me to promise more for the future of the Service. Captain Slade has been doing admirable work there and I am so glad to hear you are going to let him have more help. He deserves it and has really got more than he could do.
>
>   For another and different reason I rejoice at what you tell me, it is this. Those who are in strongest and most serious opposition to you – so far as I understand them – will find, if you carry this new idea through, the main strength of their current switched off. It is your supposed neglect of what you are now devoting yourself to that is their strongest line of attack … I am entirely at your service if there is any thing I can do to support or further your scheme.'[59]

A week later Slade sent Corbett notes tracing the origins and function of the War Course, stressing the growth of the student, body. When Slade took over in May 1904 he agreed to take up to 40 students, if he could have more assistance, which was duly provided. Reducing the course from eight months to four and concentrating on 'the study of the Art of War' had increased the tendency to cram. By 1905 he had a staff of five or six, and in November the first course was held at Devonport. By mid-1906 it had been agreed that the Course would be taught at Portsmouth, with shortened lecture programmes at the other ports. Links with Camberley included joint staff exercises on Combined Operations every spring: 'There are thus 40 or 50 officers of each service thrown together with a definite war problem before them to consider and discuss. The result is a very considerable modification of previously conceived ideas, and a much broader view of the whole subject on the part of everybody concerned.' The two men had already discussed the future development of the course, and Slade stressed:

> we are not copying the German Admiral Staff or General Staff – but that the development is going on on lines which are quite constitutional so to speak, and quite in accordance with our traditions. That is to say we are not trying to evolve a brand new department which is going to revolutionise the whole Navy & teach every body their work, but that we are merely providing a means of assisting the officer in our Admiralty scheme who holds the analogous position to that of the Chief of the Staff in a military sense, namely the First Sea Lord, by establishing a board of officers whose business it is to consider and thrash out systematically

---

[59]   Corbett to Fisher 13.5.1906: FISR 1/5 202 *FGDN II* pp. 81–82 Fisher endorsed this letter: 'Julian Corbett the best naval writer there is. This is written in 1906 and yet there are some people writing in 1912 that Sir John Fisher did not care a d…n about a war college or educating naval officers in strategy!'

all sorts of war problems, quite independently and unhampered by the routine work of an Admiralty department such as the NID.

He hoped the War College could serve this higher function without interfering with any existing institution. By combining the work of the War College and the NID the College could conduct planning exercises based on the latest intelligence, which would be quite distinct from the educational role. 'I do not think that the DNI need be in the least bit afraid of his position. It is important I think to emphasise the fact that the work of the two departments, the NID and the War College can and should proceed on absolutely parallel lines each helping & feeding the other.'[60] This link was emphasised by NID planner Captain George Ballard, top student and 'VG indeed' on the 6th War Course, March–June 1906.

Using Slade's notes Corbett produced two articles for *The Times*, suitably modified for a public audience. The course addressed the 'most serious problem' the Navy had to face, studying war at a time of radical change in materiel: 'the Navy had forgotten the art of war'. The Course had been developed by officers, not civilians, recognising the need to study strategy 'as a reasoned system, as a scientific study' to provide the language and concepts for discussions with statesmen and the framing of orders. That it took so long to start, and had been conducted in a less than systematic manner, reflected the national character. When May's initial course was split and shortened it was focused on the 'art of war' at the expense of training tasks. Even so, the first two courses, 58 Captains and Commanders, had a positive impact on the Annual Manoeuvres of 1903, manoeuvres Corbett had reported for *The Times*. Splitting the eight-month course increased the number of officers attending, and accommodated Admirals. More than 150 officers completed the 1904–5 courses, including 20 Admirals.

A second major reorganisation followed the introduction of the nucleus crew system. After initially being taught at Devonport, the Course moved to Portsmouth in 1906 and the Flag Officers' course was rolled into the regular programme. The main driver of this process was the increased size and complexity of war games, especially the strategic exercise – which could only be housed at Portsmouth and Devonport. Corbett also stressed combined staff rides with Camberley to establish unity of action between the two services. The Course, he argued in his first article, would broaden the outlook of naval officers, and ensure they understood 'the political and military' context in which they had to operate, including diplomatic, military, financial and commercial considerations – 'every factor, indeed, that goes to complicate the great game of war. Naval history is studied almost entirely from this point of view – the deflection of naval strategy by politics, and its domination by the military necessities of the case.' It only remained to engage the Foreign Office to complete the process.[61]

---

[60]   Slade to Corbett RNC Greenwich 20 May 1906: CBT 13/2/1.

[61]   J.S. Corbett. 'The Naval War Course I' *The Times* 5.6.1906: p. 6.

Four days later the second article addressed the future. Corbett stressed that, while the origins of the War Course lay in Continental General Staff systems it only prepared officers for high command, one of the three great functions of a Staff. The other two staff functions, war plans and intelligence, were handled by the Naval Intelligence Division. 'From the first it was recognised that a General Staff of the Continental pattern was not to be thought of for the Navy.' To compensate for the fact that the NID was overwhelmed with detail, the Course would produce advisory drafts from which the Board could develop war plans. At present 'there is today no machinery at the Admiralty or elsewhere for the preparation of plans of campaign ... it has to be done by the First Sea Lord himself'. The War Course could answer this need, filling a serious gap in Admiralty capabilities, without becoming a War Staff. The key was continuity.

> It must be cut free from Greenwich. It must be constituted as a sub-department, like the Intelligence Department, under a director of its own who is not hampered with the discharge of the petty administrative and disciplinary duties of the Captain of the Naval College.

A slight increase in staff would release the director to superintend a dedicated planning staff, acting under the First Sea Lord, in concert with the DNI. The planning staff would be selected Course graduates; their work would inform key policy and procurement decisions. Corbett preferred Portsmouth to Greenwich, which was ill-equipped, expensive and too close to the Admiralty. Linking planning with the War Course would provide an ideal opportunity to test ideas and concepts through syndicate work and war games. He was less concerned by the danger of losing touch with wider realities; the Course already possessed excellent external links. This organic growth would give the Navy 'the advantages of a General Staff, with none of the objections which have so long held us back'. To secure Fisher's support, he concluded that such planning support would strengthen the First Sea Lord and enable the Admiralty to present the CID with 'properly prepared' plans. Such a Course would 'probably establish relations with the General Staff of the Army, as it has already done with the Staff College'. The Course needed to speak with authority, and work in parallel with the NID; 'as though they were sections of one whole'.[62]

Delighted by such fluent advocacy of an Admiralty alternative to the 'General Staff' model he feared, Fisher acknowledged the War Course and the NID as the twin pillars of his war planning.[63] The *Manchester Guardian*, considering Corbett a 'good authority' on the success of the War Course, noted, 'We have more faith in the "war course" than in a few extra big guns or a larger "size" in battleships.' The Devonport based *Western Mercury* accepted the argument and provided a long

[62]   J.S. Corbett. 'The Naval War Course II' *The Times* 9.6.1906: p. 6.

[63]   Fisher to Corbett 11.6.1906: *FGDN II* p. 82. CBT 12/108.

quote.[64] In November the Course moved to Portsmouth, the staff being appointed to HMS *Terpsichore*, an old cruiser used for experimental duties.[65] To reflect the changes that had occurred since 1902 the course was renamed the Royal Naval War College on July 1 1907.[66]

The Green Pamphlet

To coincide with the move Corbett and Slade produced: 'Strategic Terms and Definitions used in Lectures on Naval History', the first text printed for the Course. Originally devised to establish a common language and accepted concepts to simplify the process of teaching this resume of strategic ideas and concepts – 'The Green Pamphlet' – was far more than a list of terms. Corbett subtly used it to infuse his ideas into his audience, avoiding confrontation. The notes were anything but routine; they stressed the critical importance of lines of communication, and the relative unimportance of battle. Writing in an age that anticipated fleet engagements would determine 'command of the sea', Corbett reminded his audience that there was a better measure of success, namely control of communications. It was not necessary to seek out and destroy an enemy fleet that could not challenge control of communications, even if it was still useful. Critically, Corbett stressed that the enemy could be forced to give battle by threatening a vital asset: with the strategic focus now on Germany the College began studying German Baltic trade routes, the obvious target for such operations. In 1908, three Captains, all Course graduates, were specially employed.[67] Naval Attache Captain Hugh Watson observed:

> my study of the German Navy has been a close one, extending over three years, first at the War College; then visiting German, Dutch, Danish, and Swedish naval centres; at the Intelligence Department of the Admiralty; and subsequently as naval Attaché in Berlin.[68]

Corbett's teaching was historically based, intellectually coherent, and entirely opposed to the quasi-Mahanian notions about the importance of battle, the irrelevance of blockade and other 'subordinate' methods of waging war then current in the Navy.

---

[64] *Manchester Guardian* 7.6.1906 & *Western Mercury* 3.7.1906: CBT 13/2/3–4.

[65] Terpsichore was the muse of dance. Admiralty to the President of the RNC 9.11.1906: ADM 203/10 For experiments to spot periscopes in 1909: FISR 1/9.

[66] Admiralty Order 1.7.1907 ADM 203/100.

[67] 10th War Course ADM 203/69 pp. 25–29.

[68] Watson to Admiralty 9.1.1912 in M. Seligmann (ed.). *Naval Intelligence from Germany*. Aldershot 2007 p. 367.

War Plans

At the same time Fisher employed Corbett to write an introduction to the 1906 Ballard Committee War Plans. It has been argued that the Ballard plans were a smokescreen, an idea that can be traced back to Arthur Marder and Peter Kemp. This is not credible: these plans, largely devised by the War Course and attached experts, but not Corbett, were a serious attempt to think through the nature of a major war in the light of the latest experience, especially the Russo-Japanese War. It was no accident that the Admiralty had two officers compiling an operational history of the conflict, or that it formed a major element in the teaching programme.[69] Recognising an opportunity to achieve two aims with one paper, Fisher required Corbett's 'introduction' to concentrate on the general strategic principles, which would 'add most materially' to their 'educational value'.[70] When they met a few days later Fisher stressed this 'epitome of the Art of Naval War' would be 'the Bible of the War Course'.[71] Corbett completed 'Some Principles of Naval Warfare' in April 1907, in meeting Fisher's specification he took a significant step towards the ultimate 'Bible of the War Course', his 1911 strategic study.

Because strategy is a practical art, works of strategic theory should always be considered in context. In 1907 Corbett wrote his strategic primer alongside three essays defending Fisher's naval policy: Fisher considered the first of these, 'Recent Attacks on the Admiralty', his greatest propaganda piece.[72] In March Corbett publicly challenged the anti-Fisher 'Syndicate of Discontent' defending the Dreadnought concept in the main military forum, the Royal United Services Institution.[73] It was a bold move, one that taxed his legal mind to develop an argument that would at one and the same time defeat the obscurantists and avoid giving offence to thin-skinned admirals. Carefully stressing the importance of the correct use of historical evidence, he undermined the arguments made by Custance, the leading intellect of the 'Syndicate'. A Mahanian thinker with a predilection for seizing odd pieces of evidence and making them fit his schemes, Custance was also a personal friend.[74] Three months later Corbett published another Fisherite essay in

---

[69]   A project that would ultimately involve Corbett.

[70]   Fisher to Corbett 9.3.1907: *FGDN II* p. 120 & Schurman, *Corbett* p. 67.

[71]   Fisher to Corbett 17.3.1907: FISR 1/5/ 2322 & Schurman, *Corbett* p. 67.

[72]   *The Nineteenth Century* February 1907.

[73]   J.S. Corbett. 'The Strategical Value of Speed' *JRUSI* July 1907. Delivered 6.3.1907.

[74]   Barfleur, pseud. R. Custance. *Naval Policy: A Plea for the Study of War.* London 1907. Corbett's copy of this text contains significant marginalia. Chapter IX 'The Speed of the Capital Ship' was the target of Corbett's RUSI paper. Slade to Corbett 16.4.1908: CBT 13/2/20.

the highly influential *Nineteenth Century*: 'The Capture of Private Property at Sea' set out the Admiralty case in advance of the Second Hague Peace Conference.[75]

At Portsmouth, the War College offered students a provocative combination of intellectual and practical approaches to key professional issues. Lectures and essay work were followed by tactical and strategic exercises in which the lessons learned could be exploited. The decision to teach men from four different ranks was slowly wound back; soon promising Commanders were the lowest ranking participants. The Course served another agenda: the assigned essay questions reflected current Admiralty concerns and student responses were circulated throughout the service by the DNI. There can be no doubt who was behind the question posed in March and June 1907:

> 3. What are the treaties dealing with the Baltic and the entrances thereto? What is the present political situation in that sea and how might it affect us?[76]

Or in October 1906 to January 1907:

> 8. If Germany attempts to close the Baltic in war with Great Britain how would it affect neutrals? What is the probable line of action? What were the rights of Denmark, and when and how were they given up?

In Spring 1908 Students were asked:

> 10. Discuss the best method of making use of the *Invincible* type of heavy cruisers in the case of a war with Germany. Which fleet should they be attached to, or should they act independently, and, if the latter, where?

Questions 25 and 26, 'How could we best support Denmark/Belgium should her neutrality be threatened by Germany?', provided ample scope for legal, geographical and strategic thinking. Similarly it is hard to avoid the conclusion that Fisher set the following question in the Autumn of 1908 and Spring of 1909, and drew a great deal of value from the answer.

> 18. Give a short account of the construction of the Kaiser Wilhelm Canal and its proposed alterations. How will this affect German strategy?

Geo-strategic analyst Halford Mackinder had lectured to the Course on the topography of the German and Danish coasts.[77]

---

[75] *The Nineteenth Century* June 1907: reprinted in A.T. Mahan (ed.). *Some Neglected Aspects of War*. Boston 1907 pp. 115–54.

[76] ADM 203/100 f. 19.

[77] ADM 203/100 ff. 89–91.

Starting with the 'Green Pamphlet' of November 1906, the College issued extensive handouts, reproduced from typescript using the Gestetner Cyclostyle process. A translation of Admiral Maltzhan's essay on Clausewitz appeared in 1906, a revised 'Green Pamphlet' in January 1909.[78] The College took a standing order for Navy Records Society volumes and other useful publications. In 1913, Cambridge University Press launched a 'Naval and Military Series', driven by the needs of the Naval War and Army Staff Colleges. Corbett took on the vital, if Herculean, task of general editor, and received a suitably encouraging letter from the First Lord's Naval Secretary – War College alumnus David Beatty hoped other civilian lecturers would publish: 'I shall look forward with interest to the publications.'[79] Among the select few to publish with this imprint early was Herbert Richmond, whose April–May 1911 lectures formed part of his book *The Navy in the War of 1739–48*.[80]

After 1902 the War Course/College dominated Corbett's intellectual life. His lectures were tailored to the development of naval thinking and international affairs, and he set his own work to one side so that he could concentrate on hot topics like Invasion and International Law. His work on these subjects informed Course lectures, published articles and NID submissions to the relevant CID enquiries. Corbett usually repeated his War Course lectures at Devonport, Chatham or Sheerness, ensuring a large body of officers had access to higher naval education.[81] It appears his work was highly regarded: he received £11.00 for a lecture, whereas others, like military historian John Fortescue, received only £5.00; even lawyers only charged £10.00. Corbett's fees swallowed up 40 per cent of the external speaker budget.[82]

Developing the College

In August 1907, Slade succeeded Charles Ottley as DNI: Ottley had just replaced George Clarke at the CID. He thanked Corbett for 'the help you have given me in working up the War Course to what it us now. I feel certain that without the assistance of your historical knowledge and deep reading I should not have been able to make it half the success that I feel it has been.' Their close personal and intellectual relationship would endure.[83] Slade would summon Corbett to develop

[78]   ADM 203/100 f. 59.
[79]   ADM 203/100 f. 96. Beatty to Corbett 25.11.1912: CBT 13/3/5. My copy of J. Corbett (ed.), *Naval and Military Essays* (Cambridge, 1914) bears the College stamp and that of the Imperial Defence College.
[80]   H. Richmond. *The Navy in the War of 1739–48*. 3 vols. Cambridge 1920.
[81]   ADM 203/100 ff. 11–15.
[82]   ADM 203/100 f. 25.
[83]   Slade to Corbett 17.8.1907 War College Portsmouth: CBT 13/2/11.

the Admiralty case for the 1908 invasion enquiry.[84] A shared interest in naval history and a sustained analysis of the latest strategic thinking, both British and German, ensured they kept in touch.[85] Having outgrown his original professional contacts, Corbett was well aware of his own status as a professional historian. He asked Newbolt to explain to Custance that:

> 'facts' are not history, but only its dry bones and … no one but an historian can hope to put flesh on them. I know he looks upon me as a traitor because I listened reverently to all he had to say, before performing the painful duty of shewing he was as incapable of drawing historical conclusions as I was of commanding a fleet … With all his regard for history he cannot see in it a profession as difficult, complex and absorbing as his own and that it does not begin and end with facts any more than his began and ends with guns.[86]

That Corbett preferred Fisher's detail-lite global vision to Custance's curiously pedantic approach was a sure sign of intellectual maturity.

As DNI Slade kept watch over the College, vetting his successors, and the new edition of the 'Green Pamphlet'.[87] He was not impressed:

> Between you & I Lowry has not got a real grasp of the principles, although he is better than he was. He has a lot to learn yet. He gave me his lectures to read that he is going to deliver to the next course. I had to criticise some of his statements … I don't know what to say about the strategy at the War College now, it is certainly not on a satisfactory footing, but as I said this morning I noticed a considerable advance since I last talked to them about it.[88]

In part the 'Green Pamphlet' was driven by Slade's opposition to aspects of Fisher's policy, he wanted more cruisers to protect oceanic commerce. Lowry's sudden replacement by Rear Admiral Lewis Bayly came as a complete, and far from welcome, surprise. Slades verdict was: 'an able man, but a crank. He is a nephew of Chinese Gordon and has many of his uncle's idiosyncracies. I do not think he is a well read man … He is not conspicuous for his tact.'[89] Little wonder Bayly found the two-year appointment 'a very dull time.'[90] Although he became

---

[84] Slade to Corbett 19.2.1908: CBT 13/2/16. Slade to Corbett 19.9.1908: CBT 13/2/28.
[85] Slade to Corbett 16.4.1908 5 Dawson Place: CBT 13/2/20.
[86] Corbett to Newbolt 25.5.1908: CBT 3/57.
[87] Slade to Corbett 11.9.1908: CBT 13/2/25 Slade to Corbett 18.9.1908: CBT 13/2/27.
[88] Slade to Corbett 23.9.1908 & 19.10.1908: CBT 13/2/24, 29 & 30.
[89] Slade to Corbett 16.11.1908: CBT 13/2/35.
[90] L. Bayly. *Pull Together.* London 1939 pp. 129–32.

Commander-in-Chief East Indies in 1909, Slade's interest in the War College never waned, nor did his desire for an Admiralty Staff:

> The function of the War College is not the preparation of war plans, but the investigation of war problems, on which the plans can be based. In order that the problem should be properly set, it is necessary that the conditions should be strictly limited & the question should always be formulated by the Admiralty; when the problem has been solved with one set of candidates it ought to be re-examined with a different set of candidates, not as a consequence from the past problem, but as an entirely new one.[91]

The War College essays were still circulated to the fleet, but neither they nor the Course Director impressed Slade:

> The last lot of essays … are all designed on narrow lines & deal with only one aspect & that the narrowest of the art of war. There is no attempt to make the men look deeper or wider for their inspiration than the gunnery manual & a few other kindred works. Then I hear the work with the soldiers is being stopped. That I am extremely sorry for as it is of the utmost importance for us to get to work harmoniously with them in Peace as we shall have to work very closely with them in war. I shall be very sorry indeed to see the War College become a narrow school of paper tactics and that is what I am afraid it is tending to.[92]

Fisher had Bayly produce a set of war plans in 1909, and these may have been a 'smokescreen'.[93] By 1910 Slade admitted that Bayly was 'coming round at last to see the importance of having a little education in the theory of war. He was most contemptuous about it when he started.'[94]

After 1900 Corbett's books were written for an audience of mid-career and senior naval officers; they valued his work. When *The Campaign of Trafalgar* appeared in June 1910, Wilmot Fawkes praised his strategic analysis, and his ability to show:

> what the Admiralty & the Admirals knew, the facts on which their decisions were based. How splendidly they worked together, anticipating orders & taking responsibility whenever necessary … I congratulate you most heartily & hope the book will be well studied by the rising generation of naval officers.[95]

---

[91]   Slade to Corbett HMS *Hyacinth* Colombo 5.8.1909: CBT 13/2/42
[92]   Slade to Corbett HMS *Hyacinth* at sea 29.10.1909: CBT 13/2/45
[93]   Bayly, *Pull Together* p. 131.
[94]   Slade to Corbett 4.5.1910: CBT 13/2/(50).
[95]   Admiral Wilmot Fawkes C-in-C Devonport to Corbett 29.6.1910: CBT 13/3/28.

Herbert Richmond, Captain of HMS *Dreadnought*, found it 'prodigiously interesting ... the old wars were not a mere heedless jumble of ships running about like mad dogs looking for some one to bite, but were organised concerns, planned on definite lines, and governed always by some particular objects'.[96]

Although he complained about becoming a 'hidebound bureaucrat', Corbett's enthusiasm and commitment never slackened.[97] That his brilliant exposition of national strategic doctrine, *Some Principles of Maritime Strategy* of 1911, was written, 'with some diffidence' at the behest of the Fisher,[98] might seem ironic if the purpose were not so obvious. Fisher recognised both Corbett's abilities and the need for a clear statement of national strategy based on the 'Green Pamphlet', the Ballard Committee introduction and the Report to the Invasion Enquiry of 1908.[99] Corbett's carefully calculated exposition of strategic concepts had three objects: to demolish the 'premature' incomplete and inappropriate 'naval' strategy promulgated by Mahan; to combat the Army General Staff and their 'Continental' ideas; and stress the critical role of the economic blockade in wartime. Clausewitz and other German military thinkers provided a strong conceptual framework for the naval case, demonstrating that the Army's 'German' intellectual base could equally well support a 'British' strategy. The job was quickly done, without waiting for a publisher's contract. Significantly Corbett changed his style: the strategy pamphlet and an early draft of the book employed irrefutable logic and withering scorn to demolish the fallacies of the unreflective; the book itself used less direct language, and relied on historical evidence to refute critics.[100]

Retaining the Clausewitzian form and structure of the original strategic pamphlet, suitably expanded by a broad range of historical examples – many of them from research conducted in the intervening years – Corbett repeated the argument that strategic theory was not 'a substitute for judgment and experience'. It was an educational tool that helped commanders make their own decisions, and provided them with a common set of term and concepts to convey their meaning to subordinates and colleagues.[101] Corbett's handling of Clausewitz was sophisticated and nuanced – using his theoretical framework to create a British strategy based on naval history. He developed Clausewitz's concept of limited war, a prominent feature of *England in the Seven Years' War*, by removing it from the difficult context of a European war, and elevated it into the master principle of 'The British

---

[96]   Richmond to Corbett HMS *Dreadnought* 30.6.1910: CBT 13/1/10.

[97]   Corbett to Newbolt 20.4.1909: CBT 3/7/65.

[98]   Obituary Notice by Richmond. *The Naval Review* February 1923 p. 18.

[99]   Schurman, *Corbett* p. 67, re correspondence of March 1907 between Fisher and Corbett, leading to the pamphlet 'Some Principles of Naval Warfare'. ADM 116/1043B. Corbett, *Some Principles* 1988 edn by E. Grove, p. xxiv, including the 'Green Pamphlet'. P. Kemp (ed.). *The Fisher Papers*: Vol. 2. London, NRS 1964 pp. 318–45.

[100]   Grove, 'Introduction' to *Some Principles* 1988 edn pp. xxiv–xxv.

[101]   Corbett, *Some Principles* 1911 pp. 1–8.

Way'.[102] Britain could wage limited war, using the sea to isolate enemy territory, thereby limiting the amount of force required to capture it as the ideal strategy in a war waged for limited political aims. Limited aims and the strategic use of the sea had been critical in the Russo-Japanese War. Corbett proved a far abler student of Clausewitz than of the contemporary German General Staff, which perverted his lessons on the political nature of war, creating a military solution to complex political problems. In addition, he demonstrated that decisive battle could only be secured under favourable conditions by forcing the enemy to fight, the best example was by cutting the enemy's vital trade routes. He shared Fisher's belief that Germany depended on iron ore from Sweden, so a threat to the Baltic would secure a decisive battle. An effective offensive strategy was essential if an inferior fleet was expected to give battle.

Like Clausewitz, 'Corbett wrote his strategy book as a result of rather than as a key to historical study'.[103] He reduced naval history to order, rendered the strategic issues clear for his students, and pointed up the critical fact that without professional historical research the work of strategists was inevitably flawed. Although *Some Principles* was developed from War College lectures it owed its public appearance to Fisher's anxiety to sustain his work into the post-Fisher era. While it did not please opponents of the Fisher revolution, men like Admiral Custance and Sir George Clarke, too much can be made of their futile fulminations.[104] It was intended to influence those outside the service. By 1914 Corbett's work was the basis of British strategy. This was only possible because Corbett had mastered broad swathes of naval history in breadth, depth and context. This enabled him to produce a serious, intellectually sustainable, framework for national strategy. The ideal forum for Corbett's views was the Committee of Imperial Defence. If the CID had failed as a strategic coordinating body by 1911 it was still the only place where senior politicians and service leaders met to consider Imperial questions. Fortunately the CID was run by Maurice Hankey, a junior officer with a strong sense of bureaucratic survival.[105] While Hankey could not direct or coordinate the work of the two services, he did, by sheer hard work and intellectual capacity, develop a strategic framework, and most of the details for a major war effort of Imperial scale and ambition, work was largely informed by close contact with Corbett and Richmond.[106]

For Corbett, the temporary, contingent nature of the book and the hostile response he expected from old friends like Custance made it, however necessary,

---

[102]   Ibid. pp. 54–55.

[103]   Schurman, *Corbett* p. 182.

[104]   Professor Schurman gives greater importance to the critics: *Education* pp. 183–84, & *Corbett* pp. 168–69, 177, 194.

[105]   D'Ombrain, *War Machinery* p. 273.

[106]   Ibid. p. 111. Hunt, *Sailor-Scholar* p. 42.

a 'difficult tasteless' process.[107] While he wrote *Some Principles*, Corbett taught the 16th War College Course.

The Spring 1911 War Course

By 1911 the War Course had been running for eight years, providing higher education for senior officers with a core naval staff on short-term postings and outside experts. The work was driven by real needs and examined real scenarios, links with the Army College at Camberley were good, and the Course added a critical leaven of intellectual rigour to the navy's salty professionalism. Furthermore the Admiralty took the results seriously. This new-found maturity was reflected in the appointment of Rear Admiral Sir Henry Jackson as Course Director. One of the sharpest minds in Fisher's technology group, and a key figure in the development of wireless radio, Jackson's innate modesty and tact masked a highly capable leader. He would go from the Course to become chief of the Admiralty War Staff in 1913. He was a sound and effective, if low-profile, First Sea Lord in 1915–16. His term at the War College was the ideal preparation for his Staff post, and equipped him to conduct the war at sea with economy and effect. Marder criticised his lack of drive, energy and aggression,[108] mistaking for inaction a recognisably Corbettian approach to the business of war at sea.[109]

Jackson's appointment marked a significant increase in the status of the course, and he would be the first Director to be spared Slade's criticism. Jackson's first Course ran between 6 March and 20 June. He lectured on strategy, preparation for war, cruisers, the development of modern warships and tactics. Lectures were given every morning at 9.30 and a smaller number at 10.40, leaving the rest of the day free for strategic exercises, private study, syndicate work and preparation. Course staff lectured on engineering, the operational and tactical side of the Russo-Japanese War, foreign naval developments, intelligence and submarine cables. Visiting officers discussed submarines, aircraft, Courts Martial, minelayers and naval hygiene. The wider themes were covered by external speakers: A. Pearce Higgins LLD provided twelve lectures on Maritime International Law; Douglas Owen examined aspects of merchant shipping in wartime, stop and search national economies, food supply and finance in ten lectures; Corbett examined the Russo-Japanese War, Combined Operations and the naval war after Trafalgar in twelve lectures.[110] The first week of April was spent at Camberley, joining a Joint Naval and Military Staff Exercise. The following week students took Easter leave.

---

[107]   Corbett to Newbolt 12.10.1911: CBT 3/75.

[108]   Marder, *FDSF I* p. 21.

[109]   Henry Jackson to Corbett 4.12.1916: CBT 13/3/39.

[110]   The four lectures on 'The Great War after Trafalgar' formed the basis for Corbett's last published essay of 1922. They demonstrate that before he signed the contract for *Some*

Jackson provided concise, critical analysis of the students. They were divided by rank, and then rated against their peers. Two Admirals two stood out – Vice Admiral Sir Stanley Colville and Rear Admiral Frederick Tudor Hamilton were equal top: 'very attentive and keen experienced officers'. Fifth-placed Rear Admiral David Beatty was 'smart and able, apt to be rash in conclusions'. Charles Dundas brought up the rear, being merely 'steady and attentive'. The Captains were divided by class and ranked: Alfred Chatfield was top, being 'First class, v.g. and very clever in explanation', while Henry Chatterton brought up the rear, second class, 'rather flighty and too talkative'. The two marines were only Seconds, but the two soldiers were both Firsts, and one gave a good lecture on discipline. Four officers were redeployed before they took a significant part in the Course.[111]

At the beginning of the Course Jackson circulated a question paper, and invited each section to select a topic, and decide whether to complete the task as syndicates, smaller groups, or as individuals. On this occasion the papers were not printed for circulation, possibly as a result of Slade's criticism.

R.N. WAR COLLEGE, PORTSMOUTH, Spring Session 1911

Proposed Subjects for Essays,

Section.

A

    1.   Discuss the question of the fortification of the mouth of the Scheldt, considering its bearing, if any, on the traditional policy of Great Britain – with regard to the Low Countries, and its effect on our policy as a belligerent in the narrow seas the various attitudes of Holland being taken into consideration

    2.   Discuss the proposed ratification of the Declaration of London, considering the causes which led to the Conference of 1908–9, and the advantages or disadvantages which might accrue therefrom to Great Britain as a belligerent or neutral.

B

    3.   Discuss the question of the use and necessary defences of Ports as designated in recent papers, vis : War Anchorages. Temporary Naval Bases. Defended Mercantile Ports. Coaling Stations. Ports of Refuge.

Principles, took on the *Russo-Japanese War* book and the Official History he planned to carry his historical/strategic analysis forward at least to 1815.

[111]   ADM 203/99 pp. 45–46.

4. Discuss the question of Commerce attack by Great Britain, with special reference to the general scheme of operations, visit and search of neutrals by ships and destroyers, prize crews etc.

5 Discuss the position of the Orkneys and Shetlands in a possible war with Germany, considering present and proposed communications, fortifications etc, and the possibility of a portion being seized by Germany.

6. Discuss the question of Colonial Navies and the trend of their development, and how they should be used in conjunction with our fleet for training purposes and in war.

C

7. What effect if any are Submarines and Air craft likely to have in the near future on British Naval Strategy and Tactics ?

8. Discuss the question of the best type of Conning Tower for battleships in connection with the arrangements for Control of Fire.

9. Discuss the use of Mine Layers and Mine Sweepers as an integral portion of the fleet in war, and their probable effect on the movement of the fleet.[112]

These essays, the only written work that students submitted, formed a significant element in their assessment. The subjects were all of the utmost contemporary interest, and informed by recent experience, especially the Russo-Japanese War. Corbett's 'History' was modern, and closely integrated to the rest of the course.

Corbett had achieved a striking success in generating a historically-based advanced education system for the Royal Navy, teaching the principles of strategy through Clausewitzian case studies. That he did not consider his work entirely successful, and the Royal Navy made little official reference to it, reflects the difficulties of measuring influence, not the reality.[113] His teaching influenced the men who mattered. For David Beatty the course proved highly significant, both as an intellectual stimulus and as the occasion he met Alfred Chatfield, who would be his flag captain for the rest of his seagoing service.[114] Fresh from the War Course Beatty turned down a post he considered useless as a preparation for war. Although by repute a bold huntsman with a zest for speed, Beatty was anything but an unthinking fire-eater – a type with which the pre-war Navy was amply provided.

---

[112]   ADM 203/100 p. 136

[113]   I disagree with Professor Schurman's conclusions on this issue in *Corbett* pp. 56–59.

[114]   A. Chatfield. *The Navy and Defence: The Autobiography of Admiral of the Fleet Lord Chatfield*. London 1942 p. 91.

An educated, reflective officer, widely read and suitably instructed Beatty took a serious interest in naval history, while his comprehension of Clausewitz reflected both Corbett's tuition on the War Course and his own experience of combat.[115] Similarly his definition of the attributes of a good cruiser captain was drawn almost verbatim from Corbett's *Campaign of Trafalgar*.[116]

On the next course, September to December 1911, the star was future First Sea Lord Rosslyn Wemyss who, Jackson noted, possessed a 'strong personality and has a good grasp of strategical situations' Former attaché in Berlin Captain Philip Dumas was 'very good at strategical research, and exercise work', while future Committee Chair Richard Phillimore was 'very good at policy'. In early 1913 the College moved even closer to the development of Imperial strategy, the Course Director noting

> In future officers who are considered particularly suitable for Assistant Secretaries Committee of Imperial Defence should be noted. This to include officers on staff. They must be commanders, preferably with sea time or just promoted. One will not probably be required till 1914. Cmdr [K] Dewar would probably be suitable. Dewar was retained on the Staff, perhaps pending such an opening. The next course was notable for the good discussions they took part in & for the excellent essays they wrote – not quite so keen on tactical games & strategical games as some of the other classes previously – but what they did required very little if any criticism. They all seemed to grasp sound strategical principles. The flag officers frequently assisted me in preparing schemes & researches for the Admiralty Staff, working together for a week with one staff officer to produce a combined opinion on the matter in question. This is worthwhile carrying out in future during the last 2 months of the course when not doing strategical games.

Martyn Jerram was the best Admiral, which suggests that Marder's dismissive treatment is wide of the mark.[117] However, the subsequent course starred Robert Arbuthnot: 'very good indeed. Has done exceedingly well, he has a great grasp of strategy & is very clear.' Perhaps Course performance was not the best guide to ability in combat.

The War Staff Course

The bitter clash between Fisher and Admiral Lord Charles Beresford reached a conclusion at a CID subcommittee in the summer of 1909. Beresford's latest attack on Fisher's administration prompted an unusually dramatic response from Prime Minister Asquith. Having chosen a CID Committee of key cabinet allies – Sir

---

[115]   B.M. Ranft (ed.). *The Beatty Papers* Vol. I. London NRS 1989 pp. 33 & 60.
[116]   Ranft, *Beatty I* p. 59.
[117]   Marder, *FDSF I* p. 39.

Edward Grey, Lord Haldane, Lord Morley and Lord Crewe – Asquith subjected Beresford to a sprightly legal cross-examination: finally brought face to face with facts the old windbag collapsed on almost all fronts. That said, Asquith had no intention of issuing Fisher with a blank cheque; the Admiralty was criticised for not taking Beresford into its confidence, and for not setting up a war staff along the lines adopted by the Army. This measure was considered essential to the effective coordination between the two services, which explains why Fisher was so opposed. He had no wish to become enmeshed in the Army's Continental plans. The First Lord of the Admiralty, Reginald McKenna, then consulted the CID Secretariat, Rear Admiral Sir Charles Ottley and Captain Maurice Hankey on the way ahead, given that Fisher's retirement was imminent.

Fisher responded by setting up the Navy War Council in October 1909, which had the authority to summon the President of War College, when necessary.[118] Slade considered this a farce, like other intellectuals connected with the War College such as Ottley, Corbett and Hankey, he favoured a Naval Staff acting under the direct authority of the Admiralty. The Government, especially Lord Haldane at the War Office, looked to Ottley to improve relations between the services. Despite being fobbed off by Fisher, who disliked any limit on his freedom of action, Ottley pressed on, outlining Corbett's next book:

It is submitted that the sole object of the instruction in strategy should be to throw into high relief the fundamental principles on which all sound strategy must be based. Although numerous military works on this subject exist in every language it is believed that there is no single naval treatise which could be used as a text book of strategy. These principles are of course to be found diffused through pages of writers such as Mahan, Colomb, Etc etc., but none of these have published works sufficiently concise to serve as handbooks.

In dealing with strategy therefore the Admiralty will have to trust to the discretion of the lecturer. Some guidance might be given him, however, as to the methods to be pursued …. There is reason to believe that the discussion of current strategy at both the Naval War College and the military Staff College have led to unfortunate results.

The principles of strategy can, however, be illustrated by history, or by the elucidation of imaginary problems.

The general principles of Imperial strategy, contained in various memoranda and Minutes of the Committee of Imperial Defence should be included in this part of the War Course.[119]

[118]   Ibid. p. 248.
[119]   Ottley memoranda submitted with Hankey to Fisher 10.1.1910: FISR 1/9/455.

Other subjects, notably logistics, intelligence, mobilisation and coast defence, would be taught from Admiralty and CID Memoranda. Staff duties were still being developed.[120]

In August 1911 Winston Churchill took office as First Lord of the Admiralty, with the specific brief to create an Admiralty Staff. In effect the Government forced him to adopt Ottley's concept. Churchill produced a memo on the subject in October, stressing that the best preparation for war required:

> education in the naval principles of strategy, which all historians agree to be permanent in their general application, it may perhaps be roughly estimated that a year's special course of study at the War College would answer the purpose. There is no text book at present which could be taken as the standard for such a course, but the subject is fully treated by Mahan, Colomb, Corbett and others in a manner which would suffice, if properly handled, until an authorised text book has been compiled from the material which may be extracted from their works.[121]

Within weeks the 'text book', *Some Principles*, appeared.[122] Although Fisher was out of office, and Arthur Wilson was uninterested, Churchill established an Admiralty War Staff in January 1912 which, for all its faults, placed naval planning on a secure footing, opening the possibility that Corbett's ideas would be taken seriously. That said, it was badly organised and inadequate. While Churchilll claimed it would be 'the means of sifting, developing, and applying the results of history and experiment, and of preserving them as a general stock of reasoned opinion available as an aid and as a guide for all who are called upon to determine, in peace or war, the naval policy of the country', it was not a true staff organisation. Nor did it become one until late 1917.[123]

Having created a Staff the Admiralty needed trained staff officers. The obvious solution was to add a Staff Course to the War College, sharing key elements like Corbett's history lectures, and using students as 'staff' for War Course exercises. As Course Director, Admiral Jackson was heavily involved, and additional staff were recruited. The Staff Course catered for Commanders, Lieutenant Commanders and Lieutenants and was run alongside the War Course. Trainee staff officers joined War Course exercises, as staff officers for the admirals. Between 1912 and 1914 the Staff Course trained 36 officers, including Bertram Ramsay. In 1912 Commander K.G.B. Dewar addressed the curriculum for the projected course. Under the heading 'History' he developed familiar arguments about the value of the subject for naval education:

---

[120]   Ibid.

[121]   Churchill memo. 28.10.1911: R.S. Churchill (ed.). *Winston S. Churchill. Companion Volume II part II*. London 1969 pp. 1303–12, at p. 1307.

[122]   The book was published in November 1911.

[123]   Roskill, *Hankey I* p. 100.

Any attempt to make Officers learn up historical periods or campaigns should be discouraged, the naval Officer cannot spare the time to study history for the sake of history.

He can however be taught to apply its teachings to modern problems and to get his facts as he requires them. The study of a past war should merely be viewed as a commentary on the possibilities of the future. Historical teaching should be combined with tactical and strategical instruction. The study of blockade strategy, tactical formations, commerce protection etc. should always be accompanied by brief historical investigations …

Lectures on history can be very easily overdone, nearly everything that can be said in a lecture can be found in books, and it is better to teach the student to use books, as they are available when he leaves the College. Historical teaching if properly applied will do much to guard Officers from that mire of technical materialism into which they always sink after long peace, they should learn from history that human nature is always the same and that it is the human factor that wins wars.

He feared the Admiralty had set out again

on the old Chinese road where the whole object of historical teaching is sacrificed to feats of incoherent memorialisation. What a delightfully simple but ineffective way of teaching history.

It is considered most important that the methods of teaching history to naval Officers and what they are to be taught should be decided by naval Officers. Historians are good servants but bad masters.[124]

College Flag Captain Richard Webb summarised Dewar's analysis: 'Naval History should be taught not as an exact and continuous subject, but as a means of illustrating by actual examples therefrom how various operations should be undertaken.' As this method was already in use the provision of suitable history 'might be left to Mr. Corbett'. The 1912 War Staff course prepared mid-career officers to plan, coordinate and structure the increasingly complex, interlocked operations that would be required to wage the First and Second World Wars. It was no coincidence that modern staff work reached the Grand Fleet in mid-1917, under the leadership of War College graduates Beatty, de Brock and Chatfield. The Admiralty system improved markedly when Wemyss, another War College star, became Deputy First Sea Lord, and then took the title Chief of Staff seriously. The tragedy of the War Course was that John Jellicoe, the one officer who really needed to attend, was by far the most conspicuous of those who did not.

---

[124]   K. Dewar. 'Naval War Staff Course': ADM 203/69 pp. 9–11. For a less than flattering appreciation of War and Staff Courses, see K.G.B. Dewar. *The Navy from Within*. London 1939 pp. 129–58. Even Marder considered it 'excessively critical of the Establishment.' *FDSF V* p. 374.

Conclusion

The ideas concepts and methods of modern war reached the Royal Navy in the Edwardian age, through the Naval War College; at the heart of that project lay the strategic analysis of Julian Corbett. Between the first short course in 1904 and the last pre-war intake of 1914, 616 Royal Navy Officers attended the War Course, and although not all of them completed their studies most managed to return, notably Rosslyn Wemyss.[125] Highly capable at sea and ashore, Wemyss was exactly the calibre of man the Navy needed to educate. His introduction of an effective Admiralty Staff in 1917–18 justified the entire pre-war War Course. Most of the men selected were of a high calibre, with career prospects, although Lieutenant Rooke (1907–08) rated 'Hopeless, wants in ordinary intelligence'.[126] These officers undertook a topical course of study in which Corbett's history and strategy were the largest external elements, but by no means the only ones. The programme was under constant review, and the work of the students was fed directly into Admiralty policymaking and strategy. The Course and staff were used to develop war plans, and the course informed careers. The late addition of the Staff Course, and the close links between it and the War Course, provided the Navy with a nucleus of trained staff officers just in time for a war that would see an exponential expansion in demand for staff work.

The War Course was remarkable success. It developed planning, and doctrine functions, provided a common resource of knowledge and ideas, drafted critical war plans, introduced Staff Training and built command teams, notably Beatty and Chatfield. Close contact with DNI, the Admiralty and the Army Staff College kept the teaching fresh and responsive. Outstanding officers including Beatty, Wemyss, Bacon, Chatfield, de Brock, Ballard, Pound and Ramsay acquired vital skills and insight as they prepared for high command.

Corbett's work was widely recognised: in June 1914 Fisher, Churchill, Jackson and Bethell pressed for him to be knighted.[127] He knew that *Some Principles* was a snapshot of British strategic doctrine in development, not a closed process. His dissatisfaction with the book was, much like that of his illustrious Prussian precursor, that of a man seeking certainty when everything was in flux. Had he produced the book four years earlier it would have been very different: had he been able to revisit it in 1914, or 1920, the results would have been even more startling. *Some Principles* is the opening essay of an ongoing debate, designed to open the eyes of *his* students to a higher and more effective way of thinking about war, hence the hard-fought battle to open with a discussion of theory. Nor was it intended to be a stand-alone text. It remains the basic analytical tool that all should consult *before* tackling his mature case studies, *The Seven Years' War*,

---

[125]   Lady Wemyss. *The Life and Letters of Lord Wester Wemyss*. London 1935 pp. 100, 130.
[126]   ADM 203/69 pp. 19–23.
[127]   Fisher to Corbett 22.6.1914: *FGDN II* pp. 507–8.

Trafalgar, *The Russo-Japanese War* and *Naval Operations*. Taken together, these works are vital to our understanding of pre-1914 naval education, policy and planning. That Corbett generated the definitive analysis of British strategy reflected the meeting of remarkable men: Custance and Clarke, Fisher, Jackson, Slade and Ballard leavened Corbett's elegant, incisive approach, and his quasi-religious commitment to the Navy, to ensure the results would exceed expectation. Immediate political pressures drove Corbett's work: Fisher's public relations machine, Beresford's bluster and vitriol, the Continental delusions of the Army and the threat of a protectionist government were real. They forced him to change his text, and altered the style in which it was delivered. Strategic texts should only be studied in context, such works are unique to their time, and their audience. If they retain value for other times and other audiences that is an unexpected bonus not a core requirement. Corbett wrote *Some Principles* for the War Course, he wanted to keep it up to date for the same reason.

Corbett's teaching and texts shaped British strategic thinking, and they survived khaki-clad Continentalists, academic declinists and materiel-minded sailors. Seen in its proper setting, as the jewel of the War Course and the culmination of an educational transformation, *Some Principles* assumes a significance far beyond the paltry sales and carping criticisms. After the war Corbett's pioneering work was transformed by Sir Herbert Richmond and Basil Liddell-Hart from a pragmatic, flexible response into the dogmatic prescription that is 'The British Way in Warfare', but that is another story.

Appendix 1:   Marder

The reputation of the Naval War Course/College still suffers from the pioneer judgments of an important scholar. In 1961 Professor Arthur J. Marder published the first volume of *From the Dreadnought to Scapa Flow*. He ignored the pre-1900 history and strategy courses run at Greenwich and seriously underestimated the audience for the War Course. Recognising it provided higher education, he limited the audience to Commanders and Captains. From 1904 Admirals were a key part of the audience, both for their own benefit, and for the encouragement their presence gave to lower ranks. Furthermore the Course was a full-pay appointment, attendance was compulsory.[128]

The criticism that the teaching was no better than the understanding of the experts was hardly fair, given the standing of the experts involved.[129] Like much of Marder's analysis, the approach is vitiated by his reliance on isolated voices of discontent, notably Kenneth Dewar.[130] However, among his scathing remarks Dewar admitted that 'the hours were short and the leave generous, which gave one opportunities for thought and study'. The last qualification, as Corbett and every service educator before and since has known, is the key to preparing students for the unknown, and the unpredictable. Overcrowded courses crammed with endless lectures, exercises, directed study and delivery might be easy to administer, control and assess; they generate apparently rigorous ranking orders based on numerical scores, but they are no substitute for intelligent programmes which give students the opportunity for self-development. The War Course report was based on far more than 'results', delivered by an officer of unquestioned professional expertise. It was not expressed in anything so vulgar as a numerical ranking. Men were rated as 'first class' because they had the character to lead, the ability to inspire, the judgement to get it right and the dedication to see it through. Intellectual skills were of limited utility in naval command without leadership, teamwork, powers of expression and decision.

Those who took away from the Course a combination of new ideas drawn from horizon-broadening lectures, personal study and contact with fellow officers of various ranks, went on to think about their profession in new, and more coherent, ways. They acquired a new common language in which to express their ideas, and to communicate with new colleagues who shared their concerns. The War Course was no place for hidebound thinking, narrow and prescriptive approaches or closed minds. Marder may have been influenced by jaundiced critics, notably Chatfield, whose dismissive approach to Corbett and the Course is easily understood after

---

[128]   Marder, *FDSF I* pp. 32–33.
[129]   Ibid. p. 364.
[130]   Ibid. pp. 400–401, citing Dewar, *The Navy From Within* pp. 131–33.

reading the splenetic rant he penned after reading Volume III of Corbett's *Naval Operations*.[131]

Furthermore, Marder's treatment seriously undervalued Fisher's intellectual penetration. Fisher adopted and developed the Course because he could see the need for strategic education and war planning, and he sustained it because it solved key problems that emerged in his period in office. His advanced education programme addressed major areas of concern, from International Law and changing strategic situations, to specific case studies and the development of a national strategic concept. The staff and students of the Course may not have predicted the events of 1914–18, but the War Course ensured the best brains in the Navy worked on real problems in an atmosphere conducive to study and reflection. When war came they still had much to learn, but they were better equipped to learn the practical lessons, and better able to express their understanding because of their time on the War Course.

Appendix 2:   Presidents of the Naval War College

[Col. Head ranged R]Destination

Rear Admiral Henry May   Sept. 1900–April 1904   died
Captain Edmond Slade   13.5.1904–October 1907   DNI
Rear Admiral R S Lowry   –November 1908   2nd Cruiser Squadron
Rear Admiral Lewis Bayly   22.11.1908–23.2.1911   1st Cruiser Squadron
Rear Admiral Sir Henry B Jackson KCB KCVO FRS   24.2.1911–27.1.1913   War Staff
Vice Admiral Alexander Bethell   28.1.1913–1915 (formerly DNI)

Appendix 3: Officers on the War Course/College Staff[132]

[col. Head ranged R]Destination

Capt. J.A. Fergusson   (31.12.1905) 10.1.1905–Nov. 1906   to HP
Capt. J.C. Ley (Flag Capt. 30.6.1906)   23.8.1905–15.7.1907   *Endymion*
(Temp.) Capt. B.M. Chambers   1.6.1906–3.1.1907   *Bulwark*
Lt R.E. Carr 30.1.1906–31.6.1907   HP
Lt D.T. Norris   20.1.1906–31.12.1907 when promoted Cmdr   *King Alfred*
Capt. J.H. Howell-Jones RMA (with Adml May)   1.6.1903–31.12.1906   Osb. College
Naval Instructor A.L. Veater??   1.5.1906–1.8.1911
Lt F.D. Arnold-Forster (vice Carr; post Course)   1.2.1907–22.1.1909 Cmdr   *Achilles*

---

[131]   Chatfield to Keyes *Private & Personal* January 1923: in P. Halpern (ed.). *The Keyes Papers* vol. II. London NRS 1980 pp. 85–87.
[132]   Adm 203 pp. 5 & 167.

Cmdr C.D. Carpendale   2.10.1906–31.8.1908   *Edgar* for *Hermes*

Major St.G.B. Armstrong RMLI   27.7.1907–26.7.1910   Stonehouse Depot.

Cmdr A.K. Waistell   28.2.1907–2.2.1910   *Pathfinder*

Cmdr A.N. Loxley   20.8.1907–29.3.1909   Flag Cmdr 2nd Div Home Fleet on *King Edward*.

Paymaster C.E. Batt (Staff Paymaster) (Secretary)   1.10.1907–26.11.908   *Shannon*

(Temp) Capt. J.C. Ley (Flag Capt.)   1.11.907–31.1.1908   *Endymion*

Cmdr Wilfred Henderson   6.11.1907–1.10.1909 (Capt. 30.6.1909)   HP

Capt. G.P.W. Hope (Flag Capt. vice Ley)   1.2.1908–29.3.1908 Flag Capt   *Magnificent*

Lt H.W. Longden (vice Norris)   1.1.908 Cmdr 31.12.1910– ?

Capt. R. Webb   1.2.1908–4.1.1909   *Amethyst*

Lt H.C. Watson (addl)   24.1.1908 (after War Course)–23.6.1908   *Carnarvon*

(Temp) Capt. B.M. Chambers   18.1.1908–5.11.1908   *Talbot*

Lt G.O. Stephenson (vice Watson)   5.8.1908–9.8.1910   *Cornwallis*

Cmdr H.G.E. Lane (vice Carpendale)   22.9.1908–25.3.1911   *Indomitable*

Asst Paymaster E.B. Parker (Secretary)   27.11.1908–24.2.1911   Depot.

Capt. C.F. Thorp (vice Webb)

Flag Capt. Vice Hope   24.3.1909–11.1911   *Britannia*

Lt A.L. Strange (vice Arnold-Forster)   30.1.1909–16.8.1909   *King Edward*

Cmdr P. Franklin MVO (vice Loxley)   27.3.1909–31.7.1911   RNWC Devonport

Capt. G.C. Cayley (vice Hope)   3.4.1909–11.10.1909   Naval Mobilisation Division

Cmdr C. Peel (vice Strange)   13.9.1909–7.1911   *Antrim*

Cmdr B.H. Smith (vice Waistell)   8.2.1910–

Lt C.St.C. Cameron (vice Stephenson)   9.8.1910–

Major C.L. Brooke RMA (vice Armstrong)   8.1.1911–

Staff Paymaster P.H. Francklin (Secretary)   24.2.1911–

Cmdr A.V. Vyvyan (vice Lane)   25.3.1911–5.1.1913   Admiralty

Lt R.G. Copleston RM (Ret'd) (vice N Instructor Veater)   1.8.1911–

Cmdr H.R. Norbury (vice Longden)   24.7.1911–

Cmdr K.G.B. Dewar (vice Peel)   1.8.1911–31.8.1913   HP

Cmdr W. Nunn (vice Francklin)   1.9.1911–31.8.1913

Cmdr G.P. Bigg-Wither (vice Nunn)   30.9.1912   *Espiegle*

Capt. R. Webb (vice Thorp)   11.1911–

Cmdr Arnold-Forster (vice Smith)   2.1912–

Cmdr C.S. Townsend   Feb. 1912

Cmdr A.deK.L. May   all three for War Staff Section with Major

Major L S.J. Halliday VC RMLI   Cmdr B.H. Smith as Chief Instructor

Cmdr A.D.P.R. Pound   6.1.1913   also for War Staff Section (but in place of Vyvyan)

Flag Capt R Webb 2.4.1912–15.8.1913   Admiralty

Paymaster M.G. Bennet (Secretary)   28.1.1913–

Capt. C.E. Le Mesurier   30.1.1913–

Capt B.H. Smith   8.2.1910–

Cmdr C.S. Townsend   10.1.1912–30.12.1913   Devonport War College

Cmdr F.D. Arnold-Forster   10.1.1912 –31.12.1913   *Apollo*

Cmdr A.D.P.R. Pound   6.1.1913–21.4.1914   *St Vincent*
Cmdr K.G.B. Dewar   1.8.1911–31.8.1913   HP
Cmdr G.P. Bigg-Wither   30.9.1912–
Lt R.G. Coplestone (Rtd) Librarian   11.5.1911
Lt (T) C.St C. Cameron   9.8.1910–31.1.1914   *Agamemnon*
Lt (FG) T. Fisher (Cmr 31.12.1913)   1.2.1913–
Eng. Cmdr A. Brown   6.5.1912–
Major C. Brooke RMA   8.1.1911–
Cmdr H.W.W. Hope   1.8.1913–
Cmdr C.T. Hardy   19.12.1913–
Cmdr H.G.E. Lane   1.1.1914–
Cmdr A. Rice   1.2.1914–
Capt. R.F.C. Foster RMA   23.3.1914–

Chapter 11

Financing Kitchener's
(and Everyone Else's) Armies

Kathleen Burk

In his book *The British Way in Warfare*, David French has pointed out that, during its period of great power, Great Britain exercised three weapons. They were the ability of its diplomats to put together European coalitions; the power of the Royal Navy; and the financial power which supported both. The focus of this essay is the decline in the power of this third weapon. The need to maintain the relative power of the Royal Navy before and during the war was a contributing factor, but it was the vital but crushing requirements to subsidise a growing number of impecunious allies and, for the first time in modern British history, to create a mass army, which devastated her financial power, which never recovered. By the end of the war, international financial supremacy had been surrendered to the United States, a situation which had far-reaching and long-lasting consequences.

In peacetime, a navy costs much more to build and to run than an army of equivalent size and, no matter what the wealth of Britain, from the 1880s the country would feel the strain of paying for the successive building programmes, and then the manning and the running of the fleet. It was true that Britain had the huge advantage of having been the first industrial nation, with a lead of about a century over all other European countries; even more important, it was also true that she was the greatest financial and commercial power in the world. In short, the major reason why she could afford to fight two centuries of wars, create an empire, develop the resources of the home islands and maintain a relatively liberal political system was the combination of the financial probity of the government and the financial and economic power of the private sector. This reputation for probity meant that the government could raise the money it required to equip the country with a navy and, when needed, an army; the financial power of the private sector meant that there was money to be had and that the two sectors could work together to find and provide it. Britain was thus rich and able to maintain her military forces. Over the following years, the structure would remain, but whether sufficient financial resources existed became increasingly problematic.

Until the latter part of the nineteenth century, any competing naval powers were European. This meant that the main tasks of the Royal Navy in wartime were threefold: to sweep the oceans of enemy vessels, whether warships or merchant ships; to blockade the enemy fleets in their home ports; and to attack them if they tried to escape. British command of the four 'narrow seas' – the Channel, the

North Sea, the mouth of the Mediterranean and the Suez Canal – facilitated by her control of the 'five strategic keys' which 'lock up the world' – the great naval bases at Dover, Gibraltar, Alexandria, the Cape of Good Hope and Singapore – enabled her warships to control access to and thus to command the world's oceans.[1] After 1880, however, European naval powers strengthened their fleets and new non-European naval powers arose, specifically Japan and the USA. With the safety of the shipping lanes and the Empire increasingly at risk, and given that by 1895 she imported four-fifths of her wheat,[2] did Britain dare cease trying to maintain her increasingly threatened global maritime dominance? Or should the crucial principle be to retain superiority in the home waters in order to protect the British Isles themselves, and thus give up global pretensions?

By 1901, the Admiralty had concluded that past policies and ways of thinking needed to change. There was, in fact, to be something of a diplomatic revolution over the subsequent decade, as Britain settled outstanding imperial problems with the USA, France and Russia, and signed a peacetime alliance with Japan, the first such engagement for centuries. A major reason was financial, or, rather, the fears of the Chancellor of the Exchequer, Sir Michael Hicks Beach. In despair because of his conviction that Britain was coming to the end of her resources, he had quarrelled with his service colleagues and nearly broken up the Cabinet. Britain had been engaged in a naval arms race with France and Russia since the 1880s and especially since 1889. Between that year and 1897, expenditure on the navy had increased by 65 per cent,[3] and Hicks Beach now believed that the relentless growth in naval expenditure would lead 'straight to financial ruin'. He pointed out that expenditure between 1895–96 and 1901–2 had risen by 40 per cent, over half of which was accounted for solely by increased spending on the army and navy (not including the special costs of the Boer War). Public expenditure on military forces in 1901 was 58 per cent of total government expenditure, 15 per cent of this total expenditure being spent on the navy. By 1903, with the growing German naval

---

I am very grateful to George Peden and Jeremy Wormell for reading a draft or two of this essay.

[1]   The base at Alexandria controlled the eastern Mediterranean and the Suez Canal, the base at the Cape of Good Hope enabled the control of the route to the Indian Ocean and the South Pacific, whilst Singapore kept an eye on the Far East. Admiral Sir John Fisher, quoted in A.J. Marder, *From the Dreadnought to Scapa Flow: The Royal Navy in the Fisher Era 1904–1919. Volume I: The Road to War, 1904–1914* (London, 1961), p. 41. The base which is missing is Halifax, which became the responsibility of Canada itself in December 1903. By this time, the Royal Navy had effectively turned over responsibility for the naval defence of the Western Hemisphere to the USA.

[2]   Jon Tetsuro Sumida, *In Defence of Naval Supremacy: Finance, Technology, and British Naval Policy, 1889–1914* (London, 1993 pb edn), p. 10.

[3]   Ibid., p. 18.

threat, the navy alone would account for 25 per cent of public expenditure.[4] A major reason for this was the growth in the cost of the ships themselves. Between 1895 and 1905 the cost of a first-class cruiser (a vessel with a long range and high speed that could scout ahead of the main battle fleet) nearly quadrupled.[5] With the building of the dreadnought and then the super-dreadnought, costs increased substantially. Furthermore, there was increasing competition for funding for social reforms.

Yet the British economy supported the increasing expenditure on military forces before the First World War. Clearly, the ability to finance such an increase in costs required a substantial growth in the economy so that the necessary revenue would be available. This took place. In 1904/5, total defence expenditure was £72,200,000, which was 4.4 per cent of Gross Domestic Product (adjusted to the financial year); nine years later, just before the outbreak of the war, total defence expenditure equalled £72,500,000, just £300,000 more than in 1904/5 – but this was only 3.4 per cent of GDP. Indeed, during the period 1903 to 1913, the government repaid more than one-eighth of the outstanding national debt.[6] Additionally, the Boer War had demonstrated that the government would have no difficulty in borrowing for immediate military purposes: the National War Loan of 1900, the so-called Khaki Loan, was eleven times oversubscribed, whilst the 1901 Exchequer Bonds were subscribed more than twice over.[7] Yet there was a fundamental difference between the pre-war period and that of the First World War. With regard to paying for military supplies of all types, during the former, a substantial proportion of the goods required were available in the UK and were thus paid for in sterling. In comparison, a substantial proportion of the goods required during the Great War came from abroad and especially from the United States. These had to be paid for with dollars. Finance was overwhelmingly crucial, and here it was not the ability to raise the money domestically but the ability to

---

[4]   Chancellor of the Exchequer, 'Financial Difficulties: Appeal For Economy in Estimates', October 1901, CAB 37/58, Vol. 109, p. 8; Aaron L. Friedberg, *The Weary Titan: Britain and the Experience of Relative Decline, 1895–1905* (Princeton, 1988), Table 3–1, 'Gross Expenditures 1887–1907', p. 131.

[5]   Sumida, *In Defence of Naval Supremacy*, pp. 20–21 plus Figure 1, 'Expenditure on battleships and first-class cruisers, 1889–1904'. The newer ones were so much larger that the manning requirements of the Royal Navy grew much faster after 1897 than during the previous five years: 1889–90, 65,400; 1896–97, 93,750; 1904–5, 131,100. Expendture on new works, such as barracks, docks and other port facilities, increased five times from 1897 to 1904–5. Ibid.

[6]   G.C. Peden, *Arms, Economics and British Strategy: From Dreadnoughts to Hydrogen Bombs* (Cambridge, 2007), Table 1.1, Defence expenditure as percentage of GDP, 1904/5–1913/14, p. 35; E. Victor Morgan, *Studies in British Financial Policy, 1914–1925* (London, 1952), p. 89.

[7]   The Diary of Sir Edward Hamilton, 16 March 1900, Add. MS 48676, and 11 Feb. 1901, Add. MS 48677, British Library; Kathleen Burk, *Morgan Grenfell 1838–1988: The Biography of a Merchant Bank* (London, 1989), pp. 111–23.

raise or purchase dollars: the outcome of the war for Great Britain depended on her access to dollars and to the goods they could buy.

The cause of this was a change in the traditional British way in warfare. Great Britain, in common with the other belligerents, was unprepared for the scale or duration of the war. The assumptions on which British pre-war strategy had been based were that she would utilise her superior naval power to blockade the Central Powers – the German, Austro-Hungarian, and Ottoman empires and, later, Bulgaria – and starve them of resources, sweep their ships from the oceans, and supply her own allies with subsidies and *matériel*. She would not provide a mass army of her own; rather, her allies were expected to provide the bulk of the land forces, with Britain contributing only an Expeditionary Force of six divisions, amounting to 150,000 men. Although it was planned that two divisions would remain in the country for home defence, by early September, in fact, all six divisions plus a cavalry division would be in France. Indeed, British strategic assumptions were very quickly shown to be mistaken. The Germans reached the coast of Belgium and nearly made it to Paris, until they were stopped at the Marne in mid-September. France clearly could not defeat the Germans on her own, particularly given that the Germans had already defeated the Russians at the Battle of Tannenberg, thereby lessening considerably the dangers for Germany of a two-front war. Very soon into the war, Lord Kitchener, the Secretary of State for War, succeeded in persuading the Cabinet that it was vital that Britain should after all make a Continental commitment and raise a mass army. Kitchener was almost alone in the highest reaches of the government in envisaging a long war, but such was his prestige that the Cabinet agreed to begin the necessary preparations.[8]

An army requires clothing, provisions, weapons and munitions, but only some of these supplies in the volume now required were immediately available in Britain. As noted above, roughly 80 per cent of the country's consumption of wheat was imported. Furthermore, in 1906–7, the Government Factories and Workshops Committee, under the chairmanship of Sir George Murray, Permanent Secretary of the Treasury (1903–11), recommended 'not only that the size of the state sector should be reduced, but also that the private firms should be kept short of orders so that the royal ordnance factories could be kept as fully occupied as possible'. Unfortunately for Britain, 'the consequence of the government's acceptance of the Murray Committee's recommendation was that the army's sources of supply for munitions were too limited for intensive fighting in a campaign against the German army'.[9]

In this situation, Britain had to turn elsewhere, and the natural place to turn to was the United States, home of the most powerful industrial economy in

---

[8]   Kitchener told Lord Esher that 'the war might last two or three years at least'. Diary of Lord Esher (original manuscript), 13 Aug. 1914, Vol. 2, folder 13, Esher Papers, Churchill College, Cambridge.

[9]   Clive Trebilcock, 'War and the Failure of Industrial Mobilisation', J.M. Winter, ed., *War and Economic Development* (Cambridge, 1975), pp. 139–64.

the world. President Woodrow Wilson had immediately proclaimed American neutrality, but this did not prohibit the selling of goods to the belligerents. Orders for 400,000 rifles were placed in October 1914. Within two years, the British had a purchasing mission of 10,000 men working in the USA. The latter had always been a quantity rather than a quality producer. Shells, rifles and other munitions required precision from their makers and British engineering firms were much more used to precision engineering than were American firms. The question as to whether American manufacturers could cope with the tolerances necessary in the production of guns and shells was a real one: if not, they might blow up in the faces of British, French or Russian soldiers. Therefore, British engineers travelled out to inspect likely American firms to see if they seemed competent and to advise them. Moreover, since the factories necessary to produce supplies often did not yet exist, the British government provided the capital to build them. (It did the same in Canada.) And, of course, the USA was full of Germans – a million of them had emigrated there during the 1890s alone and they were the country's largest non-English-speaking minority. Some retained their loyalty to their homeland, particularly when Germany's enemies included France and Russia; they might well be tempted to sabotage the production and shipping of these supplies. A spy ring was certainly being run by the German Embassy. There were also millions of Irish immigrants and Irish-Americans of longer standing who had no reason to love Britain. Therefore, members of British missions inspected the *matériel* as it was produced in the factories, they guarded it on the trains taking it to the docks, and they supervised its loading onto the ships.[10] Ten thousand may seem an extraordinary number of inspectors and watchers for Britain to have sent out to the States, but Britain was not only purchasing supplies for her own army, navy and civilian population. From early on in the war, she was also financing or guaranteeing the purchases in the USA and elsewhere of Russia, Italy, Belgium, Greece, Rumania and, increasingly, France;[11] as a result, by October 1916, 'Of the £5,000,000 which the Treasury have to find daily for the prosecution of the war,

[10]   For details as well as hundreds of references, see Kathleen Burk, *Britain, America and the Sinews of War 1914–1918* (London, 1985).

[11]   J.M. Keynes, then in 1D, the Finance Division of the Treasury, recognised that France tried to pay her own way, commenting in March 1916 that Britain had only one ally, France, and that the rest were mercenaries. Elizabeth Johnson, ed., *The Collected Writings of John Maynard Keynes, Volume XVI: Activities 1914–1919* (London, 1971), p. 187. Nevertheless, by mid-1916, Britain had to take over the financing of French purchases in the USA, and by April 1917 she was also paying for French purchases in Britain and the Empire, as well as supporting the French exchange against the dollar. Kathleen Burk, 'The Treasury: From Impotence to Power', Kathleen Burk, ed., *War and the State: The Transformation of British Government, 1914–1919* (London, 1982), p. 91.

about £2,000,000 has to be found in North America'.[12] Financial catastrophe was not far off.

The Treasury, therefore, had two primary concerns. The first was to raise the finance to make domestic payments, which included paying both suppliers and soldiers, and the second was to find dollars. The experience of the Boer War gave no reason to believe that it would be overwhelmingly difficult, and the initial assumption was that, on the whole, it would be 'business as usual'. This assumption would be falsified rather quickly. The methods included taxation, medium- or long-term borrowing, and short-term borrowing. Setting out the rates of taxation is complicated – as it is now – because of the sliding scale and the various allowances and abatements. In the financial year 1913–14, income tax was charged at 9*d.* (3.25p) on the pound on incomes between £160 and £2,000 and at 1*s.* (5p) on incomes of £2,000 to £3,000. (The incomes may look rather small, but Virginia Woolf, in her 1928 essay, *A Room of One's Own*, set £500 a year as the income [along with a room of one's own] which would ensure independence, at least for a female writer.) The last Budget before the war had raised the rates in order to finance social reforms, with a sliding scale ranging from 5*d.* to 1*s.*4*d.* in the pound and a supertax of 6*d.* on incomes over £3,000. On 17 November 1914, the Chancellor of the Exchequer, David Lloyd George, brought in his second Budget of the year, and the rates of income and supertax were doubled. There were no changes in these taxes in the May 1915 Budget, only a sharp increase in the tax on alcohol – and the intention here was more to restrict consumption amongst munition workers than to raise revenue.[13]

The Treasury, which feared the inflationary consequences of the need to finance the war, had wanted higher taxation, because budget deficits would be higher than the officials thought wise. They had advised Lloyd George to depend more on taxation than on borrowing: the traditional approach for paying the costs of a war was to depend on taxation for half of the required funds. Lloyd George, however, preferred the reverse. (In response to this approach, the Treasury during the war

---

[12]   This was written by Keynes in the Treasury section of a memorandum compiled by the Foreign Office as a result of the American reaction to Lloyd George's speech on 28 Sept. 1916 calling for a 'Knock-Out Blow': 'The Financial Dependence of the United Kingdom on the United States of America', 6 Nov. 1916, CAB 42/23/7. By this point, the Allies were largely or wholly dependent on the US for guns, shells, metals, explosives, machine tools, oils and petroleum, cotton, foodstuffs, raw materials and grains. Ibid. By April 1917, British support of what the Treasury called 'our less wealthy allies' totalled about £950 million, over £400 million of which went to support Russia. Treasury comment in Treasury Minute 19304/14, 14 September 1914, f. 157, T. 197/7; for amount of support, Keynes, *Collected Writings, Vol. XVI*, p. 187.

[13]   Morgan, *British Financial Policy*, pp. 89–90; Virginia Woolf, *A Room of One's Own* (Harmondsworth, 1945), p. 103. The per capita income of a female shop assistant just before 1914 was, roughly, £25/£30 per annum. Thanks to Jeremy Wormell. See also Martin Daunton, *Just Taxes: The Politics of Taxation in Britain, 1914–1979* (Cambridge, 2002), chapter 2.

would deliberately use inflation to transfer resources to the government, in the absence of effective taxation, whilst using long-term loans from time to time to prevent the inflation caused by short-term borrowing from getting out of hand.[14]) In this budget, whilst the estimated deficit was £340 million, new taxation was estimated to produce only £15.5 million. One reason for Lloyd George's decision to limit taxation was that he wished for taxpayers to feel that they had the funds available to invest in the £350 million War Loan, which he also announced in his budget speech.[15] The result, as noted below, would not be as he wished.

The Coalition Government which came to power in May 1915, with Reginald McKenna succeeding Lloyd George as Chancellor, saw a stronger but still inadequate response to the dramatic rise in expenditure. Lloyd George himself was a significant cause of this rise. As Chancellor, he had told the War Office to spend what they needed to spend and not to worry about the Treasury. Furthermore, many of the 'mushroom ministries' which were soon to be thrown up by the war – such as the Ministries of Munitions, Food, Labour and Shipping, and the Air Board – would not be subject to Treasury control over their numbers or organisations; rather, the Acts establishing these organisations left to their ministers the power to determine the size of their staffs, which multiplied according to their whims. Waste and wastage were rampant. Worst of all, the Treasury had already lost control over the domestic spending of the War Office and would soon of the new Ministry of Munitions.[16]

McKenna brought in a supplementary Budget in September 1915 which forecast expenditure in short of £1,590 million against expected revenue of £272 million. Expenditure was expected to be five times that of revenue. This clearly could not go on. Rates of income tax were raised by 40 per cent and a number of exemptions and abatements were lowered or eliminated. Excise duties were raised. The Budget also introduced an Excess Profits Duty. A choice of two bases of profits was provided from which the owner could choose, and profits of more than £200 above the standard allowed were taxed at 50 per cent. Nevertheless, the revenue raised was only £337 million, just £65 million more than the earlier estimate.[17]

The next two Budgets made very little difference, proportionately speaking. Taxes were raised a bit, but expenditure grew even faster. Treasury officials were keen to increase the rates of tax, but McKenna and his successor as Chancellor,

[14]   This reluctant acquiencence by the Treasury to what they hoped would be a limited degree of inflation should be contrasted with domestic financial policy in the Second World War (see George Peden's essay in this book: Chapter 12). G.C. Peden, *The Treasury and British Public Policy, 1906–1959* (Oxford, 2000), pp. 86–95.

[15]   Ibid., pp. 83–85.

[16]   *Parliamentary Papers 1917–18*, Vol. iii, *First Report from the Select Committee on National Expenditure*, pp. 6–10; ibid., *Second Report from the Select Committee on National Expenditure*, p. 15.

[17]   Peden, *The Treasury and British Public Policy*, pp. 90–91.

Andrew Bonar Law, both appeared to believe that there was a limit to the taxation which could be imposed without stimulating a taxpayers' revolt. Lloyd George, since 6 December 1916 the Prime Minister, was no keener. In the 1917–18 Budget, with expenditure estimated at £2,290 million and income at £613 million – 25 per cent of expenditure at least was better than 1914's 20 per cent – income tax was not raised. The last wartime Budget, however, that of 1918–19, brought significant changes. The maximum rate of income tax was raised to 6*s.* (30p) in the pound, but there were a number of concessions. Excise duties, Excess Profits Duty and supertax were all raised. Yet, even with these increases, revenue did not begin to match expenditure.[18]

The economist E. Victor Morgan, writing in 1945, expressed astonishment: 'To those who have passed through the sterner days of the Second World War, the taxation … seems very light, the deficits relatively very large, and the complacency with which the situation was regarded by successive Chancellors, little short of fantastic.'[19] He suggests three reasons for this response. First of all, there were the technical difficulties associated with imposing taxation at the rates common in the Second World War. Where were the staffs to collect the taxes and to check for evasion? Furthermore, Parliament, in spite of their abstract desire for increased taxation, often responded to vested interests' objections to specific taxes. Secondly, nineteenth-century views of taxation were still widespread, and the general public would, it was believed, have strongly resented very high taxes – hence the timidity of McKenna and Bonar Law. And finally, there was the belief that what was important was that the government raise the funds which were required, and it was just as good, if not better, to float loans on the London money market. 'The basic fact that if the Government was to purchase more of the real product of the nation, then private citizens must purchase less, was hardly ever allowed to emerge from the sea of verbiage.'[20] In defence of the Treasury, as Peden points out,

> *pace* Morgan, officials were well aware of the need to transfer purchasing power from private individuals to the government, and even used primitive national income estimates to reach figures for taxable capacity and aggregate savings of the community. However, given the tax and credit structures of the day, it was difficult to achieve the required reduction in private purchasing power.[21]

It would also have required greater political will.

So, if loans were the answer, how successful was the government in borrowing the money it needed? During the first few months of the war, money was borrowed

---

[18]   Morgan, *British Financial Policy*, pp. 90–94; Table 7, 'Adjusted Net Expenditure of the United Kingdom, 1913–14 to 1924–25', p. 101 and Table 8, 'Adjusted Net Revenue of the United Kingdom, 1913–14 to 1924–25', ibid., p. 104.

[19]   Ibid., p. 94.

[20]   Ibid., pp. 94–95, quote on p. 95.

[21]   Peden, *The Treasury and British Public Policy*, p. 80.

on Ways and Means advances and on Treasury bills. By means of the former, the government borrowed from government departmental balances and from the Bank of England in advance of revenue receipts. A cheque was drawn on the Government's account at the Bank and used to pay contractors. The problem was that this increased the money supply and was, therefore, a highly inflationary form of finance: once the cheques were cleared, the banks would be holding higher cash reserves at the Bank. They could then lend several times the amount to private sector clients or to the government, who would chase goods and services, and whose costs – obeying the laws of supply and demand – would then increase. By means of Treasury bills, the Government borrowed from the joint stock banks for thirty or sixty or ninety days, and later for six or twelve months, at which point the Government had to repay them if the banks for any reason declined to renew the bills.[22] Again, the Treasury bills could be turned into cash which could be the basis of new lending. In short, these were both inflationary methods of raising funds, a lesson which the Treasury learned and which was a method avoided in the Second World War.

The Government repaid the Ways and Means and Treasury bills from the first months of the war by 1 January 1915, with the proceeds of the first War Loan. This was an issue of £350 million of stock at 3½ per cent; it was sold at 95 and would be repaid at par (£100), between 1 March 1925 and 1 March 1928 at the Treasury's option. Therefore, the buyer earned 3½ per cent per year and another 5 per cent when it was redeemed (that is, bought back) by the government.[23] The Chancellor would have preferred an issue at par (that is, the full price of 100), but opinion in the City of London was that the issue would not be very successful if there were not some capital gain. The City turned out to be correct. Lloyd George claimed, untruthfully, that the War Loan was oversubscribed, but instead of £350 million, only £200 million was taken up. This was a deception which was described, a half-century later, as 'the Treasury's blackest secret'.[24]

In June 1915 came the second War Loan, issued at par and for an unlimited amount, with an interest rate of 4½ per cent, and repayable between 1 December 1925 and 1 December 1945. Although the loan was issued in nominal amounts of £100 at the Bank of England, the Treasury wanted also to tap the funds of small investors, so in addition the loan was issued through the Post Office in bonds of £5 and £10 and vouchers of 5s.; they also wanted to curb consumption. Another attempt was made the following February to tap the funds of those not used to investing by the issue of War Savings Certificates, which were sold at 15s.6d. (77½ pence) and which, if held for five years, would be redeemed at £1.[25] From

---

[22]   Six- and twelve-month Treasury bills were a wartime innovation.

[23]   The yield was approximately 4 per cent. Morgan, *British Financial Policy*, p. 106.

[24]   Diary of Sir Alec Cairncross, 4 February 1964, University of Glasgow Archive, quoted in Peden, *The Treasury and British Public* Policy, p. 86.

[25]   For details, see Jeremy Wormell, *The Management of the National Debt of the United Kingdom, 1900–1932* (London, 2000), chapter 5, 'The Small Saver and Continuous Borrowing'.

December 1915, the Treasury issued five-year 5 per cent Exchequer Bonds, which would be free of tax for foreign holders.[26] For the rest of the financial year, the government largely depended on Treasury bills.

From 1916, financing the war became increasingly difficult and for most of the year the Government continued to depend on Treasury bills for domestic borrowing. In October there was an issue of 6 per cent Exchequer Bonds, which carried an interest rate 20 per cent higher than those issued the previous December. The high rate was deemed necessary to draw in foreign funds and thereby lessen the pressure on the foreign exchanges, as Britain tried desperately to find foreign currency without having to sell pounds, which would weaken sterling. The third War Loan, issued in 1917, offered two types of security: 1) a 5 per cent stock issued at 95 and repayable between 1929 and 1947; and 2) a 4 per cent stock issued at par, free of income tax, and repayable between 1929 and 1942. As it happened, the take-up was £2,075 million for the 5 per cent loan but only £52 million for the 4 per cent tax-free loan: investors seemingly decided that, whilst a very high rate of income tax was distantly possible, the income resulting from an interest rate of 5 per cent was certain and therefore more immediately attractive.

From the beginning of the war, the Government had depended on long-term borrowing, interspersed with medium-term Exchequer bonds and short-term Treasury bills, filling up the cracks with Ways and Means advances. Interest rates had drifted up. After the 1917 War Loan, there were no more long-term issues until the conversion and funding loans after the war. Rather, the Government relied on short- and medium-term 'tap' issues, so-called because from April 1915 they were available – on tap – whenever an investor wished to buy them. Everything was made easier when the USA declared war in April 1917, not least because the pressure to obtain dollars lessened.[27]

From the spring of 1915, the increasingly urgent requirement for dollars grew to dominate Treasury concerns. Since the beginning of the war, Britain had been driven to a number of expedients in order to raise the necessary funds. If a government needs domestic resources, it can raise taxes, or borrow, or simply print money, all of which Britain did.[28] However, if a government requires foreign resources, it needs to pay with foreign currency, in this case US dollars. How did Britain acquire them? First of all, she shipped gold to buy them in New York: between August 1914 and mid-July 1917, Britain exported £305 million (roughly $1,450 million) in gold to the USA, which included gold borrowed or purchased from Russia and France.[29] Secondly, between August 1914 and 14 July 1917, the

---

[26]   The hope was that holders of dollars would buy the bonds, thereby providing the Treasury with more dollars for use in the USA.

[27]   Morgan, *British Financial Policy*, pp. 106–13. The point of the double-dates was that the borrowing was *either* short-/medium-term *or* long-term. Thanks to Jeremy Wormell.

[28]   Or it can commandeer goods, as Germany eventually did.

[29]   Johnson, ed., *Collected Writings of Keynes, XVI*, p. 249.

Treasury through its Financial Agent in the USA, J.P. Morgan & Co., sold $750 million of British-owned American securities, which the Treasury had acquired from their private owners first by request and later by the threat of penal taxation. And thirdly, Britain issued medium-term loans on the New York money market.[30] The situation would change when the USA joined the war.

It is worth pausing a moment to consider the unusual relationship between the British Government and the House of Morgan, the most powerful merchant/investment bank in the world. It was founded in London in 1838 by the American George Peabody, who in 1854 took another American, J.S. Morgan, as his partner. Morgan sent his son, J. Pierpont Morgan, to America to establish himself as the agent of J.S. Morgan & Co., and in 1864 the establishment of the firm of Dabney, Morgan & Co. constituted the first incarnation of what in 1893 became J.P. Morgan & Co. By the turn of the century, the New York bank had supplanted the London firm as the dominant bank, not least because of the disparity in financial resources of the separate countries. The senior partner of the firm of Morgan Grenfell in London was E.C. Grenfell, whilst after his father's death in 1913, J.P. Morgan, Jr became the head of the House of Morgan. A devoted Anglophile, he spent half of the year in England, where he moved with ease in society (his niece, Mary Burns, had married the first Viscount Harcourt), and at the outbreak of the war, turned over his country house (Dover House) to the British Government for use as a hospital.

Grenfell was a director of the Bank of England, whilst during the 1920s and early 1930s he represented the City of London in the House of Commons. He stood at the centre of the Anglo-American financial relationship, a position which was of inestimable benefit to the British Government. When in 1915 Morgans became the British Government's Purchasing and then Financial Agent in the USA, Lloyd George gave permission for Morgan Grenfell to have a secure telegraph line to J.P. Morgan and to use their own, uncensored, cypher, 'an amazing, elaborate code', something which neither the Treasury nor the War Office nor the Admiralty possessed. This was, according to Grenfell, an 'extraordinary' privilege which had been given to them in a 'fit of broadmindedness' by Lloyd George;[31] at times Lloyd George used it himself. (The ordinary channel was through the Foreign Office to the Embassy in Washington and the Consulate in New York.) Thus, by means of this line, instructions from the War Office and Admiralty went out to J.P.

---

[30]   Ibid., pp. 249–50. For a list of these loans, see Kathleen Burk, 'J.M. Keynes and the Exchange Rate Crisis of July 1917', *The Economic History Review*, Second Series, 32/3 (1979), p. 407, refs 3–4; for more details, see Wormell, *National Debt*, chapters 9–10.

[31]   For the description of the code, George Booth in Duncan Crow, *A Man of Push and Go: The Life of George Macaulay Booth* (London, 1965), p. 123; for Lloyd George's broadmindedness, Grenfell to New York partner Thomas Lamont, 14 Oct. 1915, Box Hist. 11 – Letters, file 12, Morgan Grenfell Papers, Morgan Grenfell & Co. (now probably in the Guildhall Library, London, but taken from photocopies of the documents acquired when the documents resided in Morgan Grenfell itself).

Morgan and Co.'s specially established Purchasing Department, which placed the orders. Instructions from the Treasury were of special concern to Grenfell. Each morning he walked to the Treasury, collected the draft cables, and walked back to the Morgan Grenfell office, where they were encrypted and then cabled to New York. J.P. Morgan & Co. also provided an overdraft to the British Government, which in December 1916 stood at $175 million but by 1 April 1917 totalled $358 million.[32]

It had, in fact become increasingly difficult for the British Government to raise funds in the USA. Warning signs appeared as early as December 1914, when the rate of the pound against the dollar began to fall; by 15 February 1915 it had reached $4.79½ (from $4.86), and Grenfell placed the situation before the Treasury. But nothing came of it, as Grenfell cabled New York:

> Governor Bank of England and I find it is impossible get authorities take any action in comprehensive manner on Exchange question at present (stop) Chancellor of the Exchequer and colleagues so fully occupied other matters that cannot give proper attention to this matter, and we think Exchange position may have to become worse before proper remedies taken. This may appear to you very foolish procedure but from your own experience dealing with Government officials you will understand it is often impossible make them appreciate a difficult situation, especially on such complicated matter as Exchange.[33]

The problem, of course, was that as the pound became worth less in America, the amount of goods it could buy also lessened, a problem exacerbated by US inflation. The situation did worsen. On 14 August, Grenfell wrote to Lloyd George that the proceeds of a loan of $50 million raised in New York the month before had nearly gone, that the rate of exchange of the pound had dropped to $4.70¼, and that to cover payments of $17 million due the following week, Morgans had only $4 million in hand.[34]

The fear that Britain literally would not be able to pay her bills finally galvanised the Cabinet. The following week, the Chancellor led a small group to France for discussions with his counterpart, and it was decided to send a joint mission to the USA (the Anglo-French Loan Mission), which departed on 1 September 1915, to try to raise a loan on the private money market. In spite of great efforts by the Mission and Morgans, it was not a success. The Mission had wanted to raise an unsecured

---

[32]   Burk, *Sinews of War*, pp. 20 27, 83, 95; 'Mr Bonar Law's statement on finance at the seventh meeting of the Imperial War Cabinet held ... on the 3rd April, 1917', Cab. 23/40.

[33]   United States Senate, 74th Congress, 2nd Session, Special Committee on Investigation of the Munitions Industry, *Munitions Industry*, Report no. 944, 7 vols (Washington, 1936), v. 169–70.

[34]   Morgan Grenfell & Co. to Lloyd George, 14 Aug. 1915, D/12/1/11, Lloyd George Papers.

loan (that is, not backed by collateral, such as US railway bonds) of £200 million (a little less than $ 1,000 million, or $1 billion), ideally at 4½ per cent interest, but in any case no more than 5 per cent. What they got was an unsecured five-year loan of £100 million (a bit less than $500 million) at 5 per cent interest but which, with charges and commissions, worked out at close to 6 per cent, far higher than that obtaining in Britain. Only with great reluctance did the Cabinet agree to the terms. But even worse was its failure to sell: by mid-November, only $11 million's worth of bonds had been sold, and when the underwriters' syndicate broke up on 14 December, $187 million's worth had to be taken by the underwriters; furthermore, only $33 million had been sold to ordinary, non-institutional investors.[35]

There were several reasons for this. First of all, although 1,570 banks and other institutions underwrote the loans, support was generally lacking in the Midwest, South and West – the syndicate included only one major Chicago bank. These were the areas of Scandinavian and German settlement and of the strongest isolationist sentiment, and it was the efforts of those people, as well as of organised pacifists, Irish immigrants and anti-Russian Jews (German-Jewish banks included some of the most important in the United States), backed by the Hearst press, which prevented the loan from selling successfully to the public. On a more prosaic level, Americans were not used to foreign loans and distrusted them; they were also used to collateral security and to interest rates of 5½–6 per cent on the most unimpeachable stock, whereas to the Treasury, an interest rate at that level would have implied the failure of British Government credit. The success of the Mission lay in the fact that they had convinced 1,570 banks and financial houses, often against their better judgement, that Britain and France were good for $500 million and that the public would buy that amount's worth of bonds; the failure of the loan lay in the refusal of the public to do so.

This was a turning point in the attempts by Britain to raise dollars in the USA: it was the last attempt by the British Government during the war to raise unsecured funds on the private US money market. Thereafter, Britain could only issue secured loans in the USA which were backed by collateral. In September 1916, the Government issued a two-year $250 million loan at 5 per cent, backed by $300 million's worth of Canadian, American and other foreign securities; the

[35] Marquess of Reading, *Rufus Isaacs, First Marquess of Reading, 1914–1935* (London, 1945), pp. 32, 43; Reading to Chancellor, 13 Sept. 1915, no. 130133, and Reading to Chancellor, 14 Sept. 1915, no. 131217, both FO 371/2589, Foreign Office Papers, The National Archive, Kew; Asquith to the King, 28 Sept. 1915, Series I, Vol. 8, f. 12, Asquith Papers, Bodleian Library, Oxford; Blackett to Bradbury, 20 Oct. 1915, no. 153996, FO 371/2589; Blackett to Bradbury, 27 Oct. 1915, T. 170/62, Treasury Papers, The National Archive, Kew; Reading to Homberg, 6 Nov. 1915, Harvey to Bradbury, 20 Nov. 1915, and Spring Rice to ?Grey, Private, 29 Nov. 1915, all T. 170/63; Cabinet Committee on the Co-Ordination of Military and Financial Effort, 'Memorandum', 31 Jan. 1916, Cab. 37/141/38; Arthur Link, *Wilson: The Struggle For Neutrality, 1914–1915* (Princeton, 1962), p. 628; Burk, *Sinews of War*, pp. 64–75.

other three loans, issued in 1916, 1917 and 1919, all required an interest rate of 5½ per cent. These were referred to as Collateral Notes. The total amount of British wartime Loans publicly issued in the USA came to $1,300 million.[36] It should be added that all were repaid on time and in full.

In 1916, Britain's position in US eyes darkened considerably. It became increasingly difficult to finance British purchases in the USA for herself and all of her allies. But Britain was also, unknowingly, moving into increasingly choppy political waters: President Wilson was becoming more and more exasperated by British actions against Germany which also caught Americans in the net. There was growing American disgust and anger with the shipping blockade, heightened by British mail and cable censorship. The British response to the 1916 Easter Rising in Dublin, and particularly the decision to execute the leaders, was viewed with dismay by pro-Ally Americans and with real hatred by the politically important Irish-Americans. Finally, in an incredibly maladroit move, Britain published on 18 July 1916 a blacklist of some 87 American and 350 Latin American firms accused or suspected of trading with the Central Powers. President Wilson wrote accordingly to his close adviser Colonel E.M. House on 23 July: 'I am, I must admit, about at the end of my patience with Great Britain and the Allies. This blacklist business is the last straw … I am seriously considering asking Congress to authorize me to prohibit loans and restrict exportations to the Allies.'[37] Wilson's anger with Great Britain was to have a devastating effect on the ability of Britain to raise dollars.

The British overdraft with Morgans had to be financed in December 1916, so it was suggested by Morgans that Britain issue short-term, unsecured Treasury bills to be bought by American banks and repeatedly renewed. H.P. Davison, a partner in Morgans, met with the Federal Reserve Board on 19 November 1916 to let them know what Morgans planned to do, which was to issue the Treasury bills, without limit but possibly to an amount as high as $1 billion, and as fast as the market could absorb them. The Board found this alarming: not only might this clog up the banks, since it was entirely possible that, although the bills were short-term, they might have to be funded into long-term, possibly thirty- or forty-year, bonds, but were also worried about American dependence on the war trade. The following week, an article appeared in the press restating Morgans' intention, and the Board decided to take action. They drafted a warning note to be inserted in the *Bulletin*, the organ of the Federal Reserve System, cautioning

---

[36] Burk, *Sinews of War*, Appendix II. This sum includes the November 1919 3-Year and 10-Year Collateral Note issues.

[37] Arthur S. Link, *Wilson: Campaigns for Progressivism and Peace, 1916–1917* (Princeton, 1965), pp. 10–15, 65; Thomas A. Bailey, 'The United States and the Blacklist During the Great War', *Journal of Modern History*, 6/1 (1934), pp. 14–35; J.P. Morgan & Co. wrote to Grenfell on 5 Aug. that 'In our opinion there is really strong feeling here with reference to Black List and we do not believe this feeling is political.', no. 23733, Box Hist. 2, file 11, Morgan Grenfell Papers; Box 121, E.M. House Papers, Yale University Library.

banks against investing too heavily in short-term foreign securities, which was then taken to the President for his approval. The President not only approved the action of the Board but felt that the announcement should be stronger – that this kind of security was not liquid and could therefore prove very embarrassing if there was a change in American foreign policy – and that the warning should be extended to the private investor as well as to the member banks. It appeared in the press on 28 November 1916.[38]

The reaction was strong and immediate. The price of Allied bonds and American war stocks tumbled on 28 November, and Morgans that day had to buy nearly $20 million's worth of sterling to maintain the pound/dollar exchange rate. Within a week, values in the securities market had fallen by $1 billion. On 1 December, Morgans announced that they had decided not to proceed with the issue.[39] Morgans believed that the new shadow on Britain's credit now precluded her from raising any loan at least until January 1917. This would have been bad enough if the government had had only to consider paying for orders – it had been necessary to find £38 million in the previous week alone[40] – but now the exchange was in dire straits. By mid-December the situation was perilous. Keynes wrote in 1939 a memorandum describing it:

> I remember in particular a terrific run at the end of 1916, when the daily requirement … ran for a short time in excess of £5 million, which in those days we considered simply terrific. Chalmers and Bradbury [Joint Permanent Secretaries to the Treasury] never fully confessed to ministers the extent of our extremity when it was actually upon us, though of course they had warned them, fully but unavailingly, months beforehand of what was coming. This was because they feared that, if they emphasised the real position, the policy of the peg [maintaining the rate of the pound] might be abandoned, which, they thought, would be disastrous. They had been brought up in the doctrine that in a run one must pay out one's gold reserves to the last bean.

---

[38] Davison to Grenfell, 7 Nov. 1916, no. 29868, Box Hist. 2, file 13, Morgan Grenfell Papers; Cab 37/161/9; Memorandum by Crawford, enclosed in Spring Rice to Grey, 5 Dec. 1916, no. 255636, FO 371/2800; Diary of Charles Hamlin, Vol. 4, 19 Nov. 1916, Charles Hamlin Papers, Library of Congress; US Senate, *Munitions Industry*, v. 204–5. The Governor of the Bank of England had encouraged Morgans on 30 October to issue Treasury bills, on the grounds that the Bank did so very successfully: they kept a supply of the bills on hand, and issued them 'as fast as the market would take them'. Morgan to J.P. Morgan & Co., 30 Oct. 1916, no. 24877, Box Hist. 2, file 12, Morgan Grenfell Papers.

[39] US Senate, *Munitions Industry*, vi. 132; Spring Rice to Grey, 5 Dec. 1916, no. 255636, FO 371/2800; J.P. Morgan & Co. to Grenfell, 29 Nov. 1916, no. 31778 and Chancellor to J.P. Morgan & Co., 29 Nov. 1916, no. 26788, both Box Hist. 2, file 13, Morgan Grenfell Papers; Hamlin Diary, Vol. 4, 1 Dec. 1916.

[40] Minutes of the War Committee, 28 Nov. 1916, Cab. 42/26/2.

The Asquith Coalition government fell in the midst of all of this, and at the first meeting of Lloyd George's new War Cabinet Chalmers was called to report:

> Well, Chalmers, what is the news?' said the goat [Lloyd George]. 'Splendid,' Chalmers replied in his high quavering voice, 'two days ago we had to pay out $20 million; the next day it was $10 million; and yesterday only $5 million.' He did not add that a continuance at this rate for a week could clean us out completely'.[41]

But amidst the shock, the British government wanted to know why the American government had acted as it did. They were willing to accept that there were good banking (rather than diplomatic) reasons for the Board's actions: the Board feared for the liquidity of the banks, and they desired to build up their gold reserves in place of so much paper. But then the British discovered that the State Department had approved of the warning, and the question then became, was the President behind it? There was no clear answer until February 1917, when this was confirmed to the British by the Chairman of the Federal Reserve Board. But the Foreign Secretary, Sir Edward Grey, had decided almost immediately that that was the case, and the government acted on that assumption.[42]

But why did Wilson do it? Ever since the beginning of the war, his constant desire had been to bring the war to an end by mediation, with himself acting as mediator. His motives were humanitarian, but his ruthless treatment of the British in this particular episode illustrated his feeling that by this time, relations with Britain were more strained than with Germany.[43] When Morgans' actions afforded him the opportunity to apply pressure, he was fresh from his re-election triumph and secure in power. There is no doubt that he still smarted from Lloyd George's attempt in September 1916 to forestall an earlier peace move (the 'Knock-Out Blow' speech); if the pressure were not seen to come directly from the President, it would be harder to counteract. And in November 1916, the Allies had few points more vulnerable than credit in the USA. The President – along with others in

---

[41]   Keynes, *Collected Works, XVI.* 211. Keynes' memory was only slightly at fault: the true figures were $17 million, $8 million and $4 million. Minutes of the War Cabinet, 9 Dec. 1916, Cab. 37/161/9. Purchases of £ exchange by J.P. Morgan & Co. for the British government: quarter ending Sept. 1916 – $150 million; quarter ending Dec. 1916 – nearly $350 million. 'British government Treasury accounts in America', n.n., n.d., File JPM & C. Misc. 18E/1, Morgan Grenfell Papers. 'The goat' referred to Lloyd George's sexual appetite.

[42]   Minute by Sperling, 14 Dec. 1916, on Spring Rice to FO, 1 Dec. 1916, no. 250107 and Crawford to Grey, 30 Nov. 1916, no. 242886, both FO 371/2800; Hamlin Diary, Vol. 4, 29 Nov. 1916; Warburg to Strong, 23 Nov. 1916, quoted in US Senate, *Munitions Industry*, v. 197; Minutes of the War Committee, Cab. 42/26/2.

[43]   Hamlin Diary, Vol. 4, 30 Nov. 1916.

the Administration – was certain that peace was imminent;[44] the Allies should be forced to accede to mediation; only supplies and credit from the USA kept them going; undermine this credit and there would be no choice left.

The first months of 1917 were a time of turmoil, and Britain's finances never recovered from the devastation wreaked upon them by Wilson. The Treasury was forced to scrabble for finance wherever it was to be found; a loan of $50 million was issued in Japan for credit in the USA, and Bethlehem Steel, at least, was persuaded to take Treasury notes in payment for orders. Britain managed to issue a loan in the last week of January for $250 million at 5½ per cent, repayable in one or two years, and with such attractive terms, it was naturally oversubscribed.[45] The British would worry later about how to repay it. Thus the point had been reached where Britain no longer had control over her external financial affairs, but was at the mercy of events and the American government. Whilst she waited for the USA to decide between peace and war with Germany, the Treasury and Morgans cobbled up one expedient after another to stave off disaster, sometimes with little more than a week's money in hand for American payments. By mid-March, the Treasury, with all expedients, could see little more than a month ahead.[46] But the Germans then came to the rescue with their policy of unrestricted submarine warfare, and the USA became a belligerent on 6 April 1917.

This changed everything: rather than focusing on convincing Wall Street to provide loans, Britain now had to convince the US Treasury, and especially the Secretary of the Treasury, William Gibbs McAdoo, to provide the desperately needed funds. President Wilson's son-in-law, McAdoo's Wall Street career had been less than overwhelmingly successful; he also had presidential ambitions. Therefore, the British Government had to deal with a man insecure in his command of finance and acutely concerned about his political position. He was also determined to replace the pound with the dollar as the international standard of value and medium of exchange and to see New York replace London as the centre of the international discount market.[47] Altogether, he was not overly anxious to help Britain more than was absolutely necessary.

With regard to finance and the USA, Britain had two main desires. She wanted, first of all, for the USA to take over the burden of financing the purchases of the Allies in the USA; Britain herself would continue to finance them in the rest of the

[44] Diary of Hardman Lever, 23 March 1917, f. 76, T. 172/429, Treasury Papers, The National Archive, Kew.

[45] Henry F. Grady, *British War Finance, 1914–1919* (New York, 1969, 1st pub. 1927), p. 133; Balfour to Spring Rice, 24 Feb. 1917, no. 41794, FO 371/3118 and Crawford to Balfour, 27 Jan. 1917, no. 22121, FO 371/3070; Lever's Diary, 12 Feb. 1917, ff. 30–33, T. 172/429.

[46] Keynes, 'Statement of Resources and Liabilities in America', 17 March 1917, ff. 2–4, T. 172/422.

[47] House to Wiseman, 25 Aug. 1917, 90/26, William Wiseman Papers, Yale University Library; Reading to Chancellor, 22 Sept. 1917, fos. 57–8, T. 172/433.

world. (She also hoped that the USA would reimburse Britain for the money already spent on behalf of the Allies, but this the USA refused to do.) And secondly, she needed help with maintaining the exchange rate of the pound. To her astonishment and chagrin, McAdoo refused to promise a stated amount of aid; rather, it had to be negotiated – even fought over – month by month. He objected to the apparent assumption of the Allies that they had only to ask for money and it would be given; furthermore, he preferred not to let the Allies count on certain sums of money, since their uncertainty would make them more amenable to pressure.[48] He was also under continual pressure from the Congress not to waste American money on anything not connected with the war. He believed that the Allies were trying to bleed the USA, a suspicion made clear to an astonished British Government on 12 July when he cabled to A.J. Balfour, now Foreign Secretary, that 'America's financial policy will be dictated by a desire to cooperate to the fullest extent possible with the several powers making war in common with Germany, but America's cooperation cannot mean that America can assume the entire burden of financing the war'.[49]

This cable jolted the Treasury into facing the depths of McAdoo's ignorance – a situation which was partly the Treasury's own fault, since their representative in the USA had, as a matter of principle,[50] given McAdoo as little information as possible – and the need to remedy the matter as quickly as possible. The Chancellor replied to the cable on 23 July, pointing out that Britain had given the Allies nearly £194 million from 1 April to 14 July 1917, whilst the USA had given them only £90 million. Whilst acknowledging that the US government had given Britain nearly £145 million in addition to the funds for the other Allies, the Chancellor pointed out:

> even since America came into the war financial assistance afforded to the other Allies by the United Kingdom has been *more than double* the assistance afforded them by the United States, and that the assistance the United Kingdom has afforded these other Allies much exceeds the assistance she has herself received from the United States.

McAdoo was then given a great deal of information as to how the £5,000 million which Britain had spent on the war had been raised and spent, and ended with the plea that since British resources for payments in the USA were exhausted, if the USA did not take over payments in the USA, 'the whole financial fabric of

---

[48]   Lever's Diary, 2 May 1917, fos. 105–7 and 11 May 1917, fos. 117–18, T. 172/429; McAdoo to Wilson, 30 April 1917, 2/87, Woodrow Wilson Papers, Library of Congress.

[49]   Department of State, *Papers Relating to the Foreign Relations of the United States, 1917, Supplement 2, the World War* (Washington, 1932), pp. 543–45.

[50]   Lever to Chancellor, 19 May 1917, FO 371/3114. Sir Hardman Lever was the head of the Treasury Mission in the US.

the Alliance will collapse'. The cable had the desired effect, and in the following months, financial aid came in agreed monthly advances.[51]

There were two other extraordinarily difficult contretemps which focused on the foundation of Britain as a financial power. The first was over whether or not the USA should advance funds to enable Britain to maintain the rate of the pound. One high US Treasury official believed that it was merely that the UK had a 'sentimental attachment' to the rate, and McAdoo certainly queried whether it was a 'war purpose',[52] to which Congress had restricted the use of appropriated funds. In late July 1917 matters became desperate, and when McAdoo refused to help, the UK Treasury grasped the nettle: in a choice between the rate of exchange with the dollar and the remaining gold in the Bank of England, the rate would have to give way. McAdoo was informed. The UK's argument was that the British exchange rate was the Allied exchange rate, and British failure to support it would be tantamount to a major defeat in battle. More practically, the fall in sterling would probably be so great that the loss in worldwide purchasing power by the Allies would greatly exceed the $100 million which the British estimated that they required monthly to maintain the rate. McAdoo was probably shaken by the threat that the American government would fall heir to the financial responsibility for the entire Alliance. His great problem was that he would soon be faced with the difficult task of explaining to hostile Congressional committees the payments for sustaining exchange, and he asked the British ambassador to explain his political problems to the Foreign Secretary and ask them to hold out as long as possible. Balfour cabled back immediately that he fully understood the problems McAdoo was facing – the British government had the same problems with Parliament. This cleared the air; the funds were provided, and the rate was maintained at $4.76 to the pound for the duration of the war.[53]

The other ferocious conflict took place between November 1917 and February 1918 over the demand of the US Treasury that it be subrogated to the collateral that lay behind some of the UK Treasury's money market borrowing in the USA. These were British-owned American and other securities which had been deposited by their owners with the British Treasury, and which the Treasury had deposited with Morgans as security for its $400 million overdraft and the collateral loans. The US Treasury insisted that, if it supplied the money to retire some of these obligations,

---

[51]   Chancellor to Page, 23 July 1917, FO 371/3120; Northcliffe to Chancellor, 26 July 1917, FO 371/3115; McAdoo to the President, 26 Aug. 1917, 4/194, Wilson Papers.

[52]   Crawford to FO, 26 June 1917, no. 126709, FO 371/3115.

[53]   US State Department, Foreign Relations, Supplement 2, 532–33; Keynes to Chalmers to Chancellor, prob. 28 July 1917, ff. 61–62, and Minute by Chalmers to Chancellor, f. 62, T. 172/443; War Cab. 199, 30 July 1917, Cab. 23/3; Lloyd George to Northcliffe, 30 July 1917, no. 151220 and Spring Rice to FO, 31 July 1917, no. 150775, both FO 371/3116; Chancellor to McAdoo and Northcliffe, 30 July 1917, no. 150751, FO 371/3115; Balfour to Spring Rice, 2 Aug. 1917, no. 152541, FO 371/3116; Spring Rice to Balfour, 3 Aug. 1917, ff. 413–20, FO 800/242; Burk, *Sinews of War*, pp. 197–206.

the USA should be entitled to take over all the rights to the collateral, including the right to utilise and even to sell it. The British government fought against this, arguing that it had never required this of its Allies when making loans to them and, furthermore, that the securities had only been loaned to the UK Treasury. But McAdoo made threats with regard to future financial aid which could not be ignored, and the British had to turn over the securities to the Americans.[54] The US Treasury had forced the British to resign control over their own assets, a concession symbolic of the changed financial relationship between the two countries: no one doubted any longer who had the whip hand.[55] By the end of the war, the UK Treasury owed the US Treasury $4,277 million, a large proportion of the so-called war debts. Their existence, and the failure of Britain to continue to service them after December 1932, ensured that financial aid from the USA to Britain in the next war was difficult to secure, and that the required quid pro quo – although policies this time, not money – was strongly enforced.[56]

With regard to financing the war itself in the UK, one result was the amount of inflation it had engendered. By mid-July 1919, the short-term, floating debt amounted to over £1,000 million, and the need to fund it – to turn it into long-term debt – led to the 4 per cent Victory and Funding Loans of 12 June 1919.[57] They did not solve the problem. According to Jeremy Wormell, 'it took three years and a recession to reduce the floating debt to a level at which the authorities felt comfortable'.[58] A second result was that, between 1913/14 and 1918/19, the National Debt increased almost twelve times, from £649.8 million to £7,506.9 million.[59] A third was the fall of the pound off of the gold standard in March 1919, when the US Treasury ceased to provide further dollar advances to the UK.[60] The UK would not return to gold until 1925, and it only remained on the gold standard until September 1931. But most fundamentally, and permanently, the United States and Great Britain changed positions as supreme international financial power. The UK paid a heavy price for victory in the First World War.

---

[54]   In 1923, at the time of the War Debt Funding Agreement, $300 million of the subrogated securities were released and returned to Britain. US Senate, *Munitions Industry*, viii. 177.

[55]   Kathleen Burk, 'The Diplomacy of Finance: British Financial Missions to the United States 1914–1918', *Historical Journal*, 22/2 (1979), p. 369.

[56]   Kathleen Burk, 'American Foreign Economic Policy and Lend-Lease', Ann Lane and Howard Temperley, eds, *The Rise and Fall of the Grand Alliance, 1941–5* (London, 1995), pp. 43–68.

[57]   Wormell, *National Debt*, pp. 383–401; 'The financial situation', 18 July 1919, T. 171/170, circulated as GT 7729, Cab. 24/84; Burk, 'From Impotence to Power', p. 101.

[58]   Wormell, *National Debt*, p. 407.

[59]   Peden, *The Treasury and British Public Policy*, p. 80.

[60]   Burk, 'From Impotence to Power', p. 101.

Chapter 12
Financing Churchill's Army

George Peden

Introduction

This chapter is divided into four sections. The first two deal respectively with retrenchment and rearmament in the inter-war period from the point of view of explaining why the British Army was not better prepared for war in 1939. The third explains the ways in which domestic war finance continued to be important even after manpower rather than money became the limiting factor on the expansion of the Army. The fourth section deals with overseas war finance, mainly in terms of the consequences for British power of Churchill's decision to seek victory at any cost.

It is important to distinguish between domestic finance and overseas finance. Governments could obtain the paper pounds they needed through taxation or loans. Taxes, and loans raised from savings, diverted spending power from the public to the government without inflation. Borrowing from banks, on the other hand, was potentially inflationary, if the borrowing took the form of Treasury bills, which banks regarded as nearly as liquid as cash, since the government had to repay the bills after 90 days if the banks chose not to renew them. Government reliance on Treasury bills could be expected to increase the banks' willingness to lend. As experience in the First World War had shown, the most inflationary borrowing by the government was from the Bank of England (such loans being known as 'ways and means advances'). Ways and means advances represented an increase in the money supply, and they led to further increases in the following way. A book entry would be made in the government's account at the Bank of England and cheques drawn on that account would be used to pay contractors. Once the cheques were cleared, the joint stock banks found themselves holding more cash reserves at the Bank of England and lent four or five times the increase to their customers or to the government. The result was more money chasing the supply of goods and services, and once any slack in the labour supply was taken up, prices tended to rise. Workers would then claim higher wages to protect their standard of living, and if employers resisted, production would be disrupted by strikes.

An increase in the supply of paper pounds could also have an effect on overseas finance. People abroad would be less willing to hold sterling assets if inflation was expected to erode the value of the pound compared with other currencies. As sterling assets were sold in order to buy assets in other currencies, sterling's exchange rates with these currencies would fall. In so far as imports had to be paid for in foreign currencies, the effect would be that import prices would increase in terms of sterling. Paper pounds could be used to pay for imports from the countries that used sterling for international financial transactions and for their currency reserves. These countries formed the Sterling Area, which broadly corresponded to the British Empire, with the notable exception of Canada, and their willingness to accumulate sterling balances in payment for goods and services was to be an important element in war finance. However, the countries of the Sterling Area lacked the industrial resources to produce munitions on a large scale. As in the First World War, the United Kingdom (UK) would have to turn to the United States of America (USA) for supplies on the scale necessary for a large army.

Imports from the USA had to be paid for in dollars, which could be obtained in four ways. First, the UK could export goods and services, but it was inevitable that earnings would cover a declining proportion of purchases as industrial capacity was diverted to munitions production. Second, the UK could use its gold reserves, which were greater in 1939 than in 1914, but which, even so, were small in relation to the orders that would be placed in the USA. Third, the government could take over British-owned securities that could be sold for dollars. Fourth, it might be possible to raise loans in the USA, perhaps using securities as collateral, perhaps relying on the good will of the US government. However, the UK's failure to continue payments on its war debt to the USA after 1933 led Congress to pass the Johnson Act in the following year, prohibiting further loans to all governments, including those of the UK and France, which had defaulted. The barrier to American aid was raised further from 1935 when Congress passed Neutrality Acts banning the export of arms to belligerent states and forbidding American ships from entering combat zones. Overseas finance in the Second World War came to depend on the willingness and ability of the US government to persuade Congress that it was in America's interests that the British war effort should be sustained.

Domestic and overseas finance were linked by the question of whether British public finance enjoyed the confidence of financial markets throughout the world. Wars were financed largely by increasing the National Debt, which spread the cost over more than one generation, and it had been the Treasury's boast since the eighteenth century that the British government's credit was better than that of foreign governments, with the consequence that it could borrow at comparatively low interest rates. However, the government's credit depended on its ability to service the debt without inflation. In the pre-Keynesian era financial markets expected the Chancellor of the Exchequer to be able to balance his budget for central government expenditure and revenue. Experts in public finance from Adam Smith onwards had stressed the need for parsimony after a war in order to restore the government's finances. For all but the last few years of the inter-war period the Army was subject to Treasury parsimony.

Retrenchment

In peacetime finance was a means of allocating resources between the Army, Air Force and Navy, and government policy was reflected in the annual estimates agreed between the defence departments and the Treasury. The size of the British Army in 1918 had been dependent on American economic aid, which ended early in 1919, making a reduction to something like the pre-1914 establishment an urgent necessity. Inflation during and immediately after the war highlighted the need to restore normality to the public finances. The Army was early identified as a target for economies. On 15 August 1919 the War Cabinet decided that it should be assumed that 'the British Empire will not be engaged in any great war during the next ten years, and that no Expeditionary Force is required for this purpose'.[1] One year after the Armistice there were just over 800,000 troops on the British establishment (that is, excluding those paid for by India); by November 1920 that figure had fallen 370,000. Following an enquiry in 1921–22 by a committee of businessmen chaired by Sir Eric Geddes, 22 infantry battalions were disbanded and 7 withdrawn from overseas; and the number of cavalry regiments was reduced from 28 to 20.[2] Whereas expenditure on the Army in the financial year 1921/22 had been £95.1 million, in 1922/23 it was £45.4 million.[3]

Strict Treasury control of expenditure was re-established, and in some respects tightened. Before the war the Army and Navy estimates had gone to the Cabinet for approval without previous consultation with Treasury officials, who had in any case been concerned purely with whether departments' proposals were the best ways in which to carry out government policy. In the inter-war period no proposal to increase expenditure could go to the Cabinet without first being discussed with Treasury officials, who were encouraged by the new Permanent Secretary of the Treasury, Sir Warren Fisher, to form independent views on what policy should be. A minister could, of course, appeal to the Cabinet if the Chancellor of the Exchequer withheld approval for some proposal but, so long as the budget had to be balanced, any increase in expenditure meant more taxation, or less funding for other departments, and the Chancellor usually enjoyed the support of other ministers. As before 1914, the Treasury could reserve an item in the annual estimates for further consideration, so that even although money had been voted by Parliament, permission to spend it could be withheld. The authority of the Permanent Secretary of the Treasury in Whitehall was increased in 1919 when he was recognised as head of the Civil Service. At Fisher's suggestion, the most senior civil servant in each defence department was made its accounting officer, with his appointment being subject to approval of the Board of Treasury. War

---

[1]   War Cabinet 'A' minutes, 616A, CAB 23/15, TNA.

[2]   Brian Bond, *British Military Policy between the Wars* (Oxford, 1980), pp. 21, 26–27.

[3]   Army expenditure figures in text are from *Statistical Abstract for the United Kingdom for each of the fifteen years 1913 and 1919 to 1932* (Cmd. 4489), Parliamentary Papers (PP) 1933–34, vol. xxvi, p. 1, and *1924 to 1938* (Cmd. 6232), PP 1939–40, vol. x, p. 367.

Office finance officers had in any case long had a reputation for parsimony, and it was often they rather than Treasury officials who were responsible for delays in obtaining approval for new proposals.

From 1922/3 to 1927/8 successive secretaries of state for war did battle annually with the Chancellor, but in 1927/28 expenditure was still £44.15 million, or only £1.25 million less than in 1922/23 (in a period when prices were stable or falling).[4] Churchill, as Chancellor from 1924 to 1929, pursued economy with his accustomed energy. At his suggestion, the Cabinet set up a committee under a businessman, Lord Colwyn, in 1925 to recommend economies in the 1926/7 defence estimates, but it was only in 1928/9 that there was a marked reduction in Army expenditure, to £40.5 million. In 1928, the Treasury's position was decisively strengthened by Churchill's success in persuading the Committee of Imperial Defence (CID) to lay down that 'it should be assumed for the purpose of framing the Estimates of the Fighting Services, that at any given date there will be no major war for ten years'. Even so, Churchill made clear that the assumption should be reviewed each year by the CID. Moreover, his intention was that the Ten Year Rule should not hamper the development of ideas, but would hold back mass production until the situation required it.[5]

The Army was thus free to experiment with new armoured fighting vehicles, but most of the infantry and cavalry's equipment was drawn from large stocks left over from the First World War. The financial crisis of 1931 led to further reductions in the estimates, and the Army's expenditure reached its inter-war nadir of £35.9 million in 1932/3. In March 1932, the Cabinet accepted the recommendation of the Chiefs of Staff (COS) that the assumption that there would be no major war for ten years must be cancelled in view of the situation in the Far East, but at the same time recognised the Treasury's case that this decision must not be taken to justify additional expenditure without regard to the country's very serious financial and economic position.[6] One result of prolonged retrenchment, combined with the general depression in heavy industry, was that the Army's suppliers were by no means as ready for mass production as Churchill had hoped in 1928. The problem was referred in 1933 to a committee of three industrialists, Lord Weir, Sir Arthur Balfour and Sir James Lithgow, and their report in February 1934 confirmed that the decline in the armament industry had led to a serious shortfall in capacity for munitions production. The industrialists recommended that selected engineering firms should be asked to prepare capacity, or 'shadow factories', to supplement output from the Royal Ordnance Factories in war, and that meantime educational

---

[4]   The best account of the Treasury's attempts to control defence expenditure in this period is John R. Ferris, *The Evolution of British Strategic Policy, 1919–26* (Basingstoke, 1989).

[5]   CID 236th meeting, 5 July 1928, CAB 2/5, TNA.

[6]   Cabinet conclusions (CC), 19 (32), 23 March 1932, CAB 23/70, TNA.

orders should be placed to familiarise the firms with munitions production.[7] The shortfall in capacity meant that the War Office's ability to spend was restricted by industrial bottlenecks as well as by finance.

Retrenchment also had an adverse effect on tank development. By 1931 the General Staff had decided that the Army needed three types of tanks: a medium tank with an anti-tank gun as well as a machine gun; an infantry support tank; and a light tank for reconnaissance. However, in 1932 the Director of Mechanisation decided, on financial grounds, to stop development work on a replacement for the medium tank then in service. This decision was not irreversible, but lack of tank orders had already reduced the number of firms with specialist design staff from two to one in 1928, when Vickers-Armstrong took over Carden-Loyd, and there proved to be insufficient design capacity for all the types of tanks that the Army wished to order in the 1930s. In particular, the decision in 1934 to develop two different types of tanks, one heavily armoured for infantry support and one, known as a cruiser, which was more lightly armoured than a medium tank, seems to have precluded the development of a direct replacement for the medium tank.[8]

Rearmament

The Army was in competition with the Admiralty and, in particular, the Air Force in regard both to finance and industrial resources. Between November 1933 and February 1934 the Defence Requirements Sub-committee (DRC) of the CID, comprising the COS, the Permanent Secretary of the Treasury, the Permanent Under Secretary of the Foreign Office and the Cabinet Secretary, prepared a programme for dealing with what were described as 'the worst deficiencies' in the armed forces. Its recommendations would have preserved the existing balance between the defence departments, with the Army receiving over a third of the total defence budget, or more than twice as much as the Air Force (see Table 12.1). However, during the DRC's deliberations Fisher had expressed the view that the British public would be more willing to pay for the air defence of the UK than they would for any other defensive purpose.[9] When the sub-committee's report was considered by ministers, the Chancellor of the Exchequer, Neville Chamberlain, successfully argued for a higher priority for the Air Force and a lower priority for the Army. As a result, in July 1934 the Air Force was allocated £20 million for the period 1934/5–1939/40, compared with the DRC's recommendation of £15.7

---

[7]   William Hornby, *Factories and Plant* (London, 1958), pp. 14–18, 21–23, 83–85, 147–49.

[8]   David French, *Raising Churchill's Army: The British Army and the War against Germany 1919–1945* (Oxford, 2000), pp. 96–101; J.P. Harris, *Men, Ideas and Tanks: British Military Thought and Armoured Forces, 1903–1939* (Manchester, 1995), pp. 238–41, 274–83, 298–302.

[9]   DRC 7th meeting, 25 Jan. 1934, CAB 16/109, TNA.

million, whereas the Army's recommended allocation was cut from £40 million to £20 million. Chamberlain accepted at this stage that it was essential to have an expeditionary force to keep Germany out of the Low Countries, but he did not believe in 1934 that Germany would be ready for war in 1939, and he felt that the Army's DRC programme could be spread over a longer period than five years.[10] Chamberlain also proposed that replacement of the Navy's capital ships should be postponed, but he was unable to convince his Cabinet colleagues; Stanley Baldwin, the leader of the Conservative party and the chairman of the ministerial committee considering the DRC programme, drew attention to possible activities of the Navy League in this connection.[11] There was no such organisation to support the Army.

Table 12.1:   Forecasts of annual expenditure if recommendations of Defence Requirements Sub-Committee accepted in full, 28 February 1934

Financial year	Admiralty £000s	Air Ministry £000s	War Office £000s	War Office as % of total for three services
1934/5	56,249	17,650	44,369	37.66
1935/6	60,978	18,665	44,946	36.08
1936/7	63,323	20,300	45,243	35.11
1937/8	63,844	21,300	45,468	34.81
1938/9	65,081	21,275	45,684	34.60

Source: DRC 14, CAB 16/109.

Towards the end of January 1935 intelligence reports began to reach the Treasury about the scale of German borrowing for rearmament and, at Fisher's suggestion, ministers agreed in July that the defence departments should be authorised to examine defence requirements on the assumption that they could be partly financed by a defence loan.[12] When a new Defence Requirements Sub-Committee reported in November 1935 it once more recommended that the War Office should be allocated more funds than the Air Ministry (see Table 12.2). However, when ministers in the Defence Policy and Requirements Committee came to discuss the report in January 1936, they were told by Weir that industry could not fulfil the whole programme without a semi-war organisation to overcome

---

[10]   For development of Treasury's views on the Air Force and Army in 1934–36, see G.C. Peden, *British Rearmament and the Treasury, 1932–1939* (Edinburgh, 1979), pp. 118–27, 136.

[11]   Disarmament Committee (Ministerial), 52nd meeting, 2 July 1934, CAB 27/507, TNA.

[12]   Peden, *British Rearmament*, pp. 73–74.

bottlenecks, principally shortages of skilled labour and machine tools, and that he did not believe that the controls that existed in Germany could ever be imposed in Britain. Going beyond his brief as industrial adviser, Weir expressed the view that the Army was the most expensive way of helping allies, and asked whether a contribution on land would be necessary if the Air Force were built up to be a substantial deterrent. (Weir's strategic views appear to have been based on those of Captain Basil Liddell Hart.[13]) Chamberlain took up the argument that the threat of an air offensive by the RAF might be a more effective deterrent to German aggression than defensive action by land forces. Ministers agreed that the report's programme for the Regular Army should be accepted, but that no decision should be taken for three years on the recommendation that twelve Territorial Army divisions should be prepared to reinforce the Regular expeditionary force. Meanwhile only a small sum (£250,000) would be made available to purchase training equipment for the TA.[14]

Table 12.2:   Forecasts of annual expenditure if recommendations of Third Defence Requirements Report accepted, 21 November 1935

Financial Year	Admiralty £000s	Air Ministry £000s	War Office £000s	War Office as % of total for three services
1936/7	74,900	45,000	54,000	31.05
1937/8	89,000	60,000	62,000	29.38
1938/9	90,650	64,000	72,000	31.77
1939/40	90,700	50,000	72,000	33.85
1940/1	83,300	44,000	82,000	39.18

Source: DRC 37, CAB 16/112.

The rearmament programme which the Cabinet approved in February 1936 for the three services in the financial years 1936/7 to 1941/2 was 'very tentatively' estimated to cost £394.5 million in excess of the level of expenditure represented by the original 1935 estimates. The total of the defence departments' expenditure over the five-year period was thus expected to be of the order of £1016 million. Financial restraint was eased by the Treasury's willingness to pay for rearmament by borrowing, for ministers need now no longer assume that more money for

---

[13]   Memorandum by Lord Weir, DPR (DR) 4, 9 Jan. 1936, and DPR (DR) 1st and 2nd meetings, 13 and 14 Jan. 1936, CAB 16/123. Weir had underlined passages in Liddell Hart's articles in *The Times* of 25, 26 and 27 Nov. 1935, Weir papers, 17/10, Churchill College, Cambridge.

[14]   DPR (DR) 2nd, 4th and 7th meetings, 14, 16 and 27 Jan. 1936, CAB 16/123, TNA; Neville Chamberlain diary, 19 Jan. 1936, NC 2/23A, University of Birmingham Library.

one department need mean less for another within a balanced budget. On the other hand, the Cabinet approved the rearmament programme on condition that there were to be no restrictions on the social services, and no interference with production for civil or export trade; indeed it was minuted that the maintenance of 'the general industry and trade of the country' was 'an essential element in the financing' of the programme.[15] In practice an increasing degree of priority over civil work was gradually given to rearmament orders, but it was not until after the German occupation of Austria in March 1938 that the government decided to ask that full priority be given.[16] Treasury officials could thus withhold approval of expenditure that would interfere with normal civil business. For example, the Treasury tried to stop the War Office from bringing new firms into gun production, arguing that orders should be postponed until new Royal Ordnance factories had been completed. As a result, the Director-General of Munitions Production, Sir Harold Brown, reported in July 1937 that he had been unable to place all the orders that had been authorised.[17]

Treasury control of expenditure was a political necessity, to reassure taxpayers and Parliament that rearmament would not lead to profiteering. On the other hand, financial control was relaxed to ensure that orders were placed as quickly as possible once industrial capacity had been identified. From February 1936 representatives of the three defence departments and the Treasury met frequently in the Treasury Inter-service Committee for this purpose. The defence departments were allowed to exceed the estimates agreed before the beginning of each financial year, and it became the norm for Parliament to be asked to approve supplementary estimates. To encourage civilian engineering firms to undertake munitions production, contracts were placed on a long-term basis, extending beyond a single financial year, so that the finance required in any one year depended upon the speed with which firms fulfilled contracts. Moreover, the official in charge of the Treasury division dealing with the defence departments, Edward Bridges, believed that it was impossible for the Treasury to refuse approval for additions to the rearmament programme that the services declared to be necessary on technical or strategic grounds. As a result, the forecast for the Army's programme increased from £94 million in February 1936 to £177 million in January 1937 and £214 million in June 1937, with further additions totalling £43 million under consideration at the last date. In May 1937 the Cabinet had agreed in principle that the TA should receive sufficient equipment of the same type as the Regular Army to allow all TA infantry divisions to be trained in peace time, at a cost of £9.25 millions, compared with £250,000 agreed fourteen months earlier.[18] Bridges advised that the only way in which to reassert financial discipline was to fix a sum that the defence departments could spend over the next

---

[15]   CC 10 (36), 25 Feb. 1936, and 12 (36), 2 March 1936, CAB 23/83, TNA.
[16]   CC 16 (38), 23 March 1938, CAB 23/93, TNA.
[17]   Informal Army Council minutes, 20 July 1937, item 2, WO 163/47, TNA.
[18]   CC 20 (37) 5 May 1937, CAB 23/88; CP 165, CAB 24/270, TNA.

five years. The Treasury put forward the figure of £1,500 million as the total sum of what could be afforded for all three defence departments over five years from taxation and defence loans, and in June 1937 the Cabinet agreed that decisions on major new projects should be postponed pending a review of defence expenditure in future years.

The review was conducted by Sir Thomas Inskip, the minister for co-ordination of defence, and in February 1938 the Cabinet agreed to his recommendation that a limit of £1,570 million be set for the defence departments' expenditure in the next five years.[19] It will be noted that this figure was about 55 per cent greater that the forecast for the rearmament programme approved two years earlier. Moreover, Inskip recommended that expenditure could be accelerated, provided it was related to approved programmes, and also that there should be a further review in 1939 to consider whether programmes of greater scope should be approved in the light of the international situation. As Table 12.3 shows, War Office expenditure continued to rise, and its share of total defence expenditure in 1938/9 was the same as that recommended by the DRC in November 1935 (compare Tables 12.2 and 12.3). At first sight the Inskip review does not seem to have led to severe financial restraint on the Army.

Table 12.3:   Actual expenditure by departments and War Office share of total defence expenditure, 1932/3–1938/9

Financial year	Admiralty £000s	Air Ministry £000s	War Office £000s	War Office as % of total for three services
1932/3	50,010	17,100	35,880	34.8
1933/4	53,500	16,780	37,592	34.8
1934/5	56,580	17,630	39,660	34.8
1935/6	64,806	27,496	44,647	32.6
1936/7	81,092	50,134	54,846	29.5
1937/8	101,950	82,290	77,877	29.7
1938/9	127,295	133,800	121,361	31.7

Source: *Statistical Abstract for the United Kingdom for each of the Fifteen years 1924 to 1938* (Cmd. 6232), PP 1939–40, x, 367.

---

[19]   For the origins and conduct of the Inskip review see N.H. Gibbs, *Grand Strategy* (London, 1976), pp. 465–77, and Peden, *British Rearmament*, pp. 10, 20, 38–42, 77–81, 86–92, 137–39.

However, when bringing the total of expenditure close to the Treasury's figure of £1,500 million, Inskip had accepted the arguments of the Treasury that significantly higher expenditure would undermine the UK's economic stability. Although the defence programmes were presented in purely financial terms, the Treasury was aware that what mattered was the supply of goods and services that money could buy. That in turn depended on the UK's manpower and productive capacity; its ability to pay for imports; and sterling's standing in international money markets. The COS assumed that it was only in a long war that the maritime powers, the UK and France, would be able to mobilise their resources and wear down Germany by blockade. From this perspective, economic stability could be regarded as 'a fourth arm of defence'. Inskip was persuaded that the best deterrent to Germany would be maintenance of the UK's 'staying power' in peace and war, plus an ability to avoid a 'knock-out blow' by the *Luftwaffe* at the outset of a war. In an interim report accepted by the Cabinet on 22 December 1937, he recommended that the main effort should be directed first to the UK's air defence and second to the defence of her trade routes. He placed the defence of British territories and interests overseas, as a third objective, at a lower level of priority than the first two, and said that the fourth objective, cooperation in the defence of the territories of any allies in war, should be provided for only after the first three had been met. Inskip admitted that if France were to be again in danger of being overrun by land armies it might be necessary to improvise an army to assist her, and that the Government would be criticised for having failed to anticipate so obvious a contingency.[20]

Following the Inskip Report the Army's programme for air defence of Great Britain was increased from £57 million to £68 million, but the programme for the Regular Expeditionary Force was cut from £95 million to £77 million, and provision for the Territorial Army from £52 million to £8 million.[21] The Expeditionary Force was still to comprise four infantry and one mobile division, but Inskip believed that it would no longer need the very large reserves of equipment and shells required for the intensity of fighting that experience of the Western Front in 1918 had led the War Office to assume would be necessary. On 17 March 1938, the CID approved plans for an Expeditionary Force of two infantry and one mobile division with equipment and war reserves on a Continental scale, but for defensive purposes only; two further infantry divisions with half of the reserves of that scale and ready to embark in forty days; and a pool of equipment with which to send two further divisions, which might be Regular or TA, after four months. The Chancellor of the Exchequer was able to change the War Office's specification that this force was to be prepared for 'an Eastern campaign' (meaning the defence of Egypt against the Italian army) to 'for general purposes', which allowed Treasury officials to

---

[20]   CP 316 (37), CAB 24/273, TNA.

[21]   M.M. Postan, *British War Production* (London, 1952), p. 31.

resist proposals for equipment, whether as to type or scale, for a Continental campaign.[22]

Even so, War Office expenditure on warlike and general stores more than doubled between 1937 and 1938, from £21.4 million to £44.3 million, which meant that the Army's share of such expenditure by the three defence departments rose from about one-fifth to about one-quarter.[23] Moreover, once it was clear that the Munich agreement had failed to reduce the threat of war, the Cabinet was no longer minded to respond to Treasury pleas for financial restraint. In January 1939, the COS proposed that there should be a Regular Expeditionary Force of four infantry and two mobile divisions, equipped on a Continental scale, with an immediate reserve of four TA divisions, and full training equipment for the rest of the TA. One Treasury official pointed out that the estimated cost of the Regular Expeditionary Force had risen from £72 million in October 1935, to £97 million in October 1937, and to £126 million in January 1939. Even so, on 22 February the Cabinet approved the War Office's proposals for the Expeditionary Force. The Army programme was greatly increased on 29 March when the Cabinet accepted the decision of Chamberlain and the Secretary of State for War, Leslie Hore-Belisha, to double the TA to 26 divisions, at a capital cost vaguely stated to be £80 million to £100 million, and on 19 April the Cabinet approved in principle a plan to increase industrial capacity and reserves of equipment for a 32-division force to be in the field 12 months after the outbreak of a war. The cost of this plan was £45 million for new industrial capacity and £90 million for additional equipment.[24]

Although the Treasury continued to monitor expenditure, and to hold up proposals involving expenditure of foreign exchange, the War Office's principal problem was no longer the availability of finance, but rather the speed with which industrial capacity could be brought on stream to allow all the money it had been allocated to be spent. Industrial problems were so great that the Cabinet agreed to the creation of a Ministry of Supply in peace time, although previously calls in Parliament for such a step had been resisted. The War Office thereby lost control over the design and production of its own weapons, and priority had to be given to quantity over quality.

From the Treasury's point of view, the problem in 1939 was how to adapt financial policy to the new scale of defence expenditure. Tax revenue had increased, with the standard rate of income tax being raised in the budgets of 1936, 1937 and 1938 (when it reached 5s.6d., or 27.5p, compared with 4s.6d., or 22.5p, in 1935). However, with the economy only just emerging from a recession, it was decided in 1939 to rely on increased borrowing rather than taxation. In February 1939, the government's borrowing powers, which had been set under

[22]   Peden, *British Rearmament*, pp. 143–45.

[23]   Postan, *British War Production*, pp. 12, 28.

[24]   CC 8 (39), 15 (39) and 21 (39), CAB 23/98, TNA; Note by Edmund Compton, 1 Feb. 1939, Treasury papers, series 161, box 1071, file S.42580/4 (T 161/1071/S.42580/4), TNA.

the Defence Loans Act of 1937 at £400 million, were doubled, and the Treasury intended to obtain further authority from Parliament as necessary. On 5 July 1939, the Treasury's most senior official dealing with finance, Sir Richard Hopkins, appeared before a special meeting of the Cabinet held to consider the financial situation. Hopkins advised that, as regards domestic finance, the Treasury was waiting for the economy to reach full employment, but once that point was reached – probably in the autumn – it would be necessary to ensure that all necessary savings were made available to the government. That would involve, for example, controls over advances by banks and building societies, and over companies' dividends and financial reserves. In other words, the Treasury was contemplating controls hitherto considered acceptable only in wartime, whether or not war broke out in the near future. As regards external finance, Hopkins pointed out that even armaments produced in the UK involved imports of raw materials to the value of 25 per cent to 30 per cent of the finished articles; moreover increasing rearmament orders were diverting British firms away from exports, so that the balance of trade was deteriorating. The principal reason for the disappearance of 40 per cent of sterling's gold reserves in the past 15 months was that foreigners were taking out their money; a great deal of fugitive French money which had been banked in London during the period of the Popular Front government had returned to Paris, and New York was now attracting fugitive foreign gold. Nevertheless the adverse balance of trade resulted in a steady loss of British-owned gold, and the UK was in a worse position to fight a long war than in 1914 unless the USA was prepared to help with war finance.[25]

The belated attempt to prepare a 32-division army for a Continental campaign, in addition to an Air Force that could match the *Luftwaffe*, and a Navy that could protect the British Empire from Japan and Italy as well as Germany, had financial consequences that raised the question of whether Britain would be able to sustain a long war. Financial policy thus faced major challenges, both as regards diverting production from civil to military use, and securing the overseas supplies necessary to carry out the COS's long-war strategy. As for the Army itself, rapid expansion in 1939 inevitably led to shortages of weapons and equipment.

Domestic War Finance

At the outbreak of war Parliament granted the government a vote of credit of £500 million for additional expenditure on the defence of the realm in the financial year 1939/40, a sum which proved to be £71.5 million greater than what was required. Subsequent votes of credit continued to ensure the necessary paper pounds were available. The sizes of the armed forces in wartime were determined by the supply of manpower, not finance. The Army's strength rose from 241,000 in June 1939

---

[25]   Minutes of special meeting of Cabinet, 5 July 1939, and CP 149 (39), CAB 23/100, TNA.

to 1,656,000 twelve months later; in March 1941 Churchill imposed a ceiling of about 2 million, to ensure that the Army did not absorb manpower that would be better employed in munitions production. However, with increasing deliveries of American munitions from mid-1941, the ceiling could be breached and numbers continued to rise, reaching 2,920,000 by June 1945.[26] Domestic financial policy had two major contributions to make to the war effort: first, by securing the transfer of resources from civilian to military use in ways that would be acceptable to the public; and, second, by encouraging the efficient use of these resources. Ministers and officials responsible for financing Churchill's armies had the advantage of being able to learn from experience in the First World War. One lesson from 1914–18 was that inflation should be avoided as much as possible, and domestic war finance was much more successful in this respect in the Second World War than in the first.

Of the £14,800 million borrowed within the UK by the government during the war, only £770 million resulted in an increase in the supply of bank notes. Reliance on ways and means advances was avoided. The government was able to mobilise the nation's savings, partly through the kinds of controls on banks and building societies, and on companies' dividends and financial reserves that Hopkins had outlined to the Cabinet in July 1939, but mainly because physical controls over investment (such as the allocation of steel) removed most alternatives to the purchase of government bonds. In contrast to the First World War, no attempt was made to attract savings by increasing the rate of interest on war loans. In October 1939 the Chancellor of the Exchequer and the Prime Minister took the view that it would be very difficult politically to justify a higher rate than 3 per cent, presumably because of Labour opposition to bondholders receiving returns comparable to those of the First World War. Despite the failure of the public to take up all of a £300 million issue of 3 per cent War Loan 1955–9 in March 1940, the Bank of England and the Treasury stuck to the policy of 3 per cent for long-term loans. From June 1940 varying terms relating to yields and maturities within that ceiling – for example 2.5 per cent on five- to ten-year issues – were offered to attract firms' accumulating depreciation funds and undistributed profits, a technique associated with the monetary theory of John Maynard Keynes. Firms were also encouraged to use idle funds to take up tax reserve certificates (in readiness for tax liability) at 1 per cent, while the cash reserves of the clearing banks were mopped up with Treasury deposit receipts, whereby the banks were required to lend to the Treasury for six-month periods at 1⅛ per cent. Rationing, and price controls on essential goods, reduced the public's ability to spend, and small savings, in

[26] W.K. Hancock and M.M. Gowing, *British War Economy* (London, 1949), pp. 136, 237, 288–92, 353; Central Statistical Office (CSO), *Statistical Digest of the War* (London, 1951), p. 9.

the form of Post Office Savings Bank accounts or National Savings certificates, accounted for about a quarter of the government's borrowing in the UK.[27]

The principal financial weapon against inflation was taxation. The standard rate of income tax was increased from 5s.6d. (27.5p) to 7s. (35p) in the pound in the first war budget in September 1939, and to 8s.6d. (42.5p) in the second in July 1940. Social justice demanded heavy taxation of the rich, and the top rate of surtax, which was payable in addition to the standard rate of income tax, was fixed at 9s.6d. (47.5p) in the July budget, giving a marginal tax rate for the highest earners of 18s. (90p). Even so, the April 1941 budget tightened the screw further, by raising the standard rate a further 6d. (2.5p) to 10s. (50p), 4s. (20p) higher than in 1918/19. In August 1940, Keynes had returned to the Treasury as an adviser to the Chancellor, and the April 1941 budget reflected his influence in using an analysis of national income to calculate the extent to which civilian consumption must be reduced in order to finance government expenditure without inflation. Earned income and personal allowances were reduced so as to increase the number of people liable to income tax, but these changes were made more acceptable by treating the additional tax paid as a post-war credit to be repaid at a time of the government's choosing after the war. In contrast to the First World War, direct taxation of working-class incomes was made effective through the deduction at source by employers and the development of the pay-as-you-earn (PAYE) system. The 1941 budget took direct taxation to its practical limit: six months later the Ministry of Information reported that the increase in income tax rates was reducing the willingness of workers to undertake overtime. The problem of preventing surplus purchasing power from increasing consumption had thereafter to be left to indirect taxation, which had been widened in 1940 by the introduction of purchase tax on the sale of non-essential goods. On the other hand, with a view to moderating trade union demands for wage increases, the cost of living was stabilised from 1941 by using Treasury subsidies to hold down prices of essential goods and services, such as bread, coal, gas and electricity.[28]

One particular problem that had to be addressed by taxation was the politically sensitive issue of profiteering. Chamberlain, while Chancellor, had proposed in the 1937 budget to levy what was called a National Defence Contribution, which was to be graduated according to the growth of profits. However, the measure was fiercely opposed by business and by members of the Conservative party, including Churchill, who denounced what he regarded as a tax on inventiveness and enterprise. Churchill's argument was based on the assumption that in peacetime there would be competition between firms, and he referred favourably to the excess

---

[27]   R.S. Sayers, *Financial Policy 1939–45* (London, 1956), esp. pp. 153–56, 161, 223, 494; Susan Howson, 'Cheap Money and Debt Management, 1932–51', in P.L. Cottrell and D.E. Moggridge (eds), *Money and Power: Essays in Honour of L S. Pressnell* (Basingstoke, 1988), pp. 227–89, at 250–55.

[28]   Sayers, *Financial Policy*, pp. 58–93; G.C. Peden, *The Treasury and British Public Policy, 1906–1959* (Oxford, 2000), pp. 318–27.

profits duty of the First World War as a means of dealing with profiteering in the absence of effective competition.[29] An armaments profits duty to be levied at 60 per cent of increased profits since 1937 was enacted in July 1939, but in the first war budget two months later it was merged with a new excess profits tax (EPT) at the same rate on all trade or business profits over a pre-war standard. For political reasons EPT was raised from 60 per cent to 100 per cent in the July 1940 budget, although Treasury officials were aware that the latter rate took away all incentive from businessmen to economise on resources or to take risks in new investment. The 1941 budget recognised the need to restore incentives by promising that 20 per cent of the EPT paid during the war would be repaid afterwards, on condition that the refund was ploughed back into a business. Even so, industrialists were loath to invest in additional plant on these terms, especially as they were also personally liable to pay very high rates of income tax and surtax. As a result, most new industrial capacity was financed by the government, in addition to the government-owned Royal Ordnance Factories, with private firms undertaking management for a fee.

Ideally contracts would have been negotiated, and financial control exercised, in ways designed to encourage efficient production without excess profits.[30] In 1934 the three services' Contracts Co-ordinating Committee had recommended 10 per cent on capital employed as a reasonable profit in the absence of effective competition in war time. By and large the Ministry of Supply succeeded in keeping contractors for the Army within this limit: a survey of 743 firms in 1943 showed the average rate of profit was 9.68 per cent. However, most of the Ministry's contracts relied on ascertaining costs of production after the contract was completed, plus a profit, which might be fixed in advance or be a percentage of the ascertained costs. Either way, there was little incentive to the contractor to make more efficient use of capital or labour, in contrast to the situation where the price was fixed in advance and the contractor could increase his profit by lowering costs. From 1943 the Ministry of Supply, following the earlier examples of the Admiralty and Air Ministry, began to use technical costing, whereby Ministry staff examined methods of production and negotiated a fixed price in advance. Presumably the scale of the increase in number of contracts after the outbreak of war (see Table 12.4) had stretched the resources of the Ministry too much to adopt that system earlier.

---

[29]   *Parliamentary Debates (Commons)*, 5th series, 1936–37, vol. 324, cols. 883–97.

[30]   What follows is based on William Ashworth, *Contracts and Finance* (London, 1953).

Table 12.4:   Number and value of War Office contracts (1938/9) and Ministry of
Supply contracts (1939/40–1942/3)

Financial year	Number of new orders	Index of approximate value (1938=100)
1938/9	19,000	100
1939/40	39,000	460
1940/1	57,608	898
1941/2	74,361	1,040
1942/3	99,229	1,153

Source: G.D.N. Worswick, 'A survey of war contract procedure', in University of Oxford
Institute of Statistics, *Studies in War Economics* (Oxford, 1947), 390–403, at 391.

Taken as a whole, domestic war finance was successful. War-related expenditure
rose from 7 per cent of national income in 1938 to over 50 per cent from 1941. As
a result of this transfer of resources to the government, consumer expenditure fell
by 16 per cent in real terms between 1938 and 1943.[31] Nevertheless, social peace
was preserved. In particular, the average annual number of days lost to strikes in
1940–45 was less than half the average number of 1915–18.[32] Social peace was
not, of course, solely a function of financial policy: rationing of essential goods,
and subsidies to stabilise their prices, were the most visible signs of a policy of
'fair shares for all'. Nevertheless, high taxation of the better-off played a part, as
did the absence of serious controversy over profiteering.

Overseas Finance

Anglo-French strategy in 1939 was planned on the basis of a three-year war, but, as
noted above, the UK's balance-of-payments deficit on current account was already
a source of concern to the Treasury before war broke out. President Roosevelt
persuaded Congress to pass a revised Neutrality Act on 4 November 1939
permitting Britain and France to purchase munitions in the USA on a 'cash and
carry' basis – that is, for gold and dollars, and with the requisite shipping provided
by the Allies. Since the Johnson Act prohibiting the raising of loans in the USA
remained in force, the UK's ability to draw upon American resources appeared to
be restricted to its gold and dollar reserves (about £450 million, or $1,800 million,

---

[31]   Stephen Broadberry and Peter Howlett, 'The United Kingdom: "Victory at All
Costs"', in Mark Harrison (ed.), *The Economics of World War II* (Cambridge, 1998),
pp. 43–80, at 47; CSO, *Statistical Digest*, p. 203.

[32]   Department of Employment and Productivity, *British Labour Statistics: Historical
Abstract* (London, 1971), p. 396.

in September 1939), plus sales of British-owned direct investments in the USA, plus earnings from exports.[33] However, when the Chancellor of the Exchequer, Sir John Simon, objected at the War Cabinet on 22 September 1939 to plans for greatly increasing the Army and the Air Force, Chamberlain remarked that the USA was an uncertain factor, and that it must be hoped that, if the war lasted for three years, the Americans would help with the immediate financial difficulty. The Prime Minister added that there would be no comfort, if we lost the war, in having a credit balance in dollars.[34] The financial constraint on the expansion of the Army was thus less than what a strict policy of rationing gold and dollars would have required. At a Cabinet meeting on 13 February 1940 it was pointed out that the balance-of-payments deficit on current account was greater than what could be sustained over a three-year war, and yet ministers authorised the Ministry of Supply to create industrial capacity sufficient to equip 55 divisions, being the 32 British divisions authorised before the war plus 23 divisions to be manned by the Dominions, India or prospective allies.[35] Even so, down to 10 May 1940, the day Churchill became prime minister, Treasury attempts to control expenditure of dollars impeded the speedy purchase of armaments in the USA. One of Churchill's first actions was to throw such restraint to the winds and to send a message to President Roosevelt saying: 'We shall go on paying dollars for as long as we can, but I should like to feel reasonably sure that when we can pay no more you will give us the stuff just the same.'[36]

The British and American Treasuries had been in contact regarding the financing of purchases of supplies in America since the autumn. The Secretary of the US Treasury, Henry Morgenthau, had wished to be kept informed about the marketing of British-owned securities and the possible effects on the New York stock exchange. He also advised the British Treasury to open a special account with the Federal Reserve Bank of New York (to which he would have confidential access) to handle war purchases in the USA, while also making it clear that there could be no question of any credit.[37] Churchill's message to Roosevelt seems to have prompted concern on Morgenthau's part about the scale of possible British purchases. He asked for the most senior official dealing with overseas finance in the British Treasury, Sir Frederick Phillips, to come to Washington with information about British assets and an estimate of purchasing needs in the USA for the next 12 months.[38] The figures, when Phillips presented them in July, left

---

[33]   'The Exchange Position: Inflation', memorandum by the Chancellor of the Exchequer, 8 Sept. 1939, CAB 66/1, TNA.

[34]   Sir John Simon diary, 23 Sept. 1939, Simon papers, vol. 11, Bodleian Library, Oxford.

[35]   War Cabinet conclusions, 13 Feb. 1940, CAB 65/5, TNA.

[36]   Hancock and Gowing, *British War Economy*, p. 119.

[37]   Morgenthau 'Diary', vol. 212, 30 September; vol. 219, 19 and 20 October; vol. 220, 30 October (all 1939), Franklin D. Roosevelt Library, Hyde Park, New York.

[38]   Ibid, vol. 262, 13 May, and vol. 277, 28 June (both 1940).

no doubt that the UK would need massive financial assistance in the first half of 1941, but Phillips realised that there could be no change to the American policy of 'cash and carry' before the presidential election in November 1940.[39] Britain's gold reserves were expected, in August 1940, to be exhausted by the end of the year, and the sale of requisitioned securities and even works of art could not much delay bankruptcy (although they could influence American opinion by showing that Britain had indeed paid all that she could). At the end of September 1940 the gold and dollar reserves amounted to no more than $897 million, of which $600 million was the minimum balance required to manage sterling as an international currency. In contrast British orders in the USA for aircraft and munitions were estimated to total $3,169 million, of which $759 million were for the Ministry of Munitions. Consequently no major new orders were placed by the Ministry after 15 October until Congress had passed the Lend-Lease Act on 11 March 1941 (although new contracts to the value of $75 million for munitions were authorised on 27 January). British orders placed after 11 March required no cash payment, but orders placed earlier did. Morgenthau agreed to transfer only $290 million of these 'old commitments' to lend-lease, and in order to finance the remainder the British Treasury had to resort to all manner of expedients, including borrowing $425 million from the US Reconstruction Finance Corporation, using British-owned securities as collateral.[40]

In these circumstances choices had to be made as to how gold and dollars should be spent. At first priority was given to orders for machine tools required for war production in the UK: on 30 January 1940 it was estimated that machine tools would account for 21.8 per cent of orders placed in the USA during the first year of the war.[41] Even following the loss of guns and tanks at Dunkirk, priority still was given to machine tools and raw materials for British production, since American factories would be unable to deliver munitions of British design much before 1941. However, in June 1940, $43 million was allocated for the purchase of surplus US Army equipment for immediate delivery and $240 million for new orders for delivery before the end of 1941. The Ministry of Supply was more cautious in 1940 than the Ministry of Aircraft Production in placing orders in the USA: as of November that year aircraft accounted for 69 per cent of the value of orders placed and 80 per cent of the value of orders due to be placed.[42] However, with first lend-lease and then the USA's entry into the war the British Army became increasingly reliant on American-supplied equipment: for example, from 1942

---

[39]   Telegram from Phillips; 'Conjectural Balance of Payments between the United Kingdom & USA', and 'Dollar Requirements of the United Kingdom Exchange Control', all 17 July 1940, and undated report by Phillips on his visit, Foreign Office papers (FO) 371/25209, TNA.

[40]   H. Duncan Hall, *North American Supply* (London, 1955), pp. 215–16, 250–77; Sayers, *Financial Policy*, pp. 389–97.

[41]   Hancock and Gowing, *British War Economy*, p. 106.

[42]   Hall, *North American Supply*, pp. 133–36, 162, 174–77, 212.

more than half of the British Army's new tanks came from the USA.[43] The flow of aid was not, however, one-way; even before the Anglo-American Mutual Aid Agreement of February 1942 British military stores and other goods and services were made available to the US government without payment, a procedure known as 'reciprocal aid'. Although the sheer size of the US economy ensured that lend-lease would outweigh reciprocal aid, the latter was not negligible, the respective figures being $27,023 million and $5,667 million, or about 4.75 per cent of each country's national income.[44]

The only other major overseas source of military equipment for the British Army was Canada. However, although Canada was to be responsible for 7.9 per cent of the British Commonwealth's supplies of munitions from all sources during the war, compared with 21 per cent from the USA, the dominion's arms industry only reached its full potential in 1942.[45] There was also a financial problem. About one-third of the cost of munitions produced in Canada represented imports of components and raw materials from the USA and, as Canada had a trade deficit with the USA, Canadian supplies had to be paid for partly in gold and US dollars. Thus, although the Bank of Canada provided Canadian dollars in return for sterling paid to its account at the Bank of England, and although British-owned Canadian securities were sold to raise Canadian dollars, the limiting financial factor until lend-lease supplies began to arrive in Canada from the USA in 1941 was London's gold and US dollar reserves. In January 1942, almost all of Canada's sterling balances – $700 million out of the $728 million accumulated by that date – were converted into an interest-free Canadian dollar loan. At the same time Canada gave the UK $1,000 million as a free gift. Even so, such was the scale of UK purchases in Canada by this date that the money from the gift was exhausted within the year and Canada once more accumulated sterling balances to bridge the gap while other measures were being considered. These other measures included the transfer to the Canadian government of munitions factories built in the dominion at UK government expense. The Anglo-Canadian Mutual Aid Agreement of May 1943 was supposed to do away with the dollar sign, but British orders exceeded the mutual aid funds made available by the Canadian government. In mid-1944 the Treasury instructed the Ministry of Supply and other Whitehall departments to think about alternatives to Canadian sources. In the event, Keynes was able in August 1944 to secure refunds from Canada for payments made by the UK on behalf of Canadian forces, and the scarcity of Canadian dollars was overcome down to the end of the war.[46]

Financial relations with India were conducted in sterling, but the measure of self-government achieved by India before the war made it politically inexpedient

---

[43]   CSO, *Statistical Digest*, p. 187.

[44]   Hall, *North American Supply*, p. 432; H. Duncan Hall and C.C. Wrigley, *Studies of Overseas Supply* (London, 1956), p. 2.

[45]   Hall and Wrigley, *Studies*, p. 2.

[46]   Sayers, *Financial Policy*, ch. 11.

to place the whole burden of Indian defence on the Indian taxpayer. As early as 1933 a tribunal under Sir Robert Garran, the eminent Australian lawyer, had recommended that the UK government should make some contribution towards Indian defence expenditure, mainly on the grounds that the Indian army could be deployed outside India. The sum involved was small, £1,500,000 annually, and by 1938 it was clear that modernisation of the Indian army would require larger subventions. Following Cabinet approval in June 1939 of a modernisation programme drawn up by Lord Chatfield, Inskip's successor as Minister for Co-ordination of Defence, it was accepted that the UK would pay for the initial capital expenditure and increase the Garran contribution. In February 1940 the Chancellor of the Exchequer agreed with the Secretary of State for India a formula for sharing the cost of Indian defence expenditure whereby India's share was related to its pre-war defence budget, and the remainder, including the whole cost of Indian forces serving abroad, was to be paid by the UK, as was the cost of military stores supplied by India to British forces.[47] As of 14 December 1941 – before the war in the Far East impacted on the financing of India's war effort – it was estimated that in the financial year 1941/2 the UK would bear the cost of two-thirds of Indian defence expenditure.[48] The cost to the UK increased with the numbers of Indian troops serving outside India and with inflation within India (which became rapid in 1943). Payment was made with sterling, mainly through the accumulation by India of sterling balances, but also through the repatriation of Indian debt held in the UK. Churchill complained that the British 'were being charged nearly a million pounds a day for defending India from the miseries of invasion'.[49] On the other hand, the Secretary of State for India, Leo Amery, pointed out in April 1942 that India had raised a large army, with 250,000 troops serving overseas, a figure which he thought compared favourably with the efforts of the rest of the Empire.[50] The Congress party was opposed to any major change in the 1940 agreement and, if Britain wished to exploit the military resources of India, there was no alternative to allowing India's sterling balances to increase, which they did from £295 million in mid-1942 to £1,138 million in mid-1945.[51]

With the dominion armies the general principle was that each government should pay for its own forces in the field. However, the war was unpopular among the Afrikaner population of South Africa, and the British government was aware that the government of General Smuts might lose its majority and be replaced by an Opposition pledged to making peace. While the Union government paid for South African forces deployed in East Africa in 1940–41, it claimed in 1942 that it could not afford to pay for the whole cost of South African forces in the Mediterranean theatre. After much haggling, the UK government agreed in November 1943 to

47   Ibid., p. 253.
48   Ralph Hawtrey, 'Financial History of the War', ch. 22, T208/204, TNA.
49   Winston S. Churchill, *The Second World War*, vol. iv (London, 1951), p. 181.
50   Hawtrey, 'Financial History', ch. 22.
51   Sayers, *Financial Policy*, p. 259.

subsidise South Africa by paying £5.5 million towards the estimated £17.5 million annual cost of its overseas forces.[52]

From a Treasury perspective, one of the worrying features of overseas finance was the loss of control of expenditure by the defence departments. Keynes pointed out in May 1945 that expenditure by the War Office, Air Ministry and Admiralty in the Middle East in 1944 had been £115.5 million, compared with £139.3 million in 1942, when there had been active operations against the Germans; as he remarked, 'the Major-Generals in Cairo look like becoming chronic'. Total expenditure by the defence departments outside North and South America and Europe in 1941, 1942 and 1943 had been approximately the same as the UK's total net disinvestment in these years.[53]

Did disinvestment matter? It was estimated at the end of 1945 that overseas investments worth £1,118 million had been sold or otherwise disposed of during the war, reducing the UK's income from abroad from £168 million in 1938 to £50 million in 1945, during which period prices had doubled. The UK would have to increase its exports to pay for the 1938 level of imports, but during the war British industry had been diverted from production for export to production of munitions, so that exports in 1945 were only 46 per cent of the 1938 volume. The UK had also become the greatest debtor in the world, owing £3,355 million in June 1945 compared with £476 million in August 1939. In contrast, the UK's gold and dollar reserves had fallen from £605 million to £453 million. On the other hand, apart from the US Reconstruction Finance Corporation Loan of $425 million; the $700 million no-interest loan from Canada; and a small sum owing to Portugal, all of the UK's debts were in the form of sterling balances that could be frozen until such time as the UK economy had recovered from the war.[54]

The UK's dollar debt would have been quite unmanageable if supplies made available under the Anglo-American Mutual Aid Agreement had had to be paid for in cash. It will be recalled that lend-lease supplies from the USA were valued at $27,023 million, and, even if UK reciprocal aid to the USA ($5,667 million) were deducted from that sum, the dollar debt would have been $21,356 million, equivalent to £5,339 million at the current rate of exchange, or about 160 per cent of total UK overseas debts at June 1945. However, American aid did not come in the form of an unconditional gift. The Lend-Lease Act was passed on the understanding that the USA would receive some 'consideration'. This took the form of Article VII of the Mutual Aid Agreement, which committed both countries to non-discriminatory, multilateral trade after the war. The Americans wanted the British to end the system of Imperial preference (whereby countries within the British Empire paid lower tariffs when exporting to each other than

---

[52]   Ibid., pp. 308–9.

[53]   *Collected Writings of John Maynard Keynes*, vol. 24 (Cambridge, 1979), pp. 263–65.

[54]   Ibid., pp. 257–8. Figures from 'Statistical Material Presented during the Washington Negotiations' (Cmd. 6707), PP 1945–6, vol. xxi, p. 1, and CSO, *Statistical Digest of the War*, pp. 162, 200.

foreign countries did), and Churchill's resistance to this 'consideration' was overcome only when he was told that reductions in preferences would always be linked to reductions in US tariffs. The US Treasury, under Morgenthau, and the US Foreign Economic Administration under Leo Crowley, aimed to keep the British financially dependent on the USA, and down to early 1944 they restricted growth in the UK's gold reserves during the war by taking out from lend-lease a range of civil goods such as sugar or paper, for which the British then had to pay cash.[55] Lend-lease ended with the war in August 1945, and Keynes had to go to Washington, cap in hand, to negotiate the Anglo-American Loan Agreement of December 1945 whereby the USA granted a line of credit of $3,750 million to cover the UK's expected balance-of-payments deficit while the British economy was converted from wartime to peacetime production. (In a separate agreement Canada extended a line of credit of $1,250 million dollars.) The USA also lent the UK $650 million to cover the cost to the UK of lend-lease supplies unconsumed or in transit at the end of the war. The rate of interest charged by the Americans, 2 per cent, was less important than the other terms which they imposed: sterling was to be convertible for current transactions one year after the Loan Agreement was approved by Congress; there was to be no discrimination against imports from the USA after the end of 1946; and the UK was to ratify the Bretton Woods agreements of 1944, which would mean that there could be no devaluation of sterling without the approval of the American-dominated International Monetary Fund. In the event, sterling convertibility could not be sustained on these terms in 1947, and the UK had to look for further US aid, in the form of the Marshall Plan of 1948.[56]

The Army had accounted for 38 per cent of defence expenditure during the Second World War (compared with 36 per cent for the Navy and 26 per cent for the Air Force).[57] It is reasonable to say, therefore, that the price of trying to be a major military as well as naval and air power was financial dependence on the USA, reducing the UK's position in the Anglo-American special relationship to that of junior partner. On the other hand, it is equally reasonable to say that the price was one that was well worth paying for the defeat of the Axis powers.

---

[55]   See Kathleen Burk, 'American Foreign Economic Policy and Lend-Lease', in Ann Lane and Howard Temperley (eds), *The Rise and Fall of the Grand Alliance, 1941–45* (Basingstoke, 1995), pp. 43–68.

[56]   For the Anglo-American Loan Agreement, see Roger Bullen and M.E. Pelly (eds), *Documents on British Policy Overseas*, series I, vol. III: *Britain and America: Negotiation of the United States loan 3 August–7 December 1945* (London, 1986) and L.S. Pressnell, *External Economic Policy since the War*, vol. I: *The Post-War Financial Settlement* (London, 1986), pp. 262–329. For the UK's continuing need for US aid see Kathleen Burk, 'Britain and the Marshall Plan', in Chris Wrigley (ed.), *Warfare, Diplomacy and Politics: Essays in Honour of A.J.P. Taylor* (London, 1986), pp. 210–30.

[57]   David French, *The British Way in Warfare 1688–2000* (London, 1990), p. 227.

Conclusion

Retrenchment after the First World War, and financial restrictions in line with the lower priority accorded to the Army compared with the Air Force and Navy between 1934 and 1939, were reasons why Churchill's Army was so ill-prepared for war in 1940. So too, however, was the sudden decision in March 1939 to change planning for the Army from a 6-division basis to a 32-division basis. The financial restrictions arising from the Inskip Report of December 1937 can be exaggerated: expenditure continued to rise through 1938 and domestic finance ceased to be a limiting factor from the spring of 1939. External finance likewise ceased to be a limiting factor from the spring of 1940, and indeed had been considerably eased during the Phoney War.

The role of finance during the war was to facilitate the transfer of resources, both domestic and external (such as overseas investments) from private to government use. On the whole, financial policy was successful in encouraging the efficient use of resources and in minimising non-sterling debt. The scale of the British war effort went far beyond what could have been sustained over the three years envisaged by the COS in 1937–39. The outcome was dependence on the USA. But then, as Chamberlain had remarked on 22 September 1939, there would have been no comfort in having a credit balance in dollars if the UK had lost the war.

Chapter 13

'The Method in which we were schooled by Experience': British Strategy and a Continental Commitment before 1914

T.G. Otte

[I]f we would know the truth about men and affairs, we must learn to study their history quite simply and with minds as free as we can make them from prejudice. Our preconceptions generally arise from our having unconsciously become metaphysicians.

R.B. Haldane[1]

In the beginning was the Great War. Much of the later twentieth century has been overshadowed by that conflict. It has, therefore, been tempting for scholars to argue that Britain's grand strategy revolved around a 'continental commitment'. Generational experiences of the Second World War and the subsequent Cold War have tended to harden such assumptions. It has been taken as axiomatic that, whenever a foreign Power, usually an autocratic one, pursued an aggressive, hegemonic policy, it was inherent in the logic of Britain's strategic interests for her to combine with other Powers in an effort to contain and defeat that potential hegemon. An impressive list of scholarly studies gives support to that interpretation.[2] And since Britain did go to war in August 1914, the case, it seems, is complete.

Indeed, the 1689 Mutiny Act, renewed annually, and the only, albeit vague, guideline for military planning, stipulated that the Army existed to preserve the balance of power in Europe. Tellingly, perhaps, that stipulation was dropped

---

[1] [R.B.] Viscount Haldane, 'The Meaning of Truth in History' [Creighton Lecture, 6 Mar. 1914], in *idem, The Conduct of Life and Other Addresses* (London, 1914), 46.

[2] See *inter alios* P. Guinn, *British Strategy and Politics, 1914 to 1918* (Oxford, 1963); S.R. Williamson, *Grand Strategy: Britain and France Prepare for War, 1904–1914* (Cambridge, MA, 1965); M. Howard, *The Continental Commitment: The Dilemma of British Defence Policy in the Era of the Two World Wars* (London, 1972); J. Gooch, *The Plans of War: The General Staff and the British Military, c. 1900–1916* (London, 1974); P.M. Kennedy, *The Realities behind Diplomacy: Background Influences on British External Policy, 1865–1980* (London, 1981).

in 1868 in the wake of the Cardwell reforms.[3] Assumptions of an unequivocal 'continental commitment' at the end of the long nineteenth century have been challenged recently in terms of military and diplomatic strategy.[4] But there appears to be further room for reassessing British military strategy before 1914; and the notion of a 'British way in warfare' furnishes a useful analytical tool.

To challenge the Continentalist orthodoxy might seem counter-intuitive. After all, Britain did go to war in pursuit of continental objectives; and she did so with the aid of a continental expeditionary force and on the basis of a continental war plan of a kind. The orthodox view is buttressed by a substantial body of literature. S.R. Williamson argued that the conclusion of the 1904 Anglo-French convention reshaped the international system and emerged as the driving force behind British decision-making. The pursuit of Franco-British staff talks furnished the two Powers with a form of *ersatz* alliance, substituting military exchanges for a formal combination. In Williamson's analysis, the staff talks emerge as the pivot of British decision-making.[5]

D'Ombrain's study of the defence administration between the Boer War and 1914 makes a similar point. It charts the course of the Army's growing ascendancy over the proceedings of the Committee of Imperial Defence (CID) after 1905–6, with the resultant embrace of a continental strategy.[6] John McDermott added a further nuance to the argument by arguing that British military planning was revolutionised by the internal bureaucratic dynamics within the new CID-centred defence establishment.[7]

The notion of a 'revolution in British military thinking' has been refuted by John Gooch and Edward M. Spiers. Both see the strategic reorientation in pre-1914 defence planning as evolving gradually. Their studies have de-emphasised the significance of the role played by Richard Burdon (later Viscount) Haldane, the Secretary of State for War between 1905 and 1911. Instead they pinpoint General Sir Henry Wilson's appointment, in 1910, as Director of Military Operations (DMO) as the moment of change.[8] Crucially, both identify the 114th

---

[3]   W.S. Hamer, *The British Army: Civil–Military Relations, 1885–1905* (Oxford, 1970), 31; for the Cardwell-Cairns reforms, see ibid., 1–76, and E.M. Spiers, *The Late Victorian Army, 1868–1902* (Manchester, repr. 1999), 1–28.

[4]   K. Neilson, *Britain and the Last Tsar: British Policy and Russia, 1894–1917* (Oxford, 1995); T.G. Otte, *The China Question: Great Power Politics and British Isolation, 1894–1905* (Oxford, 2007).

[5]   Williamson, *Grand Strategy, passim.*

[6]   N. d'Ombrain, *War Machinery and High Policy: Defence Administration in Peacetime Britain, 1902–1914* (Oxford, 1973), here esp. 74–114.

[7]   J. McDermott, 'The Revolution in British Military Thinking from the Boer War to the Moroccan Crisis', in P.M. Kennedy (ed.), *The War Plans of the Great Powers, 1880–1914* (Winchester, MA, 1985 (pb)), 99–117.

[8]   Gooch, *Plans of War*, 278–95; *idem, The Prospect of War: Studies in British Defence Policy, 1847–1942* (London, 1981), vii and 92–115; E.M. Spiers, *Haldane: Army Reformer* (Edinburgh, 1981), 81–84.

CID meeting of 23 August 1911 as cementing the Army's predominance over the Royal Navy in war planning: this was the final victory of the advocates of a 'continental commitment' with the focus on a British Expeditionary Force (BEF) to be deployed somewhere in Northern France.[9] More recently, Hew Strachan has advanced a more nuanced interpretation, which emphasises the inherent flaws in strategic thinking and contrasts Continentalist proclivities with the lack of proper preparations for a real continental war.[10]

A number of factors pose potential problems for analyses of British defence planning and policymaking before the Great War. The first of these is the fact that war broke out. This may sound like a perverse piece of controversialism, but it is not. As Haldane observed in his post-war reflections on the conflict, British policy had two branches. The preservation of peace by diplomatic means was the first branch: 'The second branch was concerned with what might happen if we failed in our efforts to avert war.'[11] Military plans, then, were a form of insurance policy against a whole range of possible eventualities. Conversely, the outbreak of war has invested some of these plans *ex post facto* with a new significance, and has tended to reinforce assumptions of an inevitability of war.

The second complicating factor is the disruption of the European balance of power as a result of Russia's defeat in the Russo-Japanese War of 1904–5. This may have been a regional conflict. Its ramifications, however, were global. Russia's military weakness, her financial distress and domestic instability reduced the efficacy of the existing Franco-Russian military alliance. The hitherto delicately poised balance between the *Franco-Russe* and the German-led Triple Alliance thus shifted in favour of the latter grouping. In consequence, Russia's weakness magnified the German 'threat'.[12]

The intense personal rivalries between senior officers further complicate any analysis of British military planning. These were all too common in the unreformed Army and War Office. As Sir Clinton Dawkins, a well-connected Whitehall insider and member of the Council of India who chaired the 1901 committee on War Office reform, noted: 'The real vice is not the system but persons …. It is a

---

[9]   See also Kennedy, *Realities*, 132.

[10]   H. Strachan, 'The British Army, its General Staff and the Continental Commitment, 1904–1914', in D. French and B. Holden Reid (eds), *The British General Staff: Reform and Innovation, c. 1890–1939* (London, 2002), 75–94.

[11]   [R.B.] Viscount Haldane, *Before the War* (London, 1920), 1. See also the pertinent comments by D.M. Schurman on the 'disadvantage of hindsight', *idem*, 'Historians and Britain's Imperial Stance in 1914', in J.E. Flint and G. Williams (eds), *Perspectives on Empire: Essays Presented to Gerald S. Graham* (London, 1973), 172.

[12]   For a fuller discussion, see the arguments developed in the "twin" papers by T.G. Otte, 'The Fragmenting of the Old World Order: Britain, the Great Powers and the War', in R. Kowner (ed.), *The Impact of the Russo-Japanese War* (London and New York, 2007), 91–108, and K. Neilson, 'The War and British Strategic Foreign Policy', in R. Kowner (ed.), *Rethinking the Russo-Japanese War, 1904–5* (2 vols, Folkestone, Kent, 2007) i, 307–18.

story ... of [Field Marshal Sir Garnet] Wolseley, [General Sir Redvers] Buller, [Field Marshal Sir George] White, [Field Marshall Sir Evelyn] Wood all trying to knife each other.'[13] Personal animosities within the upper echelons of the Army were no less rife in the years before 1914. Field Marshal Sir William Robertson, commandant of the Staff College and Quarter Master General in 1914, did not even mention Wilson, the DMO, in his memoirs.[14] Questions of military planning were thus frequently loaded with a wider significance on account of such personal rivalries.

Finally, clashes between rival military planners were played out against an intense public discourse on defence matters. Indeed, they frequently amplified, and were amplified by, the debates in the press and parliament. Shifts in international politics and the rapid technological transformation of modern warfare left the Edwardian political classes preoccupied with questions of home and imperial defence. Senior members of the defence establishment thus found themselves forced to engage not just with each other or their political masters but also with parliamentarians and civilian defence experts. They themselves, in fact, were adept at manipulating opinion-formers in pursuit of their own ambitions.[15]

*   *   *

To appreciate the Continentalist tendency in British military thinking it is necessary to consider the often tortuous course of efforts at military reform since 1900. The indifferent performance of the Army during the Boer War brought the shortcomings of the nation's military organisation under intense public scrutiny. Previously, the War Office itself had proved remarkably resilient against reform pressures. It was also something of a politicians' graveyard, though the two most recent secretaries of state, Sir Henry Campbell-Bannerman and the Marquess of Lansdowne, rose to higher offices afterwards, but this was largely facilitated by party-internal squabbles. The parlous state of the Army ran counter to the precepts

---

[13]   Dawkins to Curzon (private), 29 Feb. 1901, Curzon Mss, British Library Oriental and India Office Collection [hereafter BLOIOC], Mss.Eur.F.111/10. For the 1901 committee, see Hamer, *British Army*, 174–201; and *Report of the Committee appointed to enquire into War Office organisation* (Cd. 580–1, 1901).

[14]   Sir W. Robertson, *From Private to Field Marshal* (London, 1921). According to T. Travers, *The Killing Ground: The British Army, the Western Front and the Emergence of Modern Warfare, 1900–1918* (London, 1987), *passim*, the Army remained a profoundly somnolent organisation, riven with petty jealousies and factional infighting.

[15]   Corbett to Hardinge, 10 Aug. 1904, Hardinge Mss, Cambridge University Library, vol. 7. For fuller discussions, see A.J.A. Morris, *The Scaremongers: The Advocacy of War and Rearmament, 1896–1914* (London, 1984); R. Williams, *Defending the Empire: The Conservative Party and British Defence Policy, 1899–1915* (New Haven, CT, 1991).

of 'National Efficiency'. Indeed, it fuelled the debate about the need for increased competitiveness to halt the perceived danger of national decline.[16]

It fell to St John Brodrick (later Earl of Midleton), Lansdowne's successor at the War Office, to remedy the situation. At the age of forty-four he was, by the standards of the day, still youthful. Apprenticed at the War and Foreign Offices before 1900, he was a competent political operator, one of the few bright spots on an otherwise already worn-out, drab and uninspiring Unionist frontbench. Yet, if he was a young man, he was also a man in a hurry. He was imbued with a strong sense, so common among the rising Edwardian generation in British politics, of the need 'to do some real big work for the Empire'.[17] Once installed at Buckingham House, Brodrick fell to it with gusto. Some of his reform ideas were sensible, others ill-conceived and hastily executed. His idea of turning the existing cabinet defence committee into a permanent feature of policymaking, to examine prepared defence schemes, provided the necessary stimulus for moves, under the aegis of the Prime Minister-designate, Arthur James Balfour, to establish the CID in 1902.[18]

Brodrick's army reform scheme, by contrast, was overambitious, underfunded and ill-devised. Against the backdrop of the explosive growth in public expenditure following the South African conflict, there was little political appetite for additional funding for the armed forces: 'Everyone is urgent for reform, and yet is crying out at the expense.'[19] The Chancellor of the Exchequer, Sir Michael Hicks Beach, was wedded to the mid-Victorian principles of fiscal prudence; and he was casting about for ways to curb the burgeoning budget: 'these are times when every economy ought to be made'.[20] Brodrick's war of attrition with the Treasury, first under 'Black Michael' with his penchant for Billingsgate and then under the dour but doughty Aberdonian C.T. Ritchie, was one contributing factor to the ultimate

---

[16]   For a discussion of this see G.R. Searle, *The Quest for National Efficiency: A Study in British Politics and Political Thought, 1899–1914* (London and Atlantic Highlands, NJ, repr. 1990), 44–48.

[17]   Brodrick to Selborne (private), 16 Aug. 1898, Selborne Mss, Bodleian Library [hereafter Bod.], MS Selborne 2; Curzon to Brodrick, 9 Nov. 1900, Midleton Mss, British Library [hereafter BL], Add.Mss. 50074.

[18]   Brodrick to Balfour (private), 28 Oct. 1900, and reply, 31 Oct. 1900, Sandars Mss, Bod., Ms.Eng.his.c.732; see also J.S. Mackintosh, 'The Role of the Committee of Imperial Defence before 1914', *English Historical Review* lxxvii, 4 (1962), 492–93.

[19]   Brodrick to Milner (confidential), 3 Nov. 1900, C. Hedlam (ed.), *The Milner Papers* i, *South Africa, 1899–1905* (London, 1933), 159.

[20]   Beach to Brodrick, 12 Sept. 1901, St Aldwyn Mss, Gloucestershire Record Office, Gloucester, PCC/16. For a discussion of the financial situation, see also A.L. Friedberg, *The Weary Titan: Britain and the Experience of Relative Decline, 1895–1905* (Princeton, NJ, 1988), 89–134, though this author disagrees with some of the conclusions.

failure of his army reform plans: 'The only field for any … real economy appears to lie in our military system', Ritchie stressed in early 1903.[21]

In the House of Commons, meanwhile, Brodrick was assailed by the 'Hughligans' on the Unionist backbenches, so christened after this informal grouping's leader, Lord Hugh Cecil, ably seconded by another young man in a hurry, Winston Churchill. Brodrick's European preoccupations and his perceived neglect of the Army's Imperial functions had roused their ire.[22] The Secretary of State's overall aim was the introduction of a three-years service period. The Army was to be reconstituted as a mixture of Regulars, militia and yeomanry, organised in six large army corps. In parliament, Brodrick's stiff and humourless demeanour made him the perfect target for the guerrilla tactcs of the 'Hughligans'. Worse, his failure to consult senior officers and civil servants meant that he also encountered stiff opposition within his own department. By the spring of 1903, Brodrick had driven his reform cart into a political mire from which he was unable to extricate it. As the Unionist chief whip, Alec Acland-Hood, warned, 'if we persist in sticking to Brodrick's scheme … it will end in disaster in the House, and we shall have the country and the Press against us'.[23]

Combined, the need for military reforms, the lack of political progress in the matter, and the perceived growing threat to British interests caused fresh alarm. In 1901/2, the focus of defence planning was firmly on a war with Russia and/or France as the most likely eventualities. Two memoranda, drawn up in the War Office intelligence department, illuminate contemporary concerns. In the analysis of Colonel E.A. Altham, Britain's means of offence against Russia were severely curtailed. Forward action in Central Asia was practically impossible. Offensive operations in the Black Sea or the Caucasus region were equally fraught with risks. Without Turkish cooperation, and possibly under constant menace from a combined Franco-Russian fleet in the Mediterranean, it was difficult to sustain operations there. In the Far East, even if Vladivostok or Port Arthur could be taken, this would not 'force an early and advantageous conclusion to the war'. Russia's Achilles' heel was of a financial kind. Ironically, Altham's conclusion was that the chance of defeating Russia lay in extending the conflict. Only by attacking the French colonial empire, and so eliminating France as a significant factor in an

[21]   Memo. Ritchie, 'Our Financial Position', 21 Feb. 1903, The National Archives (Public Record Office) [hereafter TNA (PRO)], Cabinet Papers [hereafter CAB] 37/64/15. Brodrick's memoirs give a flavour of the strained relations with Beach, Earl of Midleton, *Records and Reactions, 1856–1939* (London, 1939), 123–26.

[22]   For Brodrick's parliamentary problems see L.J. Satre, 'St John Brodrick and Army Reform, 1901–1903', *Journal of British Studies* xv, 2 (1976), 122–24; also R. Shannon, *The Age of Salisbury, 1881–1902: Unionism and Empire* (London, 1996), 533–37.

[23]   Acland-Hood to Sandars, 1 Mar. 1903, Sandars Mss, Ms.Eng.hist.c.738; Williams, *Defence of Empire*, 10–26.

Anglo-Russian war, could Russia be deprived of the necessary financial support to sustain her own war effort.[24]

William Robertson, then Assistant Quarter Master-General in the intelligence department arrived at the same conclusion. For as long as Britain's naval predominance remained unchallenged, 'the fall of most, if not all, French Colonies would only be a question of time'. That being so, however, and taking the 'offensive spirit and best traditions' of France into account, it was likely that the French staff would seek 'a rapid solution of the war'. Robertson deduced that, provided a sufficient naval force could be assembled to establish temporary command of the Channel, the French would attempt an invasion of Britain. There would be secondary operations overseas; 'but invasion will, in all probability, remain the ultimate goal'.[25]

Britain's defence position, then, was anything but satisfactory. All the advantages seemed to lie with Russia and her ally. Her geographical proximity to key British strategic interests and her vast manpower reserves gave her the upper hand. Russia, observed the First Sea Lord, Admiral Lord Walter Kerr, was not assailable by a naval power with only a small army.[26] General Sir Henry Brackenbury, the Director of Military Intelligence (DMI) in the 1890s, was more forthright still: 'we are attempting to maintain the largest Empire the world has ever seen with armaments and reserves that would be insufficient for a third class military power.'[27] Brackenbury's acerbic comment went to the very heart of the dual nature of British power. In Asia, Britain was effectively a continental power, albeit one without the usual military accoutrements of a continental power. But British policymakers had an essentially imperial, maritime mindset that focused on sea power as the main element of British power.

If Britain's military capabilities were inadequate, and their methods of organisation wanting, the constellation of the Great Powers exacerbated her difficulties. The latent hostility of France, continually fed on colonial grievances and powerfully reinforced by the Franco-Russian alliance, and the decline of British diplomatic influence at Constantinople rendered a Crimean coalition strategy against Russia impracticable. The framework of cooperation with the two South Eastern European status quo-Powers, Austria-Hungary and Italy, under the auspices of the 1887 Mediterranean Accords, had not been maintained.

---

[24]   Memo. Altham, 'Military Needs of the Empire in a War with France and Russia', 10 Aug. 1901, TNA (PRO), War Office Papers [hereafter WO] 106/48/E3/2. For the importance of this memorandum see also K. Neilson, "Greatly Exaggerated': The Myth of the Decline of Great Britain before 1914', *IHR* xiii, 4 (1991), 713–14.

[25]   Memo. Robertson, 'The Military Resources of France, and probable Method of their Employment in a War between France and England', 27 Dec. 1901, CAB 3/1/4A; Robertson, *Private to Field Marshal*, 127–33.

[26]   Kerr to Selborne, 2 Apr. 1904, Balfour Mss, BL, Add.Mss. 49707.

[27]   Min. Brackenbury, 15 Dec. 1899, as quoted in McDermott, 'Revolution in British Military Thinking', 101.

A rapprochement with Germany had been sought between 1898 and 1901; but this had not proved durable, nor had Berlin shown itself a reliable partner against Russia. The 1902 alliance with Japan, meanwhile, driven by financial and naval considerations, was expected to have a deterrence value against Russia in Asia, but was defensive. Under these circumstances, Robertson concluded, only an alliance with Germany or the introduction of conscription provided a solution to Britain's defence problems.[28] Neither was practicable nor desirable.

True, as David French has rightly observed, British military intelligence had a pronounced propensity to overestimate Russian military power and to ignore some of Russia's fundamental weaknesses.[29] But such perceptions and estimates informed military calculations. The case for a thorough strategic defence review seemed more urgent than ever.

The famous memorandum drafted in 1888, and circulated internally in 1891, by Edward Stanhope, Secretary of State in the second Salisbury administration, offered little strategic guidance. It established a clear hierarchy of priorities of purpose for the Army. Its chief function was domestic, to assist the civilian authorities at home in maintaining law and order. Its principal external military role was that of providing soldiers for garrison duty, primarily in India, and secondarily in the other colonies and overseas fortresses and coaling stations. After providing for these imperial requirements, two corps of Regular troops, augmented by some Militia and other auxiliary forces, were reserved for home defence duties. Finally, one of these two corps was to be mobilised in the eventuality of a European war. But Stanhope added a significant rider: 'it will be distinctly understood that the probability of the employment of an Army-Corps in the field in any European war is sufficiently improbable to make it the primary duty of the military authorities to organise our forces efficiently for the defence of this country'.[30] Stanhope's ordering of priorities may well have been sufficient for the purposes of late-Victorian soldiering. But it offered little strategic guidance in the more challenging international environment after 1901. Indeed, some reform-minded officers, such as Robertson, later concluded that it was owing to Stanhope's memorandum 'that broad military plans essential for the defence of the Empire as a whole received no adequate treatment'.[31]

Against this background the CID was established in 1902. The new body provided a forum for the discussion of defence problems at a strategic level,

---

[28]   Memo. Robertson, 4 Oct. 1902, CAB 38/4/10.

[29]   D. French, *British Strategy and War Aims, 1914–1916* (London, 1986), 13.

[30]   *Paper by the Secretary of State, laying down the requirements from our army, dated 1st June 1891* (Cd. 607) (1901), XXXIX. For further discussions see the two important articles by I.F.W. Beckett: 'Edward Stanhope at the War Office, 1887–1892', *Journal of Strategic Studies* v, 2 (1982), 278–307, and 'The Stanhope Memorandum of 1888: a Reinterpretation', *Bulletin of the Institute of Historical Research* lvii, 136 (1984), 240–47.

[31]   Robertson, *Private to Field Marshal*, 92. Robertson served in the Military Intelligence department under Major-General Sir John Ardagh in the 1890s.

bringing together military and civilian experts under the superintendence of the Prime Minister. Its formation was the vital first step in the direction of providing strategic direction for the services. Its purpose was to identify potential future conflicts involving Britain or British interests, to assess their ramifications and the requirements necessary to meet these challenges.[32]

From its inception, Arthur Balfour dominated the committee's proceedings. Long interested in questions of imperial defence, he easily established a 'complete mastery ... over his colleagues', as the Foreign Office representative on the CID noted.[33] Central to Balfour's strategic concerns, and thus to the logic of CID deliberations, were Britain's imperial commitments. These were the determinants of military policy. Balfour's defence scheme revolved around the idea of a small peacetime force of Regulars, supplemented by militia troops as an efficient and economical means of reinforcing the Army. In this manner, it would be possible to despatch the 100,000 men required to reinforce the troops in India during the first year 'in a great war on the north-west frontier'.[34]

Ironically, ongoing concerns about India aside, Britain's defence position improved markedly during the final years of the Balfour administration. In November 1903, the Prime Minister concluded that an invasion of the British Isles by a foreign Power – implicitly by France – was practically impossible. An attempt to invade would require a landing force of at least 70,000. The formidable logistical requirements of such an undertaking apart, the French navy would have to establish naval supremacy in the Channel. Given the current naval balance of power and the cumbersome transport of troops across the Channel, this was an unlikely scenario.[35] Indeed, summarising the thinking behind this memorandum in the spring of 1905 in Parliament, Balfour averred: 'Serious invasion of these islands is not an eventuality we need seriously to consider.'[36]

Balfour's '*simply splendid*' invasion paper was 'a landmark in the history of modern British defence policy'.[37] Its conclusions were endorsed by Colonel Sir George Clarke, the first secretary to the CID, and Captain C.L. (later Rear-Admiral Sir Charles) Ottley, soon to be Director of Naval Intelligence. As Clarke

---

[32]   D'Ombrain, *War Machinery*, 45–67; J. Mackintosh, 'The Role of the Committee of Imperial Defence before 1914', *English Historical Review* lxxvii, 4 (1962), 490–503.

[33]   Sir J. Tilley, *London to Tokyo* (London, 1942), 40; also R.F. Mackay, *Balfour: Intellectual Statesman* (Oxford, 1985), 156–94.

[34]   Min. Balfour, 'Supplementary Note on the Military Needs of the Empire', 19 Dec. 1904, CAB 3/1/28A; also Selborne to Balfour, 5 Apr. 1903, Balfour Mss, Add.Mss. 49707; and minutes 62nd CID meeting, 17 Dec. 1904, CAB 2/1.

[35]   Memo. Balfour, 'Draft Report on the Possibility of Serious Invasion' (confidential), 11 Nov. 1903, CAB 3/1/18A. This was long in gestation, having first been discussed in April 1903, see minutes 11th CID meeting, 29 Apr. 1903, CAB 2/1.

[36]   *The Times* (12 May 1905).

[37]   Quotes from Fisher to Sandars (private), n.d. [3 Jan. 1904], Balfour Mss, Add.Mss. 49710; and Mackay, *Balfour*, 182.

observed, strengthening the Navy in home waters would be 'the cheapest and most effective policy'. Indeed, the costs of maintaining the existing volunteer force exceeded the financial outlay necessary for commissioning and building a ten-strong cruiser squadron: 'The invasion cry is therefore suicidal on the part of the volunteers. Which course would an intending enemy prefer, that we add 10 battleships to our present standard of strength, or that we should double the expenditure on Volunteers?'[38] Ottley came to a similar conclusion. The French capture of Sfax in North Africa in 1884, he noted, was preceded by a week-long bombardment, in which the entire *Escadre de la Mediterranée* participated, before French troops could safely be landed. Moreover, there had been no naval threat to the French squadron during the operation.[39] A French attempt to invade the English Channel coast, by contrast, would have to be carried out under much more adverse conditions for the invader.

If there was no serious prospect of an invasion of the British Isles, Britain's defence position in Asia was also much improved. Here, the residual Russian threat to India was much reduced, given Russia's ongoing Far Eastern entanglements – rumours of Russian troop movements and concentrations in Central Asia notwithstanding.[40] Finally, the anticipated, correctly as it turned out, destruction of the Russian fleet in the war with Japan relieved some of the naval pressure on Britain.[41]

Under Balfour's guidance, the CID thus reasserted navalist assumptions about Britain's defence requirements. It had moved away again from Brodrick's more European concerns. In the somewhat fawning judgment of one of his ministers, Balfour had 'guarded the Empire against the extravagances of both the narrow Military and the narrow Naval extremists'.[42] Even so, there was no doubt, as Dawkins emphasised, that '[t]he Navy is our first and far the most important Line'. But he added that the Navy could not be handled 'with absolute freedom and confidence, for offensive-defensive operations possibly, if the shores behind them are left crowded with an unarmed, unorganized, panic-stricken population'. It was, therefore, necessary 'to get your military forces organized, and organized

[38] Clarke to Balfour (private), 27 June 1904, and marginal comments on memo. Balfour, 'Draft Report on the Possibility of Serious Invasion', 11 Nov. 1903, Balfour Mss, Add.Mss. 49700 (quotes from latter); see also Lord Sydenham of Combe, *My Working Life* (London, 1927), 183–84.

[39] Memo. Ottley, 'The Question of Invasion', 28 June 1904, Balfour Mss, Add.Mss. 49700.

[40] Clarke to Balfour (private), 23 July 1904, ibid.

[41] Memo. Selborne, 'Naval Estimates 1904–05: possible reduction', 26 Feb. 1904, CAB 37/69/32. Austen Chamberlain, the new Chancellor of the Exchequer, was pressing for further cuts in naval expenditure, Balfour to Chamberlain, 23 Aug. 1904, Chamberlain Mss, Birmingham University Library, AC 7/1B/23.

[42] Wyndham to Balfour (private but unimportant), 14 May 1905, in J.W. Mackail and G. Wyndham, *Life and Letters of George Wyndham* (2 vols, London, n.d.) ii, 500.

economically, because the First Line (the Navy) must inevitably absorb more and more money'.[43]

This, however, was the crux of the matter, for the further reorganisation of the Army failed to materialise. Hugh Oakley Arnold-Forster, not Balfour's preferred choice as Brodrick's successor and a failure in the post to anyone but himself, focused on the manpower needs of garrisoning the Empire. Though in line with Balfour's thinking, his preferred solution to the problem merely added to its complexity. He suggested abolishing the Cardwellian system of linked battalions, which, arguably, had demonstrated its merits during the Boer War and which Brodrick had wished to preserve. He envisaged the creation of a General Service Army, largely for imperial defence purposes, and a Home Service Army, predominantly made up of volunteers. Ultimately, the necessary reforms of the militia system, entailed in this scheme, ran into immovable opposition. Although it was never taken off the *tapis*, by the time the Balfour administration collapsed in December 1905, it was nothing but an empty shell.[44]

While the reorganisation of the army was hanging fire, the existence of the CID as a form of 'clearing-house' for strategic ideas acquired additional significance. John McDermott has highlighted the importance of the bureaucratic dynamics within the defence establishment. At the root of the 'revolution in military thinking', which he detected around 1904–6, lay the interaction between bureaucratic ambitions and shifts in international politics. Though speculative in parts, the argument is not without merit. As one contemporary writer noted: 'Where there is a great executive organization, such as … our command and regimental systems, side by side with a great administrative organization like our War Office, it may be taken for granted that in the ordinary course of things the first will at best hold its own, and the second will keep on swelling until it either is pricked or bursts.'[45]

All bureaucracies have to justify their existence; they thus seek to fill the space allotted to them. The CID was no exception. From its inception, there were efforts to strengthen it. Viscount Esher, the *eminence grise* in the Edwardian defence establishment, pressed for the CID to be given the power to settle 'the *main lines* of Imperial Military policy' and to review these by means of 'constant and serious deliberation'.[46] The committee on War Office reform, headed by Esher in 1903, recommended the creation of a full-time secretariat, a permanent bureaucratic

---

[43]　Dawkins to Fisher, 12 Oct. 1903, Balfour Mss, Add.Mss. 49710.

[44]　Memo. Lyttelton, 'The Military requirements of the Empire and Mr Arnold-Forster's Army Scheme Compared', 15 Dec. 1904, CAB 3/1/27A; Williams, *Defending the Empire*, 41–58; but cf. A.V. Tucker, 'The Issue of Army Reform in the Unionist Government, 1903–1905', *Historical Journal* ix, 1 (1966), 90–100, here especially 97.

[45]　Captain O. Wheeler, *The War Office Past and Present* (London, 1914), 288.

[46]　Esher to Edward VII, 14 Feb. 1903, M.V. Brett (cont. O. Viscount Esher) (eds.), *Journals and Letters of Reginald, Viscount Esher* (3 vols, London, 1934–38) i, 376. For some of the background, see P. Fraser, *Lord Esher: A Political Biography* (London, 1973), 84–107.

apparatus to assist the CID as the principal advisory and consultative body on all matters concerned with home and overseas defence. Esher's committee also suggested the establishment of a proper General Staff. Indeed, the link between these two new bodies was crucial for the further development of British military thinking.[47] For his part, the Esher protégé Clarke appreciated that the CID was 'a machine and like most machines it is capable of good or bad work according to the way it is managed'.[48] Clarke was not slow to put his hands on the key levers of this new piece of machinery. There was, in fact, a profound irony about these developments. The prospect of war with the Franco-Russian combination had provided the necessary reform stimulus. By the time the CID was set up and the creation of a General Staff was decided upon, however, the international situation was a good deal less threatening. The Anglo-French *entente* of April 1904 had removed much of the friction that had characterised Anglo-French relations for the past two decades; and the *malaise* of Russia after the war in the Far East gave Britain a breathing space of at least a decade. Thus, while the traditional concerns of British defence planners had become less pressing, the reassertion by Balfour of an Indocentric orientation in defence policy threatened to turn the Army into an appendix of the subcontinental defence establishment. The military element in the CID secretariat and, after 1906, the General Staff sought to reverse this trend in favour of continental war-fighting plans. Ironically, Russia's weakness and the concomitant shift in the balance of power in Europe in Germany's favour, combined with the *Wilhelmstrasse*'s rather maladroit diplomacy, facilitated these efforts.

In early 1903, in examining the possibility of a war with Germany, the two AQMGs in the Military Intelligence department of the War Office had still concluded that such an eventuality was far-fetched. Robertson's attempt to talk up the possibility of an invasion was soon superseded by the CID's official decision that no invasion of Britain was possible.[49] Altham's comments on Robertson's paper reflected much more closely the then still prevailing concerns. A war between the two countries, he argued, 'would … resemble a struggle between an elephant and a whale, in which each, although supreme in its own element, would find difficulty in bringing its strength to bear on its antagonist'. Altham admitted that a German invasion of the Low Countries might force a war with Germany upon Britain. But this seemed a remote eventuality. Indeed, he concluded that, 'from a strategical point of view, an understanding with that Power on questions

---

[47]   Balfour to Arnold-Forster, 28 Oct. 1903, Balfour Mss, Add.Mss. 49722; McDermott, 'Revolution in Military Thinking', 102. For Esher's role, see Gooch, *Plans of War*, 32–61.

[48]   Clarke to Campbell-Bannerman, 3 Sept. 1907, Campbell-Bannerman Mss, BL, Add.Mss. 41213. For an appreciation of Clarke see J. Gooch, 'Sir George Clarke's Career at the Committee of Imperial Defence, 1904–1907', in *idem.*, *Prospect of War*, 73–91.

[49]   Memo. Robertson, 'The Military Resources of Germany, and Probable Method of their Employment in a War between Germany and England', 7 Feb. 1903, CAB 3/1/20A.

as to which we have common or conflicting interests would greatly strengthen our general position'.[50]

Two years later, military planning bore quite a different stamp. From the middle of 1904 onwards, Clarke sought to undermine the axioms of an Indocentric defence strategy. Russia was scarcely in a position to threaten British interests in Central Asia. He opined that in the North Western Frontier 'we have the very strongest frontier in the world', and that, in the absence of a continued Russian threat, 'we can afford to drop visionary projects, and devote ourselves to practical questions'.[51] Indeed, at the CID meeting that led to Balfour's paper on the military needs of the Empire, the DMO, Major-General Sir James Moncrieff Grierson, advocated the creation of a joint 'striking force' for overseas operations in either an Imperial or a European context.[52]

According to McDermott, this was a 'revolution in military thinking', an abrupt reorientation in British strategic planning which came to focus on Germany as a probable enemy before the first Moroccan crisis of 1905–6. This assertion is problematic on a number of counts. For one thing, it tends to ignore that, even after the conclusion of the 1904 agreement with France, diplomatic factors were considered largely irrelevant, as Balfour, who retained membership of the CID, observed in May 1908: 'I imagine that … they were [not] doing their duty if they supposed that the safety of the country could depend upon some paper instrument or a mere *entente*, however *cordiale* it might be.' The factors that were to be considered were 'of a military and naval character'.[53] By the same token, plans for a potential war with Germany ought to be seen in the same light.

It is also difficult to substantiate the assumption of an abrupt shift of focus in 1904–5. On the contrary, Germany was seen as a potential enemy well before then. By April 1902, the Admiralty and Foreign Office concluded, albeit with some hesitation, that the German naval construction programme was aimed against Britain.[54] In Army circles such concerns gained wider currency as well. Grierson, educated in Germany and a fervent admirer of Moltke, identified Germany as a potential adversary even earlier. In 1900, he was attached to the staff of the China Expeditionary Force under the Prussian Field Marshal Count Alfred von Waldersee. The experience left an indelible impression on Grierson: 'I had much

[50]   Memo. Altham, 'Memorandum of the Military Policy to be adopted in a War with Germany', 10 Feb. 1903, ibid.

[51]   Clarke to Balfour (private), 23 July 1904, Balfour Mss, Add.Mss. 49700; see also McDermott, 'Revolution in Military Thinking', 107–9, for other instances.

[52]   Minutes of 62nd CID meeting, 17 Dec. 1904, CAB 2/1.

[53]   'Statement made by Mr A.J. Balfour before the Sub-Committee on Invasion', 29 May 1908, CAB 3/2/43A; McDermott, 'Revolution in Military Thinking', 107–9.

[54]   Lascelles to Lansdowne (private), 25 Apr. 1902, Lansdowne Mss, TNA (PRO), Foreign Office Papers [hereafter FO] 800/129; Kerr to Selborne, 28 Apr. 1902, D.G. Boyce (ed.), *The Crisis of British Power: The Imperial and Naval Papers of the Second Earl of Selborne, 1895–1910* (London, 1990), 144.

higher ideas of [the Germans'] discipline, but that, like so many other illusions, is doomed to vanish.'[55] He was even more impressed by the desire, freely admitted by German officers, to create 'a future Colonial Empire, which shall rival ours'.[56] There was, then, no abrupt change in British defence planning.

As for a general reorientation away from imperial defence schemes to continental war scenarios, a closer reading of the extant archival material suggests a more complex picture. The vast bulk of CID papers and memoranda was concerned with imperial matters. Yet, the General Staff spent a great deal of effort on the continental war plans. Under Grierson's guidance and that of his successors, senior staff officers came to regard a continental war as some form of 'gold standard' of modern military thought. In January 1905, Grierson ordered a war game for the spring, based on the scenario of a German invasion of the Low Countries during a Franco-German war. A CID meeting in the summer, after the war game had been concluded, pondered the question whether Britain should guarantee the integrity of the Netherlands.[57] Concerns by senior Foreign Office officials who, rightly perhaps, preferred to deal with such potential eventualities 'in less absolute terms' than those stipulated by the General Staff, were batted aside by Clarke, who insisted that Germany was now a likely enemy, and that there was a strong temptation for her to invade Belgium.[58]

In the summer of 1905, with the Franco-German stand-off over Morocco at its height and Russia brought to the brink of defeat,[59] the CID returned to Grierson's idea of a joint strike force. For that purpose a permanent sub-committee was established to investigate the matter, and to prepare a scheme for combined operations by the two services. For the moment, a CID paper argued, 'the overwhelming extent of our maritime supremacy would permit us to undertake operations which in ordinary maritime warfare would be unjustifiable, such as close approaches to hostile ports and attacks on defended positions'. In this context, the paper toyed with 'a military expedition on a considerable scale' somewhere along the North German coast.[60]

---

55   Grierson to Knox (no. 4), 20 Nov. 1900, WO 32/6414.

56   Memo. Grierson, 'Report on the Operations of the German Contingent CEF', 11 Dec. 1900, BLOIOC, L/MIL/17/20/14. For a similar assessment, based on different evidence, see Strachan, 'General Staff', 82–83.

57   Minutes of 74th CID meeting, 6 July 1905, CAB 2/1.

58   Sanderson to Clarke, 10 Aug. 1905, CAB 17/69; and reply, 16 Aug. 1905, Lansdowne Mss, FO 800/116; and Clarke to Balfour, 1 Aug. 1905, Balfour Mss, Add.Mss. 49702.

59   The two were connected, as Clarke argued, Clarke to Balfour, 13 June 1905, Whittinghame Muniment Mss, Scottish Record Office, GD 433/2/39.

60   CID memo., 'Formation of a Permanent Sub-Committee of the Committee of Imperial Defence to consider and elaborate Schemes for Joint Naval and Military Expeditions', n.d. [c. July 1905], Chamberlain Mss, AC 7/5B/14; minutes of 77th CID meeting, 26 July 1905, CAB 2/1.

The First Sea Lord, Admiral Sir John Fisher, was initially enthusiastic about such a scheme. In 1903, he had accepted the invitation to join Esher's War Office reconstruction committee. Now, he supported combined operations. In a characteristic outburst of exuberance, he described the Army as 'a projectile fired by the Navy'.[61] During the hiatus caused by the fall of the Balfour cabinet, the formation of the Liberal Campbell-Bannerman administration, and the subsequent general election in early 1906, the sub-committee met to discuss the feasibility of joint naval-military operations. The War Office had already developed an implicit preference for despatching a force to Belgium or Northern France.[62] At the sub-committee meetings at the turn of 1905–6, however, the occupation of 'a strong pied à terre on the Baltic', presumably Christiansand in Norway, or a similar place on the North Sea was discussed at some length. The naval and military representatives agreed that such a bridgehead, combined with a 'sustained menace to the Baltic seaboard', would have considerable 'moral effect' on the enemy; it might even be utilised later 'for the advance of a combined Anglo-French army.' Even so, the discussions tended towards the conclusion that a large expeditionary force could not be despatched to the Baltic 'until the naval situation had cleared … [and] the great battles had been fought on the [Franco-German] frontier'.[63] Combined naval operations in the Baltic were thus secondary to other forms of direct military assistance to France and Belgium.

Much has been made of the staff talks, which commenced in January 1906, as the pivot around which an Anglo-French defensive partnership evolved.[64] Yet, their function in Anglo-French relations was more complex, and their significance is easily exaggerated. The conversations with the French ought properly to be seen in a political rather than a military context. They were an integral part of British diplomatic strategy. Their purpose was primarily psychological. They were intended to reassure France of British support in the face of German bullying without incurring for Britain any binding commitment. Sir Edward Grey, the new Foreign Secretary, and his senior diplomats appreciated that without such reassurances, and with Russia too weak to lend effective assistance to her French ally, Paris might be forced to yield to German diplomatic and military pressure.

---

[61] Fisher to Esher (private), 19 Nov. 1905, Esher Mss, Churchill College Archive Centre Cambridge [hereafter CCAC], ESHR 10/41; see also Fisher to Sandars (secret), 22 Oct. 1903, Balfour Mss, Add.Mss. 49710.

[62] Memo. by the General Staff, 'The Violation of the Neutrality of Belgium during a Franco-German War', 23 Sept. 1905, CAB 4/1/1/65B.

[63] 'Notes of Conferences Held at 2, Whitehall Gardens, on December 19, 1905, January 6, 1906, January 12, 1906, and January 19, 1906', CAB 18/24.

[64] Williamson, *Grand Strategy*, 79–80; also J. Gooch, 'Adversarial Attitudes: Servicemen, Politicians and Strategic Policy, 1899–1914', in P. Smith (ed.), *Government and the Armed Forces in Britain, 1856–1990* (London and Rio Grande, 1996), 63–64.

In that case, the achievements of the 1904 arrangement with France, principally Britain's newly found security in Egypt, would be reversed.[65]

The fact that the staff talks fell into abeyance after 1906, moreover, underlines their essentially political function. The French, for their part, never made a British military contribution an integral part of their war plans.[66] On the other hand, in the much narrower context of the evolution of General Staff thinking, the 1906 exchanges were significant in that they encouraged the CID to focus its planning exercises on landing two army corps in Northern France rather than at Antwerp or, indeed, somewhere in Northern Germany. This had implications for the planned combined Army-Navy operations. Above all, it implied a role reversal. Rather than firing the Army as its projectile, the Navy was now in danger of being reduced to some sort of maritime transport mule for the Army. Unsurprisingly, Fisher and the Admiralty lost interest in joint operations. Army and Navy war planning now proceeded along two quite separate trajectories.[67]

In so far as the Continentalist tendency in military thinking was concerned, two factors need to be considered: the army reforms after 1906; and the continuity of the Continentalist momentum within the General Staff. The two were linked. '[S]uccess at the War Office may very probably be the crux of the next Gov[ernmen]t?', Clarke had speculated during the twilight of the Balfour administration.[68] As it turned out, there were more pressing issues bearing down upon the Liberal administration after 1906. Even so, the new Secretary of State for War, the philosopher-lawyer Haldane, succeeded where his three Unionist predecessors had failed. Whereas Brodrick and Arnold-Forster had 'launched reckless schemes without consulting [their] officials', 'Schopenhauer' Haldane proceeded with caution. His army reforms were completed in stages.[69] Reflecting his own philosophical training and the public's demands for efficiency, he argued

---

[65]   Memo. Grey, 20 Feb. 1906, and min. Hardinge, 23 Feb. 1906, *BD* iii, no. 299. Clarke also was seized of the need to reassure the French, see Clarke to Balfour, 11 June 1905, Whittinghame Muniment Mss, GD 433/2/39. For a fuller discussion of this see T.G. Otte, "Almost a Law of Nature'?: Sir Edward Grey, the Foreign Office, and the Balance of Power in Europe, 1905–12', in E. Goldstein and B.J.C. McKercher (eds), *Power and Stability: British Foreign Policy, 1865–1965* (London, 2003), 85–87.

[66]   On this point see J. Snyder, *The Ideology of the Offensive: Military Decision Making and the Disasters of 1914* (Ithaca, NY, 1984), 94–96; D. Stevenson, *Armaments and the Coming of War: Europe, 1904–1914* (Oxford, 1996), 306–7.

[67]   R.F. Mackay, *Fisher of Kilverstone* (Oxford, 1973), 350–55; P.M. Hayes, 'Britain, Germany, and the Admiralty's Plans for Attacking German Territory, 1906–1915', in L. Freedman, P.M. Hayes and R. O'Neill (eds), *War, Strategy, and International Politics: Essays in Honour of Sir Michael Howard* (Oxford, 1992), 95–116.

[68]   Memo. Clarke, 6 Feb. 1905 (copy), Haldane Mss, National Library of Scotland, MS 5906.

[69]   Campbell-Bannerman to Edward VII, 21 Feb. and 5 July 1906, Campbell-Bannerman Mss, Add.Mss. 52512.

for a sustained effort 'to think out … those problems which concerned the Army and the Navy as a whole'.[70]

Haldane's reforms brought order into the chaos in the organisation and the confusion of purpose that he had inherited. Taking his cue from Esher, he extended the General Staff system, so far confined to the War Office, to the Army as a whole. It was to be 'a thinking department' in charge of war preparations and, if war broke out, of conducting operations. Haldane also tackled the necessary reorganisation of the Army. It was reconstituted as an expeditionary force, composed of one cavalry and six infantry divisions, and kept in constant readiness for deployment abroad. At around 150,000 men, the size of this projected 'oversea force' was subject to some controversy, and would remain so; but both Cabinet and CID accepted the scheme.[71]

More controversially, Haldane also reconfigured the militia, yeomanry and volunteers. These auxiliary forces were incorporated into the Territorial Force. The new second line consisted of fourteen mounted brigades and fourteen infantry divisions, and was designed for home defence and voluntary service abroad. Organised on a county basis, it was something of a throwback to Cromwellian times, and unsurprisingly was soon nicknamed the 'New Model'.[72] The reforms did not quite produce the 'Hegelian army', Haldane later claimed to have called into being. All the same, it was a more efficient and coherent force. And at the hands of contemporary cartoonists 'Schopenhauer' had become 'Napoleon B. Haldane', replete with the Corsican's bicornous hat.[73]

In later years, Haldane argued that the overall aim of the reforms had been the creation of a continental expeditionary force. He also highlighted the importance of the rumours of an impending Franco-German war in early 1906 at the time of

---

[70]   Haldane speech, Alnwick Corn Exchange, 12 Jan. 1906, *The Times* (13 Jan. 1906).

[71]   Minutes of 89th and 90th CID meetings, 28 June and 6 July 1906, CAB 2/2. For a detailed discussion of Haldane's reforms see Spiers, *Haldane*, *passim*, and J. Gooch, 'Mr Haldane's Army: Military Organization and Foreign Policy in England, 1906–7', in *idem*, *Prospect of War*, 92–115, who both place greater emphasis on officials than on the minister. For a different view, see S. Koss, *Lord Haldane: Scapegoat for Liberalism* (New York and London, 1969), 46–48.

[72]   Clarke to Haldane, 6 Mar. 1906, Haldane Mss, MS 5908; Sir F. Maurice, *Haldane, 1856–1915: The Life of Viscount Haldane of Cloan* (London, 1937), 204–34; D. Sommer, *Haldane of Cloan: His Life and Times, 1856–1928* (London, 1960), 189–95. For the parliamentary aspects see A.J.A. Morris, 'Haldane's Army Reforms, 1906–1908: The Deception of the Radicals', *History* lvi, 186 (1971), 17–34. It was, perhaps, no coincidence that the Cromwellian period attracted some attention at the time, see C.H. Firth, *Cromwell's Army: A History of the English Solider during the Civil Wars, the Commonwealth and the Protectorate* (London, 1902). In 1895, Haldane's fellow Liberal "Leaguer", the Earl of Rosebery, was instrumental in erecting a statue to Cromwell outside the Palace of Westminster.

[73]   E.g., *Punch* (26 June 1907), 457.

the force's inception.[74] Such rumours did indeed circulate around Whitehall and Westminster at the time; and they reinforced the perceived need to bolster French confidence.[75] The demands of a continental strategy, however, never dominated Haldane's reform scheme. Fiscal constraints and domestic political considerations made it necessary to retain the voluntary system of recruitment and to keep a tight rein on military expenditure. The Cardwellian system of linked battalions, judged sufficient for the Army's imperial duties, was thus retained. Indeed, throughout the period before August 1914, the Regular infantry battalions were deployed for imperial garrisoning in a manner not dissimilar from that employed at any stage since the 1870s.[76] Finally, the abandonment of the corps structure for the reconstituted Army, which Brodrick had favoured, and the retention of the division as the basis of organisation, meant that the new force was compatible with the Indian army. Indeed, the size of the Regulars was 'fixed by the peace requirements of India and the Colonies … [and] the requirements of the garrisons abroad'.[77] The overarching strategic objective behind the reforms, then, was flexibility, not the creation of a force for specifically continental purposes. Haldane was nearer the truth when he noted that, in opting for the format of the BEF, '[o]urs was the method in which we had been schooled by experience'.[78] That experience was imperial, not continental.

In terms of CID and General Staff planning, however, the continental impulse remained strong. The basic assumption behind British military calculations concerning European eventualities was that a renewed Franco-German contest was the most likely scenario. It was taken as axiomatic that in such an eventuality the German army would invade the Low Countries. A General Staff memorandum by Major R.S. Gorton in the spring of 1907 stressed that the military requirements of the Empire included the preservation of Belgium's integrity. There also lay serious danger to British interests in 'the absorption of the Netherlands by some other Power', especially if that Power had significant naval capabilities. Neither the Belgian nor the Dutch army was in a position to repel a German invasion without outside assistance. As regarded the Netherlands, Gorton suggested either direct reinforcements of the Dutch army or the landing of an expeditionary force on the Dutch coast to defend the Dutch right flank. As for Belgium, the choice lay between direct assistance for the Belgians or cooperation with France.[79] Reports on

---

[74]   Haldane, *Before the War*, 164–69.

[75]   Grey to Haldane, 8 Jan. 1906, Haldane Mss, MS 5907; also R.F.V. Heuston, *Lives of the Lord Chancellors* (Oxford, 1964), 205.

[76]   On this important point see the pertinent comments by Strachan, 'General Staff', 91, on which the above is based.

[77]   Minutes 90th and 95th CID meeting, 6 July 1906 and 21 Feb. 1907, CAB 2/2 (quote from latter).

[78]   Haldane, *Before the War*, 178–79.

[79]   Memo. Gorton, 'Our Position as regards the Low Countries', 5 Apr. 1907, WO 106/46/E2/13; also memo. MO 1A, 'The Netherlands, Germany and the United Kingdom'

the Belgian manoeuvres cast doubt on the reliability and efficiency of the Belgian army; they thus helped to focus General Staff thinking on closer Anglo-French military cooperation as more likely to halt a German onslaught.[80]

In 1908, a second CID enquiry was held into the problem of an invasion of the British Isles. As before, the CID concluded that 'so long as our naval supremacy is assured ..., invasion is impracticable'.[81] That remained the CID's position until August 1914.[82] This latest re-examination of the invasion question came against the backdrop of renewed international turmoil. In the Balkans, Austria-Hungary's annexation of Bosnia-Herzegovina pitted the Habsburg and Romanov empires against each other for the first time since 1887. A minor spat over deserters from the French Foreign Legion, the so-called Casablanca Incident, saw France and Germany at loggerheads over Morocco once more; and the public outcry in Germany after the Kaiser's injudicious '*Daily Telegraph* interview' suggested that the government in Berlin might willingly accept the escalation of any of the current foreign crises in order to divert attention from its domestic travails. It was 'not a time when any nation can safely strike sparks'.[83]

Renewed international uncertainty encouraged the CID to re-examine the 'military needs of the Empire'. A sub-committee under the new premier, H.H. Asquith, soon concluded that a naval blockade of Germany was unlikely to yield immediate results, and that hit-and-run attacks on German ports and coastal installations or blocking the Elbe estuary were fraught with unacceptable risks. The General Staff emphasised the signal importance of the early battles in any continental war, and suggested that an expeditionary force of four divisions and one cavalry division, amounting to some 110,000 men and possibly later augmented to 160,000, had to be deployed swiftly along the left flank of the French army. This decision, the sub-committee concurred, should not be made 'to turn on the mere point of violation of Belgian neutrality'. Even so, there was to be no automaticity.

(secret), 29 June 1908, WO 106/48/E2/12.

[80] General Staff memo., 'Our Position as regards the Low Countries', 16 Apr. 1907, ibid. E2/13; see also J. Gooch, 'Adversarial Attitudes: Servicemen, Politicians and Strategic Policy, 1899–1914', in P. Smith (ed.), *Government and the Armed Forces in Britain, 1856–1990* (London, 1996), 68.

[81] Minutes of 100th CID meeting, 22 Oct. 1908, CAB 2/2; 'Report of the Sub-Committee to Reconsider the Question of Oversea Attack', 22 Oct. 1908, CAB 3/2/44A; also Tweedmouth to Campbell-Bannerman, 7 Aug. 1907, Campbell-Bannerman Mss, Add. Mss. 41231.

[82] In 1911, the CID concluded that there was no case for reopening the enquiry into the question of invasion, see minutes of 109th CID meeting, 24 Mar. 1911, CAB 2/2; see also 'Memorandum on the Principles Governing the Defence of the United Kingdom, as Amended by the Home Ports Defence Committee', Apr. 1911, CAB 3/2/49A.

[83] Grey to Goschen (private), 5 Nov. 1908, Grey Mss, FO 800/61; D. French, 'Spy Fever in Britain, 1900–1915', *Historical Journal* xxi, 2 (1978), 355–70; T.G. Otte, "'An Altogether Unfortunate Affair': Great Britain and the Daily Telegraph Affair', *Diplomacy & Statecraft* v, 2 (1995), 296–333.

The final decision whether to support France and, if so, how, was 'a matter of policy which can only be determined when the occasion arises'.[84] There was, then, no single coherent continental strategy; there was, indeed, no continental commitment.

Strategic discussions at CID level lacked internal coherence. To a large extent this reflected the disparate interests and ambitions of the two service departments. But it is also suggestive of a more profound failure 'to think out', as Haldane had promised to do in 1906, Britain's defence requirements. On the one hand, as David French has rightly pointed out, British defence planners tended to overestimate the impact of sea power in the next war.[85] Grey merely expressed a general consensus when he stressed the maritime foundations of British policy during CID discussions in 1911. Indeed, the use of naval pressure as an instrument of economic warfare was generally recognised to be 'our only effective weapon in a war with Germany'.[86] On the other hand, the Foreign and War Offices thought a blockade too slow and not sufficiently effective against Germany. The attritional effect of sea power, moreover, was visited upon the enemy and neutrals alike – that had been one of the lessons of the Napoleonic wars, though one that was, perhaps, not sufficiently appreciated by CID planners.[87]

The 1909 re-examination of Britain's imperial defence requirements was indicative of the extent to which the internal balance of influence within the CID had shifted in favour of the General Staff. Similarly, the arrival of General Sir Henry Wilson as DMO in August 1910 was far less significant as a 'stimulus to move military strategy ... to detailed military planning'.[88] Wilson advocated the early despatch of the BEF to the theatre of war on the grounds of its expected psychological boost to the French, which he deemed vital. But there were also strategic reasons, based on the assumption that the opening encounters between the German and French armies were likely to be decisive. In consequence, Wilson

---

[84]   'Report of the Sub-Committee of the Committee of Imperial Defence on the Military Needs of the Empire', 24 July 1909, CAB 4/3/109B. The minutes of the sub-committee can be found in CAB 16/5. For the Admiralty's views see also Hayes, 'Plans for Attacking Germany', 107–9.

[85]   French, *Strategy and War Aims*, 14.

[86]   Clarke to Campbell-Bannerman, 26 May 1906, Campbell-Bannerman Mss, Add. Mss. 42213; CID memo., 'Capture of Private Property of belligerents at Sea', 4 May 1906, CAB 4/2/73B; Foreign Office memo., 'The Attitude of Great Britain towards Belgium in the event of a violation of Belgian Territory by Germany in Time of War', 27 Feb. 1912, CAB 4/4/33. For Grey's exposition of foreign policy to the colonial premiers, see minutes of 111th CID meeting, 26 May 1911, CAB 2/2/2.

[87]   Oppenheimer to Grey (no. 2, political), 28 Sept. 1909, FO 371/673/37070; War Office memo., 'Military policy in a War with Germany', 2 July 1908, CAB 16/5. The best examinations of the economic blockade remain D. French, *British Economic and Strategic Planning, 1905–1915* (London, 1982), 22–84, and A. Offer, *The First World War: An Agrarian Interpretation* (Oxford, 1991 (pb)), 285–317.

[88]   The argument most succinctly developed in Gooch, *Plans of War*, 289.

calculated, it was necessary to minimise the numerical advantage the Germans were likely to have in the West. By implication, this made the introduction of conscription in Britain desirable, a measure which Wilson had strongly supported for some time. But in all other respects Wilson's arguments embodied the essential continuity in General Staff thinking.[89]

In this context the 114th meeting of the CID on 23 August 1911 has been invested with much significance by scholars. It has been argued that the meeting gave official CID imprimatur to a continental strategy. Indeed, in one recent piece of perverse controversialism, this gathering, rather than the so-called German 'war council' of 8 December 1912, has even been described as the true war council.[90] In fact, a more nuanced, if prosaic, reading of the evidence suggests itself. The General Staff's submission to the meeting stressed the necessity of supporting France from the outset of a Franco-German war. The outcome of the 'opening moves' of the campaign would decide whether the German onslaught could be halted. The longer the war lasted, the more difficult it would be for Germany to sustain her war effort, argued General Sir William Nicholson, the Chief of the Imperial General Staff. In a note on Nicholson's memorandum Wilson stressed the need for the simultaneous mobilisation of the BEF with the French and German armies, and for detailed advance planning of mobilisation, concentration and transport.[91]

As for the meeting itself, much has been made of the lack of cooperation between the two services that became apparent at the meeting, and of the lacklustre performance by the First Sea Lord, Admiral Sir Arthur Wilson. But in terms of actual policy decisions, as Hankey observed after the meeting, 'the great point is that no decision was arrived at – this means ... defeat of our opponents [Henry Wilson and the General Staff]'.[92] Leaving aside the DMO's own serious underestimation of the strength of the German army in the West and the speed at which it would move, Wilson's contribution to the debate was concerned with the logistics of mobilisation and transport, and, in fact, created more confusion than clarity. Although the meeting appeared to back his assertion of the need for the speedy deployment of the BEF, it was significant primarily because it shifted the

---

[89]   Memo. Wilson, 'The Necessity for Cooperation with France in the Event of War between It and Germany', 11 Aug. 1911, WO 106/47/E2/23; D'Ombrain, *War Machinery*, 81–89.

[90]   The orthodox interpretation is best summarised in Williamson, *Grand Strategy*, 187–93; and Gooch, *Plans of War*, 290–92. For Niall Ferguson's scatter-gun iconoclasm, see his *Pity of War* (London, 1999).

[91]   Memo. Nicholson, 'The Military Aspect of the Continental Problem', 11 Aug. 1911, and 'Note by the Director of Military Operations', 12 Aug. 1911, CAB 4/3/130B.

[92]   Hankey to Fisher, 24 Aug. 1911, Fisher Mss, CCAC, FISR 1/10/530a. For some of the background see S. Roskill, *Hankey: Man of Secrets* (3 vols, London, 1970–74) i, 101–3; K.M. Wilson, 'Hankey's Appendix: Some Admiralty Manoeuvres During and After the Agadir Crisis, 1911', *War in History* i, 1 (1994), 81–97.

focus of planning from a possible landing in Belgium to tacking the BEF onto the left wing of the French army. This in itself, of course, reflected Belgium's recent reassertion of her neutrality in any future war. Even so, the meeting did not approve a continental strategy. Considering the rumours of an immediate outbreak of a Franco-German War, which were then current, this outcome of the CID meeting is remarkable, and underlines further the limits of the General Staff's influence.[93]

If anything, the most important consequence of the August 1911 CID meeting was institutional. Admiral Wilson's uninspiring performance led to his unceremonious sacking, and Asquith set about reorganising the Admiralty. This involved moving Churchill to the Admiralty – the other candidate for the post was Haldane – and led to the creation of an Admiralty Staff.[94] True, the Admiralty under Churchill cooperated more smoothly with the General Staff; true also, by March 1913, Wilson and his French counterpart, General Joseph Joffre, had settled plans for the deployment of the BEF in the area around Maubeuge.[95] This did not, however, imply automatic support for France. Indeed, even the French focus of advance planning was not sacrosanct. In the spring of 1912, a CID meeting raised again the possibility of an operation centred on Antwerp. Similarly, the assumption, seemingly confirmed in August 1911, that all six divisions would be despatched to France did not go unchallenged when the decision for war was forced upon the government three years later.[96] If anything, at the handful of CID meetings in the last eighteen months before 1914, the prospect of a continental war seemed to recede; technical issues and problems of colonial defence preoccupied the minds of ministers and their advisers.

British planning and policy was essentially reactive until the outbreak of the Great War. In July–August 1914, it remained unclear until the very last moment whether Britain would join the conflict. The decision to do so rested with the Cabinet, and the ministers did not consult with the military planners: 'No CID has been held, no military opinion has been asked for by this Cabinet, who are deciding on a question of war', Wilson noted in his diary as the July crisis was moving towards its denouement.[97] Even when war had been decided upon, senior

---

[93]   Haldane to mother, 21 Aug. 1911, Haldane Mss, MS 5986; minutes of the 114th CID meeting, 23 Aug. 1914, CAB 2/2/2. For the Belgian aspect, see memo. Hurst, 'Attitude to be adopted towards Belgium in event of Germany Violating her Neutrality during Anglo-German War', 16 Feb. 1912, FO 371/1557/7014; M.E. Thomas, 'Anglo-Belgian Military Relations and the Congo Question, 1911–1913', *Journal of Modern History* xxx, 2 (1953), 157–65.

[94]   Haldane to Grey, 2 Oct. 1911, and Asquith to Haldane (confidential), 10 Oct. 1911, Haldane Mss, MS 5909.

[95]   For a detailed discussion, see Williamson, *Grand Strategy*, 300–327.

[96]   Minutes of 116th CID meeting, 25 Apr. 1912, CAB 2/2/3; for 1914, see Williamson, *Grand Strategy*, 364–67.

[97]   Wilson diary 30 July 1914, as quoted in C.E. Callwell, *Field Marshall Sir Henry Wilson: His Life and Diaries* (2 vols, London, 1927) i, 153.

officers like General Douglas Haig thought that the BEF should not be despatched immediately. By then, the immediate mobilisation, simultaneous with that of the French army, was not possible at any rate.[98] Indeed, although the BEF was mobilised and despatched speedily, this was only part of the Army's experience of the war. During the early stages of the conflict the BEF suffered a serious defeat. In consequence, British strategy had to revert to its traditional form of holding aloof from the land war, whilst acting as the financier and supplier of the coalition.[99] There was no realistic alternative. Having embraced a continental strategy before 1914, the General Staff now had create the continental army needed to execute it.

---

[98]   Haig diary, 4–5 Aug. 1914, G. Sheffield and J. Bourne (eds), *Douglas Haig: War Diaries and Letters, 1914–1918* (London, 2005), 53–54.

[99]   The best analysis of these developments is to be found in the two studies by David French, *Strategy and War Aims* and *The Strategy of the Lloyd George Coalition, 1916–1918* (Oxford, 1996).

Chapter 14

The British Empire vs. The Hidden Hand: British Intelligence and Strategy and 'The CUP-Jew-German-Bolshevik combination', 1918–1924

John Ferris

On 6 January 1920, at 17 Knaussestrasse in Grunewald, a leafy suburb of Berlin, Ivor Hedley had an interview with Enver Pasha. Hedley was an officer of British military intelligence. Enver, until recently the leader of Turkey, but now in hiding for his role in the Armenian genocide of 1915–16:

> said he was above all a patriot. The war had been lost, and as far as he was concerned as a soldier, that finished the question of the war. Now as a Turk, he wanted to get his own country together again. He said that in Turkey they have a proverb which roughly translated means – 'To be good friends one must have quarreled well'. He had to look to his late enemies to find a real friend for Turkey. It was, therefore, to England that he turned, considering her to be the strongest nation in the world.

In return for territorial concessions on the peace treaty with Turkey, 'the re-establishment of the old Unionist Party which he says is as strong, united and patriotic as ever, and which he can "mobilize" at once', and 'an independent Turkey closely and secretly associated with Great Britain', Enver would help to solve 'our difficulties and dangers in Egypt and other Mahommedan countries further East … It will not be possible to convert them to be entirely anti-Bolshevik, as the thing has gone too far already; but it will be possible, to a large extent to remove, the Anti-English feeling.' Enver would return to Berlin by 12 January, for 24 hours, to receive 'the "Yes or No" answer of His Majesty's Government, giving roughly what they are prepared to do for Turkey and what they will require in return'.[1]

---

[1]   Material from the CAB, FO and WO series are held at The National Archives, Kew, and the L/MIL and L/PS series at The India Office Records and Library, The British Museum. Citations from these series are made with the permission of The Controller of Her Majesty's Stationery Office. Material from the papers of Arthur Balfour (The British Library), David Lloyd George (The Parliamentary Archive), Maurice Hankey (Churchill

This incident seems odd. So does the issue it opens: the role of conspiracies in power politics and British strategy after the First World War. Much of the evidence on this matter has long been known, though some has become open only since 1990. Scholars of Turkish Nationalism think it valuable, while those of British strategy find it difficult.[2] Quite what is one to do when the Chief of the Imperial General Staff, Henry Wilson, writes as follows, in January 1922:

> We have definite evidence of a world-wide conspiracy fomented by all the elements most hostile to British interests – Sinn Feiners and Socialists at our own doors, Russian Bolsheviks, Turkish and Egyptian Nationalists and Indian Seditionists. Up to the present we have been lucky in not having experienced trouble in more than one theatre at the same time, but when it is remembered that the hostile combination is working with the connivance – if not under the active direction of – the German Foreign Office, it would be folly to ignore the probability of better co-ordinated attacks in the future.[3]

The answer is simple. One should take such evidence seriously. One cannot understand British strategy between 1919 and 1923 without accounting for it. That evidence reflected real issues, often accurately, and shaped assessments and actions at the highest of levels. Even when misleading or misinterpreted, it mattered. This evidence can be understood only when it is parsed properly, by taking care about periodisation and overgeneralisation.

During the Great War, Germany, Turkey and Muslims from European colonies strove to subvert the Entente empires. This threat was checked by the weakness of its participants, and Entente strength in security and political warfare. Britain, for example, combined effective counter-intelligence in India, with a cautious policy toward Afghanistan, so helping Emir Habibullah contain internal and external intrigues; a seizure of power in Persia through bribery and paramilitary forces; and a military and political offensive against Turkey. Britain believed that Islam and nationalism could shape the political self-consciousness of Muslims, but also were mutually exclusive: the stronger one movement was, the weaker the other must be. It patronised Arab nationalism, especially through cooperation with the Sherif of

---

College, Cambridge), Henry Wilson (The Imperial War Museum), Charles Hardinge (The Cambridge University Library) and Horace Rumbold (The Bodleian Library) appears with permission of the copyright holders.

Memorandum by Hedley, 6.1.20, 'Notes on an Interview with Enver Pasha', WO 32/5620.

[2] A.L. Macfie, 'British Intelligence and the Causes of Unrest in Mesopotamia, 1919–21', and 'British Views of the Turkish Nationalist Movement, 1919–22', *Middle Eastern Studies*, 35/1 (1999) and 38/3 (2002); Timothy J. Paris, 'British Middle East Policy-Making after the First World War: The Lawrentian and Wilsonian Schools', *The Historical Journal*, 41/2 (1998), p. 791.

[3] CP 3619, CAB 24/32.

Mecca, as a sword against Turkey and a shield against Pan Islam, to prevent, as the Director of Naval Intelligence, Admiral Hall, wrote, 'a combination between the Turco-German forces and the Arabs, the direct result of which would produce something like a serious general Moslem *jehad* directed against us'.[4] This threat was real. In 1919, two months after Habibullah was assassinated, his successor, Emir Amanallah, declared war and *jihad* against the Raj. That might have been more inconvenient in 1916. Though soldiers were Britain's main tool against Turkey, subversion was a major adjunct. Equally, German armies were aided by cooperation with nationalist and left-wing opponents of the Tsarist regime. After seizing power, the Bolsheviks sought to subvert all capitalist states by working with revolutionary movements in their metropoles and empires.

The armistice did not end the war in the Middle East. British forces were strong but stretched while several rivals remained powerful, especially the Bolsheviks and the ostensibly beaten Turks. British authorities appreciated these facts. In October 1918, after thinking the Committee of Union and Progress (CUP), the military-political party which ruled Turkey, might 'fight to the death' in Istanbul or 'rejoin the money they had deposited in Switzerland', the Secret Intelligence Service (SIS), quite accurately, saw 'indications' that Enver 'contemplates a third course – to retreat to the Eastern Caucasus and wage a guerrilla warfare there, in repetition of his exploits in the interior of Tripoli' during 1912, hoping to exploit Turkish power, Pan-Islamic and Pan-Turanian sentiment, and the Russian collapse to seize the Caucasus and Central Asia. 'The C.U.P., in fact, have not given up the game. The war may lead to the opening of the Straits and the partition of the Ottoman Empire. But it has immensely weakened the orderly forces of civilization, and loosened the hold of Europe over large areas of the Moslem world. There may still be room in this world for Enver.'[5] Members of the Eastern Committee, which oversaw Britain's war in western Asia, shared these fears.[6] During the next year, as statesmen in Paris, overwhelmed by other matters, failed to define a peace treaty for the Middle East, British authorities warned that Allied strength was waning and Turkish hostility and power reviving. Even in December 1918, referring to Turkish protests at British orders, the War Office noted, 'apparently the Turks have still to learn that they are a defeated nation'. In March 1919, the second minister in command at the Foreign Office, Lord Curzon, warned that Britain's position rested not on power but 'bluff' and the 'the calculating self-interest of the Turks'.

---

[4]   'Memorandum on the Proposed Agreement with the French', 12.1.16, Admiral Hall, FO 371/2767, 8116; J.R. Ferris, 'The Internationalism of Islam: British Perceptions of a Muslim Menace, 1840–1951', *Intelligence and National Security* 24/1 (2009), pp. 57–77; Richard Popplewell, *Intelligence and Imperial Defence, British Intelligence and the Defence of the Indian Empire, 1904–1924* (London, 1995), pp. 165–297.

[5]   EC 1852, EC 2132, EC 2157, CAB 27/34.

[6]   37th and 40th meetings of the Eastern Committee, 29.10.18, 2.12.18, CAB 27/24.

The CUP was powerful. Turks accepted the loss of Arabia, but might revolt rather than lose Anatolia.[7]

Even so, decision-makers still thought Britain could dominate Arabs, Persians and Turks. Their main debate of 1919 over this issue combined assessments of the political power of Islam, with the question of whether Turkey should be allowed to retain Istanbul. The Foreign Office argued that Britain's victory had killed Pan Islam. Curzon held 'this war has applied a wonderful test-stone to the solidarity of Islam', and shown it did not exist.[8] A senior official, Eyre Crowe, agreed that to take Istanbul from Turkey would provoke 'agitation by active sections of Moslem opinion', but also wreck 'the legend of Turkish military prowess, which has for so long been the mainspring of Pan-Islamic propaganda, and … encourage Moslems to seek elsewhere for the figure-head of their religion … Moslem mentality would be more impressed by a categorical anti-Turkish issue than it would be placated by a policy of temporization and compromise.'[9] The Foreign Secretary of the Government of India, Hamilton Grant, later retorted:

> How profoundly the Moslem world has been moved has been demonstrated by events in Egypt, in Kurdistan, in India and by the present Afghan War with its concomitant tribal outbursts. But we have by no means plumbed the depth of what the pent up ira religiosa of Islam may mean to us. That there are other forces at work I do not for a moment deny: general unrest, high prices, awakened nationalism, class and race hate, and Bolshevism. But in India and surrounding Moslem countries the basic cause of trouble is outraged Islam, and the belief that it is now our policy to crush if not utterly destroy it. And incidentally I may mention that I noticed in England some justification for this belief. The war with Turkey has obviously reawakened in many quarters a dormant crusading passion typified in the desire to see the cross once more on St Sophia.[10]

Initially, such views were limited to the government of India, and the India Secretary, Edwin Montagu; they were rejected even by Arthur Hirtzel, the Permanent Secretary to the India Office.[11] During 1919, however, these attitudes waxed in influence while those of diplomats declined, as concern grew about British weakness and its enemies' strength. Foes with loose and bewildering connections – German revisionists, Bolsheviks, the CUP, nationalists in Turkey and other Muslim countries – waged subterranean war against Britain. In 1918, every anti-British Muslim movement worked with Germany. In 1919, they all

---

[7]   EC 2911, CAB 27/39, GT 7037, CAB 24/77.

[8]   Meeting of the Eastern Committee, EC 46, 23.12.18, CAB 27/24.

[9]   EC 2822, CAB 27/39.

[10]   Hamilton Grant to Balfour, 7.7.19, Arthur Balfour Papers, Add. Ms. 49749, British Library.

[11]   Minute by Hirtzel, 20.12.18, L/PS/10/623; 46th meeting of the Eastern Committee, 23.12.18, CAB 27/24.

turned to the Bolsheviks. Germans were linked to Bolsheviks, the CUP, and Muslim nationalist émigrés in Europe, who were joined to each other and to groups in their homelands. The Bolsheviks were connected to revolutionaries in Britain, Germans, the CUP, and Turkish Nationalists, who had contacts with Arab leaders, including Sherifians like Emirs Feisal and Abdulla. Enver was linked to everyone. The Khilifat movement of Indian Muslims was connected to Muslim nationalists and to the Congress Party.

These developments triggered well-honed reflexes among British intelligence officers and officials. They were used to waging political warfare and to fighting conspirators, to the ideas that Islam and nationalism rallied Muslim masses, and could work for or against Britain, which must gain Arab support by working with its leaders. They also were well informed on their enemies. British intelligence centred on the Middle East. Above all else, SIS was an Imperial counter-espionage organisation, working with able security services in Egypt and India, and with Indian Political Intelligence (IPI) abroad. They easily penetrated revolutionary movements within the Empire and without, learning of their plots and links to external foes. British codebreakers mastered Soviet ciphers and intercepted all telegraph and telephone traffic within occupied Turkey. The problem was interpretation. Britain suffered from too much and too little intelligence, and a complex foe. Its enemies were in a real conspiracy, but a dysfunctional one, resting on opportunism and ignorance. They lied to each other, and enabled one another's fantasies. There was not just one fantasy, or conspiracy, but many of both. The conspiracy was more dangerous in its parts, than the whole; even so, it was a problem, which might become serious. Britain had good intelligence on the conspiracy, which it understood better than did any of its members, but this blessing was mixed. It understood real dangers; equally, excellent intelligence on fantasy made the British fantasists as well. With imagination and forged documents, the conspiracy could reach the heavens, or at least, Ireland.

Both these outcomes were entangled in the best-known aspect of that issue: British concern with German and Bolshevik involvement in this conspiracy. During 1917–18, these two groups had been linked in ways the British knew they did not fathom, and conducted subversion against Britain. In 1919–20, their centrality in this alignment was magnified, because much of the action Britain could observe occurred in Berlin and Switzerland, an old haunt for German influence and British intelligence. In 1919, British officials thought it significant that only 'the intervention of the new German Minister at Berne', had freed 'Parvus', 'one of the most active and unscrupulous Bolshevik agents' (Alexander Helfand, a socialist and key link between German authorities, the CUP and Bolsheviks), from a Swiss jail, enabling contacts with émigré Muslim politicians.[12] Moscow's initial efforts to subvert India were organised by M.N. Roy, a nationalist who had allied with Germans in 1916–18, and were executed through Muslims who left India during

---

[12] Foreign Office to Legation, Berne, No. 218, 14.2.19, minute by Tyrrell, 17.2.19, FO 608/180.

1916 on a *hejira* to join the Turco-German *jihad* in Afghanistan.[13] Enver noisily claimed to combine communism, nationalism and Islam. He was tied to Bolsheviks and Germans, and a claimant to rule the Turkish Nationalist movement, which was led by officers whom he had commanded as soldiers and members of the CUP. These external forces claimed to be fomenting unrest within the British Empire, and sometimes were known to be trying to do so. Their links to riots in Egypt, rebellion in Iraq, and Khilifat demonstrations in India, were hard to determine, because that aim required a powerful grip on the intentions of many conspirators and the attitudes of many peoples. In 1920, noting that investigation showed no connections and much mistrust between Turkish Nationalists and Bolsheviks, the SIS chief in Istanbul wrote:

> I do not think we can say Bolshevism does not exist because we can certify that no *Bolshevist organization* exists. We are looking for something far more elusive and intangible than that, viz: tendencies and sympathies on the part of the Turks or any of the peoples of Turkey, which foreshadows a fusion with Bolshevism or may end directly or indirectly, morally or materially, in aiding the Bolshevik cause to our detriment … There have in fact been a number of incidents relevant to the subject, which, with the concomitant evil of Pan-Islamism, seem to fill the near horizon day by day with greater power of disturbing the British world.[14]

Given these circumstances, British intelligence reports often seem slightly crazed. In June 1919, an experienced intelligence officer, Hugh Whitall, warned that:

> the temporarily suppressed rising in EGYPT and INDIA were but a tentative experiment, a sort of rehearsal for the expected REVOLT of ISLAM which … is still being indefatigably prepared by the united efforts of the enemies of GREAT BRITAIN in order to disturb British rule in INDIA and the EAST generally, and thereby eventually, it is hoped, bring about a downfall of the British Moslem Empire … Defeated GERMANY still appears to have a control over this revolutionary Moslem organization which she helped to create during the war, and her interests, it is quite possible, prompt her to use it to-day to revenge herself on the victors. The GERMANS and their MOSLEM friends have found moreover new and powerful allies in the RUSSIAN BOLSHEVIKS, whose fear and hatred of ENGLAND rivals their own, and who likewise plan to undermine British power by rousing the EAST to rebellion … This union is principally GERMANY's work,

---

[13]   India Office to Foreign Office, 9.7.23, FO 371/9262, N 6991.
[14]   'Political Report', SIS CX /3452, 5.5.20, 'Connection of Nationalists and Pan-Islamists with Russian Bolshevists', FO 371/5178, E 4689, FO 371/5178, E 4689.

but still there was 'LENIN'S HAND IN THE GAME'.[15] This statement sounds as if it came from *The Boy Allies*, but it was an accurate account of talk by conspirators in Switzerland and Istanbul. Whitall was cautious on points where he was uncertain or, as events proved, wrong. He accurately represented the intentions of conspirators, but overstated their coherence and capabilities, as would many of his colleagues in coming months. These officers did not distort (as against, mistake) the facts about conspiracy, revolt, Pan Islam and nationalism. Their interpretations were reasonable, but often wrong, sometimes weird. Intelligence officers had been looking for the threat so long it was easy to see. They suffered from the professional deformation of alarmism. They overemphasised the power of conspiracies, which were defined by declaration rather than capability, and the role of Germany, because of recent experiences and their residual ability to follow activities which continued after the Armistice. Their reports, which Whitehall took seriously, sharpened the sense of general menace and the concern with links in the conspiratorial chain, such as Enver, and dragged concern from local causes to external ones. Thus, the Indian army detected 'evidence that German brains are behind' the alliance between Bolsheviks and Turks.[16] The War Office thought the Iraq revolt of 1920 had widespread local support, but its 'origin' was 'external and part of a general attack on British Empire'. Similarly, the India Office's chief intelligence analyst, Norman Bray, thought key parts of the rebellion were 'organized through various societies and directed by outside influence through the medium of BERLIN and Moscow', with strings leading through Switzerland: 'Because we find the threads leading to BERLIN and MOSCOW it by no means proves that we have reached the end of our investigations, we have only commenced them.'[17] Whitehall accepted these arguments.

Such comments have made all British analyses of this conspiracy seem risible, therefore to be ignored. In fact, these errors were hard to avoid, influential in effect, and generally cheap in cost. They led Britain to misconstrue German and Soviet influence over events and Muslims abroad, so producing a sense of hooded menace which drew more attention to the topic than it might otherwise have received. They also shaped British efforts to solve these problems. It is harder to show that these analyses or actions caused mistakes.

By 1921, as Parvus dwindled and Enver left Berlin, though some CUP leaders remained behind, the fears of Germany declined. Its government pledged to avoid

---

[15]   Memorandum by Hugh G.G. Whitall, 'The Nearer East and the British Empire', 7.6.19, FO 141/433/2.

[16]   CP 412, CAB 24/96.

[17]   War Office to Commander in Chief, India, 86244, 10.9.20, L/MIL 5/764; Major Bray, 14.9.20, 'Mesopotamia, Preliminary Report on Causes of Unrest': FO 141/433–2; A.L. Macfie, 'Causes of Unrest', and 'Turkish Nationalist Movement'. Notably, in 1918, documents captured from a German officer showed Britain 'that German activities were the direct cause of the present disturbances at Najef', the great Shi'ite shrine in Iraq, EC 125, CAB 27/25.

intrigues with Islam, which the British could verify by monitoring nationalist conspirators in Europe.[18] Intelligence became less apocalyptic and more accurate, focusing on the intentions and capabilities of specific parties, combined with a sense that Islamic sentiments moved Muslim peoples. It monitored relations between Germans, the CUP and Bolsheviks, and expected a German-Russian alliance eventually to emerge, but was not alarmed even by the alignment between them which emerged from the Genoa Conference in 1922. Intelligence focused on other conspirators, Bolshevik and Muslim, some of whom did have the intention and capability to cause specific threats. Thus, Soviet leaders hoped to hustle the East. In 1919, the Red Army had plans to create 'a cavalry corps (30.000 to 40.000 riders) with the idea of launching it against India'. During a bad patch in the Russian Civil War, the War Minister, Leon Trotsky, held that, although 'our Red Army' had been 'driven from the West to the East', it still:

> constitutes an incomparably more powerful force in the Asian terrain of world politics than in the European terrain … The road to India may prove at the given moment to be more readily possible and shorter for us than the road to Soviet Hungary … the road to Paris and London lies via the towns of Afghanistan, the Punjab and Bengal.[19]

In order to do so, the Bolsheviks must develop forces in Asia and 'indigenous revolutionaries'. Vladimir Lenin moved in that direction by committing Soviet power to an Asian-based enterprise, working through crooked timber like Enver and Roy, and the Baku Conference of 1920, where the Bolsheviks tried to raise and seize control over nationalists across the Muslim world. Ultimately, these efforts failed, but they were a real problem and bound to cause concerns about a conspiracy.

These matters were the greatest single concern for British intelligence between 1919–24, on which it had excellent and overlapping sources. The evidence came mostly from human sources, which were good on the CUP, the Soviets, Arab and Indians, less so on the Turkish Nationalists. The most alarming of these reports, such as claims that Sherifian leaders were working with Turkish Nationalists and the Egyptian nationalist party, the Wafd, to launch an anti-British *jihad*, came from sources whose reliability was uncertain, or who lacked reason to speak truth to power, like Abdul Aziz ibn Saud.[20] British authorities discounted such bias, helped by hard evidence. Rarely has any state been so well served with stolen documents and signals intelligence as was Britain in these cases, especially from the Turkish

---

[18]   British embassy, Berlin, to Foreign Office, No. 902, 5.7.21, FO 371/6498, E 7992.

[19]   Leon Trotsky, *The Trotsky Papers, Volume One, 1917–1919*, ed. Jan M. Meijer, (The Hague, 1964), pp. 632–37.

[20]   'Note for the Conference at No. 6 Sh.Kasr-al-hil on Monday, 22nd December, at 5 pm', Residency Bagdad to High Commission Cairo, telegram, 28.4.20, Consulate Jeddah telegram to Foreign Office No 413, 14.12.20, FO 141/433/2.

Nationalists and organs of the Soviet state, though forged papers were plentiful and occasionally believed. Those harder sources reduced uncertainty and error but could not eliminate them. They illustrated the intentions of states: solutions of Soviet and Turkish traffic showed their alignment was close, but strained. These sources were weaker about conspiracies, where they tended to confirm and never disproved the worst fears. Solutions of Turkish Nationalist traffic, for example, supported the idea of a Pan Islamic crusade against England, by showing that Mustafa Kemal was 'preaching Holy War' to Arabs, while his chief of staff, Fevzi Cakmak, told the commander of the Eastern Front, 'Please report at once the negotiation with the Arab chiefs. Also how are you going to ensure that arms ammunition and money will be supplied to them. With reference to the attack they will make on the British please send me a plan.'[21]

During 1920–21, intelligence provided a consistent and alarming picture. Turkish Nationalists had allied with the Bolsheviks. They were striving to do so with Pan Islamic conspirators, Sherifians, the Wafd and the Khilifat movement, which were manoeuvring on their own. The alignment between Muslims and Bolsheviks was opportunistic, however, especially on Kemal's part. Thus, in December 1920 Bray defined Kemal as a 'moderate'. He wanted to revise Sèvres, rather than destroy the British empire, 'he hoped, and still hopes, to be able to break away when the time comes' from the Bolsheviks, but his position was weak. Kemal 'is striving to hold the balance between the pro and anti Bolshevik parties' in Ankara. 'The great danger therefore in Anatolia is the possible complete triumph of the Unionist-Bolshevik party.' 'Unless the position of Mustapha Kemal and the non-Bolshevik party be strengthened considerably in the near future, there is a grave danger of complete Bolshevik control eventuating.'[22] Meanwhile, evidence pointed to divisions among British enemies. In 1920 the War Office informed commanders that a 'most secret source which is apparently reliable', but which required further confirmation to absolutely prove its accuracy, reported that Soviet authorities in Moscow had told those in the Caucasus it would not cooperate with 'Young Turks or encourage the imperialism of the latter'.It also advised that 'Pan Islam is considered dangerous to Bolshevik movement as it is a counterrevolutionary force and sooner or later Bolsheviks will have to fight against it'. As the SIS office in Cairo wrote, relations between all these parties were 'almost entirely selfish, financial and military, and not political or sentimental', lasting 'as the one party asks and the other gives, but immediately the demand or the supply ceases, the fabric crashes. Either of these contingencies might happen at almost any moment, and this cannot be lost sight of in attempting to compute the bulk and weight of the

---

[21]   War Office to Bagdad, 87609 21.1.21, 15.11, High Commissioner Cairo to Jeddah, 8.2.21, FO 141/433/3. Martin Thomas, *Empires of Intelligence, Security Services and Colonial Disorder after 1914* (London, 2008) pp 79–90, otherwise excellent, is sometimes misleading on British perceptions of Pan Islam.

[22]   B. 360, Very Secret', 'Middle East. Turco-Bolshevik Activities: Note by Political Intelligence Officer Attached to India Office', 10.12.20, FO 141/433/3.

Bolshevik-cum-Islam danger.'[23] Nor did Britain think that Bolshevism attracted Muslims. Still, by acting through Enver, Moscow might seize control over Muslim nationalists in Turkey, and the world.

These views exaggerated Enver's bondage to Bolsheviks and his influence in Turkey, and the closeness of relations between Turkish Nationalists and Soviets. Until 1921, these parties were aligned with but not allied to each other. None the less, this interpretation was fairly accurate and not unreasonable even where it was wrong. There were conspiracies. They were linked, if less systematically than Whitehall supposed. A sense of common identity and interests did bind Muslims, though this was only one dimension of their identity, and not always a strong or the dominant one. Enver did have influence in Ankara, a chance to take power there, and remarkable connections. During 1918, his chief staff officer had been Hans von Seeckt who, by 1920, as head of the *Reischwehr*, still wanted to subvert British power in Asia. After Turkey surrendered, Enver fled to Germany. German generals, retired and serving, concluded he could help them – and harm Britain – more, if based among Bolsheviks. After several failed efforts, they passed Enver to Moscow by air.[24] During this period, Enver contacted Hedley. The Prime Minister, David Lloyd George, had Hedley's report assessed by a group of Ministers, chaired by the Deputy Prime Minister, Andrew Bonar Law. After discussing Enver's 'influence' in Turkey, Egypt and 'in Asia with special reference to his alleged organization of Anti British Mohammedan forces under the auspices of the Bolshevist Govt.', this group offered mixed conclusions. Hedley should return immediately to Berlin and tell Enver 'that we are prepared to deal as fairly as possible with Turkey … that he is wanted for Atrocities; that we must know before going any further exactly what he can and will do to help'; meanwhile, Britain should check 'what he is doing against us & whether his influence would be of any value if he took our side'.[25] Britain also should inform France of any actions it took, making this an Allied matter rather than the secret Anglo-Turkish negotiation which Enver advocated.

Curzon and Lloyd George, however, rejected any deal with Enver, whom they thought a war criminal and 'one of our most desperate enemies', his price too high and reliability too low As Curzon said, 'To deal with such a man is a matter calling for great caution. To deal with him through such an intermediary as we saw

---

[23]   War Office to Allenby, personally only, 16.3.20, No 31951, FO 141/433–2; Memorandum by Hulme Beaman, 20.6.21, 'Liaison between Kemalists, Pan-Islamists and Bolsheviks', FO 141/433/3.

[24]   Hans Ulrich Seidt, *Berlin Kabul Moskau: Oskar von Niedermayer und Deutschlands Geopolitik* (Munich, 2002).

[25]   'Meeting in the Prime Minister's Room Claridge's Hotel on Sunday January 11th, 1920, at 6 PM, CAB 1/29. This meeting supported the idea of negotiation with Enver more than Curzon later suggested it had done, Curzon to Thwaites, 14.3.20, WO 32/5620.

yesterday would be very perilous.'[26] Montagu still favoured such an arrangement, so as to split the conspiracy: 'Enver Pasha has low motives. But we have often used low people before and with Italian allies it does not befit us to make many bones about low motives.' He later described reports that Enver was in Afghanistan as 'another fruit of the decision we took to have nothing to do with this man'.[27] Meanwhile, Enver, unwilling to take 'No' for an answer, met Hedley four more times. He claimed that he preferred to work with England but, if it refused, would turn to Moscow; that he could split the Caucasus and Central Asia from the USSR, or use them as a base to support the Soviet 'campaign against India'. Kemal 'was willing … to take his orders from Enver if necessary, thus though appearing to be still enemies, they would in reality be working for the same ends for their country'. As part of his grand bargain, Britain must commit itself to independence for Egypt and self-determination for other Arab countries. Enver took these talks seriously but overplayed his hand, as he would do in 1922, when he ordered the Bolsheviks either to leave Turkistan or fight: they chose war.[28] His claims reinforced British tendencies to see Enver as central to events, when he merely stood next to their centre. Whitehall remained uncertain of his influence in Turkey, sometimes thinking it powerful, or else 'almost negligible. His treachery, dishonesty, cruelty, conceit and subservience to Germans have destroyed it.'[29] However, it continued to fear the link between Enver, Ankara and the Bolsheviks, with reason. When Enver finally reached Moscow, he immediately entered an alliance of convenience with the Bolsheviks, and attempted to create one between Berlin and Moscow: in fact, he built the first post-war links which led to the secret military ties between their governments. He prepared actively to grapple with Kemal in Ankara, through political intrigue and attempts to maintain an army in the Caucasus. He might have seized power had Greece defeated Turkey during the 1921 campaign. Certainly the British commander in Turkey, General Harington, thought 'Enver is doubtless scheming to be the Deus ex Machina and repeat his sensational performance of ?1913 when he re-entered Adrianople. Enver hopes to enter arena at the head of his Bolshevik reinforcements after Mustapha Kemal has taken strain of the Greek attack.'[30]

Nor were Turks and Bolsheviks the only problem. Britain took contact between Turks and Arabs, including Sherifians, for granted, even in the absence of evidence. In 1918, when British authorities were talking to Turks, they knew Feisal was doing so too. Gilbert Clayton, head of the Arab Bureau, noted, 'Feisal

[26] Curzon to Lloyd George, 21.1.20, CAB 1/29; Curzon to Thwaites, 14.3.20, WO 32/5620; cf. FO 371/5211, E 1311.
[27] Montagu to Hankey, 11.1.20, CAB 21/184; Montagu to Curzon, 17.2.20, FO 800/157.
[28] Memorandum by Hedley, 'Notes on a Second Interview with Enver Pasha', n.d., *passim*, WO 32/5620.
[29] GHQ Constantinople to War Office, 11.2.21, I 9850, FO 371/6498, E 1974.
[30] Harington to War Office, telegram 593, 13.7.21, FO 371/6473, E 8447.

is a strong Moslem and as such may not regard the destruction of Turkey as a great Moslem power with complete equanimity.'[31] By November 1919, the Military Intelligence Department (MID) wrote, 'We shall be glad to hear of any actual details of collusion between Arabs and Mustapha Kemal. Of course one feels fairly certain that a good deal of it goes on, but we do not get many actual details.'[32] Almost immediately, a 'very secret source' informed authorities in Istanbul about a Pan Islamic conference at Sivas, which was 'clearly an organization evolved by the CUP, and Turkish Nationalists, with the object of enlisting the support and coordinating the efforts of all anti-foreign and disaffected elements in Islamic countries'. The 'Mouvahidin Society', on whose executive sat Kemal, aimed 'to procure by any and every means the complete and immediate emancipation of all Muslim countries at present under foreign protection or domination, and to unite them in a kind of world-wide Islamic Confederacy under the Presidency of the Ottoman Khalifate'. This 'Holy Warrior Society', intelligence at Istanbul reported, 'in its infancy', might lack roots in British colonies, and seem impotent because of 'the boundless ambition of its aims and the grandiloquence of its language'. Still, 'the Islamic situation, wherever we may look, is at present peculiarly adapted for the promotion of political agitation on false religious grounds'.[33] Such reports shaped a sense that Kemal's movement was both nationalist and Pan Islamic. Concern with the Mouvahidin Society fell, but during 1920 SIS and IPI continued to follow links between Kemal and Arab religious and political leaders, including Sherifians.[34] British authorities thought no Arab party or prince, including the Wafd and Sherifians, had much power, but that many had influence on a large and volatile population. From June 1920, when France threw Feisal from Syria, British authorities viewed the Sherifians, and Arab nationalism, as a free agent, with the potential to help or harm; and nine months before, Feisal had warned Britain that, if driven from Damascus, 'he would make such a war a religious one against both us and the French'.[35] They doubted he was working actively against them, but rumours abounded, especially of Sherifian involvement in the Iraq revolt.[36]

Britain estimated another Semitic people in similar, if broader, terms. Social anti-Semitism marked British decision-makers before 1914, but probably less than any other elite on earth. British concern about Jewish influence on world politics stemmed primarily from practical experience during the Great War, when Jewish

---

[31]   E C 19, 66, CAB 27/25.

[32]   Gribbon to Lt Colonel Bois, 13.11.19, WO 106/5133.

[33]   High Commissioner Constantinople to High Commissioner, Cairo, telegram No. 250, 3.12.19, 'Note on Pan-Islamism and Bolshevism', n.d. *c.* 22.12.19, Memorandum by High Commission, Constantinople, 10.1.20, No 122/M/2279, Courteney, to Chancery, 6.2.20; Hulme Beaman, for director, 26.2.20, FO 141/433–2.

[34]   SIS CX/1755/V, Cons 23.3.20, T/26, ' A Turkish Mission to the Arabs', FO 371/5046, E 3494; W (92)/Misc., 3.2.20, 'Asiatic Islamic federation', WO 32/5620.

[35]   Colonel French to War Office, 3.9.19, No. 417: L/PS/11/155, P 4966.

[36]   Paris, 'Lawrentian and Wilsonian Schools'.

people or parties hampered British interests. Jews were an important interest group in the United States, generally anti-Tsarist and often pro German. They were seen as culturally and politically close to Germans, and also to Turks, because some CUP leaders descended from Jewish converts to Islam, while the party was associated with secret societies. The Foreign Office Historical Section noted that CUP leaders were 'without exception freemasons'; the SIS station at Istanbul thought 'Jewish Free Masonic elements' dominated the CUP, while the Cabinet secretary, Maurice Hankey, described the Nationalists as being just that 'whole crypto-Judaic neo-Turk gang', the CUP.[37] At war's end, Crowe took reports of efforts by the Chief Rabbi of the Ottoman Empire, Chaim Nahum, to build support for Turkey among his co-religionists in the United States as 'a further illustration of the Jewish intrigues in favour of the CUP Turks'.[38] Again, during 1917–18, Jews emerged as powerful factors in Russian politics, especially as leaders of the Bolshevik Party, and revolutionary socialists abroad.

Britons viewed Jews as belonging to something between a charmed circle and a secret society. This attitude, combined with experience of the trouble Jews could cause and hopes for the help they might offer, was the primary cause behind the Balfour Declaration that Britain would make Palestine a national home for the Jews, delivered to Lord Rothschild, often seen as the leader of the world's Jews. This link between Britain and Zionism, and the prominence of English Jews in the debate over policy toward Muslims (especially Montagu, an anti-Zionist, but disliked and dismissed as 'that arch Anglo-Saxon' or 'that timid Jew'), reminded Whitehall of the Jewish factor in world politics.[39] The strongest, and fairly equal, responses were social anti-Semitism, philo-Semitism, indifference and echoes of *The Protocols of the Elders of Zion*, widely circulated and not yet discredited. Thus, Crowe wrote:

> with regard to our pro-Zionist policy and our general sympathy for Jewish communities – that the heart and soul of all revolutionary and terrorist movements have invariably been the Jews, the Bolsheviks and the Turkish Committee of Union and Progress being the most notorious examples. There is also every indication that the extreme socialists in Germany are led and organized entirely by Jews. We are facing a powerful international organization …[40]

---

[37]   Foreign Office Historical Section, 1.19, No 96, 'The Pan-Islamic Movement', FO 373/5/6; Memorandum 676/V, 12.8.20, 'From our representative, Constantinople', 'Affairs in Anatolia' FO 371/4946, E 11702 ; Maurice Hankey Diary, entry 3.1.21, Maurice Hankey Papers, Churchill College, Cambridge.

[38]   Minute by Crowe, undated, FO 371/3451, 190942.

[39]   Gribbon to Muspratt, 25.11.19, WO 106/5133; Hardinge to Chirol, 12.1.20, Hardinge Papers, Volume 42.

[40]   Minute by Crowe, 18.11.18, FO 371/4369, N 513.

These views often took odd forms. Zionist arguments incorporated anti-Semitic logic, while anti-Semites were Zionists. Balfour ridiculed views of 'this Jewish international conspiracy which seems equally interested in accumulating money in the west and cutting throats in the east'. Later, he wrote, 'though the Jews undoubtedly constitute a most formidable power whose manifestations are not by any means always attractive, the balance of wrong-doing seems to me on the whole to be greatly on the Christian side'. One intelligence officer stated, 'It looks at present as if the Jews, who are running Bolshevism as well as all other mischief in the world, are trying to organize a Pan-Islamic move toward India'; yet he also supported Zionism, and had worked with it in political warfare against Turkey.[41] Nor are anti-Semitic statements always what they seem. During one meeting of the Eastern Committee, the Director of Military Intelligence, General MacDonogh, noted that the key to Palestine was its role as

> the home of the Jewish people, and therefore interesting the whole of the Jews all over the world. I see a good many of the Zionists, and one suggested to me the day before yesterday that if the Jewish people did not get what they were asking for in Palestine we should have the whole of Jewry turning Bolsheviks and supporting Bolshevism in all the other countries as they have done in Russia.

To which the second minister in command at the Foreign Office, Robert Cecil, Balfour's nephew and no anti-Semite, replied, 'Yes. I can conceive the Rothschilds leading a Bolshevist mob!'[42] The Zionist leader offering this warning, using an anti-Semitic argument to support Zionism, was Chaim Weizmann. Who is to blame if Britons believed it?

These ideas and errors mattered. During 1920–22, statesmen viewed a chaotic world, with the greatest danger being the rise of a revisionist alliance between Germany, the USSR, Turkey, anti-British nationalist movements, and perhaps Japan. That idea usually is thought a chimera. It had substance. It stemmed from a belief the defeated powers would revive and challenge the status quo; and from signs of that development. Such signs were more plentiful than at any time before 1933, centred on Bolshevism, Pan Islam, nationalism, Enver and Kemal. These fears reached a crescendo in July 1921. Only in late 1922 did Whitehall begin to abandon them. It mentioned a revisionist alliance so often because it thought that a real possibility. These ideas and intelligence did not affect the first shift of British policy in the Middle East. The decision of 1920 to abandon the Caucasus and the protectorate over Persia stemmed from a recognition of British military weakness, the Bolshevik revival, and the attitudes of the Iranian elite. Intelligence, however, in alloy with military weakness and external danger, did affect all other British decisions in the region between 1920 and 1923. The danger concerned

[41]   Ibid., minute by Balfour, undated; Balfour to Lloyd George, 19.2.19. Lloyd George Papers, F/3/4/12; Gribbon to Muspratt, 25.11.19, WO 106/5133.
[42]   EC 41, 5.12.18, CAB 27/24.

all decision-makers, including Curzon, the Foreign Secretary, despite his track record for disparaging the power of Pan Islam, but particularly Montagu and Churchill, Secretary for War (1919–20) and Colonies (1921–22), the Government of India, and the British and Indian armies. Statesmen used intelligence to justify their policies far more than in any other case of that time. Their arguments characteristically used dramatic pieces of intelligence as razor or teaser, to cut off contradictory arguments or to allude to severe consequences, depending on the desired effect or influence being sought. All supporters of compromise with any Muslim group cited the danger of Pan Islam and the links between the USSR, the CUP and Turkish Nationalists. They applied the sword and shield logic of the Arab Revolt to the Turkish Nationalists, whom they described as a formidable force which must either be ally, or enemy. Only by appeasing nationalism could one sap the popular power of Islam. Opponents of such compromises also accepted the danger of these links, though they focused on conspirators and minimised the issue of popular feelings.

These issues affected British decisions across Asia, including Britain's greatest strategic decision of 1920–21. Discussions of the renewal of the Anglo-Japanese Alliance turned on the question of whether a Russo-German alliance would emerge, which was affected by knowledge that a Russo-Turkish alignment existed, with tenuous links to Berlin. Notably, however, Britain abandoned the Anglo-Japanese Alliance for other reasons.[43]

After the Third Anglo-Afghan War of 1919, the Government of India sought 'to let Afghanistan down light; to forgive and if possible to educate its truculent young Ruler, who has already been tainted by the catchwords of Bolshevism'.[44] These attitudes were bolstered by intelligence on relations between Bolsheviks and Muslims, ranging from decryption of Russian traffic in Central Asia to reports from the Baku conference. Characteristically, the Indian Army thought 'Moscow schemers' and Islamic nationalists a threat to India. By manipulating anti-British forces, especially in Afghanistan, the Bolsheviks aimed to wreck 'British prestige in Asia' and consolidate 'their position on the borders of India, so that they may finally be able to create a revolution in this country'. That knowledge and fear drove policy toward Afghanistan during 1920. Intelligence helped to widen the breach which Kabul and Moscow built between themselves, by showing Britain where to place the wedge, especially when officials gave Amanullah transcripts of Soviet messages which disparaged his country, and himself.[45]

---

[43] J.R. Ferris, 'Armaments and Allies: The British Military Services and the Anglo-Japanese Alliance, 1911–21', in Phillips O'Brien (ed.), *The Anglo-Japanese Alliance* (Routledge, 2003).

[44] Hamilton Grant to Balfour, 7.7.19, Arthur Balfour Papers, British Library, Add Ms 49749.

[45] Indian Military Requirements Committee. Memorandum No. 1, *passim*, CAB 16/38.

In the Middle East, intelligence shaped Imperial politics by backing more basic trends. Britain ruled much of its Empire indirectly, leaving great power to protectorates. Between 1884and 1917, Britain also gave increasing political representation and power to indigenous peoples in its most advanced colony, India, so as to bring emerging political forces into its system rather than force them to attack it from outside. So too, from 1916, it patronised nationalism among Muslims, viewing it as a prophylactic against Pan Islam rather than a threat. As Hirtzel wrote in 1919:

> Panislamism is undoubtedly a danger – or rather a potential danger ... The antidote is nationalism ... we ought to ... make the Moslem of India find his spiritual home in India, & regard himself not as an Indian Moslem but as a Moslem Indian. Similarly in Arabia – the nationalist movement if properly guided & controlled will tend against Panislamism by keeping the Arab's thoughts at home.[46]

During 1920–21, intelligence on the links between Germans, Soviets, Turks and Muslim nationalists shaped British policy toward political reform in Egypt, and even more Churchill's reorganisation of British power in the Middle East. It convinced him that Britain faced dangers against which it needed local friends.[47] The candidates were obvious. All decision-makers agreed the Sherifians had some influence and preferred to work with Britain, but if necessary would join its foes.[48] Meanwhile, British intelligence acquired secret Soviet documents which described Zionism as a bitter enemy, confirming private claims by Weizman and public statements by Trotsky that these movements were irreconcilable rivals, and that to support one would be to weaken the other.[49] When Zionists and Bolsheviks told this same tale, Churchill believed it, leading him to the public statement that these movements were involved in 'a Struggle for the Soul of the Jewish People', who 'are beyond all question the most formidable and the most remarkable race which has ever appeared in the world'. Sometimes these views are called anti-Semitic: in fact, they were mainstream Zionist.[50] He built politics for the Mandates in Iraq, Palestine and Trans-Jordan, around Zionism and two Sherifian princes, Feisal and Abdulla, by combining practices of indirect rule, principles of national self-determination, and the logic of sword and shield. These forces either could bolster the British order, or sap it; by working with them, Britain tried to strip Jews and Arabs from the ranks of the conspiracy and make them allies.

---

[46]   Minute by Hirtzel, 26.8.19, L/PS/10/576.

[47]   CP 2387, CAB 24/117.

[48]   FO 800/155. Wilson to Curzon, 22.10.20.

[49]   Winston Churchill, Cabinet Paper, 5.21, 'The Paole Zion', CAB 1/29.

[50]   Winston Churchill, 'Zionism versus Bolshevism, A Struggle for the Soul of the Jewish People', *Illustrated Sunday Herald*, 8 February 1920, p. 5.

Similar ideas shaped Britain's debate about its relations with Turkey, but less conclusively, because policy took many twists, decision-makers were divided and intelligence told a shifting story. Intelligence was not irrelevant; it mattered so much that its influence checked itself. Combined with assessments drawn from realpolitik, it reinforced every competing aim. In 1920, by promoting the idea of a Pan Islamic danger, intelligence convinced decision-makers that the Treaty of Sèvres, intended to settle the peace in the Middle East, must leave Istanbul under Turkey. Subsequent policy was driven by impotence and stasis. [51] Britain lacked the force to control Anatolia, where it depended on the Greek army. Yet simply to leave Turkey presented obvious dangers so long as Turks remained aligned to Moscow. Soldiers, Indian officials and Montagu argued that Britain could overcome that dilemma, and the endangering alliance, only through great concessions to Turkey, by abandoning the Treaty of Sèvres and what the commander of the Indian Army, Henry Rawlinson, called 'the suicidal policy of backing the Greeks'.[52] Between October 1919 to December 1921, Wilson's views migrated from the idea of keeping Istanbul while 'mak(ing) love to the Turks as being the only way to ever get any peace in Arabia, in Egypt, in Aden, in Mesopotamia, and in India', to concluding 'we shall never have peace, comfort or safety in Palestine, Egypt, Mesopotamia or India until we have on our side a strong and friendly Turkey stretching from Smyrna to Baku and from Adrianople to the borders of Mosul'.[53] In hindsight, such views were the best on offer: they foreshadowed what would happen because their authors best understood the realities at hand. However, to act on these ideas would have forced the Lloyd George government, and the Foreign Office, to admit that it was on their watch England had been beaten by a defeated and odious enemy. As the Cabinet noted in 1920, 'to retire from Constantinople before a bandit like Mustapha Kemal would deal a shattering blow to our prestige in the East, and … this could not possibly be contemplated'.[54]

Such arguments remained a minority. They were opposed by the strongest faction on the issue, albeit each with different aims, Lloyd George, Curzon and the Foreign Office, backed by the most powerful swing vote among ministers, Churchill. During December 1920, so as to cause a change in policy on Turkey, the MID prepared a draft Cabinet Paper for Churchill's signature. It compiled public and secret intelligence on Kemal's position, which was described essentially as the

---

[51] Keith Jeffery, *The British Army and the Crisis of Empire, 1919–1922*, (Manchester, 1982); John Darwin, *Britain, Egypt and the Middle East: Imperial Policy in the Aftermath of War, 1918–1922*, (London, 1981).

[52] GT 8292, CAB 24/89; CP 156, CAB 24/93; CP 547, CAB 24/97; CP 966, CAB 24/102; CP 2210, CAB 24/116; CP 3402, CAB 24/109; Rawlinson to Wilson, 2.12.20, Henry Wilson Papers, 73/1/19/13C.

[53] Wilson to Sackville-West, 11.10.19, 73/1/18/12E, Wilson to Secretary of State, 19.12.21, 73/1/14/46B, Henry Wilson Papers; Wilson to Worthington Evans, 23.3.21, WO 32/5233.

[54] Cabinet 53/20, 30.9.20, CAB 23/22.

National Pact, the official position of the Turkish Nationalists. Churchill, although critical of official policy, refused to circulate these 'insolent' demands, which would 'undo all the good movement of opinion which has lately manifested itself in the cabinet'. [55] He rejected the National Pact as a basis for talks, much as he wanted a deal with Turkey. This brought his position close to that of Lloyd George, Curzon, and the Foreign Office, who, though more sympathetic to Greece than he, were willing to negotiate with Kemal and to revise the Treaty of Sèvres, though not to accept the National Pact. They took this step because, between September 1920 and June 1921, intelligence produced the widespread belief that Kemal, fearing the CUP and Bolsheviks, might be willing to compromise with Britain.[56] As one official summarised intelligence on this topic:

> there are two parties in Anatolia & not only one. The weaker is that of Mustafa Kemal & the Nationalists, who, imbued by patriotic and religious motives, have been, & are, endeavouring to resist the Peace terms & the resultant dismemberment of Turkey & reduction of the prestige of the Ottoman Khalifate. They have failed & their adherents are going over to the other & far more dangerous party, that of Enver & Talaat & the CUP-Jew-German-Bolshevik combination. The latter are not concerned with the defence of Turkey but with the Pan-Islamic offensive of Bolshevism throughout the East, primarily directed against Great Britain. The plans for this offensive have recently been discussed at Baku. Enver & his associates have sacrificed Turkey to the Bolshevik conception of Pan-Islam, have accepted the principles of lenine sic and are disseminating them by means of the Green propagandist army. Mustafa Kemal on the other hand has rejected Lenin's sic principles & is consequently about to be discarded in favour of Enver & Talaat ... Mustafa Kemal must therefore be aware that his cause is a lost one & might well be disposed in his dilemma to consider it more politic for the sake of Turkey & the Sultan to accept the Treaty, & with it the support of Great Britain & the Allies as an alternative to acquiescence in the complete eclipse of Turkey & the House of Othman for the sake of the spread of Bolshevism & the very dubious overthrow of British power in the East.[57]

In January 1921, the Cabinet thought:

> Mustapha was opposed to the Bolsheviks and to Enver and the other extremists, but was afraid to quarrel with Moscow so long as he was in want of money. It seemed possible that the fear of a revived Russia, which was already threatening

---

[55]   Churchill to DMI, 9.12.20, WO 32/5743.
[56]   Rumbold to Curzon, 6.12.20, de Robeck to Rumbold, 23.12.20, Horace Rumbold papers, Vol. 28, Bodleian Library; third meeting of The Future of Constantinople Committee, 9.1.21, CAB 27/133; minute by Crowe, 7.1.21, War Office to Foreign Office, 16.1.21, FO 371/6464, E 508, E 743.
[57]   Minute by D.G. Osbourne, 23.9.20, FO 371/4946, E 11702.

Persia and might soon become a menace to Turkey, might induce Mustapha
Kemal to seek reasonable terms from the Allies.[58]

Britain made several overtures in this direction over coming months. They failed,
while codebreaking and public statements showed Kemal's intransigence on the
National Pact. Britain could only wait on the struggle between Turkey and Greece,
with small influence and hostage to events. Even when making these overtures to
Ankara, Whitehall recognised that Kemal might be less rational or more radical
than they hoped, and work with Russia against England. Events soon strengthened
this view. The failure of the Greek offensive of 1921 deflated Enver's position,
driving him from Turkey to Turkistan, to break with the Soviets, and to die in
battle against their forces, to the astonishment of British intelligence. Precisely as
that happened, human intelligence, loosely supported by codebreaking, suggested
that Kemal had adopted Enver's platform, becoming slave to Moscow and apostle
of Pan Islam.

   Britain could not avoid seeing Kemal as an echo of Enver, interpreting his
aims in the context of Bolshevism and Pan Islam. As Enver's position evaporated,
Kemal saw key ground opening on his left and seized it. Mistrusting, manipulating
and needing the USSR, he veered toward it temporarily and formed an alliance,
which provided much political and military support while alarming many of his
colleagues. Britain misconstrued the attitudes of Kemal and company toward the
USSR: they merely used Moscow, and vice versa. Their attitudes toward Muslims,
however, were less narrow and nationalist than is commonly believed. Judging
from later disputes, during 1919–23 many – indeed, most – Nationalist leaders did
have Pan Islamic sentiments. Kemal claimed he always had wished to break the
Sultanate and Caliphate, but kept such ideas 'to myself in my own consciousness
as a national secret'. Since these institutions alone could rally 'the whole nation
and the army into a state of rebellion', he postponed efforts to abolish them until
the war was won, meanwhile exploiting their power.[59] One may wonder whether
Kemal was quite so prescient during 1919–22 as he later suggested. During that
time, he sympathised with Muslims under western imperialism, exploited religious
sentiments to strengthen Turkish influence among them and his hold at home,
expressed Pan Islamic views, and perhaps held them. Britain had reason to smell
Pan Islamism in Turkish nationalism. So it did.

   During the spring of 1922, after assessing all public and secret intelligence
available to Britain, a fairly level-headed group of officials and intelligence
officers, the Inter Departmental Committee on Eastern Unrest, concluded:

> the fundamental cause of unrest in Eastern Countries is an intense nationalism,
> which may be briefly described as the attempt on the part of the various Eastern

---

[58]   Cabinet meeting, 3 (21) 21.1.21, CAB 23/23.
[59]   *A Speech delivered by Ghazi Mustapha Kemal, President of the Turkish Republic,
October 1927* (Leipzig, 1929), pp. 16–20.

peoples to emancipate themselves from any form of control by Europeans. Consequently it is not surprising to find an anti-European fanaticism prevalent throughout the East.

This nationalism was indigenous; external causes – whether Germany, the USSR, Pan Islam or Bolshevism – were 'contributing factors', not fundamental ones. However, the combination of tinder and sparks still constituted a 'grave danger':

> Whereas the majority of those expressing Nationalist sentiments are capable of realizing that final goal towards which they are striving can only be reached by gradual and progressive means, there are certain extremist sections in each State, and certain external agencies working to exploit the national movements for other purposes, which are in part responsible for unrest and are, in some cases, instrumental in either preventing an amicable settlement of existing difficulties or are actively engaged in fostering discontent and creating an atmosphere suitable to active revolt.

Gravest of these internal-external threats was Pan Islam. That idea 'forms an integral part of the Turkish Nationalist policy'. Many Turkish leaders were firmly Pan Islamic, bound to 'association with rebellion in the East' and to 'the idea of a Turkish hegemony of Moslem States'. Kemal, more modestly, thought Turkey must assist 'the development of Moslem consciousness as an instrument for encouraging other Moslem Communities to obtain their independence', and help them to 'obtain their independence under the political and religious primacy of Turkey, rather than that they should be welded into one great Mohamedan Empire'. This policy had power: 'Pan-Islamic intrigue is more apparent in local fanaticism than in any world-wide combination' but it 'does provide an added and dangerous element to Eastern unrest'.[60]

So too, the Nationalists were seen as bound to Moscow. Around the time of the Genoa Conference, several agents reported that the Soviets aimed to form an 'Eastern Entente' with Muslims throughout the world. A Foreign Office official noted, 'The scheme is grandiose and the authority poor – but it is not impossible that some such design may inspire Bolshevik activities in central and s.-w. Asia.'[61] A few months later, a Foreign Office assessment of human and signals intelligence showed widespread Soviet activities among Muslim nationalists. The Bolsheviks supported the 'pan-Asiatic and pan-Islamic schemes of the Turkish Nationalists', though the two groups were mutually suspicious. Curzon retorted that this information must be incomplete; much more must be happening. He told the leader of the Conservative Party, Austen Chamberlain:

---

[60]   Interim report of Inter-Departmental Committee on Eastern Unrest, 24.5.22, FO 371/7790.

[61]   SIS Section 1 to Gregory, CX/1434/1, 23.3.22, minutes by PM Roberts, 27.2, Lindsey, undated, FO 371/10943, N 2848.

I do not know if you have studied the Secret Service Reports and telegrams lately with sufficient closeness to realise that that combination has been growing much firmer – that Mustapha Kemal is tight in the grip of the Bolsheviks – that his truculence as regards the Paris terms arises from his reliance on their support – that a Secret Treaty has almost certainly been concluded between them; and that this is what Litvinoff meant in his allusion in the intercepted telegram to the 'trump card' which it was still in the power of the Russians to play at Genoa.[62]

In 1920–21, intelligence and its interpretation shaped an idea of a German, Bolshevik and CUP alliance, against which Arab and Turkish nationalism seemed an ally, promoting attempts at compromise which worked with Feisal but not with Kemal. In 1921–22, the danger seemed narrower but deeper. Arab countries and Germany were quiet, but the Turkish Nationalists were yoked to the USSR, wielding the sword of Islam, while France and Italy were betraying Britain. This intelligence produced bitter anger, and caused Whitehall to underrate the opportunism in Turko-Soviet relations and the differences between them. It led decision-makers to overestimate the stakes at risk: thus, Crowe, by then Permanent Under Secretary to the Foreign Office, thought 'The Turk reestablished, as a result of military victory on his part, means the loss of practically the whole fruits of our victorious campaign in which Turkey was completely defeated. The political consequences of such a consummation can hardly be overestimated': it would bolster Pan Islam and shake British rule across Asia. Curzon spoke in similar terms.[63] Until August 1922, those emotions and analyses did not upset Britain's attempt to escape its weak position in Turkey by having Greeks and Nationalists accept the 'Paris terms', which abandoned the Treaty of Sèvres without embracing the National Pact. During the Chanak crisis of 1922, after these efforts miscarried, as Turkey smashed Greece in Anatolia, and British prestige was broken by a bandit, attitudes changed. Anger, and the belief that Ankara was bound to Moscow and the destruction of the British Empire, now shaped Whitehall's assessments and actions, leading it to almost start a world war.[64] Though that danger was averted, fear of links between the Turkish Nationalists and Pan Islam shaped Imperial policy until 1924, when Turkey abolished the Caliphate, and its claims to pre-eminence over Islam.[65]

Between 1918 and 1924, British intelligence overstated the importance of a conspiracy between Pan Islam and Bolshevism, Jews, Turks, Germans, Arabs and

---

[62] Memorandum by Leeper, 19.5.22, 'Anti-British Activities of the Soviet Government', minute by Curzon, 30.5.22, FO 371/8193; Curzon to Austen Chamberlain, 13.5.22, AC 23/6, Austen Chamberlain Papers.

[63] *Documents on British Foreign Policy, Volume XVII* (London, 1963), pp 207, 245.

[64] J.R. Ferris, 'Far Too Dangerous a Gamble?: British Intelligence and Policy During the Chanak Crisis, September–October 1922', *Diplomacy & Statecraft*, 14/3 (July 2003), pp. 139–84.

[65] Ferris, 'Internationalism of Islam'.

Russians. Yet it provided accurate reports on, and powerful analyses of, different conspiratorial and sociological groups, warned against overrating their coherence, and emphasised that opposition to Britain stemmed from local nationalism. Under the circumstances, errors were inevitable. Those made by British authorities were hard to avoid. They could have done better only through mindreaders or seers, able to see issues like the ideas Kemal kept 'to myself in my own consciousness as a national secret'. The great flaws in British policy stemmed not from intelligence and ideas, but too little power and too many problems. Still, intelligence shaped the way Britain pursued its policy in the Middle East. On occasion, this led Britain to box shadows rather than rivals, and so to inferior moves, and at Chanak almost to disaster, but generally the effect was neutral, and sometimes beneficial. More broadly, intelligence guided a Whig political strategy in the Empire, by letting Britain monitor and neutralise irreconcilable political threats while identifying which ones could be bought off and how. It reinforced British tendencies, during a key period, to patronise nationalism, so strengthening such movements in the long term. Britain took these actions not because it thought nationalism strong, but precisely because it thought those forces weak, and a useful counter to a greater problem: Pan Islam. Britain's greatest intelligence failure during these events was to overrate the immaturity of colonial nationalism and its own willingness to suppress such forces.

Index